COMMON CORE MATHEMATICS

A Story of Ratios

Grade 6, Module 4: Expressions and Equations

consider the source

JB JOSSEY-BASS™

A Wiley Brand

WELCOME

Dear Teacher,

Thank you for your interest in Common Core's curriculum in mathematics. Common Core is a non-profit organization based in Washington, DC dedicated to helping K-12 public schoolteachers use the power of high-quality content to improve instruction.[1] We are led by a board of master teachers, scholars, and current and former school, district, and state education leaders. Common Core has responded to the Common Core State Standards' (CCSS) call for "content-rich curriculum"[2] by creating new, CCSS-based curriculum materials in mathematics, English Language Arts, history, and (soon) the arts. All of our materials are written by teachers who are among the nation's foremost experts on the new standards.

In 2012 Common Core won three contracts from the New York State Education Department to create a PreKindergarten–12th grade mathematics curriculum for the teachers of that state, and to conduct associated professional development. The book you hold contains a portion of that work. In order to respond to demand in New York and elsewhere, modules of the curriculum will continue to be published, on a rolling basis, as they are completed. This curriculum is based on New York's version of the CCSS (the CCLS, or Common Core Learning Standards). Common Core will be releasing an enhanced version of the curriculum this summer on our website, commoncore.org. That version also will be published by Jossey-Bass, a Wiley brand.

Common Core's curriculum materials are not merely aligned to the new standards, they take the CCSS as their very foundation. Our work in math takes its shape from the expectations embedded in the new standards— including the instructional shifts and mathematical progressions, and the new expectations for student fluency, deep conceptual understanding, and application to real-life context. Similarly, our ELA and history curricula are deeply informed by the CCSS's new emphasis on close reading, increased use of informational text, and evidence-based writing.

Our curriculum is distinguished not only by its adherence to the CCSS. The math curriculum is based on a theory of teaching math that is proven to work. That theory posits that mathematical knowledge is most coherently and

---

1. Despite the coincidence of name, Common Core and the Common Core State Standards are not affiliated. Common Core was established in 2007, prior to the start of the Common Core State Standards Initiative, which was led by the National Governors Association and the Council for Chief State School Officers.
2. *Common Core State Standards for English Language Arts & Literacy in History/Social Studies, Science, and Technical Subjects* (Washington, DC: Common Core State Standards Initiative), 6.

effectively conveyed when it is taught in a sequence that follows the "story" of mathematics itself. This is why we call the elementary portion of this curriculum "A Story of Units," to be followed by "A Story of Ratios" in middle school, and "A Story of Functions" in high school. Mathematical concepts flow logically, from one to the next, in this curriculum. The sequencing has been joined with methods of instruction that have been proven to work, in this nation and abroad. These methods drive student understanding beyond process, to deep mastery of mathematical concepts. The goal of the curriculum is to produce students who are not merely literate, but fluent, in mathematics.

It is important to note that, as extensive as these curriculum materials are, they are not meant to be prescriptive. Rather, they are intended to provide a basis for teachers to hone their own craft through study, collaboration, training, and the application of their own expertise as professionals. At Common Core we believe deeply in the ability of teachers and in their central and irreplaceable role in shaping the classroom experience. We strive only to support and facilitate their important work.

The teachers and scholars who wrote these materials are listed beginning on the next page. Their deep knowledge of mathematics, of the CCSS, and of what works in classrooms defined this work in every respect. I would like to thank Louisiana State University professor of mathematics Scott Baldridge for the intellectual leadership he provides to this project. Teacher and trainer Jill Diniz, who is the lead writer for grades 6–12, has brought extraordinary intelligence and judgment to this work. Jill's ability to thrive in situations in which others would be lucky just to persevere, is uncommon.

Finally, this work owes a debt to project director Nell McAnelly that is so deep I'm confident it never can be repaid. Nell, who leads LSU's Gordon A. Cain Center for STEM Literacy, oversees all aspects of our work for NYSED. She has spent days, nights, weekends, and many cancelled vacations toiling in her efforts to make it possible for this talented group of teacher-writers to produce their best work against impossible deadlines. I'm confident that in the years to come Scott, Robin, and Nell will be among those who will deserve to be credited with putting math instruction in our nation back on track.

Thank you for taking an interest in our work. Please join us at www.commoncore.org.

Lynne Munson
President and Executive Director
Common Core
Washington, DC
October 25, 2013

Common Core's 6-12 Math Staff

Scott Baldridge, Lead Mathematician and Writer
Robin Ramos, Lead Writer, PreKindergarten–5
Ben McCarty, Mathematician

Nell McAnelly, Project Director
Tiah Alphonso, Associate Director
Jennifer Loftin, Associate Director
Catriona Anderson, Curriculum Manager, PreKindergarten–5
Jill Diniz, Lead Writer, 9-11 and Curriculum Manager

Sixth Grade

Erika Silva, Lead
Debby Grawn
Glenn Gebhard
Krysta Gibbs

Sixth and Seventh Grade

Anne Netter, Lead
Beau Bailey
Saki Milton
Hester Sutton
David Wright
Korinna Sanchez

Seventh Grade

Julie Wortmann, Lead
Joanne Choi
Lori Fanning
Bonnie Hart

Eighth Grade

Stefanie Hassan, Lead
Winnie Gilbert
Sunil Koswatta, Mathematician

Ninth Grade

Miki Alkire
Chris Bejar
Carlos Carrera
Melvin Damaolao
Joe Ferrantelli
Jenny Kim
Athena Leonardo

Rob Michelin
Noam Pillischer
Alex Sczesnak

Tenth Grade

Pia Mohsen, Lead
Bonnie Bergstresser
Ellen Fort
Terrie Poehl

Ninth, Tenth, and Eleventh Grade

Kevin Bluount
Wendy DenBesten
Abe Frankel
Thomas Gaffey
Kay Gleenblatt
Sheri Goings
Pam Goodner
Selena Oswalt
William Rorison
Chris Murcko
Surinder Sandhu
Pam Walker
Darrick Wood

Statistics

Henry Kranendonk, Lead
Michael Allwood
Gail Burrill
Beth Chance
Brian Kotz
Kathy Kritz
Patrick Hopsfensperger
Jerry Moren
Shannon Vinson

Document Management Team

Kristen Zimmerman

Advisors

Richard Askey
Roger Howe
James Madden
Roxy Peck
James Tanton

Table of Contents[1]

Expressions and Equations

Topics A through E (assessment 1 day, return 1 day, remediation or further applications 3 days)

---

[1] Each lesson is ONE day and ONE day is considered a 45 minute period.

Grade 6 • Module 4

Expressions and Equations

OVERVIEW

In Module 4, students extend their arithmetic work to include using letters to represent numbers. Students understand that letters are simply "stand-ins" for numbers and that arithmetic is carried out exactly as it is with numbers. Students explore operations in terms of verbal expressions and determine that arithmetic properties hold true with expressions because nothing has changed—they are still doing arithmetic with numbers. Students determine that letters are used to represent specific but unknown numbers and are used to make statements or identities that are true for all numbers or a range of numbers. Students understand the importance of specifying units when defining letters. Students say, "Let K = Karolyn's weight in pounds" instead of "Let K = Karolyn's weight" because weight cannot be a specific number until it is associated with a unit, such as pounds, ounces, grams, etc. They also determine that it is inaccurate to define K as Karolyn because Karolyn is not a number. Students conclude that in word problems, each letter (or variable) represents a number and its meaning is clearly stated.

To begin this module, students are introduced to important identities that will be useful in solving equations and developing proficiency with solving problems algebraically. In Topic A, students understand the relationships of operations and use them to generate equivalent expressions (**6.EE.A.3**). By this time, students have had ample experience with the four operations since they have worked with them from kindergarten through Grade 5 (**1.OA.B.3**, **3.OA.B.5**). The topic opens with the opportunity to clarify those relationships, providing students with the knowledge to build and evaluate identities that are important for solving equations. In this topic, students discover and work with the following identities: $w - x + x = w$, $w + x - x = w$, $a \div b \cdot b = a$, $a \cdot b \div b = a$ (when $b \neq 0$), and $3x = x + x + x$. Students will also discover that if $12 \div x = 4$, then $12 - x - x - x = 0$.

In Topic B, students experience special notations of operations. They determine that $3x = x + x + x$ is not the same as x^3, which is $x \cdot x \cdot x$. Applying their prior knowledge from Grade 5, where whole number exponents were used to express powers of ten (**5.NBT.A.2**), students examine exponents and carry out the order of operations, including exponents. Students demonstrate the meaning of exponents to write and evaluate numerical expressions with whole number exponents (**6.EE.A.1**).

Students represent letters with numbers and numbers with letters in Topic C. In past grades, students discovered properties of operations through example (**1.OA.B.3**, **3.OA.B.5**). Now, they use letters to represent numbers in order to write the properties precisely. Students realize that nothing has changed because the properties still remain statements about numbers. They are not properties of letters, nor are they new rules introduced for the first time. Now, students can extend arithmetic properties from manipulating numbers to manipulating expressions. In particular, they develop the following identities: $a \cdot b = b \cdot a$, $a + b = b + a$, $g \cdot 1 = g$, $g + 0 = g$, $g \div 1 = g$, $g \div g = 1$, and $1 \div g = \frac{1}{g}$. Students understand that a letter in an expression represents a number. When that number replaces that letter, the expression can be evaluated to one number. Similarly, they understand that a letter in an expression can represent a number. When that number is replaced by a letter, an expression is stated (**6.EE.A.2**).

In Topic D, students become comfortable with new notations of multiplication and division and recognize their equivalence to the familiar notations of the prior grades. The expression $2 \times b$ is exactly the same as $2 \cdot b$ and both are exactly the same as $2b$. Similarly, $6 \div 2$ is exactly the same as $\frac{6}{2}$. These new conventions are practiced to automaticity, both with and without variables. Students extend their knowledge of GCF and the distributive property from Module 2 to expand, factor, and distribute expressions using new notation (**6.NS.B.4**). In particular, students are introduced to factoring and distributing as algebraic identities. These include: $a + a = 2 \cdot a = 2a$, $(a + b) + (a + b) = 2 \cdot (a + b) = 2(a + b) = 2a + 2b$, and $a \div b = \frac{a}{b}$.

In Topic E, students express operations in algebraic form. They read and write expressions in which letters stand for and represent numbers (**6.EE.A.2**). They also learn to use the correct terminology for operation symbols when reading expressions. For example, the expression $\frac{3}{2x-4}$ is read as "the quotient of three and the difference of twice a number and four." Similarly, students write algebraic expressions that record operations with numbers and letters that stand for numbers. Students determine that $3a + b$ can represent the story "Martina tripled her money and added it to her sister's money" (**6.EE.A.2b**). A Mid-Module Assessment follows Topic E.

Students write and evaluate expressions and formulas in Topic F. They use variables to write expressions and evaluate those expressions when given the value of the variable (**6.EE.A.2**). From there, students create formulas by setting expressions equal to another variable. For example, if there are 4 bags containing c colored cubes in each bag with 3 additional cubes, students use this information to express the total number of cubes as $4c + 3$. From this expression, students develop the formula $t = 4c + 3$, where t is the total number of cubes. Once provided with a value for the amount of cubes in each bag ($c = 12$ cubes), students can evaluate the formula for t: $t = 4(12) + 3$, $t = 48 + 3$, $t = 51$. Students continue to evaluate given formulas such as the volume of a cube, $V = s^3$ given the side length, or the volume of a rectangular prism, $V = l \cdot w \cdot h$ given those dimensions (**6.EE.A.2c**).

In Topic G, students are introduced to the fact that equations have a structure similar to some grammatical sentences. Some sentences are true: "George Washington was the first president of the United States." or "$2 + 3 = 5$." Some are clearly false: "Benjamin Franklin was a president of the United States." or "$7 + 3 = 5$." Sentences that are always true or always false are called closed sentences. Some sentences need additional information to determine whether they are true or false. The sentence "She is 42 years old" can be true or false depending on who "she" is. Similarly, the sentence "$x + 3 = 5$" can be true or false depending on the value of x. Such sentences are called open sentences. An equation with one or more variables is an open sentence. The beauty of an open sentence with one variable is that if the variable is replaced with a number, then the new sentence is no longer open: it is either *clearly true* or *clearly false*. For example, for the open sentence $x + 3 = 5$:

> If x is replaced by 7, the new closed sentence, $7 + 3 = 5$, is false because $10 \neq 5$.
> If x is replaced by 2, the new closed sentence, $2 + 3 = 5$, is true because $5 = 5$.

From here, students conclude that solving an equation is the process of determining the number(s) that, when substituted for the variable, result in a true sentence (**6.EE.B.5**). In the previous example, the solution for $x + 3 = 5$ is obviously 2. The extensive use of bar diagrams in Grades K–5 makes solving equations in

Topic G a fun and exciting adventure for students. Students solve many equations twice, once with a bar diagram and once using algebra. They use identities and properties of equality that were introduced earlier in the module to solve one-step, two-step, and multistep equations. Students solve problems finding the measurements of missing angles represented by letters (**4.MD.C.7**) using what they learned in Grade 4 about the four operations and what they now know about equations.

In Topic H, students use their prior knowledge from Module 1 to contruct tables of independent and dependent values in order to analyze equations with two variables from real-life contexts. They represent equations by plotting the values from the table on a coordinate grid (**5.G.A.1**, **5.G.A.2**, **6.RP.A.3a**, **6.RP.A.3b**, **6.EE.C.9**). The module concludes with students referring to true and false number sentences in order to move from solving equations to writing inequalities that represent a constraint or condition in real-life or mathematical problems (**6.EE.B.5**, **6.EE.B.8**). Students understand that inequalities have infinitely many solutions and represent those solutions on number line diagrams.

An End-of-Module Assessment follows Topic H.

Focus Standards

Apply and extend previous understandings of arithmetic to algebraic expressions.

6.EE.A.1   Write and evaluate numeric expressions involving whole-number exponents.

6.EE.A.2   Write, read, and evaluate expressions in which letters stand for numbers

     a.   Write expressions that record operations with numbers and with letters standing for numbers. *For example, express the calculation "Subtract y from 5" as $5 - y$.*

     b.   Identify parts of an expression using mathematical terms (sum, term, product, factor, quotient, coefficient); view one or more parts of an expression as a single entity. *For example, describe the expression $2(8 + 7)$ as a product of two factors; view $(8 + 7)$ as both a single entity and a sum of two terms.*

     c.   Evaluate expressions at specific values of their variables. Include expressions that arise from formulas used in real-world problems. Perform arithmetic operations, including those involving whole-number exponents, in the conventional order when there are no parentheses to specify a particular order (Order of Operations). *For example, use the formulas $V = s^3$ and $A = 6s^2$ to find the volume and surface area of a cube with sides of length $s = 1/2$.*

6.EE.A.3   Apply the properties of operations to generate equivalent expressions. *For example, apply the distributive property to the expression $3(2 + x)$ to produce the equivalent expression $6 + 3x$; apply the distributive property to the expression $24x + 18y$ to produce the equivalent expression $6(4x + 3y)$; apply properties of operations to $y + y + y$ to produce the equivalent expression $3y$.*

6.EE.A.4   Identify when two expressions are equivalent (i.e., when the two expressions name the same number regardless of which value is substituted into them). *For example, the expressions $y + y + y$ and $3y$ are equivalent because they name the same number regardless of which number y stands for.*

	Module 4:	Expressions and Equations
	Date:	12/11/13

Reason about and solve one-variable equations and inequalities.

6.EE.B.5   Understand solving an equation or inequality as a process of answering a question; which values from a specified set, if any, make the equation or inequality true? Use substitution to determine whether a given number in a specified set makes an equation or inequality true.

6.EE.B.6   Use variables to represent numbers and write expressions when solving a real-world or mathematical problem; understand that a variable can represent an unknown number, or, depending on the purpose at hand, any number in a specified set.

6.EE.B.7   Solve real-world and mathematical problems by writing and solving equations in the form $x + p = q$ and $px = q$ for cases in which p, q and x are all nonnegative rational numbers.

6.EE.B.8   Write an inequality of the form $x > c$ or $x < c$ to represent a constraint or condition in a real-world mathematical problem. Recognize that inequalities of the form $x > c$ or $x < c$ have infinitely many solutions; represent solutions of such inequalities on number line diagrams.

Represent and analyze quantitative relationships between dependent and independent variables.

6.EE.C.9   Use variables to represent two quantities in a real-world problem that change in relationship to one another; write an equation to express one quantity, thought of as the dependent variable, in terms of the other quantity, thought of as the independent variable. Analyze the relationship between the dependent and independent variables using graphs and tables, and relate these to the equation. *For example, in a problem involving motion at constant speed, list and graph ordered pairs of distances and times, and write the equation $d = 65t$ to represent the relationship between distance and time.*

Foundational Standards

Understand and apply properties of operations and the relationship between addition and subtraction.

1.OA.B.3   Apply properties of operations as strategies to add and subtract.[2] *Examples: If $8 + 3 = 11$ is known, then $3 + 8 = 11$ is also known. (Commutative property of addition.) To add $2 + 6 + 4$, the second two numbers can be added to make a ten, so $2 + 6 + 4 = 2 + 10 = 12$. (Associative property of addition.)*

Understand properties of multiplication and the relationship between multiplication and division.

3.OA.B.5   Apply properties of operations as strategies to multiply and divide.[2] *Examples: If $6 \times 4 = 24$ is known, then $4 \times 6 = 24$ is also known. (Commutative property of multiplication.) $3 \times 5 \times 2$ can be found by $3 \times 5 = 15$, then $15 \times 2 = 30$, or by $5 \times 2 = 10$, then $3 \times 10 = 30$. (Associative property of multiplication.) Knowing that $8 \times 5 = 40$ and*

---

[2] Students need not use formal terms for these properties.

$8 \times 2 = 16$, *one can find* 8×7 *as* $8 \times (5 + 2) = (8 \times 5) + (8 \times 2) = 40 + 16 = 56$
(Distributive property.)

Gain familiarity with factors and multiples.

4.OA.B.4   Find all factors for a whole number in the range 1–100. Recognize that a whole number is a multiple of each of its factors. Determine whether a given whole number in the range 1–100 is a multiple of a given one-digit number. Determine whether a given whole number in the range 1–100 is prime or composite.

Geometric measurement: understand concepts of angle and measure angles.

4.MD.C.5   Recognize angles as geometric shapes that are formed wherever two rays share a common endpoint, and understand concepts of angle measurement:

     a.   An angle is measured with reference to a circle with its center at the common endpoint of the rays, by considering the fraction of the circular arc between the points where the two rays intersect the circle. An angle that turns through 1/360 of a circle is called a "one-degree angle," and can be used to measure angles.

     b.   An angle that turns through n one-degree angles is said to have an angle measure of n degrees.

4.MD.C.6   Measure angles in whole-number degrees using a protractor. Sketch angles of specified measure.

4.MD.C.7   Recognize angle measure as additive. When an angle is decomposed into non-overlapping parts, the angle measure of the whole is the sum of the angle measures of the parts. Solve addition and subtraction problems to find unknown angles on a diagram in real world and mathematical problems, e.g., by using an equation with a symbol for the unknown angle measure.

Write and interpret numerical expressions.

5.OA.A.2   Write simple expressions that record calculations with numbers, and interpret numerical expressions without evaluating them. *For example, express the calculation "add 8 and 7, then multiply by 2" as* $2 \times (8 + 7)$. *Recognize that* $3 \times (18932 + 921)$ *is three times as large as* $18932 + 921$, *without having to calculate the indicated sum or product.*

Analyze patterns and relationships.

5.OA.B.3   Generate two numerical patterns using two given rules. Identify apparent relationships between corresponding terms. Form ordered pairs consisting of corresponding terms from the two patterns, and graph the ordered pairs on a coordinate plane. *For example, given the rule "Add 3" and the starting number 0, and given the rule "Add 6" and the starting number 0, generate terms in the resulting sequences, and observe that the terms in one sequence are twice the corresponding terms in the other sequence. Explain informally why this is so.*

	Module 4:	Expressions and Equations
	Date:	12/11/13

Understand the place value system.

5.NBT.A.2   Explain patterns in the number of zeros of the product when multiplying a number by powers of 10, and explain patterns in the placement of the decimal point when a decimal is multiplied or divided by a power of 10. Use whole-number exponents to denote powers of 10.

Graph points on the coordinate plane to solve real-world and mathematical problems.

5.G.A.1   Use a pair of perpendicular number lines, called axes, to define a coordinate system, with the intersection of the lines (the origin) arranged to coincide with the 0 on each line and given point the plane located by using an ordered pair of numbers, called its coordinates. Understand that the first number indicates how far to travel from the origin in the direction of one axis, and the second number indicates how far to travel in the direction of the second axis, with the convention that the names of the two axes and the coordinates correspond (e.g., x-axis and x-coordinate, y-axis and y-coordinate).

5.G.A.2   Represent real world and mathematical problems by graphing points in the first quadrant of the coordinate plane, and interpret coordinate values of points in the context of the situation.

Understand ratio concepts and use ratio reasoning to solve problems.

6.RP.A.3   Use ratio and rate reasoning to solve real-world and mathematical problems, e.g., by reasoning about tables of equivalent ratios, tape diagrams, double number line diagrams, or equations.

    a.   Make tables of equivalent ratios relating quantities with whole-number measurements, find missing values in the tables, and plot the pairs of values on the coordinate plane. Use tables to compare ratios.

    b.   Solve unit rate problems including those involving unit pricing and constant speed. *For example, if it took 7 hours to mow 4 lawns, then at that rate, how many lawns could be mowed in 35 hours? At what rate were lawns being mowed?*

Compute fluently with multi-digit numbers and find common factors and multiples.

6.NS.B.4   Find the greatest common factor of two whole numbers less than or equal to 100 and the least common multiple of two whole numbers less than or equal to 12. Use the distributive property to express a sum of two whole numbers 1–100 with a common factor as a multiple of a sum of two whole numbers with no common factor. *For example, express 36 + 8 as* $4(9 + 2)$.

Focus Standards for Mathematical Practice

MP.2   **Reason abstractly and quantitatively.** Students connect symbols to their numerical referents. They understand exponential notation as repeated multiplication of the base number. Students realize that 3^2 is represented as 3×3, with a product of 9, and explain how 3^2 differs from 3×2, where the product is 6. Students determine the meaning of a variable within a real-life context. They write equations and inequalities to represent mathematical situations. Students manipulate equations using the properties so that the meaning of the symbols and variables can be more closely related to the real-world context. For example, given the expression $12x$ represents how many beads are available to make necklaces, students rewrite $12x$ as $4x + 4x + 4x$ when trying to show the portion each person gets if there are three people, or rewrite $12x$ as $6x + 6x$ if there are two people sharing. Students recognize that these expressions are equivalent. Students can also use equivalent expressions to express the area of rectangles and to calculate the dimensions of a rectangle when the area is given. Also, students make connections between a table of ordered pairs of numbers and the graph of those data.

MP.6   **Attend to Precision.** Students are precise in defining variables. They understand that a variable represents one number. For example, students understand that in the equation $a + 4 = 12$, the variable a can only represent one number to make the equation true. That number is 8, so $a = 8$. When variables are represented in a real-world problem, students precisely define the variables. In the equation $2w = 18$, students define the variable as weight in pounds (or some other unit) rather than just weight. Students are precise in using operation symbols and can connect between previously learned symbols and new symbols (3×2 can be represented with parentheses $3(2)$ or with the multiplication dot $3 \cdot 2$; similarly $3 \div 2$ is also represented with the fraction bar $\frac{3}{2}$). In addition, students use appropriate vocabulary and terminology when communicating about expressions, equations, and inequalities. For example, students write expressions, equations, and inequalities from verbal or written descriptions. "A number increased by 7 is equal to 11" can be written as $x + 7 = 11$. Students refer to $7y$ as a term or expression, whereas $7y = 56$ is referred to as an equation.

MP.7   **Look for and make use of structure**. Students look for structure in expressions by deconstructing them into a sequence of operations. They make use of structure to interpret an expression's meaning in terms of the quantities represented by the variables. In addition, students make use of structure by creating equivalent expressions using properties. For example, students write $6x$ as $x + x + x + x + x + x$, $4x + 2x$, $3(2x)$, or other equivalent expressions. Students also make sense of algebraic solutions when solving an equation for the value of the variable through connections to bar diagrams and properties. For example, when there are two copies of $a + b$, this can be expressed as either $(a + b) + (a + b)$, $2a + 2b$, or as $2(a + b)$. Students use tables and graphs to compare different expressions or equations to make decisions in real-world scenarios. These models also create structure as students gain knowledge in writing expressions and equations.

MP.8   **Look for and express regularity in repeated reasoning**. Students look for regularity in a repeated calculation and express it with a general formula. Students work with variable expressions while focusing more on the patterns that develop than the actual numbers that the variable represents. For example, students move from an expression such as $3 + 3 + 3 + 3 = 4 \cdot 3$ to the general form $m + m + m + m = 4 \cdot m$, or $4m$. Similarly, student move from expressions such as $5 \cdot 5 \cdot 5 \cdot 5 = 5^4$ to the general form $m \cdot m \cdot m \cdot m = m^4$. These are especially important when moving from the general form back to a specific value for the variable.

Terminology

New or Recently Introduced Terms

- **Simple Expression** (A *simple expression* is a number, a letter which represents a number, a product whose factors are either numbers or letters involving whole number exponents, or sums and/or differences of such products. Each product in a simple expression is called a *term*, and the evaluation of the numbers in the product is called the *coefficient of the term*.)

- **Linear Expression** (A *linear expression* is a product of two simple expressions where only one of the simple expressions has letters and only one letter in each term of that expression or sums and/or differences of such products.)

- **Equivalent Expressions** (Two simple expressions are *equivalent* if both evaluate to the same number for every substitution of numbers into all the letters in both expressions.) [Note: This description is not very precise—this needs to be described using lots of examples.]

- **Equation** (An *equation* is a statement of equality between two expressions.)

- **Truth Values of a Number Sentence** (A number sentence is said to be *true* if both numerical expressions are equivalent; it is said to be *false* otherwise. *True* and *false* are called *truth values*.)

- **Exponential Notation for Whole Number Exponents** (Let m be a non-zero whole number. For any number a, we define a^m to be the product of m factors of a, i.e., $a^m = \underbrace{a \cdot a \cdot a \cdot a \ldots \cdot a}_{m \text{ times}}$. The

number a is called the *base,* and m is called the *exponent,* or *power* of a.)

Familiar Terms and Symbols[3]

- Sum
- Product
- Factor
- Quotient
- Expand
- Term
- Distribute
- Variable or Unknown Number
- Number Sentence
- True or False Number Sentence
- Properties of operations (distributive, commutative, associative)

---

[3] These are terms and symbols students have seen previously.

Suggested Tools and Representations

- Bar model
- Geometric figures
- Protractors

Assessment Summary

Assessment Type	Administered	Format	Standards Addressed
Mid-Module Assessment Task	After Topic E	Constructed response with rubric	6.EE.A.1, 6.EE.A.2, 6.EE.A.3, 6.EE.A.4
End-of-Module Assessment Task	After Topic H	Constructed response with rubric	6.EE.A.2c, 6.EE.B.5, 6.EE.B.6, 6.EE.B.7, 6.EE.B.8, 6.EE.C.9

Topic A:
Relationships of the Operations

6.EE.A.3

Focus Standard:	6.EE.A.3	Apply the properties of operations to generate equivalent expressions. *For example, apply the distributive property to the expression $3(2 + x)$ to produce the equivalent expression $6 + 3x$; apply the distributive property to the expression $24x + 18y$ to produce the equivalent expression $6(4x + 3y)$; apply properties of operations to $y + y + y$ to produce the equivalent expression $3y$.*
Instructional Days:	4	
	Lesson 1:	The Relationship of Addition and Subtraction (S)[1]
	Lesson 2:	The Relationship of Multiplication and Division (E)
	Lesson 3:	The Relationship of Multiplication and Addition (S)
	Lesson 4:	The Relationship of Division and Subtraction (S)

Prior to this module, students have worked with numbers and operations from Kindergarten through Grade 5. In Topic A, students further discover and clarify the relationships of the operations using models. From these models, students build and evaluate identities that are useful in solving equations and developing proficiency with solving problems algebraically.

To begin, students will use models to discover the relationship between addition and subtraction. In Lesson 1, for example, a model could represent the number three. Students notice that if two are taken away, there is a remainder of one. However, when the students replace the two units, they notice the answer is back to the original three. Hence, students first discover the identity $w - x + x = w$ and later discover that $w + x - x = w$.

In Lesson 2, students also model the relationship between multiplication and division. They note that when they divide eight units into two equal groups, they find a quotient of four. They discover that if they multiply that quotient by the number of groups, then they return to their original number, eight, and ultimately build the identities $a \div b \cdot b = a$ and $a \cdot b \div b = a$, when $b \neq a$.

Students continue to discover identities in Lesson 3, where they determine the relationship between multiplication and addition. Using tape diagrams from previous modules, students are assigned a diagram

---

[1] Lesson Structure Key: **P**-Problem Set Lesson, **M**-Modeling Cycle Lesson, **E**-Exploration Lesson, **S**-Socratic Lesson

with three equal parts, where one part is assigned a value of four. They note that since there are three equal parts, they can add four three times to determine the total amount. They relate to multiplication and note that three groups with four items in each group produces a product of twelve, determining that $3 \cdot g = g + g + g$.

Finally in Lesson 4, students relate division to subtraction. They notice that dividing eight by two produces a quotient of four. They experiment and find that if they subtract the divisor from the dividend four times (the quotient), they will find a remainder of zero. They continue to investigate with other examples and prove that if they continually subtract the divisor from the dividend, they will determine a difference, or remainder, of zero. Hence, $12 \div x = 4$ means $12 - x - x - x - x = 0$.

Lesson 1: The Relationship of Addition and Subtraction

Student Outcomes

- Students build and clarify the relationship of addition and subtraction by evaluating identities such as $w - x + x = w$ and $w + x - x = w$.

Lesson Notes

Teachers need to create square pieces of paper in order for students to build tape diagrams. Each pair of students will need ten squares to complete the activities. If the teacher has square tiles, these can be used in place of paper squares.

The template for the squares and other shapes used in the lesson are provided at the end of the lesson. Teachers will need to cut out the shapes.

Fluency Exercise (5 minutes)

White Board Exchange: Multiplication of Decimals

Classwork

Opening Exercises (5 minutes)

Opening Exercises

a. Draw a tape diagram to represent the following expression: $5 + 4$.

    Answer:

b. Write an expression for each tape diagram.

    i.

    ii.

Discuss the answers with the class. If students struggled with either Opening Exercise, provide more examples before moving into the discussion.

Discussion (15 minutes)

Provide each pair of students with a collection of 10 squares so they can use these squares to create tape diagrams throughout the lesson.

- If each of the squares represents 1 unit, represent the number 3 using the squares provided.
  - □ ⬚⬚⬚

- Add two more squares to your tape diagram.
  - □ ⬚⬚⬚⬚⬚

- Write an expression to represent how we created a tape diagram with 5 squares.
  - □ ⬚⬚⬚⬚⬚

    $3 + 2$

- Remove two squares from the tape diagram.
  - □ ⬚⬚⬚

- Alter our original expression $3 + 2$ to create an expression that represents what we did with the tape diagram.
  - □ $3 + 2 - 2$

- Evaluate the expression.
  - □ 3

- Let's start a new diagram. This time, create a tape diagram with 6 squares.
  - □ ⬚⬚⬚⬚⬚⬚

- Use your tiles to demonstrate $6 + 4$.
  - □ ⬚⬚⬚⬚⬚⬚⬚⬚⬚⬚

- Remove 4 squares from the tape diagram.
  - □ ⬚⬚⬚⬚⬚⬚

- Alter our original expression $6 + 4$ to create an expression to represent the tape diagram.
  - □ $6 + 4 - 4$

- How many tiles are left on your desk?
  - □ 6

- Evaluate the expression.
  - □ 6

- How many tiles did we start with?
  - □ 6

- What effect did adding four tiles then subtracting the four tiles have on the number of tiles?
  - □ *Adding and then subtracting the same number of tiles resulted in the same number that we started with.*

- What if I asked you to add 215 tiles to the six tiles we started with and then subtract 215 tiles? Do you need to actually add and remove these tiles to know what the result will be? Why is that?
  - □ *We do not actually need to do the addition and subtraction because we now know that it will result in the same amount of tiles that we started with.*

| Lesson 1: | The Relationship of Addition and Subtraction |
| Date: | 12/11/13 |

15

- What do you notice about the expressions we created with the tape diagrams?

  - *Possible Answer: When we add one number and then subtract the same number we get our original number.*

- Write a number sentence, using variables, to represent what we just demonstrated with tape diagrams. Remember that a variable is a letter that represents a number. Use the shapes provided to create tape diagrams to demonstrate this number sentence.

Provide students time to work with their partners to write a number sentence.

  - *Possible answer: $w + x - x = w$. Emphasize that both w's represent the same number and the same rule applies to the x's.*

- Why is the number sentence $w + x - x = w$ called an identity?

  - *Possible answer: The number sentence is called an identity because the variables can be replaced with any numbers and the sentence will always be true.*

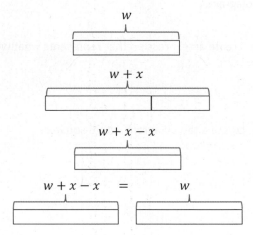

Exercises 1–5 (12 minutes)

Students will use their knowledge gained in the discussion to create another number sentence using identities. Allow students to continue to work with their partners and the squares.

> **Scaffolding:**
> The exercise could be completed as a class if students are struggling with the concept.

Exercises

1. Predict what will happen when a tape diagram has a large number of squares, some squares are removed, but then the same amount of squares are added back on.

   Possible Answer: When some squares are removed from a tape diagram, but then the same amount of squares are added back on, the tape diagram will end up with the same amount of squares that it started with.

2. Build a tape diagram with 10 squares.

   a. Remove 6 of them. Write an expression to represent the tape diagram.

   $10 - 6$

   b. Add 6 squares onto the tape diagram. Alter the original expression to represent the current tape diagram.

   $10 - 6 + 6$

 COMMON CORE

Lesson 1:	The Relationship of Addition and Subtraction
Date:	12/11/13

16

c. Evaluate the expression.

10

3. Write a number sentence, using variables, to represent the identities we demonstrated with tape diagrams.

Possible Answer: $w - x + x = w$

4. Using your knowledge of identities, fill in each of the blanks.

a. $4 + 5 - \underline{\quad} = 4$

5

b. $25 - \underline{\quad} + 10 = 25$

10

c. $\underline{\quad} + 16 - 16 = 45$

45

d. $56 - 20 + 20 = \underline{\quad}$

56

5. Using your knowledge of identities, fill in each of the blanks.

a. $a + b - \underline{\quad} = a$

b

b. $c - d + d = \underline{\quad}$

c

c. $e + \underline{\quad} - f = e$

f

d. $\underline{\quad} - h + h = g$

g

Closing (3 minutes)

- In every problem we did today, why did the final value of the expression equal the initial expression?

- Initially, we added an amount and then subtracted the same amount. Later in the lesson, we subtracted an amount and then added the same amount. Did this alter the outcome?

- Why were we able to evaluate the final expression even when we did not know the amount we were adding and subtracting?

Exit Ticket (5 minutes)

Name _____   Date _____

Lesson 1: The Relationship of Addition and Subtraction

Exit Ticket

1. Draw tape diagrams to represent each of the following number sentences.
    a. $3 + 5 - 5 = 3$

    b. $8 - 2 + 2 = 8$

2. Fill in each blank.

    a. $65 + \_\_\_\_ - 15 = 65$

    b. $\_\_\_\_ + g - g = k$

    c. $a + b - \_\_\_\_ = a$

    d. $367 - 93 + 93 = \_\_\_\_$

Exit Ticket Sample Solutions

1. Draw a series of tape diagrams to represent the following number sentences.

    a. $3 + 5 - 5 = 3$

    b. $8 - 2 + 2 = 8$

2. Fill in each blank.

    a. $65 + \underline{\quad} - 15 = 65$

        15

    b. $\underline{\quad} + g - g = k$

        k

    c. $a + b - \underline{\quad} = a$

        b

    d. $367 - 93 + 93 = \underline{\quad}$

        367

Problem Set Sample Solutions

1. Fill in each blank

    a. $\underline{\quad} + 15 - 15 = 21$ b. $450 - 230 + 230 = \underline{\quad}$ c. $1289 - \underline{\quad} + 856 = 1289$

        21   450   856

2. Why are the number sentences $w - x + x = w$ and $w + x - x = w$ called identities?

    Possible answer: These number sentences are called identities because the variables can be replaced with any numbers and the sentences will always be true.

White Board Exchange: Multiplication of Decimals

Progression of Exercises:	Answers:
1. 0.5×0.5	0.25
2. 0.6×0.6	0.36
3. 0.7×0.7	0.49
4. 0.5×0.6	0.3
5. 1.5×1.5	2.25
6. 2.5×2.5	6.25
7. 0.25×0.25	0.0625
8. 0.1×0.1	0.01
9. 0.1×123.4	12.34
10. 0.01×123.4	1.234

Fluency work such as this exercise should take 5–12 minutes of class.

How to Conduct a White Board Exchange:

All students will need a personal white board, white board marker, and a means of erasing their work. An economical recommendation is to place card stock inside sheet protectors to use as the personal white boards and to cut sheets of felt into small squares to use as erasers.

It is best to prepare the problems in a way that allows you to reveal them to the class one at a time. For example, use a flip chart or PowerPoint presentation; write the problems on the board and cover with paper beforehand, allowing you to reveal one at a time; or, write only one problem on the board at a time. If the number of digits in the problem is very low (e.g., 12 divided by 3), it may also be appropriate to verbally call out the problem to the students.

The teacher reveals or says the first problem in the list and announces, "Go." Students work the problem on their personal white boards, holding their answers up for the teacher to see as soon as they have them ready. The teacher gives immediate feedback to each student, pointing and/or making eye contact with the student and responding with an affirmation for correct work such as, "Good job!", "Yes!", or "Correct!" For incorrect work, respond with guidance such as "Look again!", "Try again!", or "Check your work!"

If many students have struggled to get the answer correct, go through the solution of that problem as a class before moving on to the next problem in the sequence. Fluency in the skill has been established when the class is able to go through each problem in quick succession without pausing to go through the solution of each problem individually. If only one or two students have not been able to get a given problem correct when the rest of the students are finished, it is appropriate to move the class forward to the next problem without further delay; in this case, find a time to provide remediation to that student before the next fluency exercise on this skill is given.

$$w + x$$

w	x

w	x

$$w + x$$

w	x

w	x

Lesson 2: The Relationship of Multiplication and Division

Student Outcomes

- Students build and clarify the relationship of multiplication and division by evaluating identities such as $a \div b \cdot b = a$ and $a \cdot b \div b = a$.

Lesson Notes

Students will use the squares that were used in Lesson 1; however, each pair of students should receive 20 squares for this lesson. Also, students will need large paper to complete the exploratory challenge.

Fluency Exercise (5 minutes)

Division of Fractions Sprint

Classwork

Opening (2 minutes)

Remind students of the identities they learned the previous day. Discuss the relationship between addition and subtraction. Inform students that the relationship between multiplication and division will be discussed today.
P.2 Have students make predictions about this relationship using their knowledge gained in the previous lesson.

Opening Exercise (5 minutes)

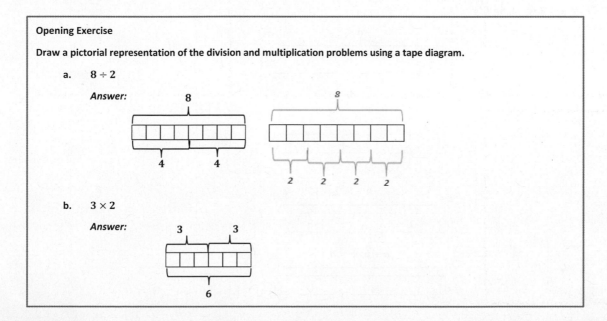

Opening Exercise

Draw a pictorial representation of the division and multiplication problems using a tape diagram.

a. $8 \div 2$

b. 3×2

Discussion (optional—see scaffolding notes)

Provide each pair of students with a collection of 20 squares which they will use to create tape diagrams throughout the lesson.

- Build a tape diagram to represent 9 units.
  - ▫ ⬛⬛⬛⬛⬛⬛⬛⬛⬛

- Divide the 9 units into three equal groups.
  - ▫ ⬛⬛⬛ ⬛⬛⬛ ⬛⬛⬛

- Write an expression to represent the process you modeled with the tape diagram.
  - ▫ $9 \div 3$

- Evaluate the expression.
  - ▫ 3

- Use your squares to demonstrate what it would look like to multiply 3 by 3.
  - ▫ ⬛⬛⬛⬛⬛⬛⬛⬛⬛

- Alter our original expression $9 \div 3$ to create an expression that represents what we did with the tape diagram.
  - ▫ $9 \div 3 \times 3$

- Evaluate the expression
  - ▫ 9

- What do you notice about the expression of the tape diagram?
  - ▫ *Possible Answer: When we divide by one number then multiply by the same number, we end up with our original number.*

- Write a number sentence, using variables, to represent the identities we demonstrated with tape diagrams. Use the variable tiles you were provided to demonstrate this number sentence with a series of tape diagrams.
  - ▫ *Provide students time to work with pairs.*
  - ▫ *Possible Answers: $a \div b \times b = a$. Emphasize that both a's represent the same number and the same rule applies to the b's.*

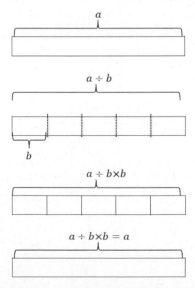

> **Scaffolding:**
> The discussion is provided if students struggled during Lesson 1. If the discussion is included in the lesson, the Exploratory Challenge will be shortened because students will only develop one number sentence.

Exploratory Challenge (23 minutes)

Students will work in pairs or small groups to determine number sentences to show the relationship between multiplication and division. They will use tape diagrams to provide support for their findings.

Exploratory Challenge

Work in pairs or small groups to determine number sentences to show the relationship between multiplication and division. Use tape diagrams to provide support for your findings.

1. Create two number sentences to show the relationship between multiplication and division. These number sentences should be identities and include variables. Use the squares to develop these number sentences.

2. Write your number sentences on large paper. Show a series of tape diagrams to defend each of your number sentences.

   Possible Answer: $a \times b \div b = a$

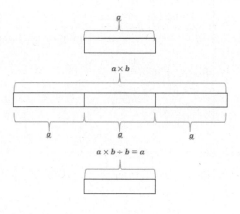

   Possible Answer: $a \div b \times b = a$

When students complete their work on the large paper, hang the papers around the room. Provide time for students to walk around and critique their peers' work. While examining the other posters, students should be comparing the number sentences and tape diagrams to their own.

Use the following rubric to critique other posters.

1. Name of group you are critiquing.
2. Number sentence you are critiquing.
3. Whether or not you believe their number sentences are true and reasons why.

Closing (5 minutes)

- What did you determine about the relationship of multiplication and division?
- What number sentences can be used to show the relationship of multiplication and division?

Exit Ticket (5 minutes)

Lesson 2:	The Relationship of Multiplication and Division
Date:	12/11/13

Name _____ Date _____

Lesson 2: The Relationship of Multiplication and Division

Exit Ticket

1. Fill in the blank to make each number sentence true.

   a. $12 \div 3 \times$ _____ $= 12$

   b. $f \times h \div h =$ _____

   c. $45 \times$ _____ $\div 15 = 45$

   d. _____ $\div r \times r = p$

2. Draw a series of tape diagrams to represent the following number sentences.

   a. $12 \div 3 \times 3 = 12$

   b. $4 \times 5 \div 5 = 4$

Exit Ticket Sample Solutions

1. Fill in the blank to make each number sentence true.

   a. $12 \div 3 \times \underline{\quad} = 12$

      3

   b. $f \times h \div h = \underline{\quad}$

      f

   c. $45 \times \underline{\quad} \div 15 = 45$

      15

   d. $\underline{\quad} \div r \times r = p$

      p

2. Draw a series of tape diagrams to represent the following number sentences.

   a. $12 \div 3 \times 3 = 12$

   b. $4 \times 5 \div 5 = 4$

Problem Set Sample Solutions

1. Fill in each blank.

   a. $132 \div 3 \times 3 = \underline{\quad}$ b. $\underline{\quad} \div 25 \times 25 = 225$

      132   **225**

   c. $56 \times \underline{\quad} \div 8 = 56$ d. $452 \times 12 \div \underline{\quad} = 452$

      8   **12**

2. How are the relationships of addition and subtraction similar to the relationship of multiplication and division?

   Possible answer: Both relationships create identities.

Division of Fractions – Round 1

Number Correct: _____

Directions: Determine the quotient of the fractions.

1.	$\frac{1}{2} \div \frac{3}{5}$		16.	$6\frac{7}{8} \div 11\frac{2}{3}$	
2.	$\frac{5}{6} \div \frac{1}{5}$		17.	$5\frac{5}{6} \div 3\frac{1}{2}$	
3.	$\frac{3}{7} \div \frac{6}{11}$		18.	$10\frac{5}{8} \div 12\frac{3}{7}$	
4.	$\frac{2}{5} \div \frac{8}{9}$		19.	$9\frac{1}{3} \div 8\frac{2}{5}$	
5.	$\frac{1}{6} \div \frac{9}{10}$		20.	$\frac{3}{4} \div 6\frac{7}{10}$	
6.	$\frac{11}{12} \div \frac{8}{9}$		21.	$2\frac{1}{3} \div 3\frac{5}{6}$	
7.	$\frac{5}{6} \div \frac{10}{13}$		22.	$2\frac{4}{5} \div 7\frac{9}{10}$	
8.	$\frac{7}{8} \div \frac{13}{15}$		23.	$5\frac{8}{9} \div 3\frac{3}{5}$	
9.	$\frac{3}{5} \div \frac{7}{9}$		24.	$12\frac{5}{9} \div 5$	
10.	$\frac{14}{17} \div \frac{13}{20}$		25.	$1\frac{5}{6} \div 2\frac{6}{7}$	
11.	$3\frac{1}{2} \div 4\frac{4}{5}$		26.	$10 \div 5\frac{8}{9}$	
12.	$6\frac{1}{5} \div 6\frac{3}{4}$		27.	$14\frac{3}{5} \div 10$	
13.	$2\frac{1}{4} \div 3\frac{1}{8}$		28.	$7\frac{9}{11} \div 1\frac{9}{10}$	
14.	$1\frac{3}{5} \div \frac{7}{8}$		29.	$15\frac{2}{3} \div 24$	
15.	$\frac{1}{5} \div 4\frac{1}{2}$		30.	$32 \div 12\frac{6}{7}$	

Division of Fractions – Round 1 [KEY]

Directions: Determine the quotient of the fractions.

1.	$\dfrac{1}{2} \div \dfrac{3}{5}$	$\dfrac{5}{6}$	16.	$6\dfrac{7}{8} \div 11\dfrac{2}{3}$	$\dfrac{165}{280} = \dfrac{33}{56}$	
2.	$\dfrac{5}{6} \div \dfrac{1}{5}$	$\dfrac{25}{6} = 4\dfrac{1}{4}$	17.	$5\dfrac{5}{6} \div 3\dfrac{1}{2}$	$\dfrac{70}{42} = 1\dfrac{2}{3}$	
3.	$\dfrac{3}{7} \div \dfrac{6}{11}$	$\dfrac{33}{42}$	18.	$10\dfrac{5}{8} \div 12\dfrac{3}{7}$	$\dfrac{595}{696}$	
4.	$\dfrac{2}{5} \div \dfrac{8}{9}$	$\dfrac{18}{40} = \dfrac{9}{20}$	19.	$9\dfrac{1}{3} \div 8\dfrac{2}{5}$	$\dfrac{140}{126} = 1\dfrac{1}{9}$	
5.	$\dfrac{1}{6} \div \dfrac{9}{10}$	$\dfrac{10}{54} = \dfrac{5}{27}$	20.	$\dfrac{3}{4} \div 6\dfrac{7}{10}$	$\dfrac{30}{268} = \dfrac{15}{134}$	
6.	$\dfrac{11}{12} \div \dfrac{8}{9}$	$\dfrac{99}{96} = 1\dfrac{1}{32}$	21.	$2\dfrac{1}{3} \div 3\dfrac{5}{6}$	$\dfrac{42}{69} = \dfrac{14}{23}$	
7.	$\dfrac{5}{6} \div \dfrac{10}{13}$	$\dfrac{65}{60} = 1\dfrac{1}{12}$	22.	$2\dfrac{4}{5} \div 7\dfrac{9}{10}$	$\dfrac{140}{395} = \dfrac{28}{79}$	
8.	$\dfrac{7}{8} \div \dfrac{13}{15}$	$\dfrac{105}{104} = 1\dfrac{1}{104}$	23.	$5\dfrac{8}{9} \div 3\dfrac{3}{5}$	$\dfrac{265}{162} = 1\dfrac{103}{162}$	
9.	$\dfrac{3}{5} \div \dfrac{7}{9}$	$\dfrac{27}{35}$	24.	$12\dfrac{5}{9} \div 5$	$\dfrac{113}{45} = 2\dfrac{23}{45}$	
10.	$\dfrac{14}{17} \div \dfrac{13}{20}$	$\dfrac{280}{221} = 1\dfrac{59}{221}$	25.	$1\dfrac{5}{6} \div 2\dfrac{6}{7}$	$\dfrac{77}{120}$	
11.	$3\dfrac{1}{2} \div 4\dfrac{4}{5}$	$\dfrac{35}{48}$	26.	$10 \div 5\dfrac{8}{9}$	$\dfrac{90}{53} = 1\dfrac{37}{53}$	
12.	$6\dfrac{1}{5} \div 6\dfrac{3}{4}$	$\dfrac{124}{135}$	27.	$14\dfrac{3}{5} \div 10$	$\dfrac{73}{50} = 1\dfrac{23}{50}$	
13.	$2\dfrac{1}{4} \div 3\dfrac{1}{8}$	$\dfrac{72}{100} = \dfrac{18}{25}$	28.	$7\dfrac{9}{11} \div 1\dfrac{9}{10}$	$\dfrac{860}{209} = 4\dfrac{24}{209}$	
14.	$1\dfrac{3}{5} \div \dfrac{7}{8}$	$\dfrac{64}{35} = 1\dfrac{29}{35}$	29.	$15\dfrac{2}{3} \div 24$	$\dfrac{47}{72}$	
15.	$\dfrac{1}{5} \div 4\dfrac{1}{2}$	$\dfrac{2}{45}$	30.	$32 \div 12\dfrac{6}{7}$	$\dfrac{224}{90} = 2\dfrac{22}{45}$	

COMMON CORE™

Lesson 2: The Relationship of Multiplication and Division
Date: 12/11/13

29

Division of Fractions – Round 2

Number Correct: _____

Improvement: _____

Directions: Determine the quotient of the fractions.

1.	$\frac{1}{2} \div \frac{3}{4}$	
2.	$\frac{3}{5} \div \frac{1}{7}$	
3.	$\frac{5}{6} \div \frac{1}{8}$	
4.	$\frac{3}{8} \div \frac{5}{9}$	
5.	$\frac{1}{4} \div \frac{2}{5}$	
6.	$\frac{7}{8} \div \frac{9}{10}$	
7.	$\frac{8}{11} \div \frac{4}{5}$	
8.	$\frac{5}{6} \div \frac{7}{12}$	
9.	$\frac{3}{4} \div \frac{8}{9}$	
10.	$\frac{7}{11} \div \frac{4}{7}$	
11.	$1\frac{3}{4} \div \frac{1}{2}$	
12.	$\frac{1}{10} \div 2\frac{3}{4}$	
13.	$5\frac{2}{3} \div \frac{7}{9}$	
14.	$\frac{5}{6} \div 6\frac{1}{2}$	
15.	$\frac{6}{7} \div 2\frac{1}{3}$	

16.	$\frac{7}{8} \div 2\frac{1}{4}$	
17.	$\frac{3}{4} \div 2\frac{3}{5}$	
18.	$4\frac{1}{5} \div 2\frac{1}{3}$	
19.	$4\frac{3}{8} \div \frac{2}{7}$	
20.	$\frac{4}{5} \div 2\frac{1}{8}$	
21.	$1\frac{1}{2} \div 3\frac{5}{6}$	
22.	$3\frac{2}{3} \div 2\frac{1}{4}$	
23.	$4\frac{3}{5} \div 1\frac{3}{4}$	
24.	$7\frac{1}{2} \div 6\frac{1}{3}$	
25.	$3\frac{4}{5} \div 2\frac{9}{10}$	
26.	$3\frac{5}{6} \div 2\frac{1}{2}$	
27.	$3\frac{3}{4} \div 4\frac{1}{8}$	
28.	$5 \div 4\frac{5}{6}$	
29.	$3\frac{1}{4} \div 2$	
30.	$8 \div 5\frac{1}{3}$	

Division of Fractions – Round 2 [KEY]

Directions: Determine the quotient of the fractions.

1.	$\dfrac{1}{2} \div \dfrac{3}{4}$	$\dfrac{4}{6} = \dfrac{2}{3}$	16.	$\dfrac{7}{8} \div 2\dfrac{1}{4}$	$\dfrac{28}{72} = \dfrac{7}{18}$
2.	$\dfrac{3}{5} \div \dfrac{1}{7}$	$\dfrac{21}{5} = 4\dfrac{1}{5}$	17.	$\dfrac{3}{4} \div 2\dfrac{3}{5}$	$\dfrac{15}{52}$
3.	$\dfrac{5}{6} \div \dfrac{1}{8}$	$\dfrac{40}{6} = 6\dfrac{2}{3}$	18.	$4\dfrac{1}{5} \div 2\dfrac{1}{3}$	$\dfrac{63}{35} = 1\dfrac{4}{5}$
4.	$\dfrac{3}{8} \div \dfrac{5}{9}$	$\dfrac{27}{40}$	19.	$4\dfrac{3}{8} \div \dfrac{2}{7}$	$\dfrac{245}{16} = 15\dfrac{5}{16}$
5.	$\dfrac{1}{4} \div \dfrac{2}{5}$	$\dfrac{5}{8}$	20.	$\dfrac{4}{5} \div 2\dfrac{1}{8}$	$\dfrac{32}{85}$
6.	$\dfrac{7}{8} \div \dfrac{9}{10}$	$\dfrac{70}{72} = \dfrac{35}{36}$	21.	$1\dfrac{1}{2} \div 3\dfrac{5}{6}$	$\dfrac{18}{46} = \dfrac{9}{23}$
7.	$\dfrac{8}{11} \div \dfrac{4}{5}$	$\dfrac{40}{44} = \dfrac{10}{11}$	22.	$3\dfrac{2}{3} \div 2\dfrac{1}{4}$	$\dfrac{44}{27} = 1\dfrac{17}{27}$
8.	$\dfrac{5}{6} \div \dfrac{7}{12}$	$\dfrac{60}{42} = 1\dfrac{3}{7}$	23.	$4\dfrac{3}{5} \div 1\dfrac{3}{4}$	$\dfrac{92}{35} = 2\dfrac{22}{35}$
9.	$\dfrac{3}{4} \div \dfrac{8}{9}$	$\dfrac{27}{32}$	24.	$7\dfrac{1}{2} \div 6\dfrac{1}{3}$	$\dfrac{45}{38} = 1\dfrac{7}{38}$
10.	$\dfrac{7}{11} \div \dfrac{4}{7}$	$\dfrac{49}{44} = 1\dfrac{5}{44}$	25.	$3\dfrac{4}{5} \div 2\dfrac{9}{10}$	$\dfrac{190}{145} = 1\dfrac{9}{29}$
11.	$1\dfrac{3}{4} \div \dfrac{1}{2}$	$\dfrac{14}{4} = 3\dfrac{1}{2}$	26.	$3\dfrac{5}{6} \div 2\dfrac{1}{2}$	$\dfrac{46}{30} = 1\dfrac{8}{15}$
12.	$\dfrac{1}{10} \div 2\dfrac{3}{4}$	$\dfrac{4}{110} = \dfrac{2}{55}$	27.	$3\dfrac{3}{4} \div 4\dfrac{1}{8}$	$\dfrac{120}{132} = \dfrac{10}{11}$
13.	$5\dfrac{2}{3} \div \dfrac{7}{9}$	$\dfrac{153}{21} = 7\dfrac{2}{7}$	28.	$5 \div 4\dfrac{5}{6}$	$\dfrac{30}{29} = 1\dfrac{1}{29}$
14.	$\dfrac{5}{6} \div 6\dfrac{1}{2}$	$\dfrac{10}{78} = \dfrac{5}{39}$	29.	$3\dfrac{1}{4} \div 2$	$\dfrac{13}{8} = 1\dfrac{5}{8}$
15.	$\dfrac{6}{7} \div 2\dfrac{1}{3}$	$\dfrac{18}{49}$	30.	$8 \div 5\dfrac{1}{3}$	$\dfrac{24}{16} = 1\dfrac{1}{2}$

Lesson 3: The Relationship of Multiplication and Addition

Student Outcomes

- Students build and clarify the relationship of multiplication and addition by evaluating identities such as $3 \cdot g = g + g + g$.

Lesson Notes

Students will continue to use the squares from Lessons 1 and 2 to create tape diagrams. Each pair of students will need 30 squares to complete the activities.

Classwork

Opening Exercise (5 minutes)

> **Opening Exercise**
>
> Write two different expressions that can be depicted by the tape diagram shown. One expression should include addition, while the other should include multiplication.
>
> a. □□□ □□□ □□□
>
>   *Possible Answers:* $3 + 3 + 3$ *or* 3×3
>
> b. □□□□□□□□ □□□□□□□□
>
>   *Possible Answers:* $8 + 8$ *or* 2×8
>
> c. □□□□□ □□□□□ □□□□□
>
>   *Possible Answers:* $5 + 5 + 5$ *or* 3×5

Discussion (17 minutes)

Provide each pair of students with a collection of 30 squares which they will use to create tape diagrams throughout the lesson.

- One partner builds a tape diagram to represent the expression $2 + 2 + 2 + 2$ while the other partner builds a tape diagram to represent 4×2.

  $2 + 2 + 2 + 2$

  $4 \quad\quad 4$

- What do you notice about the two tape diagrams you created?
  - *Possible answer: Although the tape diagrams represent two different expressions, they each have the same number of squares.*
- Why are the two tape diagrams the same? What does it say about the value of the expressions?
  - *The two tape diagrams are the same because the values of the expressions are equivalent.*
- If both expressions yield the same values, is there an advantage to using one over the other?
  - *Answers will vary.*
- Since each tape diagram has the same number of squares, can we say the two expressions are equivalent? Why or why not?
  - *Possible answer: The two expressions are equivalent because they represent the same value. When evaluated, both expressions will equal 8.*
- Therefore, $2 + 2 + 2 + 2 = 4 \times 2$. Let's build a new set of tape diagrams. One partner builds a tape diagram to represent the expression 3×4 while the other partner builds a tape diagram to represent the expression $4 + 4 + 4$.

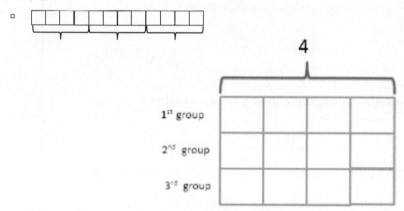

- Is 3×4 equivalent to $4 + 4 + 4$? Why or why not?
  - *Possible answer: The two expressions are equivalent because when each of them is evaluated they equal 12 as we can see with our tape diagrams.*
- Using variables, write a number sentence to show the relationship of multiplication and addition.

Provide students with time to create a number sentence.

  - *Possible answer: $3g = g + g + g$. Emphasize that each g represents the same number.*

- $3g$ is the same as writing $3 \times g$, but we no longer use the $\times$ for multiplication because it looks like a variable and can become confusing. When a number is next to a variable with no sign, multiplication is implied.

- In the two previous lessons, we talked about identities. Is the number sentence $3g = g + g + g$ also an identity? Why or why not?

  □ *Possible Answer: The number sentence $3g = g + g + g$ is an identity because we can replace g with any letter and the sentence will always be true.*

Exercises (15 minutes)

Students can continue to work with the given squares and with their partner to answer the following questions.

Exercises

1. Write the addition sentence that describes the model and the multiplication sentence that describes the model.

   $5 + 5 + 5$ *and* 3×5

2. Write an equivalent expression to demonstrate the relationship of multiplication and addition.

   a. $6 + 6$

   2×6

   b. $3 + 3 + 3 + 3 + 3 + 3$

   6×3

   c. $4 + 4 + 4 + 4 + 4$

   5×4

   d. 6×2

   $2 + 2 + 2 + 2 + 2 + 2$

   e. 4×6

   $6 + 6 + 6 + 6$

   f. 3×9

   $9 + 9 + 9$

   g. $h + h + h + h + h$

   $5h$

   h. $6y$

   $y + y + y + y + y + y$

---

3. Roberto is not familiar with tape diagrams and believes that he can show the relationship of multiplication and addition on a number line. Help Roberto demonstrate that the expression 3×2 is equivalent to $2 + 2 + 2$ on a number line.

Possible Answer: The first number line shows that there are 3 groups of 2, resulting in 6. The second number line shows the sum of $2 + 2 + 2$, resulting in 6.

Since both number lines start at zero and end at 6, the expressions are equivalent.

4. Tell whether the following number sentences are true or false. Then explain your reasoning.

a. $x + 6g - 6g = x$

The number sentence is true because it demonstrates the addition identity.

b. $2f - 4e + 4e = 2f$

The number sentence is true because it demonstrates the subtraction identity.

5. Write an equivalent expression to demonstrate the relationship between addition and multiplication.

a. $6 + 6 + 6 + 6 + 4 + 4 + 4$

$4 \times 6 + 3 \times 4$

b. $d + d + d + w + w + w + w + w$

$3d + 5w$

c. $a + a + b + b + b + c + c + c + c$

$2a + 3b + 4c$

Closing (4 minutes)

- Create a diagram that models 3 groups of size b.
- Write two equivalent expressions that represent this model.
  - *Possible answers: $3b$, $b + b + b$*
- Peter says that since the addition expression yields the same value as the multiplication expression, he will always choose to use the addition expression when solving these types of problems. Convince Peter that he may want to reconsider his position.
  - *Answers will vary, but should include the idea that when the group size is large, it is more advantageous to multiply instead of add.*

Exit Ticket (4 minutes)

Lesson 3: The Relationship of Multiplication and Addition
Date: 12/11/13

Name _____   Date _____

Lesson 3: The Relationship of Multiplication and Addition

Exit Ticket

Write an equivalent expression to show the relationship of multiplication and addition.

1. $8 + 8 + 8 + 8 + 8 + 8 + 8 + 8 + 8$

2. 4×9

3. $6 + 6 + 6$

4. $7h$

5. $j + j + j + j + j$

6. $u + u + u + u + u + u + u + u + u + u$

Exit Ticket Sample Solutions

Write an equivalent expression to show the relationship of multiplication and addition.

1. $8 + 8 + 8 + 8 + 8 + 8 + 8 + 8 + 8$

   9×8

2. 4×9

   $9 + 9 + 9 + 9$

3. $6 + 6 + 6$

   3×6

4. $7h$

   $h + h + h + h + h + h + h$

5. $j + j + j + j + j$

   $5j$

6. $u + u + u + u + u + u + u + u + u + u$

   $10u$

Problem Set Sample Solutions

Write an equivalent expression to show the relationship of multiplication and addition.

1. $10 + 10 + 10$

   3×10

2. $4 + 4 + 4 + 4 + 4 + 4 + 4$

   7×4

3. 8×2

   $2 + 2 + 2 + 2 + 2 + 2 + 2 + 2$

4. 3×9

   $9 + 9 + 9$

5. $6m$

   $m + m + m + m + m + m$

6. $d + d + d + d + d$

   $5d$

Lesson 4: The Relationship of Division and Subtraction

Student Outcomes

- Students build and clarify the relationship of division and subtraction by determining that $12 \div x = 4$ means $12 - x - x - x - x = 0$.

Lesson Notes

Students will continue to use the squares from Lessons 1–3 to create tape diagrams. Each pair of students will need 30 squares to complete the activities.

Classwork

Discussion (20 minutes)

Provide each pair of students with a collection of 30 squares so they can use these squares to create tape diagrams throughout the lesson.

- Build a tape diagram that has 20 squares.

- Divide the tape diagram into 4 equal sections.

- How many squares are in each of the 4 sections?
  - 5

- Write a number sentence to demonstrate what happened.
  - $20 \div 4 = 5$

- Combine your squares again to have a tape diagram with 20 squares.

- Now subtract 4 squares from your tape diagram.

- Write an expression to demonstrate what happened.
  - $20 - 4$

- Subtract 4 more squares and alter your expression to represent the new tape diagram.

  - $20 - 4 - 4$

- Subtract 4 more squares and alter your expression to represent the new tape diagram.

  - $20 - 4 - 4 - 4$

- Subtract 4 more squares and alter your expression to represent the new tape diagram.

  - $20 - 4 - 4 - 4 - 4$

- Last time, subtract 4 more squares and alter your expression to represent a number sentence showing the complete transformation of the tape diagram.

  - *No squares should remain.*

  - $20 - 4 - 4 - 4 - 4 - 4 = 0$

- Let's take a look at the process we took to determine the difference to be zero.

Discuss the process step by step to determine that the number of times the divisor was subtracted from the dividend is the same number as the quotient.

$$\left.\begin{array}{l} 20 - 4 = 16 \\ 16 - 4 = 12 \\ 12 - 4 = 8 \\ 8 - 4 = 4 \\ 4 - 4 = 0 \end{array}\right\} \quad \begin{array}{l} \text{Subtracted 5 times.} \\ \text{Quotient is 5.} \end{array}$$

- Do you recognize a relationship between $20 \div 4 = 5$ and $20 - 4 - 4 - 4 - 4 - 4 = 0$? If so, what is it?

  - *Possible answer: If you subtract the divisor from the dividend 5 times (the quotient) there will be no remaining squares.*

- Let's take a look at a similar problem, $20 \div 5 = 4$, to see if the quotient is the number of times the divisor is subtracted from the dividend.

- Let's create a number sentence when we subtract the divisor.

  - $20 - 5 - 5 - 5 - 5 = 0$

Discuss the process to determine that the number of times the divisor is subtracted from the dividend is the same number as the quotient.

$$\left.\begin{array}{l} 20 - 5 = 15 \\ 15 - 5 = 10 \\ 10 - 5 = 5 \\ 5 - 5 = 0 \end{array}\right\} \quad \begin{array}{l} \text{Subtracted 4 times.} \\ \text{Quotient is 4.} \end{array}$$

- Determine the relationship between $20 \div 5 = 4$ and $20 - 5 - 5 - 5 - 5 = 0$.

  - $20 \div 5 = 4$ *is the same as* $20 - 5 - 5 - 5 - 5 = 0$.

- Is this relationship always true? Let's try to prove that it is.

Model the following set of tape diagrams with leading questions for discussion.

- x is a number. What does $20 \div x = 5$ mean?

  - *Exactly five x's can be subtracted from twenty.*

$20 \div x = 5$

$20 - x$

$20 - x - x$

$20 - x - x - x$

$20 - x - x - x - x$

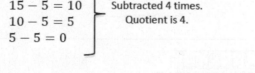

$20 - x - x - x - x - x = 0$

Lesson 4:   The Relationship of Division and Subtraction
Date: 12/11/13

- What must x be in this division sentence?
  - *Four.*
- Let's keep taking x away until we reach zero.

Model taking each x away and creating subtraction expressions to record.

- Build a subtraction expression.
  - $20 - x - x - x - x - x = 0$
- Is $20 - 4 - 4 - 4 - 4 - 4 = 0$?
  - *Yes*

MP.2

- Develop two number sentences using numbers and letters to show the relationship of division and subtraction.
  - *Possible answers:* $20 \div x = 5$ *and* $20 - x - x - x - x - x = 0$

- Or, $20 \div x = 5$ means that 5 can be subtracted exactly x number of times from 20. Is it true when $x = 4$? Subtract five from twenty four times.

- Let's keep taking x away until we reach zero.

  Model taking each x away and creating subtraction expressions to record.
- Build a subtraction expression.
  - $20 - 5 - 5 - 5 - 5 = 0$

- What two operations are we relating in the problems we completed?
  - *Division and subtraction*

Exercise 1 (10 minutes)

Students work in partners to answer the following questions.

Exercise 1

Build subtraction expressions using the indicated equations. The first example has been completed for you.

Division Equation	Divisor Indicates the Size of the Unit	Tape Diagram	What is x, y, z?
$12 \div x = 4$	$12 - x - x - x - x = 0$	$12 - 3 - 3 - 3 - 3 = 0; x = 3$ *units in each group*	$x = 3$
$18 \div x = 3$	$18 - x - x - x = 0$	$18 - 6 - 6 - 6 = 0; x = 6$ *units in each group*	$x = 6$
$35 \div y = 5$	$35 - y - y - y - y - y = 0$	$35 - 7 - 7 - 7 - 7 - 7 = 0; y = 7$ *units in each group*	$y = 7$
$42 \div z = 6$	$42 - z - z - z - z - z - z = 0$	$42 - 7 - 7 - 7 - 7 - 7 - 7 = 0; z = 7$ *units in each group*	$z = 7$

 | Lesson 4: | The Relationship of Division and Subtraction |
| Date: | 12/11/13 |

40

Division Equation	Divisor Indicates the Number of Units	Tape Diagram	What is x, y, z?
$12 \div x - 4$	$12 - 4 - 4 - 4 = 0$	$12 - 4 - 4 - 4 = 0; x = 3$ groups	$x = 3$
$18 \div x = 3$	$18 - 3 - 3 - 3 - 3 - 3 - 3 = 0$	$18 - 3 - 3 - 3 - 3 - 3 - 3 = 0; x = 6$ groups	$x = 6$
$35 \div y = 5$	$35 - 5 - 5 - 5 - 5 - 5 - 5 - 5 = 0$	$35 - 5 - 5 - 5 - 5 - 5 - 5 - 5 = 0; y = 7$ groups	$y = 7$
$42 \div z = 6$	$42 - 6 - 6 - 6 - 6 - 6 - 6 - 6 = 0$	$42 - 6 - 6 - 6 - 6 - 6 - 6 - 6 = 0; z = 7$ groups	$z = 7$

Exercise 2 (5 minutes)

Exercise 2

Answer each question using what you have learned about the relationship of division and subtraction.

    a.   If $12 \div x = 3$, how many times would x have to be subtracted from 12 in order for the answer to be zero? What is the value of x?

        Three; $x = 4$

    b. $36 - f - f - f - f = 0$. Write a division sentence for this repeated subtraction sentence. What is the value of f?

        $36 \div 4 = f; f = 9$

    c.   If $24 \div b = 12$, which number is being subtracted twelve times in order for the answer to be zero?

        Two

Closing (5 minutes)

Display the graphic organizer provided at the end of the lesson. Copies of the organizer can be made for students to follow along and record.

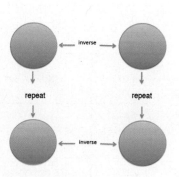

- In each of the circles, we can place an operation to satisfy the organizer. In the last four lessons, we have discovered that each operation has a relationship with other operations, whether they are inverse operations or they are repeats of another.

Place the addition symbol in the upper left hand circle.

- Let's start with addition. What is the inverse operation of addition?
  - *Subtraction.*

Place the subtraction symbol in the upper right hand circle.

- ■ After our discussion today, repeated subtraction can be represented by which operation?

  - ▫ *Division.*

Place the division symbol in the lower right hand circle.

- ■ Which operation is the inverse of division?

  - ▫ *Multiplication.*

Place the multiplication symbol in the lower left hand circle.

- ■ Let's see if this is correct. Is multiplication the repeat operation of addition?

  - ▫ *Yes.*

Understanding the relationships of operations is going to be instrumental when solving equations later in this unit.

Exit Ticket (5 minutes)

Name _____   Date _____

Lesson 4: The Relationship of Division and Subtraction

Exit Ticket

1.   Represent $56 \div 8 = 7$ using subtraction. Explain your reasoning.

2.   Explain why $30 \div x = 6$ is the same as $30 - x - x - x - x - x - x = 0$. What is the value of x in this example?

Exit Ticket Sample Solutions

1. Represent $56 \div 8 = 7$ using subtraction. Explain your reasoning.

   $56 - 7 - 7 - 7 - 7 - 7 - 7 - 7 - 7 = 0$

   $56 - 7 = 49; \ 49 - 7 = 42; \ 42 - 7 = 35; \ 35 - 7 = 28; \ 28 - 7 = 21; \ 21 - 7 = 14; \ 14 - 7 = 7; \ 7 - 7 = 0$

   OR

   $56 - 8 - 8 - 8 - 8 - 8 - 8 - 8 = 0$

   $56 - 8 = 48; \ 48 - 8 = 40; \ 40 - 8 = 32; \ 32 - 8 = 24; \ 24 - 8 = 16; \ 16 - 8 = 8; \ 8 - 8 = 0$

2. Explain why $30 \div x = 6$ is the same as $30 - x - x - x - x - x = 0$. What is the value of x in this example?

   $30 \div 5 = 6$, *so* $x = 5$. *When I subtract 5 from 30 six times, the result is zero. Division is a repeat operation of subtraction.*

Problem Set Sample Solutions

Build subtraction expressions using the indicated equations.

	Division Equation	Divisor Indicates the Size of the Unit	Tape Diagram	What is x, y, z?
1.	$24 \div x = 4$	$24 - x - x - x - x = 0$	$24 - x - x - x - x = 0; x = 6$ *units in each group*	$x = 6$
2.	$36 \div x = 6$	$36 - x - x - x - x - x - x = 0$	$36 - x - x - x - x - x - x = 0; x = 6$ *units in each group*	$x = 6$
3.	$28 \div y = 7$	$28 - y - y - y - y - y - y - y = 0$	$28 - y - y - y - y - y - y - y = 0; y = 4$ *units in each group*	$y = 4$
4.	$30 \div y = 5$	$30 - y - y - y - y - y = 0$	$30 - y - y - y - y - y = 0; y = 6$ *units in each group*	$y = 6$
5.	$16 \div z = 4$	$16 - z - z - z - z = 0$	$16 - z - z - z - z = 0; z = 4$ *units in each group*	$z = 4$

	Division Equation	Divisor Indicates the Number of Units	Tape Diagram	What is x, y, z?
1.	$24 \div x = 4$	$24 - 4 - 4 - 4 - 4 - 4 - 4 = 0$	$24 - 4 - 4 - 4 - 4 - 4 - 4 = 0; x = 6\ groups$	$x = 6$
2.	$36 \div x = 6$	$36 - 6 - 6 - 6 - 6 - 6 - 6 = 0$	$36 - 6 - 6 - 6 - 6 - 6 - 6 = 0; x = 6\ groups$	$x = 6$
3.	$28 \div y = 7$	$28 - 7 - 7 - 7 - 7 = 0$	$28 - 7 - 7 - 7 - 7 = 0; y = 4\ groups$	$y = 4$
4.	$30 \div y = 5$	$30 - 5 - 5 - 5 - 5 - 5 - 5 = 0$	$30 - 5 - 5 - 5 - 5 - 5 - 5 = 0; y = 6\ groups$	$y = 6$
5.	$16 \div z = 4$	$16 - 4 - 4 - 4 - 4 = 0$	$16 - 4 - 4 - 4 - 4 = 0; z = 4\ groups$	$z = 4$

Graphic Organizer Reproducible

Topic B:
Special Notations of Operations

6.EE.A.1, 6.EE.A.2c

Focus Standard:	6.EE.A.1	Write and evaluate numeric expressions involving whole-number exponents.
	6.EE.A.2c	Write, read, and evaluate expressions in which letters stand for numbers.
		c. Evaluate expressions at specific values of their variables. Include expressions that arise from formulas used in real-world problems. Perform arithmetic operations, including those involving whole-number exponents, in the conventional order when there are no parentheses to specify a particular order (Order of Operations). *For example, use the formulas $V = s^3$ and $A = 6s^2$ to find the volume and surface area of a cube with sides of length $s = 1/2$.*
Instructional Days:	2	
Lesson 5:	Exponents (S)[1]	
Lesson 6:	The Order of Operations (P)	

In Topic B, students differentiate between the product of two numbers and whole numbers with exponents. They differentiate between the two through exploration of patterns, specifically noting how squares grow from a 1×1 measure. They determine that a square with a length and width of three units in measure is constructed with nine square units. This expression is represented as 3^2 and is evaluated as the product of $3 \times 3 = 9$, not the product of the base and exponent, 6. They further differentiate between the two by comparing the areas of two models with similar measures, as shown below:

$2a$
When $a = 3$ the
area of the
rectangle is 6
square units.

a^2
When $a = 3$ the area of
the rectangle is 9
square units.

---

[1] Lesson Structure Key: **P**-Problem Set Lesson, **M**-Modeling Cycle Lesson, **E**-Exploration Lesson, **S**-Socratic Lesson

Once students understand that the base is multiplied by itself the number of times as stated by the exponent, they make a smooth transition into bases that are represented with positive fractions and decimals. They know that for any number, a, we define a^m to be the product of m factors of a. The number a is the base and m is called the exponent (or the power) of a.

In Lesson 6, students build on their previous understanding of the order of operations by including work with exponents. They follow the order of operations to evaluate numerical expressions. They recognize in the absence of parentheses that exponents are evaluated first. Students identify when the order of operations is incorrectly applied and determine the applicable course to correctly evaluate expressions. They understand that the placement of parentheses can alter the final solution when evaluating expressions, as in the following example:

$$2^4 \cdot (2 + 8) - 16 \qquad 2^4 \cdot 2 + 8 - 16$$

$$2^4 \cdot 10 - 16 \qquad 16 \cdot 2 + 8 - 16$$

$$16 \cdot 10 - 16 \qquad 32 + 8 - 16$$

$$160 - 16 \qquad 40 - 16$$

$$144 \qquad 24$$

Students continue to apply the order of operations throughout the module as they evaluate numerical and algebraic expressions.

Lesson 5: Exponents

Student Outcomes

- Students discover that $3x = x + x + x$ is not the same thing as x^3 which is $x \cdot x \cdot x$.
- Students understand that a base number can be represented with a positive whole number, positive fraction, or positive decimal and that for any number a, we define a^m to be the product of m factors of a. The number a is the base and m is called the exponent or power of a.

Lesson Notes

In 5th grade, students are introduced to exponents. Explain patterns in the number of zeros of the product when multiplying a number by powers of 10, and explain patterns in the placement of the decimal point when a decimal is multiplied or divided by a power of 10. Use whole-number exponents to denote powers of 10 (**5.NBT.A.2**).

In this lesson, students will use new terminology (base, squared, and cubed), and practice moving between exponential notation, expanded notation, and standard notation. The following terms should be displayed, defined, and emphasized throughout Lesson 5: base, exponent, power, squared, and cubed.

Fluency Exercise (5 minutes)

Multiplication of Decimals White Board Exchange

Classwork

Opening Exercise (2 minutes)

> **Opening Exercise**
>
> As you evaluate these expressions, pay attention to how you arrive at your answers.
>
> $4 + 4 + 4 + 4 + 4 + 4 + 4 + 4 + 4 + 4$
>
> $9 + 9 + 9 + 9 + 9$
>
> $10 + 10 + 10 + 10 + 10$

Socratic Discussion (15 minutes)

- How many of you solved the problems by "counting on"? That is, starting with 4, you counted on 4 more each time $(5, 6, 7, \mathbf{8}, 9, 10, 11, \mathbf{12}, 13, 14, 15, \mathbf{16} \dots)$
- If you did not find the answer that way, could you have done so?
  - *Yes, but it is time-consuming and cumbersome.*
- Addition is a faster way of "counting on."

- How else could you find the sums using addition?
  - *Count by 4, 9, or 10.*
- How else could you solve the problems?
  - *Multiply 4 times 10; multiply 9 times 5; multiply 10 times 5.*
- Multiplication is a faster way to add numbers when the addends are the same.
- When we add five groups of 10, we use an abbreviation and a different notation, called multiplication. $10 + 10 + 10 + 10 + 10 = 5 \times 10$.
- If multiplication is a more efficient way to represent addition problems involving the repeated addition of the same addend, do you think there might be a more efficient way to represent the repeated multiplication of the same factor, as in $10 \times 10 \times 10 \times 10 \times 10 = ?$

MP.2 & MP.7

Allow students to make suggestions; some will recall this from previous learning.

$$10 \times 10 \times 10 \times 10 \times 10 = 10^5$$

- We see that when we add 5 groups of 10, we write 5×10, but when we multiply 5 copies of 10, we write 10^5. So, multiplication by 5 in the context of addition corresponds exactly to the exponent 5 in the context of multiplication.

Make students aware of the correspondence between addition and multiplication because what they know about *repeated addition* will help them learn exponents as *repeated multiplication* as we go forward.

- The little 5 we write is called an exponent and is written as a superscript. The numeral 5 is written only half as tall and half as wide as the 10, and the bottom of the 5 should be halfway up the number 10. The top of the 5 can extend a little higher than the top of the zero in 10. Why do you think we write exponents so carefully?
  - *It reduces the chance that a reader will confuse 10^5 with 105.*

> *Scaffolding:*
> When teaching students how to write an exponent as a **super**script, compare and contrast the notation with how to write a **sub**script, as in the molecular formula for water, H_2O, or carbon dioxide, CO_2. Here the number is again half as tall as the capital letters, and the top of the 2 is halfway down it. The bottom of the subscript can extend a little lower than the bottom of the letter. Ignore the meaning of a chemical subscript.

Examples 1–5 (5 minutes)

Work through Examples 1–5 as a group, supplement with additional examples if needed.

Examples 1–5

Example 1

$5 \times 5 \times 5 \times 5 \times 5 = 5^5$

Example 2

$2 \times 2 \times 2 \times 2 = 2^4$

Example 3

$8^3 = 8 \times 8 \times 8$

Example 4

$10^6 = 10 \times 10 \times 10 \times 10 \times 10 \times 10$

Example 5

$g^3 = g \times g \times g$

- The repeated factor is called the **base** and the exponent is also called the **power**. Say the numbers in examples 1–5 to a partner.

Check to make sure students read the examples correctly:

- *Five to the sixth power, two to the fourth power, eight to the third power, ten to the sixth power, and g to the third power.*

Go back to Examples 1–4 and use a calculator to evaluate the expressions.

Example 1

$5 \times 5 \times 5 \times 5 \times 5 = 5^5 = 3,125$

Example 2

$2 \times 2 \times 2 \times 2 = 2^4 = 16$

Example 3

$8^3 = 8 \times 8 \times 8 = 512$

Example 4

$10^6 = 10 \times 10 \times 10 \times 10 \times 10 \times 10 = 1,000,000$

What is the difference between $3g$ and g^3?

$3g = g + g + g$ or 3 times g ; $g^3 = g \times g \times g$

Take time to clarify this important distinction.

- The base number can also be written in decimal or fraction form. Try Examples 6, 7, and 8. Use a calculator to evaluate the expressions.

Example 6–8 (4 minutes)

Example 6

$3.8^4 = 3.8 \times 3.8 \times 3.8 \times 3.8 = 208.5136$

Example 7

$2.1 \times 2.1 = 2.1^2 = 4.41$

Example 8

$0.75 \times 0.75 \times 0.75 = (0.75)^3 = 0.421875$

Note to teacher:

If students need additional help multiplying fractions, refer to the first four modules of Grade 5.

The base number can also be a fraction. Convert the decimals to fractions in Examples 7 and 8 and evaluate. Leave your answer as a fraction. Remember how to multiply fractions!

Example 9–10 (1 minute)

Example 9	Example 10
$\dfrac{1}{2} \times \dfrac{1}{2} \times \dfrac{1}{2} = \left(\dfrac{1}{2}\right)^3 = \dfrac{1}{8}$	$\left(\dfrac{2}{3}\right)^2 = \dfrac{2}{3} \times \dfrac{2}{3} = \dfrac{4}{9}$

- There is a special name for numbers raised to the second power. When a number is raised to the second power, it is called *squared*. Remember that in geometry, squares have the same two dimensions: length and width. For $b > 0$, b^2 is the area of a square with side length b.

- What is the value of 5 squared?
  - □ 25

- What is the value of 7 squared?
  - □ 49

- What is the value of 8 squared?
  - □ 64

- What is the value of 1 squared?
  - □ 1

> **Note to Teacher:**
>
> If students ask about exponent values of n that are not positive integers, let them know that positive and negative fractional exponents will be introduced in Algebra II and that negative *integer* exponents will be discussed in eighth grade.

A multiplication chart is included at the end of this lesson. Post or project it as needed.

- Where are square numbers found on the multiplication table?
  - □ *On the diagonal.*

- There is also a special name for numbers raised to the third power. When a number is raised to the third power, it is called *cubed*. Remember that in geometry, cubes have the same three dimensions: length, width, and height. For $b > 0$, b^3 is the volume of a cube with edge length b.

- What is the value of 1 cubed?
  - □ $1 \times 1 \times 1 = 1$

- What is the value of 2 cubed?
  - □ $2 \times 2 \times 2 = 8$

- What is the value of 3 cubed?
  - □ $3 \times 3 \times 3 = 27$

- In general, for any number x, $x^1 = x$, and for any positive integer $n > 1$, x^n is by definition,
  $$x^n = \underbrace{(x \cdot x \cdots x)}_{n\ times}.$$

- What does the x represent in this expression?
  - □ *The x represents the factor that will be repeatedly multiplied by itself.*

MP.6

- What does the n represent in this expression?
  - □ *n represents the number of times x will be multiplied.*

- Let's look at this with some numbers. How would we represent 4^n?
  - □ $4^n = \underbrace{(4 \cdot 4 \cdots 4)}_{n\ times}$

- What does the 4 represent in this expression?
  - The 4 represents the factor that will be repeatedly multiplied by itself.
- What does the n represent in this expression?
  - *n represents the number of times 4 will be multiplied.*
- What if we were simply multiplying? How would we represent $4n$?

  MP.6
  - *Because multiplication is repeated addition, $4n = \underbrace{(4 + 4 \cdots 4)}_{n\ times}$*
- What does the 4 represent in this expression?
  - The 4 represents the addend that will be repeatedly added to itself.
- What does the n represent in this expression?
  - *n represents the number of times 4 will be added.*

Exercise 1–4 (8 minutes)

Ask students to fill in the chart, supplying the missing expressions.

Exercises 1–4

1. Fill in the missing expressions for each row. For whole number and decimal bases, use a calculator to find the standard form of the number. For fraction bases, leave your answer as a fraction.

   Sample solutions are in italics.

Exponential Form	Written as a multiplication expression having repeated factors	Standard Form
3^2	3×3	9
2^6	$2 \times 2 \times 2 \times 2 \times 2 \times 2$	64
4^5	$4 \times 4 \times 4 \times 4 \times 4$	$1,024$
$\left(\dfrac{3}{4}\right)^2$	$\dfrac{3}{4} \times \dfrac{3}{4}$	$\dfrac{9}{16}$
1.5^2	1.5×1.5	2.25

2. Write "five cubed" in all three forms: exponential form, written as a series of products, standard form.

   5^3 ; $5 \times 5 \times 5$; 125

3. Write "fourteen and seven tenths squared" in all three forms.

   14.7^2 ; 14.7×14.7 ; 216.09

4. One student thought two to the third power was equal to six. What mistake do you think they made and how would you help them fix their mistake?

   The student multiplied the base (2) by the exponent (3). This is wrong because the exponent never multiplies bases; the exponent tells how many copies of the base are to be used as factors.

Closing (2 minutes)

- We use multiplication as a quicker way to do repeated addition if the addends are the same. We use exponents as a quicker way to multiply if the factors are the same.
- Carefully write exponents as superscripts to avoid confusion.

Lesson Summary

<u>Exponential Notation for Whole Number Exponents:</u> Let m be a non-zero whole number. For any number a, the expression a^m is the product of m factors of a, i.e.,

$$a^m = \underbrace{a \cdot a \cdots \cdots a}_{m \ times}.$$

The number a is called the *base,* and m is called the *exponent* or *power* of a.

When m is 1, "the product of one factor of a" just means a, i.e., $a^1 = a$. Raising any non-zero number a to the power of 0 is defined to be 1, i.e., $a^0 = 1$ for all $a \neq 0$.

Exit Ticket (3 minutes)

Name _____   Date_____

Lesson 5: Exponents

1.   What is the difference between $6z$ and z^6?

2.   Write 10^3 as a multiplication expression having repeated factors.

3.   Write $8 \times 8 \times 8 \times 8$ using exponents.

Exit Ticket Sample Solutions

> **1.** What is the difference between $6z$ and z^6?
>
> $6z = z + z + z + z + z + z$ or **6 times** z ; $z^6 = z \times z \times z \times z \times z \times z$
>
> **2.** Write 10^3 as a series of products.
>
> $10 \times 10 \times 10$
>
> **3.** Write $8 \times 8 \times 8 \times 8$ using an exponent.
>
> 8^4

Problem Set Sample Solutions

> **1.** Complete the table by filling in the blank cells. Use a calculator when needed.
>
> | Exponential Form | Written as a series of products | Standard Form |
> |---|---|---|
> | 3^5 | $3 \times 3 \times 3 \times 3 \times 3$ | 243 |
> | 4^3 | $4 \times 4 \times 4$ | 64 |
> | 1.9^2 | 1.9×1.9 | 3.61 |
> | $\left(\dfrac{1}{2}\right)^5$ | $\dfrac{1}{2} \times \dfrac{1}{2} \times \dfrac{1}{2} \times \dfrac{1}{2} \times \dfrac{1}{2}$ | $\dfrac{1}{32}$ |
>
> **2.** Why do whole numbers raised to an exponent get greater while fractions raised to an exponent get smaller?
>
> *As whole numbers are multiplied by themselves, products are larger because there are more groups. As fractions of fractions are taken, the product is smaller. A part of a part is less than how much we started with.*
>
> **3.** The powers of 2 that are in the range 2 through $1,000$ are $2, 4, 8, 16, 32, 64, 128, 256,$ and 512. Find all the powers of 3 that are in the range 3 through $1,000$.
>
> $3, 9, 27, 81, 243, 729$
>
> **4.** Find all the powers of 4 in the range 4 through $1,000$.
>
> $4, 16, 64, 256$
>
> **5.** Write an equivalent expression for $n \times a$ using only addition.
>
> $\underbrace{(a + a + \cdots a)}_{n\ times}$
>
> **6.** Write an equivalent expression for w^b using only multiplication.
>
> $w^b = \underbrace{(w \cdot w \cdots w)}_{b\ times}$

a. Explain what *w* is in this new expression.

w is the factor that will be repeatedly multiplied by itself.

b. Explain what *b* is in this new expression.

b is the number of times w will be multiplied.

7. What are the advantages to using exponential notation?

It is a shorthand way of writing a multiplication expression if the factors are all the same.

8. What is the difference between $4x$ and x^4? Evaluate both of these expressions when $x = 2$.

$4x$ means four times x, this is the same as $x + x + x + x$. On the other hand, x^4 means x to the fourth power, or $x \times x \times x \times x$.

When $x = 2$, $4x = 4 \times 2 = 8$

When $x = 2$, $x^4 = 2 \times 2 \times 2 \times 2 = 16$

White Board Exchange: Multiplication of Decimals

Progression of Exercises:	Answers:
1. 0.5×0.5	0.25
2. 0.6×0.6	0.36
3. 0.7×0.7	0.49
4. 0.5×0.6	0.3
5. 1.5×1.5	2.25
6. 2.5×2.5	6.25
7. 0.25×0.25	0.0625
8. 0.1×0.1	0.01
9. 0.1×123.4	12.34
10. 0.01×123.4	1.234

Fluency work such as this exercise should take 5–12 minutes of class.

How to Conduct a White Board Exchange:

All students will need a personal white board, white board marker, and a means of erasing their work. An economical recommendation is to place card stock inside sheet protectors to use as the personal white boards and to cut sheets of felt into small squares to use as erasers.

It is best to prepare the problems in a way that allows you to reveal them to the class one at a time. For example, use a flip chart or PowerPoint presentation; write the problems on the board and cover with paper beforehand, allowing you to reveal one at a time; or, write only one problem on the board at a time. If the number of digits in the problem is very low (e.g., 12 divided by 3), it may also be appropriate to verbally call out the problem to the students.

The teacher reveals or says the first problem in the list and announces, "Go." Students work the problem on their personal white boards, holding their answers up for the teacher to see as soon as they have them ready. The teacher gives immediate feedback to each student, pointing and/or making eye contact with the student and responding with an affirmation for correct work such as, "Good job!", "Yes!", or "Correct!" For incorrect work, respond with guidance such as "Look again!", "Try again!", or "Check your work!"

If many students have struggled to get the answer correct, go through the solution of that problem as a class before moving on to the next problem in the sequence. Fluency in the skill has been established when the class is able to go through each problem in quick succession without pausing to go through the solution of each problem individually. If only one or two students have not been able to get a given problem correct when the rest of the students are finished, it is appropriate to move the class forward to the next problem without further delay; in this case, find a time to provide remediation to that student before the next fluency exercise on this skill is given.

Lesson 5:	Exponents
Date:	12/11/13

58

Lesson 6: Order of Operations

Student Outcomes

- Students evaluate numerical expressions. They recognize that in the absence of parentheses, exponents are evaluated first.

Classwork

Opening (5 minutes)

Take a few minutes to review the problem set from the previous lesson. Clarify any misconceptions about the use and evaluation of exponents.

Opening Exercise (5 minutes)

Post the following expression on the board and ask students to evaluate it:

$$3 + 4 \times 2$$

Ask students to record their answer and report it using individual whiteboards, cards, or electronic vote devices, etc. Students who arrive at an answer other than 11 or 14 should recheck their work.

Discussion (5 minutes)

- How could you evaluate the expression $3 + 4 \times 2$?
  - $3 + 4$ *could be added first for a sum of 7; then,* $7 \times 2 = 14$.
  - 4×2 *could be multiplied first for a product of 8, then,* $8 + 3 = 11$.
- Only one of these can be correct. When we evaluate expressions, we must agree to use one set of rules so that everyone arrives at the same correct answer.
- During the last lesson, we said that addition was a shortcut to "counting on."

  How could you think about subtraction?
  - *Subtraction is a shortcut to "counting back."*
- These were the first operations that you learned because they are the least complicated. Next, you learned about multiplication and division.
- Multiplication can be thought of as repeated addition. Thinking back on Lesson 4, how could you think about division?
  - *Division is repeated subtraction.*
- Multiplication and division are more powerful than addition and subtraction, which led mathematicians to develop the order of operations in this way. When we evaluate expressions that have any of these four operations, we always calculate multiplication and division before doing any addition or subtraction. Since multiplication and division are equally powerful, we simply evaluate these two operations as they are written in the expression, from left to right.

Lesson 6:	Order of Operations
Date:	12/11/13

59

- Addition and subtraction are at the same level in the order of operations and are evaluated from left to right in an expression. Now that these rules of Order of Operations are clear, can you go back and evaluate the expression $3 + 4 \times 2$ as 11?

- The diagram correctly models the expression $3 + 4 \times 2$.
- With addition we are finding the sum of two addends. In this example the first addend is the number 3. The second addend happens to be the number that is the value of the expression 4×2, so before we can add we must determine the value of the second addend.

Example 1 (5 minutes): Expressions with Only Addition, Subtraction, Multiplication, and Division

> **Example 1: Expressions with Only Addition, Subtraction, Multiplication, and Division**
>
> **What operations are evaluated first?**
>
> *Multiplication and division, from left to right.*
>
> **What operations are always evaluated last?**
>
> *Addition and subtraction, from left to right.*

Ask students to evaluate the expressions.

Exercises 1–3

> **Exercises**
>
> 1. $4 + 2 \times 7$
>
> $4 + 14$
>
>   **18**
>
> 2. $36 \div 3 \times 4$
>
> 12×4
>
>   **48**
>
> 3. $20 - 5 \times 2$
>
> $20 - 10$
>
>   **10**

- In the last lesson, you learned about exponents, which are a way of writing repeated multiplication. So, exponents are more powerful than multiplication or division. If exponents are present in an expression, they are evaluated before any multiplication or division.

- When we evaluate expressions, we must agree to use one set of rules so that everyone arrives at the same correct answer. These rules are based on doing the most powerful operations first (exponents), then the less powerful ones (multiplication and division, going from left to right), and finally the least powerful ones last (addition and subtraction, going from left to right).

- Evaluate the expression $4 + 6 \times 6 \div 8$.
    - $4 + (6 \times 6) \div 8$
    - $4 + (36 \div 8)$
    - $4 + 4.5$
    - 8.5

- Now evaluate the expression $4 + 6^2 \div 8$.
    - $4 + 36 \div 8$
    - $4 + (36 \div 8)$
    - $4 + 4.5$
    - 8.5

- Why was your first step to find the value of 6^2?
    - *Because exponents are evaluated first.*

Example 2 (5 minutes): Expressions with Four Operations and Exponents

Display the following expression.

> **Scaffolding:**
> Some students may benefit from rewriting the expression on successive lines, evaluating only one or two operations on each line.

Example 2: Expressions with Four Operations and Exponents

$$4 + 9^2 \div 3 \times 2 - 2$$

What operation is evaluated first?

Exponents ($9^2 = 9 \times 9 = 81$)

What operations are evaluated next?

Multiplication and division, from left to right ($81 \div 3 = 27$; $27 \times 2 = 54$)

What operations are always evaluated last?

Addition and subtraction, from left to right ($4 + 54 = 58$; $58 - 2 = 56$)

What is the final answer?

56

- Evaluate the next two Exercises.

While the answers are provided, it is extremely important to circulate to ensure that students are using the correct order of operations to achieve the answer. For example, in Exercise 5, they should show 4^3 first, followed by 2×8.

COMMON CORE™ | Lesson 6:   Order of Operations   **61**
                | Date: 12/11/13

Exercises 4–5

> **Exercises 4–5**
>
> 4. $90 - 5^2 \times 3$
>
>   15
>
> 5. $4^3 + 2 \times 8$
>
>   80

Example 3 (5 minutes): Expressions with Parentheses

- The last important rule in the order of operations involves grouping symbols (usually parentheses). These tell us that in certain circumstances or scenarios, we need to do things out of the usual order. Operations inside grouping are always evaluated first, before exponents.

> **Example 3: Expressions with Parentheses**
>
> Consider a family of 4 that goes to a soccer game. Tickets are $\$5.00$ each.   The mom also buys a soft drink for $\$2.00$. How would you write this expression?
>
> $4 \times 5 + 2$
>
> **How much will this outing cost?**
>
> $\$22$

- Here is a model of the scenario:

> Consider a different scenario: The family goes to the game like before, but each of the family members wants a drink. How would you write this expression?
>
> $4 \times (5 + 2)$
>
> Why would you add the 5 and 2 first?
>
> *Because we need to determine how much each of them are spending. Each one spends $\$7$, then we multiply by 4 people to figure out the total cost.*
>
> **How much will this outing cost?**
>
> $\$28$

- Here is a model of the second scenario:

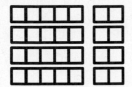

How many groups are there?
4
What is each group comprised of?
\$5 + \$2 *or* \$7

- The last complication that can arise is that if two or more sets of parentheses are ever needed, evaluate the innermost parentheses first, and work outward.

- Try Exercises 6 and 7.

Exercises 6–7

Exercises 6–7
6. $2 + (9^2 - 4)$
79
7. $2 \cdot (13 + 5 - 14 \div (3 + 4))$
32

If students are confused trying to divide 14 by 3, reiterate the rule about nested parentheses.

Example 4 (5 minutes): Expressions with Parentheses and Exponents

- Let's take a look at how parentheses and exponents work together. Sometimes a problem will have parentheses and the values inside the parentheses have an exponent. Let's evaluate this expression:

Place the expression on the board:

- We will evaluate the parentheses first.

Example 4: Expressions with Parentheses and Exponents
$2 \times (3 + 4^2)$

Which value will we evaluate first within the parentheses?

First, evaluate 4^2 which is sixteen, then add three. The value of the parentheses is nineteen.

$$2 \times (3 + 4^2)$$
$$2 \times (3 + 16)$$
$$2 \times 19$$

Evaluate the rest of the expression.

$$2 \times 19 = 38$$

Place the expression on the board:

What do you think will happen when the exponent in this expression is outside of the parentheses?

$$2 \times (3 + 4)^2$$

Will the answer be the same?

Answers will vary

Which should we evaluate first? Evaluate.

Parentheses

$$2 \times (3 + 4)^2$$
$$2 \times (7)^2$$

What happened differently here than in our last example?

The four was not raised to the second power because it did not have an exponent. We simply added the values inside the parentheses.

What should our next step be?

We need to evaluate the exponent next.

$$7^2 = 7 \times 7 = 49$$

Evaluate to find the final answer.

$$2 \times 49$$
$$98$$

What do you notice about the two answers?

The final answers were not the same.

What was different between the two expressions?

Answers may vary. In the first problem, a value inside the parentheses had an exponent and that value was evaluated first because it was inside of the parentheses. In the second problem, the exponent was outside of the parentheses and we evaluated what was in the parentheses first, and then raised that value to the power of the exponent.

> What conclusions can you draw about evaluating expressions with parentheses and exponents?
>
> *Answers may vary. Regardless of where the exponent is in the expression, evaluate the parentheses first. Sometimes there will be values with exponents inside the parentheses. If the exponent is outside the parentheses, evaluate the parentheses first, and then evaluate to the power of the exponent.*

- Try Exercises 8 and 9.

Exercises 8–9

> **Exercises 8–9**
>
> 8. $7 + (12 - 3^2)$
>
>   10
>
> 9. $7 + (12 - 3)^2$
>
>   88

Closing (5 minutes)

- When we evaluate expressions, we use one set of rules so that everyone arrives at the same correct answer. Grouping symbols like parentheses tell us to evaluate whatever is inside them before moving on. These rules are based on doing the most powerful operations first (exponents), then the less powerful ones (multiplication and division, going from left to right), and finally the least powerful ones last (addition and subtraction, going from left to right).

> **Lesson Summary**
>
> **Numerical Expression:** A *numerical expression* is a number, or it is any combination of sums, differences, products or divisions of numbers that evaluates to a number.
>
> Statements like, "3 +" or "3 ÷ 0," are not numerical expressions because neither represents a point on the number line. Note: Raising numbers to whole number powers are considered numerical expressions as well, since the operation is just an abbreviated form of multiplication, e.g., $2^3 = 2 \cdot 2 \cdot 2$.
>
> **Value of a Numerical Expression:** The *value* of a numerical expression is the number found by evaluating the expression.
>
> For example: $\frac{1}{3} \cdot (2 + 4) + 7$ is a numerical expression and its value is 9.

Note: Please do not stress words over meaning here. It is okay to talk about the "number computed," "computation," "calculation," etc. to refer to the value as well.

Exit Ticket (5 minutes)

Name _____ Date _____

Lesson 6: Order of Operations

Exit Ticket

1. Evaluate this expression: $39 \div (2 + 1) - 2 \times (4 + 1)$

2. Evaluate this expression: $12 \times (3 + 2^2) \div 2 - 10$

3. Evaluate this expression: $12 \times (3 + 2)^2 \div 2 - 10$

Exit Ticket Sample Solutions

1. Evaluate this expression: $39 \div (2 + 1) - 2 \times (4 + 1)$

   3

2. Evaluate this expression: $12 \times (3 + 2^2) \div 2 - 10$

   32

3. Evaluate this expression: $12 \times (3 + 2)^2 \div 2 - 10$

   140

Problem Set Sample Solutions

Evaluate each expression:

1. $3 \times 5 + 2 \times 8 + 2$

   33

2. $(\$1.75 + 2 \times \$0.25 + 5 \times \$0.05) \times 24$

   $60.00

3. $(2 \times 6) + (8 \times 4) + 1$

   45

4. $((8 \times 1.95) + (3 \times 2.95) + 10.95) \times 1.06$

   37.524

5. $((12 \div 3)^2 - (18 \div 3^2)) \times (4 \div 2)$

   28

Topic C:

Replacing Letters and Numbers

6.EE.A.2c, 6.EE.A.4

Focus Standard:	6.EE.A.2c	Write, read, and evaluate expressions in which letters stand for numbers.
		c. Evaluate expressions at specific values of their variables. Include expressions that arise from formulas used in real-world problems. Perform arithmetic operations, including those involving whole-number exponents, in the conventional order when there are no parentheses to specify a particular order (Order of Operations). *For example, use the formulas $V = s^3$ and $A = 6s^2$ to find the volume and surface area of a cube with sides of length $s = 1/2$.*
	6.EE.A.4	Identify when two expressions are equivalent (i.e., when the two expressions name the same number regardless of which value is substituted into them). *For example, the expressions $y + y + y$ and $3y$ are equivalent because they name the same number regardless of which number y stands for.*
Instructional Days:	2	
Lesson 7:	Replacing Letters with Numbers (P)[1]	
Lesson 8:	Replacing Numbers with Letters (S)	

Students begin substituting, or replacing, letters with numbers and numbers with letters in Topic C in order to evaluate expressions with a given number and to determine expressions to create identities. In Lesson 7, students replace letters with a given number in order to evaluate the expression to one number. They continue to practice with exponents in this lesson in order to determine the area of squares and rectangles as shown below.

---

[1] Lesson Structure Key: **P**-Problem Set Lesson, **M**-Modeling Cycle Lesson, **E**-Exploration Lesson, **S**-Socratic Lesson

$A = l \cdot w$
$A = x\ cm \cdot x\ cm$
$A = x^2 cm^2$

$A = l \cdot w$
$A = 4\ cm \cdot 4\ cm$
$A = 4^2 cm^2$
$A = 16\ cm^2$

Width = 9 cm
Width = b cm
b = 9cm

Length = x cm
Length = 4 · 5 cm
Length = 20 cm
x = 20 cm

$A = l \cdot w$
$A = x \cdot b$
$A = 20\ cm \cdot 9\ cm$
$A = 180\ cm^2$

In Lesson 8, students understand that a number in an expression can be replaced with a letter to determine identities. Through replacement of numbers, students discover and build identities such as $a + b = b + a$, $a \times b = b \times a$, $g \times 1 = g$, $g + 0 = g$, $g \div 1 = g$, $g \div g = 1$, $1 \div g = \frac{1}{g}$. These identities will aid in solving equations with variables, as well as problem solving with equations.

$4 \times 1 = 4$
$4 \div 1 = 4$
$4 \times 0 = 4$
$1 \div 4 = \frac{1}{4}$

$\longrightarrow$

$g \times 1 = g$
$g \div 1 = g$
$g \times 0 = 0$
$1 \div g = \frac{1}{g}$

$3 + 4 = 4 + 3$
$3 \times 4 = 4 \times 3$
$3 + 3 + 3 + 3 = 4 \times 3$
$3 \div 4 = \frac{3}{4}$

$\longrightarrow$

$a + 4 = 4 + a$
$a \times 4 = 4 \times a$
$a + a + a + a = 4 \times a$
$a \div 4 = \frac{a}{4}$

Lesson 7: Replacing Letters with Numbers

Student Outcomes

- Students understand that a letter represents one number in an expression. When that number replaces the letter, the expression can be evaluated to one number.

Lesson Notes

Before this lesson, make it clear to students that just like 3×3 is 3^2 or three squared, units $\times$ units is units^2 or units squared (also called square units).

It may be helpful to cut and paste some of the figures from this lesson onto either paper or an interactive whiteboard application. Each of the basic figures is depicted two ways: one has side lengths that can be counted and the other is a similar figure without grid lines. Also, ahead of time, draw a 23 cm square on a chalkboard, whiteboard, or interactive board.

There is a square in the student materials that is approximately 23 mm square, or 529 mm^2.

Classwork

Example 1 (10 minutes)

Draw or project the square shown.

Example 1

What is the length of one side of this square?

3 *units*

What is the formula for the area of a square?

$A = s^2$

What is the square's area as a multiplication expression?

3 *units* $\times$ 3 *units*

What is the square's area?

9 *square units*

We can count the units. However, look at this other square. Its side length is 23 cm. That is just too many tiny units to draw. What expression can we build to find this square's area?

23 cm

$23\ cm \times 23\ cm$

What is the area of the square? Use a calculator if you need to.

$529\ cm^2$

- A letter represents <u>one</u> number in an expression. That number was 3 in our first square and 23 in our second square. When that number replaces the letter, the expression can be evaluated to <u>one</u> number. In our first example, the expression was evaluated to be 9, and in the second example, the expression was evaluated to be 529.

Make sure students understand that 9 is one number, but 529 is also one number. (It happens to have 3 digits, but it is still one number.)

Exercise 1 (5 minutes)

Ask students to work both problems from Exercise 1 in their student materials. Make clear to the students that these drawings are not to scale.

Exercise 1

Complete the table below for both squares. Note: These drawings are not to scale.

$s = 4$

$s = 25$ in.

Lesson 7:   Replacing Letters with Numbers
Date: 12/11/13

Length of One Side of the Square	Square's Area Written as an Expression	Square's Area Written as a Number
4 units	4 units × 4 units	16 square units
25 in.	25 in. × 25 in.	625 in²

Make sure students have the units correctly recorded in each of the cells of the table. When units are not specified, keep the label "unit" or "square unit".

Example 2 (10 minutes)

Example 2

- The formula $A = l \times w$ is an efficient way to find the area of a rectangle without being required to count the area units in a rectangle.

> **What does the letter b represent in this blue rectangle?**
>
> $b = 8$

Give students a short time for discussion of the next question among partners, and then ask for an answer and an explanation.

> **With a partner, answer the following question: Given that the second rectangle is divided into four <u>equal</u> parts, what number does the x represent?**
>
> $x = 8$
>
> **How did you arrive at this answer?**
>
> *We reasoned that each width of the 4 congruent rectangles must be the same. Two 4 cm lengths equals 8 cm.*
>
> **What is the total length of the second rectangle? Tell a partner how you know.**
>
> *The length consists of 4 segments that each has a length of 4 cm. 4×4 cm $= 16$ cm.*

Lesson 7:	Replacing Letters with Numbers
Date:	12/11/13

> If the two large rectangles have equal lengths and widths, find the area of each rectangle.
>
> 128 cm²
>
> Discuss with your partner how the formulas for the area of squares and rectangles can be used to evaluate area for a particular figure.

- Remember, a letter represents <u>one</u> number in an expression. When that number replaces the letter, the expression can be evaluated to <u>one</u> number.

Exercise 2 (5 minutes)

Ask students to complete the table for both rectangles in their student materials. Using a calculator is appropriate.

Exercise 2

Length of Rectangle	Width of Rectangle	Rectangle's Area Written as an Expression	Rectangle's Area Written as a Number
7 units	4 units	7 units × 4 units	28 square units
46 m	32 m	46 m × 32 m	1,472 m²

Example 3 (3 minutes)

- The formula $V = l \times w \times h$ is a quick way to determine the volume of right rectangular prisms.
- Take a look at the right rectangular prisms in your student materials.

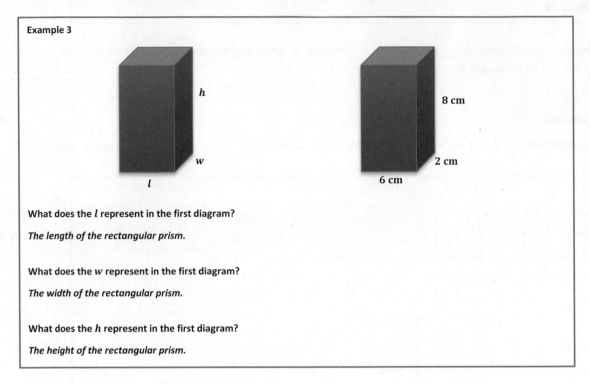

Example 3

What does the l represent in the first diagram?

The length of the rectangular prism.

What does the w represent in the first diagram?

The width of the rectangular prism.

What does the h represent in the first diagram?

The height of the rectangular prism.

- Notice that the right rectangular prism in the second diagram is an exact copy of the first diagram.

Since we know the formula to find the volume is $V = l \times w \times h$, what number can we substitute for the l in the formula? Why?

6, because the length of the second right rectangular prism is 6 cm.

What other number can we substitute for the l?

No other number can replace the l. Only one number can replace one letter.

What number can we substitute for the w in the formula? Why?

2, because the width of the second right rectangular prism is 2 cm.

What number can we substitute for the h in the formula?

8, because the height of the second right rectangular prism is 8 cm.

Determine the volume of the second right rectangular prism by replacing the letters in the formula with their appropriate numbers.

$V = l \times w \times h; V = 6\ cm \times 2\ cm \times 8\ cm = 96\ cm^3$

Exercise 3 (5 minutes)

Ask students to complete the table for both figures in their student materials. Using a calculator is appropriate.

Exercise 3

15 units

5 units

12 units

7 cm

4 cm

23 cm

Length of Rectangular Prism	Width of Rectangular Prism	Height of Rectangular Prism	Rectangular Prism's Volume Written as an Expression	Rectangular Prism's Volume Written as a Number
12 *units*	5 *units*	15 *units*	12 *units* × 5 *units* × 15 *units*	900 *cubic units*
23 *cm*	4 *cm*	7 *cm*	23 *cm* × 4 *cm* × 7 *cm*	644 *cm*³

Closing (2 minutes)

- How many numbers are represented by one letter in an expression?
  - *One.*

- When that number replaces the letter, the expression can be evaluated to what?
  - *One number.*

Lesson Summary

Expression: An *expression* is a numerical expression, or it is the result of replacing some (or all) of the numbers in a numerical expression with variables.

There are two ways to build expressions:

1. We can start out with a numerical expression, such as $\frac{1}{3} \cdot (2 + 4) + 7$, and replace some of the numbers with letters to get $\frac{1}{3} \cdot (x + y) + z$.

2. We can build such expressions from scratch, as in $x + x(y - z)$, and note that if numbers were placed in the expression for the variables x, y, and z, the result would be a numerical expression.

COMMON CORE™

Lesson 7:	Replacing Letters with Numbers
Date:	12/11/13

75

The key is to strongly link expressions back to computations with numbers.

The description for *expression* given above is meant to work nicely with how students in 6th and 7th grade learn to manipulate expressions. In these grades, a lot of time is spent *building expressions* and *evaluating expressions*. Building and evaluating helps students see that expressions are really just a slight abstraction of arithmetic in elementary school. Building often occurs by thinking about examples of numerical expressions first, and then replacing the numbers with letters in a numerical expression. The act of evaluating for students at this stage means they replace each of the variables with specific numbers and then compute to obtain a number.

Exit Ticket (5 minutes)

Name _____   Date _____

Lesson 7: Replacing Letters with Numbers

Exit Ticket

1. In the drawing below, what do the letters *l* and *w* represent?

2. What does the expression $l + w + l + w$ represent?

3. What does the expression $l \cdot w$ represent?

4. The rectangle below is congruent to the rectangle shown in Problem 1. Use this information to evaluate the expressions from Problems 2 and 3.

Exit Ticket Sample Solutions

1. In the drawing below, what do the letters l and w represent?

   Length and width of the rectangle

2. What does the expression $l + w + l + w$ represent?

   Perimeter of the rectangle, or the sum of the sides of the rectangle.

3. What does the expression $l \cdot w$ represent?

   Area of the rectangle

4. The rectangle below is congruent to the rectangle shown in Problem 1. Use this information to evaluate the expressions from Problems 2 and 3.

   $l = 5$ *and* $w = 2$ $P = 14$ *units* $A = 10$ *units*^{2}

Problem Set Sample Solutions

1. Replace the side length of this square with 4 in. and find the area.

   S

   The student should draw a square, label the side 4 in., and calculate the area to be 16 in.^{2}*.*

2. Complete the table for each of the given figures.

23 m

36 m

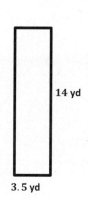

14 yd

3. 5 yd

Length of Rectangle	Width of Rectangle	Rectangle's Area Written as an Expression	Rectangle's Area Written as a Number
36 m	23 m	$36\,m \times 23\,m$	$828\,m^2$
14 yd	3. 5 yd	$14\,yd \times 3.5\,yd$	$49\,yd^2$

3. Find the perimeter of each quadrilateral in Problems 1 and 2.

$P = 16\ in.$ $P = 118\ m$ $P = 35\ yd$

4. Using the formula $V = l \times w \times h$, find the volume of a right rectangular prism when the length of the prism is 45 cm, the width is 12 cm, and the height is 10 cm.

$V = l \times w \times h; V = 45\ cm \times 12\ cm \times 10\ cm = 5,400\ cm^3$

Lesson 7:   Replacing Letters with Numbers
Date: 12/11/13

Lesson 8: Replacing Numbers with Letters

Student Outcomes

- Students understand that a letter in an expression or an equation can represent a number. When that number is replaced with a letter, an expression or an equation is stated.
- Students discover the commutative properties of addition and multiplication, the additive identity property of zero, and the multiplicative identity property of one. They determine that $g \div 1 = g$, $g \div g = 1$, and $1 \div g = \frac{1}{g}$.

Fluency Exercise (10 minutes)

Division of Fractions Sprint

Classwork

Opening Exercise (5 minutes)

Write this series of equations on the board:

Opening Exercise

$$4 + 0 = 4$$

$$4 \times 1 = 4$$

$$4 \div 1 = 4$$

$$4 \times 0 = 0$$

$$1 \div 4 = \frac{1}{4}$$

Discussion (5 minutes)

How many of these statements are true?

All of them.

How many of those statements would be true if the number 4 was replaced with the number 7 in each of the number sentences?

All of them.

Would the number sentences be true if we were to replace the number 4 with any other number?

MP.3

- Let students make conjectures about substitutions.

P.3

> **What if we replaced the number 4 with the number 0? Would each of the number sentences be true?**
>
> *No. The first four are true but the last one, dividing by zero, is not true.*

- Division by zero is *undefined*. You cannot make zero groups of objects, and group size cannot be zero.
- It appears that we can replace the number 4 with any non-zero number and each of the number sentences will be true.
- A letter in an expression can represent a number. When that number is replaced with a letter, an expression is stated.

> **What if we replace the number 4 with a letter g? Please write all 4 expressions in your student materials, replacing each 4 with a g.**
>
> $$g + 0 = g$$
> $$g \times 1 = g$$
> $$g \div 1 = g$$
> $$g \times 0 = 0$$
> $$1 \div g = \frac{1}{g}$$
>
> **Are these all true (except for $g = 0$) when dividing?**
>
> *Yes.*

- Let's look at each of these a little closer and see if we can make some generalizations.

Example 1 (5 minutes): Additive Identity Property of Zero

> **Example 1: Additive Identity Property of Zero**
>
> $$g + 0 = g$$
>
> **Remember a letter in a mathematical expression represents a number. Can we replace g with any number?**
>
> *Yes.*
>
> **Choose a value for g and replace g with that number in the number sentence. What do you observe?**
>
> *The value of g does not change when 0 is added to g.*
>
> **Repeat this process several times, each time choosing a different number for g.**

Allow students to experiment for about a minute. Most will quickly realize the additive identity property of zero: Any number added to zero equals itself. The number's identity does not change.

Lesson 8:   Replacing Numbers with Letters
Date: 12/11/13

81

Is the number sentence true for all values of g?

Yes.

Write the mathematical language for this property below:

$g + 0 = g$, *Additive identity property of zero. Any number added to zero equals itself.*

Example 2 (5 minutes): Multiplicative Identity Property of One

Example 2: Multiplicative Identity Property of One

$$g \times 1 = g$$

Remember a letter in a mathematical expression represents a number. Can we replace g with any number?

Yes.

Choose a value for g and replace g with that number in the number sentence. What do you observe?

The value of g does not change when g is multiplied by **1.**

Allow students to experiment for about a minute with the next question. Most will quickly realize the multiplicative identity property of one: Any number multiplied by 1 equals itself. The number's identity does not change.

Is the number sentence true for all values of g? Experiment with different values before making your claim.

Yes.

Write the mathematical language for this property below:

$g \times 1 = g$, *Multiplicative identity property of one. Any number multiplied by one equals itself.*

Example 3 (10 minutes): Commutative Property of Addition and Multiplication

Example 3: Commutative Property of Addition and Multiplication

$$3 + 4 = 4 + 3$$
$$3 \times 4 = 4 \times 3$$
$$3 + 3 + 3 + 3 = 4 \times 3$$
$$3 \div 4 = \frac{3}{4}$$

Replace the 3s in these equations with the letter a.

$$a + 4 = 4 + a$$
$$a \times 4 = 4 \times a$$
$$a + a + a + a = 4 \times a$$
$$a \div 4 = \frac{a}{4}$$

Lesson 8:   Replacing Numbers with Letters
Date: 12/11/13

82

> Choose a value for a and replace a with that number in each of the number sentences. What do you observe?
>
> *The number sentences are all true.*

Allow students to experiment for about a minute with the next question. Most will quickly realize that the first two equations are examples of the commutative property of addition and commutative property of multiplication. These are sometimes called the "any-order properties".

> Are the number sentences true for all values of a? Experiment with different values before making your claim.
>
> *Yes, any number, even zero, can be used in place of the variable a*
>
> Now write the number sentences again, this time replacing the number 4 with a variable, b.
>
> $$a + b = b + a$$
> $$a \times b = b \times a$$
> $$a + a + a + a = b \times a$$
> $$a \div b = \frac{a}{b}$$
>
> Are the first two number sentences true for all values of a and b? Experiment with different values before making your claim.
>
> *Yes.*
>
> Write the mathematical language for this property below:
>
> $a + b = b + a$, *Commutative property of addition. Order does not matter when adding.*
>
> $a \times b = b \times a$, *Commutative property of multiplication. Order does not matter when multiplying.*

- Models are useful for making abstract ideas more concrete.

3 groups — 4 in each group

4 groups — 3 in each group

Display and discuss the models above as they relate to the commutative property of addition and the commutative property of multiplication. When finished, pose a new question:

- Is the third number sentence in Example 3 true for all values of a and b? Experiment with different values before making your claim.

Allow students to experiment for about a minute. They should discover that any value can be substituted for the variable a, but only 4 can be used for b, since there are exactly 4 copies of a in the equation.

- Summarize your discoveries with a partner.
  - *In the equation $a + a + a + a = b \times a$, any value can be substituted for the variable a, but only 4 can be used for b, since there are exactly 4 copies of a in the equation.*
- Finally, consider the last equation, $a \div b = \frac{a}{b}$. Is this true for all values of a and b?
  - It is true for all values of a and all values of $b \neq 0$.

Closing (2 minutes)

- Tell your partner which of these properties of numbers is the easiest for you to remember?

Allow sharing for a short time.

- Now tell your partner which of these properties of numbers is the hardest for you to remember?

Allow sharing for a short time.

- Although these properties might seem simple, we apply them in many different ways in mathematics. If you have a good grasp on them, you will recognize them and use them in many applications.
- With a partner, create two different division problems that supports the following: $g \times 1 = g$, and be ready to explain your reasoning.
  - $g \div g = 1$; $5 \div 5 = 1$; $34 \div 34 = 1$; $2\frac{7}{8} \div 2\frac{7}{8} = 1$; etc.
  - *Any non-zero number divided by itself equals 1.*
  - *If a number g is divided into g equal parts, each part will have a size equal to one.*
  - *If g items are divided into groups of size g, there will be one group.*

 COMMON CORE™   Lesson 8: Replacing Numbers with Letters   84
                       Date: 12/11/13

- What about any number divided by 1? What does this mean?
  - $g \div 1 = g$
  - *If a number g is divided into 1 part, then the size of that part will be g.*
  - *Or if g items are divided into 1 group, there will be g items in that group.*

Exit Ticket (5 minutes)

Name _____   Date _____

Lesson 8: Replacing Numbers with Letters

Exit Ticket

1. State the commutative property of addition, and provide an example using two different numbers.

2. State the commutative property of multiplication, and provide an example using two different numbers.

3. State the additive property of zero, and provide an example using any other number.

4. State the multiplicative identity property of one, and provide an example using any other number.

Exit Ticket Sample Solutions

1. State the commutative property of addition, and provide an example using two different numbers.

   Any two different addends can be chosen, such as $5 + 6 = 6 + 5$.

2. State the commutative property of multiplication, and provide an example using two different numbers.

   Any two different factors can be chosen, such as $4 \times 9 = 9 \times 4$.

3. State the additive property of zero, and provide an example using any other number.

   Any non-zero addend can be chosen, such as $3 + 0 = 3$.

4. State the multiplicative identity property of one, and provide an example using any other number.

   Any non-zero factor can be chosen, such as $12 \times 1 = 12$.

Problem Set Sample Solutions

1. State the commutative property of addition using the variables a and b.

   $a + b = b + a$

2. State the commutative property of multiplication using the variables a and b.

   $a \times b = b \times a$

3. State the additive property of zero using the variable b.

   $b + 0 = b$

4. State the multiplicative identity property of one using the variable b.

   $b \times 1 = b$

5. Demonstrate the property listed in the first column by filling in the third column of the table.

Commutative Property of Addition	$25 + c =$	$c + 25$
Commutative Property of Multiplication	$l \times w =$	$w \times l$
Additive Property of Zero	$h + 0 =$	h
Multiplicative Identity Property of One	$v \times 1 =$	v

6. Why is there no commutative property for subtraction or division? Show examples.

   Answers will vary. Examples should show reasoning and proof that the community property does not work for subtraction and division. An example would be $8 \div 2$ and $2 \div 8$. $8 \div 2 = 4$, but $2 \div 8 = \frac{1}{4}$.

Lesson 8:   Replacing Numbers with Letters
Date: 12/11/13

Division of Fractions – Round 1

Number Correct: _____

Directions: Determine the quotient of the fractions.

1.	$\dfrac{4}{10} \div \dfrac{2}{10}$	
2.	$\dfrac{9}{12} \div \dfrac{3}{12}$	
3.	$\dfrac{6}{10} \div \dfrac{4}{10}$	
4.	$\dfrac{2}{8} \div \dfrac{3}{8}$	
5.	$\dfrac{2}{7} \div \dfrac{6}{7}$	
6.	$\dfrac{11}{9} \div \dfrac{8}{9}$	
7.	$\dfrac{5}{13} \div \dfrac{10}{13}$	
8.	$\dfrac{7}{8} \div \dfrac{13}{16}$	
9.	$\dfrac{3}{5} \div \dfrac{7}{10}$	
10.	$\dfrac{9}{30} \div \dfrac{3}{5}$	
11.	$\dfrac{1}{3} \div \dfrac{4}{5}$	
12.	$\dfrac{2}{5} \div \dfrac{3}{4}$	
13.	$\dfrac{3}{4} \div \dfrac{5}{9}$	
14.	$\dfrac{4}{5} \div \dfrac{7}{12}$	
15.	$\dfrac{3}{8} \div \dfrac{5}{2}$	

16.	$3\dfrac{1}{8} \div \dfrac{2}{3}$	
17.	$1\dfrac{5}{6} \div \dfrac{1}{2}$	
18.	$\dfrac{5}{8} \div 2\dfrac{3}{4}$	
19.	$\dfrac{1}{3} \div 1\dfrac{4}{5}$	
20.	$\dfrac{3}{4} \div 2\dfrac{3}{10}$	
21.	$2\dfrac{1}{5} \div 1\dfrac{1}{6}$	
22.	$2\dfrac{4}{9} \div 1\dfrac{3}{5}$	
23.	$1\dfrac{2}{9} \div 3\dfrac{2}{5}$	
24.	$2\dfrac{2}{3} \div 3$	
25.	$1\dfrac{3}{4} \div 2\dfrac{2}{5}$	
26.	$4 \div 1\dfrac{2}{9}$	
27.	$3\dfrac{1}{5} \div 6$	
28.	$2\dfrac{5}{6} \div 1\dfrac{1}{3}$	
29.	$10\dfrac{2}{3} \div 8$	
30.	$15 \div 2\dfrac{3}{5}$	

Division of Fractions – Round 1 [KEY]

Directions: Determine the quotient of the fractions.

1.	$\dfrac{4}{10} \div \dfrac{2}{10}$	$\dfrac{4}{2} = 2$	16.	$3\dfrac{1}{8} \div \dfrac{2}{3}$	$\dfrac{75}{16} = 4\dfrac{11}{16}$
2.	$\dfrac{9}{12} \div \dfrac{3}{12}$	$\dfrac{9}{3} = 3$	17.	$1\dfrac{5}{6} \div \dfrac{1}{2}$	$\dfrac{22}{6} = \dfrac{11}{3} = 3\dfrac{2}{3}$
3.	$\dfrac{6}{10} \div \dfrac{4}{10}$	$\dfrac{6}{4} = \dfrac{3}{2}$	18.	$\dfrac{5}{8} \div 2\dfrac{3}{4}$	$\dfrac{20}{88} = \dfrac{5}{22}$
4.	$\dfrac{2}{8} \div \dfrac{3}{8}$	$\dfrac{2}{3}$	19.	$\dfrac{1}{3} \div 1\dfrac{4}{5}$	$\dfrac{5}{27}$
5.	$\dfrac{2}{7} \div \dfrac{6}{7}$	$\dfrac{2}{6} = \dfrac{1}{3}$	20.	$\dfrac{3}{4} \div 2\dfrac{3}{10}$	$\dfrac{30}{92} = \dfrac{15}{46}$
6.	$\dfrac{11}{9} \div \dfrac{8}{9}$	$\dfrac{11}{8} = 1\dfrac{3}{8}$	21.	$2\dfrac{1}{5} \div 1\dfrac{1}{6}$	$\dfrac{66}{35} = 1\dfrac{31}{66}$
7.	$\dfrac{5}{13} \div \dfrac{10}{13}$	$\dfrac{5}{10} = \dfrac{1}{2}$	22.	$2\dfrac{4}{9} \div 1\dfrac{3}{5}$	$\dfrac{110}{72} = \dfrac{55}{36} = 1\dfrac{19}{55}$
8.	$\dfrac{7}{8} \div \dfrac{13}{16}$	$\dfrac{14}{13} = 1\dfrac{1}{13}$	23.	$1\dfrac{2}{9} \div 3\dfrac{2}{5}$	$\dfrac{55}{153}$
9.	$\dfrac{3}{5} \div \dfrac{7}{10}$	$\dfrac{6}{7}$	24.	$2\dfrac{2}{3} \div 3$	$\dfrac{8}{9}$
10.	$\dfrac{9}{30} \div \dfrac{3}{5}$	$\dfrac{9}{18} = \dfrac{1}{2}$	25.	$1\dfrac{3}{4} \div 2\dfrac{2}{5}$	$\dfrac{35}{48}$
11.	$\dfrac{1}{3} \div \dfrac{4}{5}$	$\dfrac{5}{12}$	26.	$4 \div 1\dfrac{2}{9}$	$\dfrac{36}{11} = 3\dfrac{3}{11}$
12.	$\dfrac{2}{5} \div \dfrac{3}{4}$	$\dfrac{8}{15}$	27.	$3\dfrac{1}{5} \div 6$	$\dfrac{16}{30} = \dfrac{8}{15}$
13.	$\dfrac{3}{4} \div \dfrac{5}{9}$	$\dfrac{27}{20} = 1\dfrac{7}{20}$	28.	$2\dfrac{5}{6} \div 1\dfrac{1}{3}$	$\dfrac{51}{24} = 2\dfrac{3}{24} = 2\dfrac{1}{8}$
14.	$\dfrac{4}{5} \div \dfrac{7}{12}$	$\dfrac{48}{35} = 1\dfrac{13}{35}$	29.	$10\dfrac{2}{3} \div 8$	$\dfrac{32}{24} = \dfrac{4}{3} = 1\dfrac{1}{3}$
15.	$\dfrac{3}{8} \div \dfrac{5}{2}$	$\dfrac{6}{40} = \dfrac{3}{20}$	30.	$15 \div 2\dfrac{3}{5}$	$\dfrac{75}{13} = 5\dfrac{10}{13}$

Division of Fractions – Round 2

Number Correct: _____

Improvement: _____

Directions: Determine the quotient of the fractions.

1.	$\dfrac{10}{2} \div \dfrac{5}{2}$		16.	$\dfrac{5}{8} \div 1\dfrac{3}{4}$	
2.	$\dfrac{6}{5} \div \dfrac{3}{5}$		17.	$\dfrac{1}{4} \div 2\dfrac{2}{5}$	
3.	$\dfrac{10}{7} \div \dfrac{2}{7}$		18.	$2\dfrac{3}{5} \div \dfrac{3}{8}$	
4.	$\dfrac{3}{8} \div \dfrac{5}{8}$		19.	$1\dfrac{3}{5} \div \dfrac{2}{9}$	
5.	$\dfrac{1}{4} \div \dfrac{3}{12}$		20.	$4 \div 2\dfrac{3}{8}$	
6.	$\dfrac{7}{5} \div \dfrac{3}{10}$		21.	$1\dfrac{1}{2} \div 5$	
7.	$\dfrac{8}{15} \div \dfrac{4}{5}$		22.	$3\dfrac{1}{3} \div 1\dfrac{3}{4}$	
8.	$\dfrac{5}{6} \div \dfrac{5}{12}$		23.	$2\dfrac{2}{5} \div 1\dfrac{1}{4}$	
9.	$\dfrac{3}{5} \div \dfrac{7}{9}$		24.	$3\dfrac{1}{2} \div 2\dfrac{2}{3}$	
10.	$\dfrac{3}{10} \div \dfrac{3}{9}$		25.	$1\dfrac{4}{5} \div 2\dfrac{3}{4}$	
11.	$\dfrac{3}{4} \div \dfrac{7}{9}$		26.	$3\dfrac{1}{6} \div 1\dfrac{3}{5}$	
12.	$\dfrac{7}{10} \div \dfrac{3}{8}$		27.	$3\dfrac{3}{5} \div 2\dfrac{1}{8}$	
13.	$4 \div \dfrac{4}{9}$		28.	$5 \div 1\dfrac{1}{6}$	
14.	$\dfrac{5}{8} \div 7$		29.	$3\dfrac{3}{4} \div 5\dfrac{1}{2}$	
15.	$9 \div \dfrac{2}{3}$		30.	$4\dfrac{2}{3} \div 5\dfrac{1}{4}$	

Division of Fractions – Round 2 [KEY]

Directions: Determine the quotient of the fractions.

1.	$\dfrac{10}{2} \div \dfrac{5}{2}$	$\dfrac{10}{5} = 2$	16.	$\dfrac{5}{8} \div 1\dfrac{3}{4}$	$\dfrac{20}{56} = \dfrac{5}{14}$
2.	$\dfrac{6}{5} \div \dfrac{3}{5}$	$\dfrac{6}{3} = 2$	17.	$\dfrac{1}{4} \div 2\dfrac{2}{5}$	$\dfrac{5}{48}$
3.	$\dfrac{10}{7} \div \dfrac{2}{7}$	$\dfrac{10}{2} = 5$	18.	$2\dfrac{3}{5} \div \dfrac{3}{8}$	$\dfrac{104}{15} = 6\dfrac{14}{15}$
4.	$\dfrac{3}{8} \div \dfrac{5}{8}$	$\dfrac{3}{5}$	19.	$1\dfrac{3}{5} \div \dfrac{2}{9}$	$\dfrac{72}{10} = 7\dfrac{2}{10} = 7\dfrac{1}{5}$
5.	$\dfrac{1}{4} \div \dfrac{3}{12}$	$\dfrac{3}{3} = 1$	20.	$4 \div 2\dfrac{3}{8}$	$\dfrac{32}{19} = 1\dfrac{13}{19}$
6.	$\dfrac{7}{5} \div \dfrac{3}{10}$	$\dfrac{14}{3} = 4\dfrac{2}{3}$	21.	$1\dfrac{1}{2} \div 5$	$\dfrac{3}{10}$
7.	$\dfrac{8}{15} \div \dfrac{4}{5}$	$\dfrac{8}{12} = \dfrac{2}{3}$	22.	$3\dfrac{1}{3} \div 1\dfrac{3}{4}$	$\dfrac{40}{21} = 1\dfrac{19}{21}$
8.	$\dfrac{5}{6} \div \dfrac{5}{12}$	$\dfrac{10}{5} = 2$	23.	$2\dfrac{2}{5} \div 1\dfrac{1}{4}$	$\dfrac{48}{25} = 1\dfrac{23}{25}$
9.	$\dfrac{3}{5} \div \dfrac{7}{9}$	$\dfrac{27}{35}$	24.	$3\dfrac{1}{2} \div 2\dfrac{2}{3}$	$\dfrac{21}{16} = 1\dfrac{5}{16}$
10.	$\dfrac{3}{10} \div \dfrac{3}{9}$	$\dfrac{27}{30} = \dfrac{9}{10}$	25.	$1\dfrac{4}{5} \div 2\dfrac{3}{4}$	$\dfrac{36}{55}$
11.	$\dfrac{3}{4} \div \dfrac{7}{9}$	$\dfrac{27}{28}$	26.	$3\dfrac{1}{6} \div 1\dfrac{3}{5}$	$\dfrac{95}{48} = 1\dfrac{47}{48}$
12.	$\dfrac{7}{10} \div \dfrac{3}{8}$	$\dfrac{56}{30} = \dfrac{28}{15} = 1\dfrac{13}{15}$	27.	$3\dfrac{3}{5} \div 2\dfrac{1}{8}$	$\dfrac{144}{85} = 1\dfrac{59}{85}$
13.	$4 \div \dfrac{4}{9}$	$\dfrac{36}{4} = 9$	28.	$5 \div 1\dfrac{1}{6}$	$\dfrac{30}{7} = 4\dfrac{2}{7}$
14.	$\dfrac{5}{8} \div 7$	$\dfrac{5}{56}$	29.	$3\dfrac{3}{4} \div 5\dfrac{1}{2}$	$\dfrac{30}{44} = \dfrac{15}{22}$
15.	$9 \div \dfrac{2}{3}$	$\dfrac{27}{2} = 13\dfrac{1}{2}$	30.	$4\dfrac{2}{3} \div 5\dfrac{1}{4}$	$\dfrac{56}{63} = \dfrac{8}{9}$

Topic D:

Expanding, Factoring, and Distributing Expressions

6.EE.A.2a, 6.EE.A.2b, 6.EE.A.3, 6.EE.A.4

Focus Standard:	6.EE.A.2a	Write, read, and evaluate expressions in which letters stand for numbers.
	6.EE.A.2b	a. Write expressions that record operations with numbers and with letters standing for numbers. *For example, express the calculation "Subtract y from 5" as $5 - y$.*
		b. Identify parts of an expression using mathematical terms (sum, term, product, factor, quotient, coefficient); view one or more parts of an expression as a single entity. *For example, describe the expression $2(8 + 7)$ as a product of two factors; view $(8 + 7)$ as both a single entity and a sum of two terms.*
	6.EE.A.3	Apply the properties of operations to generate equivalent expressions. *For example, apply the distributive property to the expression $3(2 + x)$ to produce the equivalent expression $6 + 3x$; apply the distributive property to the expression $24x + 18y$ to produce the equivalent expression $6(4x + 3y)$; apply properties of operations to $y + y + y$ to produce the equivalent expression $3y$.*
	6.EE.A.4	Identify when two expressions are equivalent (i.e., when the two expressions name the same number regardless of which value is substituted into them). *For example, the expressions $y + y + y$ and $3y$ are equivalent because they name the same number regardless of which number y stands for.*
Instructional Days:	6	
Lesson 9:	Writing Addition and Subtraction Expressions (P)[1]	
Lesson 10:	Writing and Expanding Multiplication Expressions (P)	
Lesson 11:	Factoring Expressions (P)	
Lesson 12:	Distributing Expressions (P)	
Lessons 13–14:	Writing Division Expressions (S, P)	

---

[1] Lesson Structure Key: **P**-Problem Set Lesson, **M**-Modeling Cycle Lesson, **E**-Exploration Lesson, **S**-Socratic Lesson

In Topic D, students formally utilize their understanding of expressions in order to expand, factor, and distribute. In Lesson 9, students write expressions that record addition and subtraction operations with numbers through the use of models. With a bar diagram, students understand that any number a plus any number b is the same as adding the numbers $b + a$. Students also use bar diagrams to differentiate between the mathematical terms "subtract" and "subtract from." For instance, when subtracting b from a, they know they must first represent a in order to take away b, leading to an understanding that the expression must be written $a - b$.

This concept deters students from writing the incorrect expression $b - a$, which is a common misconception because the number b is heard first in the expression "subtract b from a." Students continue to write expressions by combining operations with the use of parentheses.

In Lesson 10, students identify parts of an expression using mathematical terms for multiplication. They view one or more parts of an expression as a single entity. They determine that through the use of models, when a is represented 6 times, the expression is written as one entity: $6 \times a$, $6 \cdot a$, or $6a$.

In Lesson 11, students bring with them their previous knowledge of GCF and the distributive property from Module 2 to model and write expressions using the distributive property. They move from a factored form to an expanded form of an expression, while in Lesson 12, they move from an expanded form to a factored form. In Lesson 11, students are capable of moving from the expression $2a + 2b$ to $a + b$ written twice as $(a + b) + (a + b)$ and conclude that $2a + 2b = 2(a + b)$. Conversely, students determine in lesson twelve that $(a + b) + (a + b) = 2a + 2b$ through the following model:

Finally, in Lessons 13 and 14, students write division expressions in two forms: $dividend \div divisor$ and $\dfrac{dividend}{divisor}$, noting the relationship between the two. They determine from the model below that $1 \div 2$ is the same as $\dfrac{1}{2}$. They make an intuitive connection to expressions with letters and also determine that $a \div 2$ is the same as $\dfrac{a}{2}$.

	Topic D:	Expanding, Factoring, and Distributing Expressions
	Date:	12/11/13

Lesson 9: Writing Addition and Subtraction Expressions

Student Outcomes

- Students write expressions that record addition and subtraction operations with numbers.

Lesson Notes

This lesson requires the use of a white board for each student.

Classwork

Example 1 (3 minutes)

Example 1

Create a bar diagram to show 3 plus 5.

$$3 + 5$$

How would this look if you were asked to show 5 plus 3?

There would be 5 tiles and then 3 tiles.

Are these two expressions equivalent?

Yes, both 3 + 5 and 5 + 3 have a sum of 8.

MP.2

Example 2 (3 minutes)

Example 2

How can we show a number increased by 2?

$a + 2$ or $2 + a$

$$a + 2$$

Can you prove this using a model?

Yes, I can use a bar diagram.

$$2 + a$$

Example 3 (3 minutes)

Example 3

Write an expression to show the sum of m and k.

$m + k$ or $k + m$

Which property can be used in Examples 1–3 to show that both expressions given are equivalent?

The commutative property of addition.

Example 4 (3 minutes)

Example 4

How can we show 10 minus 6?

- Draw a bar diagram to model this expression.

10

What expression would represent this model?

$10 - 6$

- Could we also use $6 - 10$?

No, if we started with 6 and tried to take 10 away, the models would not match.

Example 5 (3 minutes)

Example 5

How can we write an expression to show 3 less than a number?

- Start by drawing a diagram to model the subtraction. Are we taking away from the 3 or the unknown number?

- We are starting with some number and then subtracting away 3.

- What expression would represent this model?

So, the answer is $n - 3$.

P.2

Example 6 (3 minutes)

> **Example 6**
>
> How would we write an expression to show the number c being subtracted from the sum of a and b?
>
> - Start by writing an expression for the sum of a and b.
>
> $a + b \ or \ b + a$
>
> - Now show c being subtracted from the sum.
>
> $a + b - c \ or \ b + a - c$

Example 7 (3 minutes)

MP.2

> **Example 7**
>
> Write an expression to show c minus the sum of a and b.
>
> $c - (a + b)$
>
> Why are parentheses necessary in this example and not the others?
>
> *Without the parentheses only a is being taken away from c, where the expression says that $a + b$ should be taken away from c.*
>
> Replace the variables with numbers to see if $c - (a + b)$ is the same as $c - a + b$.

If students do not see the necessity for the parentheses, you can have them replace the variables with numbers to see whether $c - (a + b)$ is the same as $c - a + b$.

Here is a sample of what they could try:

$$a = 1, b = 2, c = 3$$
$$3 - (1 + 2) \qquad\qquad 3 - 1 + 2$$
$$3 - 3 \qquad or \qquad 2 + 2$$
$$0 \qquad\qquad\qquad 4$$

Exercises (12 minutes)

These questions can be done on the worksheet. However, if white boards, small chalk boards, or some other personal board is available, the teacher can get instant feedback as students show their boards after each question.

> **Exercises**
>
> 1. Write an expression to show the sum of 7 and 1.5.
>
> $7 + 1.5 \ or \ 1.5 + 7$

2. Write two expressions to show w increased by 4. Then draw models to prove that both expressions represent the same thing.

   $w + 4$ *and* $4 + w$

w	4

4	w

3. Write an expression to show the sum of a, b, and c.

   Any of the following answers are acceptable.

   $a + b + c$ $b + c + a$ $c + b + a$

   $a + c + b$ $b + a + c$ $c + a + b$

4. Write an expression and a model showing 3 less than p.

   $p - 3$

5. Write an expression to show the difference of 3 and p.

   $3 - p$

6. Write an expression to show 4 less than the sum of g and 5.

   $g + 5 - 4$ *or* $5 + g - 4$

7. Write an expression to show 4 decreased by the sum of g and 5.

   $4 - (g + 5)$ *or* $4 - (5 + g)$

8. Should Exercises 6 and 7 have different expressions? Why or why not?

   The expressions are different because one includes the word "decreased by" and the other has the words "less than". The words "less than" give the amount that was taken away first where the word "decreased by" gives us a starting amount and then the amount that was taken away.

Closing (7 minutes)

▪ Write the following in words.

    □ $m + k$ *Answers will vary; the sum of* m *and* k

    □ $k + m$ *Answers will vary; the sum of* k *and* m

    □ $m - k$ *Answers will vary;* m *minus* k

    □ $k - m$ *Answers will vary;* k *minus* m

Lesson 9:	Writing Addition and Subtraction Expressions
Date:	12/11/13

- Is $m + k$ equivalent to $k + m$? Is $m - k$ equivalent to $k - m$? Explain.

  □ *$m + k$ is equivalent to $k + m$. Both of these expressions have the same result. However, $m - k$ and $k - m$ will not have the same result. I would be starting with a new total amount and taking away a different amount as well. This will give different solutions. For example, $4 + 6 = 10$, and $6 + 4 = 10$. However, $6 - 4 = 2$, but $4 - 6$ does not.*

Exit Ticket (5 minutes)

Name _____   Date _____

Lesson 9: Writing Addition and Subtraction Expressions

Exit Ticket

1. Write an expression showing the sum of 8 and a number f.

2. Write an expression showing 5 less than the number k.

3. Write an expression showing the sum of a number h and a number w minus 11.

Lesson 9:	Writing Addition and Subtraction Expressions
Date:	12/11/13

Exit Ticket Sample Solutions

1. Write an expression showing the sum of 8 and a number f.

   $8 + f$ or $f + 8$

2. Write an expression showing 5 less than the number k.

   $k - 5$

3. Write an expression showing the sum of a number h and a number w minus 11.

   $h + w - 11$

Problem Set Sample Solutions

1. Write two expressions to show a number increased by 11. Then draw models to prove that both expressions represent the same thing.

   $a + 11$ and $11 + a$

a	11

11	a

2. Write an expression to show the sum of x and y.

   $x + y$ or $y + x$

3. Write an expression to show h decreased by 13.

   $h - 13$

4. Write an expression to show k less than 3.5.

   $3.5 - k$

5. Write an expression to show the sum of g and h reduced by 11.

   $g + h - 11$

6. Write an expression to show 5 less than y, plus g.

   $y - 5 + g$

7. Write an expression to show 5 less than the sum of y and g.

   $y + g - 5$

 COMMON CORE™

Lesson 9:   Writing Addition and Subtraction Expressions
Date: 12/11/13

Lesson 10: Writing and Expanding Multiplication Expressions

Student Outcomes

- Students identify parts of an expression using mathematical terms for multiplication. They view one or more parts of an expression as a single entity.

Classwork

Discussion (4 minutes)

When we want to show multiplication of two numbers, like 5 and 7, we typically write 5×7, using the "×" to show the operations. When we start to use variables with multiplication, we can use other forms.

1. $a \times b$
2. $a \cdot b$
3. ab
4. $(a)(b)$

- Why might we want to use a form other than the × when variables are involved?
  - *The × can be confused for a variable instead of a symbol for an operation.*
- Which of the three models can be used to show multiplication where there are no variables involved?
  - *We can use method 1, 2, and 4.*
  - $5 \times 7, 5 \cdot 7$ *and* $(5)(7)$, *but not* 57 *because it looks like the number fifty-seven.*

Example 1 (10 minutes)

- When writing expressions using the fewest number of symbols, we will have to refrain from using the symbols ×, •, or ( ).
- We will also be using math terms to describe expressions and the parts of an expression. We will be using words like factor, product, quotient, coefficient, and term.
- A term is a part of an expression that can be added to or subtracted from the rest of the expression. In the expression $7g + 8h + 3$, what are examples of terms?
  - $7g, 8h$, and 3 are all terms
- A coefficient is a constant factor in a variable term. For example, in the term $4m$, 4 is the coefficient and it is multiplied with m.

Example 1

Write each expression using the fewest number of symbols and characters. Use math terms to describe the expressions and parts of the expressions.

    a. $6 \times b$

        6b, the 6 is the coefficient and a factor, the b is the variable and a factor. We can call 6b the product and we can also call it a term.

    b. $4 \cdot 3 \cdot h$

        12h, the 12 is the coefficient and a factor, the h is the variable and a factor. We can call 12h the product, and we can also call it a term.

    c. $2 \times 2 \times 2 \times a \times b$

        8ab, 8 is the coefficient and a factor; a and b are both variables and factors, and 8ab is the product and also a term.

- In this example, the variables should follow the numbers and be written in alphabetical order.

    d. $5 \times m \times 3 \times p$

        15mp, 15 is the coefficient and factor; m and p are the variables and factors; 15mp is the product and also a term.

- If it is helpful, you can gather the numbers together and the variables together. You can do this because of the commutative property of multiplication.

    □ $5 \times 3 \times m \times p$

MP.7

    e. $1 \times g \times w$

        1gw or gw, g and w are the variables and factors, 1 is the coefficient and factor if it is included, and gw is the product and also a term.

- What happens when you multiply by 1?

    □ *Multiplying by 1 is an example of the identity property. Any number times 1 is equal to that number. Therefore, we don't always need to write the one because $1 \times gw = gw$.*

Example 2 (5 minutes)

Example 2

To expand multiplication expressions we will rewrite the expressions by including the "•" back into the expressions.

    a. $5g$

        $5 \cdot g$

    b. $7abc$

        $7 \cdot a \cdot b \cdot c$

---

c.   **12g**

$12 \cdot g$ or $2 \cdot 2 \cdot 3 \cdot g$

d.   **3$h \cdot 8$**

$3 \cdot h \cdot 8$

e.   **7$g \cdot 9h$**

$7 \cdot g \cdot 9 \cdot h$

Example 3 (5 minutes)

Example 3

a.   **Find the product of $4f \cdot 7g$.**

- It may be easier to see how we will use the fewest number of symbols and characters by expanding the expression first.

$4 \cdot f \cdot 7 \cdot g$

- Now we can multiply the numbers and then multiply the variables.

$4 \cdot 7 \cdot f \cdot g$

$28fg$

b.   **Multiply $3de \cdot 9\,yz$.**

- Let's start again by expanding the expression. Then we can rewrite the expression by multiplying the numbers and then multiplying the variables.

$3 \cdot d \cdot e \cdot 9 \cdot y \cdot z$

$3 \cdot 9 \cdot d \cdot e \cdot y \cdot z$

$27deyz$

c.   **Double the product of $6y$ and $3bc$.**

- We can start by finding the product of $6y$ and $3bc$.

$6 \cdot y \cdot 3 \cdot b \cdot c$

$6 \cdot 3 \cdot b \cdot c \cdot y$

$18bcy$

COMMON CORE™

Lesson 10:   Writing and Expanding Multiplication Expressions
Date: 12/11/13

103

MP.7

- What does it mean to double something?
  - It means to multiply by 2.

$2 \cdot 18bcy$

$36bcy$

Exercises (15 minutes)

Students will be matching expressions on a BINGO board. Some of the expressions will be simplified and some will be expanded. Students will be given a BINGO board with some of the squares filled in to save time. Have the remaining answers written on a smart board, chalkboard, or overhead projector so that students can randomly place them on the BINGO board. If there is not enough time for the BINGO game, you can also use these questions on white boards, chalkboards, or some form of personal boards.

Here are the clues to be given during the game, followed by the answers that will be on the board.

Questions/Clues	Answers	
1. $10m$	$2 \cdot 5 \cdot m$	
2. $8 \cdot 3 \cdot m$	$24m$	
3. Has a coefficient of 11.	$11mp$	
4. $14mp$	$2 \cdot 7 \cdot m \cdot p$	
5. $(3m)(9p)$	$27mp$	
6. $11m \cdot 2p$	$22mp$	These answers have already been included on pre-made BINGO boards to save time. The other answers can be randomly placed in the remaining spaces.
7. $36m$	$2 \cdot 2 \cdot 3 \cdot 3 \cdot m$	
8. $2 \cdot 2 \cdot 2 \cdot 5 \cdot p$	$40p$	
9. $7mp \cdot 5t$	$35mpt$	
10. $18pt$	$2 \cdot 3 \cdot 3 \cdot p \cdot t$	
11. $7 \cdot 2 \cdot t \cdot 2 \cdot p$	$28pt$	
12. Has a coefficient of 5	$5mpt$	
13. $3 \cdot 3 \cdot 5 \cdot m \cdot p$	$45mp$	
14. $5m \cdot 9pt$	$45mpt$	
15. $10mp \cdot 4t$	$40mpt$	
16. $1mpt$	mpt	
17. $45mp$	$3 \cdot 3 \cdot 5 \cdot m \cdot p$	
18. $(4mp)(11)$	$44mp$	
19. $54mpt$	$3 \cdot 3 \cdot 3 \cdot 2 \cdot m \cdot p \cdot t$	
20. Has a coefficient of 3	$3m$	
21. $2 \cdot 2 \cdot 2 \cdot 3 \cdot m \cdot p$	$24mp$	
22. $(5m)(3p)(2t)$	$30mpt$	
23. $13mp$	$(1mp)(13)$	
24. Has a coefficient of 2.	$2p$	

Closing (3 minutes)

- What is the difference between simplifying and expanding?
  - *When we simplify the expression, we get rid of the operation symbol for multiplication and we write the factors next to each other. Sometimes we might have to multiply numbers together before writing it next to the variable(s). Expanding means that we write the expression as a product of the factors using the "•" symbol for multiplication.*
- How would you describe the following terms?
  1. Factor
     - *A number or variable that is multiplied to get a product.*
  2. Variable
     - *A letter used to represent a number.*
  3. Product
     - *The solution when two factors are multiplied.*
  4. Coefficient
     - *The factor that multiplies the variable.*

Lesson Summary

An Expression in Expanded Form: An expression that is written as sums (and/or differences) of products whose factors are numbers, variables, or variables raised to whole number powers is said to be in *expanded form*. A single number, variable, or a single product of numbers and/or variables is also considered to be in expanded form.

Note: Each summand of an expression in expanded form is called a *term*, and the number found by multiplying just the numbers in a term together is called the *coefficient of the term*. After the word "term" is defined, students can be shown what it means to "collect like terms" using the distributive property.

Expressions in expanded form are analogous to polynomial expressions that are written as a sum of monomials. There are two reasons for introducing this term instead of the word polynomial. (1) In the Common Core State Standards, the word "polynomial" cannot be formally defined before high school but we need the idea behind the word much sooner. (2) The progressions are very clear about not asking problems that state, "Simplify." However, they do describe "standard form" in the progressions, so we may ask students to put their answers in standard form. To get to standard form, we ask students to expand the expression and then collect like terms.

An Expression in Standard Form: An expression that is in expanded form where all like-terms have been collected is said to be in *standard form*.

Note: We cannot ask students to "Simplify," but we can ask them to "Put an expression in standard form," or "Expand the expression and collect all like terms."

Exit Ticket (5 minutes)

Name _____   Date _____

Lesson 10: Writing and Expanding Multiplication Expressions

Exit Ticket

1. Rewrite the expression using the fewest number of symbols and characters possible.

   a. $5g \cdot 7h$

   b. $3 \cdot 4 \cdot 5 \cdot m \cdot n$

2. Name the parts of the expression. Then expand.

   a. $14b$

   b. $30jk$

Exit Ticket Sample Solutions

1. Rewrite the expression using the fewest number of symbols and characters possible.

   a. $5g \cdot 7h$

      $35gh$

   b. $3 \cdot 4 \cdot 5 \cdot m \cdot n$

      $60mn$

2. Name the parts of the expression. Then expand.

   a. $14b$

      $14 \cdot b$ or $2 \cdot 7 \cdot b$

      14 is the coefficient, b is the variable, and $14b$ is the product of $14 \times b$.

   b. $30jk$

      $30 \cdot j \cdot k$ or $2 \cdot 3 \cdot 5 \cdot j \cdot k$

      30 is the coefficient, j and k are the variables, and $30jk$ is the product of $30 \cdot j \cdot k$.

Problem Set Sample Solutions

1. Rewrite the expression using the fewest number of symbols and characters possible.

   a. $5 \cdot y$

      $5y$

   b. $7 \cdot d \cdot e$

      $7de$

   c. $5 \cdot 2 \cdot 2 \cdot y \cdot z$

      $20yz$

   d. $3 \cdot 3 \cdot 2 \cdot 5 \cdot d$

      $90d$

2. Expand the following expressions.

   a. $3g$

      $3 \cdot g$

   b. $11mp$

      $11 \cdot m \cdot p$

Lesson 10:	Writing and Expanding Multiplication Expressions
Date:	12/11/13

c.   **20yz**

20 · y · z or 2 · 2 · 5 · y · z

d.   **15abc**

15 · a · b · c or 3 · 5 · a · b · c

3. **Find the product.**

a.   **5d · 7g**

35dg

b.   **12ab · 3cd**

36abcd

		★		

$2 \bullet 5 \bullet m$				$35mpt$
$45mp$	$40p$		$24m$	$2 \bullet 3 \bullet 3 \bullet p \bullet t$
	$2 \bullet 7 \bullet m \bullet p$	★		$11mp$
$28pt$			$22mp$	$2 \bullet 2 \bullet 3 \bullet 3 \bullet m$
$27mp$		$5mpt$		$45mpt$

$22mp$		$40p$		
	$28pt$		$2 \bullet 5 \bullet m$	$2 \bullet 2 \bullet 3 \bullet 3 \bullet m$
	$45mp$	★		$35mpt$
$24m$			$45mpt$	$27mp$
$2 \bullet 7 \bullet m \bullet p$	$5mpt$		$11mp$	$2 \bullet 3 \bullet 3 \bullet p \bullet t$

$45mp$	$40p$			$24m$
$2 \bullet 3 \bullet 3 \bullet p \bullet t$	$5mpt$	$22m$		
$11mp$			$45mpt$	$2 \bullet 2 \bullet 3 \bullet 3 \bullet m$
	$27mp$	$2 \bullet 7 \bullet m \bullet p$		$28pt$
	$2 \bullet 5 \bullet m$		$35mpt$	

Lesson 11: Factoring Expressions

Student Outcomes

- Students model and write equivalent expressions using the distributive property. They move from an expanded form to a factored form of an expression.

Fluency Exercise (5 minutes)

GCF Sprint

Classwork

Example 1 (8 minutes)

Example 1

a. Use the model to answer the following questions.

How many fives are in the model?

2

How many threes are in the model?

2

What does the expression represent in words?

The sum of two groups of five and two groups of three.

What expression could we write to represent the model?

2 × 5 + 2 × 3

b. Use the new model and the previous model to answer the next set of questions.

MP.7

> **Scaffolding:**
> For students struggling with variables, you can further solidify the concept by having students replace the variables with whole numbers to prove that the expressions are equivalent.

How many fives are in the model?

2

How many threes are in the model?

2

What does the expression represent in words?

Two groups of the sum of five and three.

What expression could we write to represent the model?

$(5 + 3) + (5 + 3)$ *or* $2(5 + 3)$

c.   Is the model in part (a) equivalent to the model in part (b)?

Yes, because both expressions have two 5s and two 3s. Therefore, $2 \times 5 + 2 \times 3 = 2(5 + 3)$.

d.   What relationship do we see happening on either side of the equal sign?

On the left hand side, 2 is being multiplied times 5 and then times 3 before adding the products together. On the right hand side, the 5 and 3 are added first and then multiplied by 2.

e.   In 5th grade and in Module 2 of this year, you have used similar reasoning to solve problems. What is the name of the property that is used to say that $2(5 + 3)$ is the same as $2 \times 5 + 2 \times 3$?

The distributive property.

MP.7

Example 2 (5 minutes)

Example 2

Now, we will take a look at an example with variables. Discuss the questions with your partner.

What does the model represent in words?

a plus a plus b plus b, two a's plus two b's, two times a plus two times b

What does $2a$ mean?

$2a$ means that there are 2 a's or $2 \times a$.

How many a's are in the model?

2

How many b's are in the model?

2

Lesson 11:	Factoring Expressions
Date:	12/11/13

What expression could we write to represent the model?

$2a + 2b$

How many a's are in the expression?

2

How many b's are in the expression?

2

What expression could we write to represent the model?

$(a + b) + (a + b) = 2(a + b)$

Are the two expressions equivalent?

Yes, both models include 2 a's and 2 b's. Therefore, $2a + 2b = 2(a + b)$

P.7 Example 3 (8 minutes)

Example 3

Use GCF and the distributive property to write equivalent expressions.

1. $3f + 3g =$ _____ $3(f + g)$ _____

   What is the question asking us to do?

   We need to rewrite the expression as an equivalent expression in factored form which means the expression is written as the product of factors. The number outside of the parentheses will be the GCF.

   How would Problem 1 look if we expanded each term?

   $3 \cdot f + 3 \cdot g$

   What is the GCF in Problem 1?

   3

   How can we use the GCF to rewrite this?

   3 goes on the outside and $f + g$ will go inside the parentheses. $3(f + g)$

■   Let's use the same ideas for Problem 2. Start by expanding the expression and naming the GCF.

---

2. $6x + 9y =$ _____ $3(2x + 3y)$ _____

What is the question asking us to do?

We need to rewrite the expression as an equivalent expression in factored form which means the expression is written as the product of factors. The number outside of the parentheses will be the GCF.

How would Problem 2 look if we expanded each term?

$2 \cdot 3 \cdot x + 3 \cdot 3 \cdot y$

What is the GCF in Problem 2?

The GCF is 3.

How can we use the GCF to rewrite this?

I will factor out the 3 from both terms and place it in front of the parentheses. I will place what is left in the terms inside the parentheses: $3(2x + 3y)$.

3. $3c + 11c =$ _____ $c(3 + 11)$ _____

Is there a greatest common factor in Problem 3?

Yes, when I expand I can see that each term has a common factor c.

$3 \cdot c + 11 \cdot c$

Rewrite the expression using the distributive property.

$c(3 + 11)$

4. $24b + 8 =$ _____ $8(3b + 1)$ _____

Explain how you used GCF and the distributive property to rewrite the expression in Problem 4.

I first expanded each term. I know that 8 goes into 24, so used it in the expansion.

$2 \cdot 2 \cdot 2 \cdot 3 \cdot b + 2 \cdot 2 \cdot 2$

I determined that $2 \cdot 2 \cdot 2$, or 8, is the common factor. So, on the outside of the parentheses I wrote 8, and on the inside I wrote the leftover factor, $3b + 1$. $8(3b + 1)$.

Why is there a 1 in the parentheses?

When I factor out a number, I am leaving behind the other factor that multiplies to make the original number. In this case, when I factor out an 8 from 8, I am left with a 1 because $8 \times 1 = 8$.

How is this related to the first two examples?

In the first two examples, we saw that we could rewrite the expressions by thinking about groups.

We can either think of $24b + 8$ as 8 groups of $3b$ and 8 groups of 1 or as 8 groups of the sum of $3b + 1$. This shows that $8(3b) + 8(1) = 8(3b + 1)$ is the same as $24b + 8$.

MP.7

Exercises (12 minutes)

If times allows, you could have students practice these questions on white boards or small personal boards.

Exercises

1. **Apply the distributive property to write equivalent expressions.**

    a. $7x + 7y$

          $7(x + y)$

    b. $15g + 20h$

          $5(3g + 4h)$

    c. $18m + 42n$

          $6(3m + 7n)$

    d. $30a + 39b$

          $3(10a + 13b)$

    e. $11f + 15f$

          $f(11 + 15)$

    f. $18h + 13h$

          $h(18 + 13)$

    g. $55m + 11$

          $11(5m + 1)$

    h. $7 + 56y$

          $7(1 + 8y)$

2. **Evaluate each of the expressions below.**

    a. $6x + 21y$ and $3(2x + 7y)$ $x = 3$ and $y = 4$

          $6(3) + 21(4)$ $3(2 \cdot 3 + 7 \cdot 4)$

            $18 + 84$ $3(6 + 28)$

              102 $3(34)$

              102 102

    b. $5g + 7g$ and $g(5 + 7)$ $g = 6$

          $5(6) + 7(6)$ $6(5 + 7)$

            $30 + 42$ $6(12)$

              72 72

Lesson 11:   Factoring Expressions
Date: 12/11/13

c. $14x + 2$ and $2(7x + 1)$ $x = 10$

$14(10) + 2$ $2(7 \cdot 10 + 1)$

$140 + 2$ $2(70 + 1)$

142                      $2(71)$

142   142

d.   Explain any patterns that you notice in the results to parts (a)–(c).

Both expressions in parts (a)–(c) evaluated to the same number when the indicated value was substituted for the variable. This shows that the two expressions are equivalent for the given values.

e.   What would happen if other values were given for the variables?

Because the two expressions in each part are equivalent, they evaluate to the same number, no matter what value is chosen for the variable.

Closing (3 minutes)

How can use you use your knowledge of GCF and the distributive property to write equivalent expressions?

Find the missing value that makes the two expressions equivalent.

$4x + 12y$ ____ 4 $(x + 3y)$

$35x + 50y$ ____ 5 $(7x + 10y)$

$18x + 9y$ ____ 9 $(2x + y)$

$32x + 8y$ ____ 8 $(4x + y)$

$100x + 700y$ ____ 100 $(x + 7y)$

Explain how you determine the missing number.

I would expand each term and determine the greatest common factor. The greatest common factor is the number that is placed on the blank line.

> **Lesson Summary**
>
> <u>An Expression in Factored Form</u>: An expression that is a product of two or more expressions is said to be in *factored form*.

Exit Ticket (4 minutes)

Name _____   Date _____

Lesson 11: Factoring Expressions

Exit Ticket

Use greatest common factor and the distributive property to write equivalent expressions.

1. $2x + 8y$

2. $13ab + 15ab$

3. $20g + 24h$

Exit Ticket Sample Solutions

> Use greatest common factor and the distributive property to write equivalent expressions.
>
> 1. $2x + 8y$
>
> $2(x + 4y)$
>
> 2. $13ab + 15ab$
>
> $ab(13 + 15)$
>
> 3. $20g + 24h$
>
> $4(5g + 6h)$

Problem Set Sample Solutions

> 1. Use models to prove that $3(a + b)$ is equivalent to $3a + 3b$.
>
>
>
>
>
> 2. Use greatest common factor and the distributive property to write equivalent expressions for the following expressions.
>
>   a. $4d + 12e$
>
> $4(d + 3e)$ or $4(1d + 3e)$
>
>   b. $18x + 30y$
>
> $6(3x + 5y)$
>
>   c. $21a + 28y$
>
> $7(3a + 4y)$
>
>   d. $24f + 56g$
>
> $8(3f + 7g)$

Greatest Common Factor – Round 1

Number Correct: _____

Directions: Determine the greatest common factor of each pair of numbers.

1.	GCF of 10 and 50		16.	GCF of 45 and 72	
2.	GCF of 5 and 35		17.	GCF of 28 and 48	
3.	GCF of 3 and 12		18.	GCF of 44 and 77	
4.	GCF of 8 and 20		19.	GCF of 39 and 66	
5.	GCF of 15 and 35		20.	GCF of 64 and 88	
6.	GCF of 10 and 75		21.	GCF of 42 and 56	
7.	GCF of 9 and 30		22.	GCF of 28 and 42	
8.	GCF of 15 and 33		23.	GCF of 13 and 91	
9.	GCF of 12 and 28		24.	GCF of 16 and 84	
10.	GCF of 16 and 40		25.	GCF of 36 and 99	
11.	GCF of 24 and 32		26.	GCF of 39 and 65	
12.	GCF of 35 and 49		27.	GCF of 27 and 87	
13.	GCF of 45 and 60		28.	GCF of 28 and 70	
14.	GCF of 48 and 72		29.	GCF of 26 and 91	
15.	GCF of 50 and 42		30.	GCF of 34 and 51	

Greatest Common Factor – Round 1 [KEY]

Directions: Determine the greatest common factor of each pair of numbers.

1.	GCF of 10 and 50	**10**	16.	GCF of 45 and 72	**9**
2.	GCF of 5 and 35	**5**	17.	GCF of 28 and 48	**4**
3.	GCF of 3 and 12	**3**	18.	GCF of 44 and 77	**11**
4.	GCF of 8 and 20	**4**	19.	GCF of 39 and 66	**3**
5.	GCF of 15 and 35	**5**	20.	GCF of 64 and 88	**8**
6.	GCF of 10 and 75	**5**	21.	GCF of 42 and 56	**14**
7.	GCF of 9 and 30	**3**	22.	GCF of 28 and 42	**14**
8.	GCF of 15 and 33	**3**	23.	GCF of 13 and 91	**13**
9.	GCF of 12 and 28	**4**	24.	GCF of 16 and 84	**4**
10.	GCF of 16 and 40	**8**	25.	GCF of 36 and 99	**9**
11.	GCF of 24 and 32	**8**	26.	GCF of 39 and 65	**13**
12.	GCF of 35 and 49	**7**	27.	GCF of 27 and 87	**3**
13.	GCF of 45 and 60	**15**	28.	GCF of 28 and 70	**14**
14.	GCF of 48 and 72	**12**	29.	GCF of 26 and 91	**13**
15.	GCF of 50 and 42	**2**	30.	GCF of 34 and 51	**17**

Greatest Common Factor – Round 2

Number Correct: _____

Improvement: _____

Directions: Determine the greatest common factor of each pair of numbers.

1.	GCF of 20 and 80		16.	GCF of 33 and 99	
2.	GCF of 10 and 70		17.	GCF of 38 and 76	
3.	GCF of 9 and 36		18.	GCF of 26 and 65	
4.	GCF of 12 and 24		19.	GCF of 39 and 48	
5.	GCF of 15 and 45		20.	GCF of 72 and 88	
6.	GCF of 10 and 95		21.	GCF of 21 and 56	
7.	GCF of 9 and 45		22.	GCF of 28 and 52	
8.	GCF of 18 and 33		23.	GCF of 51 and 68	
9.	GCF of 12 and 32		24.	GCF of 48 and 84	
10.	GCF of 16 and 56		25.	GCF of 21 and 63	
11.	GCF of 40 and 72		26.	GCF of 64 and 80	
12.	GCF of 35 and 63		27.	GCF of 36 and 90	
13.	GCF of 30 and 75		28.	GCF of 28 and 98	
14.	GCF of 42 and 72		29.	GCF of 39 and 91	
15.	GCF of 30 and 28		30.	GCF of 38 and 95	

Greatest Common Factor – Round 2 [KEY]

Directions: Determine the greatest common factor of each pair of numbers.

1.	GCF of 20 and 80	**20**	16.	GCF of 33 and 99	**33**
2.	GCF of 10 and 70	**10**	17.	GCF of 38 and 76	**38**
3.	GCF of 9 and 36	**9**	18.	GCF of 26 and 65	**13**
4.	GCF of 12 and 24	**12**	19.	GCF of 39 and 48	**3**
5.	GCF of 15 and 45	**15**	20.	GCF of 72 and 88	**8**
6.	GCF of 10 and 95	**5**	21.	GCF of 21 and 56	**7**
7.	GCF of 9 and 45	**9**	22.	GCF of 28 and 52	**4**
8.	GCF of 18 and 33	**3**	23.	GCF of 51 and 68	**17**
9.	GCF of 12 and 32	**4**	24.	GCF of 48 and 84	**12**
10.	GCF of 16 and 56	**8**	25.	GCF of 21 and 63	**21**
11.	GCF of 40 and 72	**8**	26.	GCF of 64 and 80	**16**
12.	GCF of 35 and 63	**7**	27.	GCF of 36 and 90	**18**
13.	GCF of 30 and 75	**15**	28.	GCF of 28 and 98	**14**
14.	GCF of 42 and 72	**6**	29.	GCF of 39 and 91	**13**
15.	GCF of 30 and 28	**2**	30.	GCF of 38 and 95	**19**

Lesson 12: Distributing Expressions

Student Outcomes

- Students model and write equivalent expressions using the distributive property. They move from a factored form to an expanded form of an expression.

Classwork

Opening Exercise (3 minutes)

Opening Exercise

a.   Create a model to show 2×5.

5	5

b.   Create a model to show $2 \times b$, or $2b$.

b	b

Example 1 (8 minutes)

Example 1

Write an expression that is equivalent to $2(a + b)$.

- In this example we have been given the factored form of the expression.
- To answer this question we can create a model to represent $2(a + b)$.
- Let's start by creating a model to represent $(a + b)$.

Create a model to represent $(a + b)$.

The expression $2(a + b)$ tells us that we have 2 of the $(a + b)$'s. Create a model that shows 2 groups of $(a + b)$.

> **How many a's and how many b's do you see in the diagram?**
>
> *There are 2 a's and 2 b's.*
>
> **How would the model look if we grouped together the a's, and then grouped together the b's?**
>
>
>
> **What expression could we write to represent the new diagram?**
>
> $2a + 2b$

- This expression is written in expanded form.

> **What conclusion can we draw from the models about equivalent expressions?**
>
> $2(a + b) = 2a + 2b$

- To prove that these two forms are equivalent, let's plug in some values for a and b and see what happens.

> **Let $a = 3$ and $b = 4$.**
>
> | $2(a + b)$ | $2a + 2b$ |
> | --- | --- |
> | $2(3 + 4)$ | $2(3) + 2(4)$ |
> | $2(7)$ | $6 + 8$ |
> | 14 | 14 |

MP.7

- Note, if students do not believe yet that the two are equal you can continue to plug in more values for a and b until they are convinced.

> **What happens when we double $(a + b)$?**
>
> *We double a and we double b.*

Example 2 (5 minutes)

> **Example 2**
>
> **Write an expression that is equivalent to double $(3x + 4y)$.**
>
> **How can we rewrite double $(3x + 4y)$?**
>
> *Double is the same as multiplying by two.*
>
> $2(3x + 4y)$

Is this expression in factored form, expanded form, or neither?

This expression is in factored form.

Let's start this problem the same way that we started the first example. What should we do?

We can make a model of $3x + 4y$.

3x	4y

How can we change the model to show $2(3x + 4y)$?

We can make two copies of the model.

3x	4y	3x	4y

Are there terms that we can combine in this example?

3x	3x	4y	4y

Yes, there are 6 x's and 8 y's.

So the model is showing $6x + 8y$

What is an equivalent expression that we can use to represent $2(3x + 4y)$?

$2(3x + 4y) = 6x + 8y$

This is the same as $2(3x) + 2(4y)$.

Summarize how you would solve this question without the model.

When there is a number outside the parentheses, I would multiply it by the terms on the inside.

Example 3 (3 minutes)

Example 3

Write an expression in expanded form that is equivalent to the model below.

What factored expression is represented in the model?

$y(4x + 5)$

> **How can we rewrite this expression?**
>
> $y(4x) + y(5)$
>
> $4xy + 5y$

Example 4 (3 minutes)

MP.7

- How can we use our work in the previous examples to write the following expression?

> **Example 4**
>
> Write an expression that is equivalent to $3(7d + 4e)$.
>
> *We will multiply* $3 \times 7d$ *and* $3 \times 4e$.
>
> *We would get* $21d + 12e$. *So,* $3(7d + 4e) = 21d + 12e$.

Exercises (15 minutes)

> **Exercises**
>
> Create a model for each expression below. Then write another equivalent expression using the distributive property.
>
> 1. $3(x + y)$

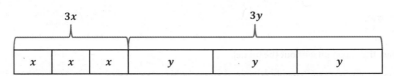

> $3x + 3y$
>
> 2. $4(2h + g)$

> $8h + 4g$

Apply the distributive property to write equivalent expressions.

3. $8(h + 3)$

   $8h + 24$

4. $3(2h + 7)$

   $6h + 21$

5. $5(3x + 9y)$

   $15x + 45y$

6. $4(11h + 3g)$

   $44h + 12g$

7.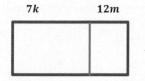

   $7k$ $12m$

   j

   $7jk + 12jm$

8. $a(9b + 13)$

   $9ab + 13a$

Closing (3 minutes)

- State what the expression $a(b + c)$ represents.
  - *a groups of the quantity b plus c.*
- Explain in your own words how to write an equivalent expression in expanded form when given an expression in the form of $a(b + c)$. Then create your own example to show off what you know.
  - *To write an equivalent expression, I would multiply a times b and a times c. Then, I would add the two products together.*
  - *Examples will vary.*
- State what the equivalent expression in expanded form represents.
  - *ab + ac means a groups of size b plus a groups of size c.*

Exit Ticket (5 minutes)

Name _____   Date _____

Lesson 12: Distributing Expressions

Exit Ticket

Use the distributive property to expand the following expressions.

1. $2(b + c)$

2. $5(7h + 3m)$

3. $e(f + g)$

Exit Ticket Sample Solutions

> **Use the distributive property to expand the following expressions.**
>
> 1. $2(b + c)$
>
> $2b + 2c$
>
> 2. $5(7h + 3m)$
>
> $35h + 15m$
>
> 3. $e(f + g)$
>
> $ef + eg$

Problem Set Sample Solutions

The following problems can be used for extra practice or for homework.

> 1. **Use the distributive property to expand the following expressions.**
>
>   a. $4(x + y)$
>
> $4x + 4y$
>
>   b. $8(a + 3b)$
>
> $8a + 24b$
>
>   c. $3(2x + 11y)$
>
> $6x + 33y$
>
>   d. $9(7a + 6b)$
>
> $63a + 54b$
>
>   e. $c(3a + b)$
>
> $3ac + bc$
>
>   f. $y(2x + 11z)$
>
> $2xy + 11yz$

2. Create a model to show that $2(2x + 3y) = 4x + 6y$.

Lesson 13: Writing Division Expressions

Student Outcomes

- Students write numerical expressions in two forms, $dividend \div divisor$ and $\dfrac{dividend}{divisor}$, and note the relationship between the two.

Classwork

Discussion (8 minutes)

The discussion will serve as a chance for students to show what they know about division and what division looks like. The discussion should conclude with the overall idea that writing $a \div b$ as $\dfrac{a}{b}$ is a strategic format when working algebraically.

- How can we write or show 8 divided by 2? (You can allow students to explain or even draw examples for class to see.
  - *Answers will vary. Students can draw models, arrays, use the division symbol and some may even use a fraction.*

- When working with algebraic expressions, are any of these expressions or models more efficient than others?
  - *Writing a fraction to show division is more efficient.*

- Is $\dfrac{8}{2}$ the same as $\dfrac{2}{8}$?
  - *No, they are not the same. $\dfrac{8}{2} = 4$, while $\dfrac{2}{8} = \dfrac{1}{4}$.*

- How would we show a divided by h using a fraction?
  - $\dfrac{a}{b}$

Example 1 (5 minutes)

Example 1

Write an expression showing $1 \div 2$ without the use of the division symbol.

- Let's start by looking at a model of $1 \div 2$.
  - *We can make a bar diagram.*

From the model what can we determine?

$1 \div 2$ *is the same as* $\frac{1}{2}$.

Example 2 (5 minutes)

> **Example 2**
>
> Write an expression showing $a \div 2$ without the use of the division symbol.

- Here we have a variable being divided by 2. Let's start by looking at a model of $a \div 2$.
  - *We can make a bar diagram.*

MP.6

From the model what can we determine?

$a \div 2$ *is the same as* $\frac{a}{2}$.

When we write division expressions using the division symbol we represent _dividend ÷ divisor_.

How would this look when we write division expressions using a fraction?

$$\frac{dividend}{divisor}$$

Example 3 (8 minutes)

> **Example 3**
>
> a.   Write an expression showing $a \div b$ without the use of the division symbol.

- How can we use what we just learned in Examples 1 and 2 to help us with this example?
  - *The dividend is the numerator and the divisor is the denominator.*

$$\frac{a}{b}$$

b.   Write an expression for g divided by the quantity h plus 3.

- How would this look with the division symbol?
  - $g \div (h + 3)$
- Now let's rewrite this using a fraction.

$$\frac{g}{h+3}$$

c.   Write an expression for the quotient of the quantity m reduced by 3 and 5.

- Let's start again by writing this using a division symbol first.
  - $(m - 3) \div 5$
- Next, we will rewrite it using the fraction bar.

$$\frac{m-3}{5}$$

Exercises 1–8 (10 minutes)

Have students use a white board or small board to practice the following questions.

Exercises

Write each expression two ways: using the division symbol and as a fraction.

1.   12 divided by 4.

   $12 \div 4$ *and* $\dfrac{12}{4}$

2.   3 divided by 5.

   $3 \div 5$ *and* $\dfrac{3}{5}$

3. a divided by 4.

   $a \div 4$ *and* $\dfrac{a}{4}$

4.   The quotient of 6 and m.

   $6 \div m$ *and* $\dfrac{6}{m}$

---

5. Seven divided by the quantity x plus y.

    $7 \div (x + y)$ *and* $\dfrac{7}{x + y}$

6. y divided by the quantity x minus 11.

    $y \div (x - 11)$ *and* $\dfrac{y}{x - 11}$

7. The sum of the quantity h and 3 divided by 4.

    $(h + 3) \div 4$ *and* $\dfrac{h + 3}{4}$

8. The quotient of the quantity k minus 10 and m.

    $(k - 10) \div m$ *and* $\dfrac{k - 10}{m}$

Closing (4 minutes)

- Explain to your neighbor how you would rewrite any division problem using a fraction.
    - *The dividend would become the numerator and the divisor would become the denominator.*

Exit Ticket (5 minutes)

Lesson 13:	Writing Division Expressions
Date:	12/11/13

Name _____   Date _____

Lesson 13: Writing Division Expressions

Exit Ticket

Rewrite the expressions using the division symbol and as a fraction.

1. The quotient of m and 7.

2. Five divided by the sum of a and b.

3. The quotient of k decreased by 4 and 9.

Exit Ticket Sample Solutions

Rewrite the expressions using the division symbol and as a fraction.

1. The quotient of m and 7.

    $m \div 7$ *and* $\dfrac{m}{7}$

2. Five divided by the sum of a and b.

    $5 \div (a + b)$ *and* $\dfrac{5}{(a+b)}$

3. The quotient of the quantity k decreased by 4 and 9.

    $(k - 4) \div 9$ *and* $\dfrac{(k-4)}{9}$

Problem Set Sample Solutions

1. Rewrite the expressions using the division symbol and as a fraction.

    a. Three divided by 4.

       $3 \div 4$ *and* $\dfrac{3}{4}$

    b. The quotient of m and 11.

       $m \div 11$ *and* $\dfrac{m}{11}$

    c. 4 divided by the sum of h and 7.

       $4 \div (h + 7)$ *and* $\dfrac{4}{h+7}$

    d. The quantity x minus 3 divided by y.

       $(x - 3) \div y$ *and* $\dfrac{x-3}{y}$

2. Draw a model to show that $x \div 3$ is the same as $\dfrac{x}{3}$.

Lesson 14: Writing Division Expressions

Student Outcomes

- Students write numerical expressions in two forms, *dividend ÷ divisor* and $\frac{dividend}{divisor}$, and note the relationship between the two.

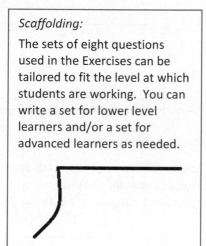

Scaffolding:

The sets of eight questions used in the Exercises can be tailored to fit the level at which students are working. You can write a set for lower level learners and/or a set for advanced learners as needed.

Lesson Notes

This is the second day of a two-day lesson.

Fluency Exercise (5 Minutes)

Long Division Algorithm White Board Exchange

Classwork

Example 1 (5 minutes)

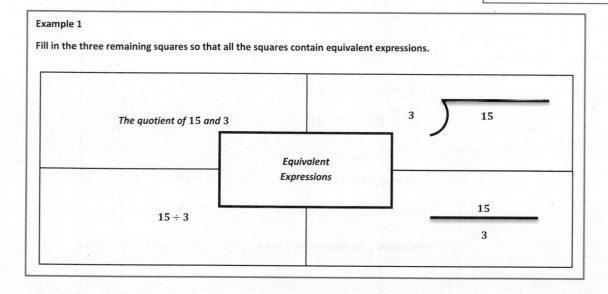

Example 1

Fill in the three remaining squares so that all the squares contain equivalent expressions.

The quotient of 15 and 3

3 ⟌ 15

Equivalent Expressions

15 ÷ 3

$\frac{15}{3}$

Example 2 (3 minutes)

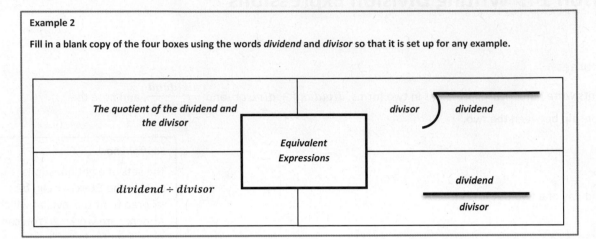

Example 2

Fill in a blank copy of the four boxes using the words *dividend* and *divisor* so that it is set up for any example.

Exercises (20 minutes)

Students will work in pairs. Each pair will be given a set of expressions to work on. There are several different versions that can be printed and used so that a variety of questions can be used throughout the classroom. The students will fill in the four rectangles, one with the given information and three with equivalent expressions.

Set A	Answers
1. $5 \div p$	5 divided by p, $\dfrac{5}{p}$, $p \overline{)5}$
2. The quotient of g and h	$g \div h$, $\dfrac{g}{h}$, $h \overline{)g}$
3. $w \overline{)23}$	23 divided by w, $23 \div w$, $\dfrac{23}{w}$
4. $\dfrac{y}{x+8}$	y divided by the sum of x and 8, $y \div (x + 8)$, $x + 8 \overline{)y}$
5. 7 divided by the quantity a minus 6	$7 \div (a - 6)$, $\dfrac{7}{a-6}$, $a - 6 \overline{)7}$
6. $3 \overline{)m+11}$	The sum of m and 11 divided by 3, $(m + 11) \div 3$, $\dfrac{m+11}{3}$
7. $(f + 2) \div g$	The sum of f and 2 divided by g, $\dfrac{f+2}{g}$, $g \overline{)f + 2}$
8. $\dfrac{c-9}{d+3}$	The quotient of c minus 9 and d plus 3, $(c - 9) \div (d + 3)$, $d + 3 \overline{)c - 9}$

Set B	Answers:
1. $h \div 11$	The quotient of h and 11, $11 \overline{)h}$, $\dfrac{h}{11}$
2. The quotient of m and n	$m \div n$, $n \overline{)m}$, $\dfrac{m}{n}$
3. $5 \overline{)j}$	The quotient of j and 5, $j \div 5$, $\dfrac{j}{5}$

Lesson 14:	Writing Division Expressions
Date:	12/11/13

140

4. $\dfrac{h}{m-4}$ *h divided by the quantity m minus 4*, $h \div (m-4)$, $m-4\overline{)h}$

5.   *f divided by the quantity g minus 11* $f \div (g-11)$, $g-11\overline{)f}$, $\dfrac{f}{g-11}$

6. $18\overline{)a+5}$ *The sum of a and 5 divided by 18*, $(a+5) \div 18$, $\dfrac{a+5}{18}$

7. $(y-3) \div x$ *The quantity y minus 3 divided by x*, $x\overline{)y-3}$, $\dfrac{y-3}{x}$

8. $\dfrac{(g+5)}{(h-11)}$ *The quantity g plus 5 divided by the quantity h minus 11*,

                                $(g+5) \div (h-11)$, $h-11\overline{)g+5}$

Set C   *Answers:*

1. $6 \div k$ *6 divided by k*, $k\overline{)6}$, $\dfrac{6}{k}$

2.   *The quotient of j and k* $j \div k$, $k\overline{)j}$, $\dfrac{j}{k}$

3. $10\overline{)a}$ *a divided by 10*, $a \div 10$, $\dfrac{a}{10}$

4. $\dfrac{15}{f-2}$ *15 divided by the quantity f minus 2*, $15 \div (f-2)$, $f-2\overline{)15}$

5.   *13 divided by the sum of h and 1* $13 \div (h+1)$, $h+1\overline{)13}$, $\dfrac{13}{h+1}$

6. $3\overline{)c+18}$ *The sum of c plus 18 divided by 3*, $(c+18) \div 3$, $\dfrac{c+18}{3}$

7. $(h-2) \div m$ *The quantity h minus 2 divided by m*, $m\overline{)h-2}$, $\dfrac{h-2}{m}$

8. $\dfrac{4-m}{n+11}$ *The quantity 4 minus m divided by the sum of n and 11*,

                                $(4-m) \div (n+11)$, $n+11\overline{)4-m}$

Closing (7 minutes)

- Have two pairs of students trade pages to check each other's work. If all of the boxes are correct, students will need to write a sentence that summarizes why the expressions are equivalent. If there are mistakes, the students will need to write sentences to explain how to correct it.

- Then have students evaluate some of the expressions. Many answers will need to be written as a fraction or decimal answer.

       Set A: $p = 3, w = 5, a = 10$

       Set B: $h = 4, j = 8, a = 10$

       Set C: $k = 2, a = 10, c = 6$

Exit Ticket (3 minutes)

Name _____   Date _____

Lesson 14: Writing Division Expressions

Exit Ticket

1. Write the division expression in words and as a fraction.

$$(g + 12) \div h$$

2. Write the following division expression using the division symbol and as a fraction: f divided by the quantity h minus 3.

Exit Ticket Sample Solutions

> 1. Write the division expression in words and as a fraction.
>
> $$(g + 12) \div h$$
>
> The sum of g and 12 divided by h, $\frac{g+12}{h}$.
>
> 2. Write the following division expression using the division symbol and as a fraction: f divided by the quantity h minus 3.
>
> $f \div (h - 3)$ and $\frac{f}{h-3}$

Problem Set Sample Solutions

Complete the missing spaces in each rectangle set.

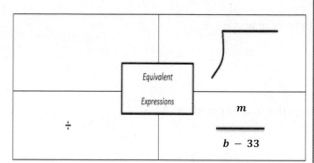

Answers: The quotient of h and 16, $16\overline{)h}$, $\frac{h}{16}$

Answers: m divided by the quantity b minus 33, $b-33\overline{)m}$, $m \div (b - 33)$

Answers: $x\overline{)7}$, $7 \div x$, $\frac{7}{x}$

Answers: The sum of y and 13 divided by 2, $(y + 13) \div 2$, $\frac{y+13}{2}$

  | Lesson 14:   Writing Division Expressions
                    Date: 12/11/13

Exercise Handout

Set A

1. $5 \div p$

2. The quotient of g and h

3. $w \overline{)23}$

4. $\dfrac{y}{x+8}$

5. 7 divided by the quantity a minus 6

6. $3 \overline{)m+11}$

7. $(f + 2) \div g$

8. $\dfrac{c-9}{d+3}$

Set B

1. $h \div 11$

2. The quotient of m and n

3. $5 \overline{)j}$

4. $\dfrac{h}{m-4}$

5. f divided by the quantity g minus 11

6. $18 \overline{)a+5}$

7. $(y - 3) \div x$

8. $\dfrac{(g+5)}{(h-11)}$

Set C

1. $6 \div k$

2. The quotient of j and k

3. $10 \overline{)a}$

4. $\dfrac{15}{f-2}$

5. 13 divided by the sum of h and 1

6. $3 \overline{)c+18}$

7. $(h - 2) \div m$

8. $\dfrac{4-m}{n+11}$

White Board Exchange: Long Division Algorithm

Progression of Exercises:	Answers:
1. 3,282 ÷ 6	547
2. 2,712 ÷ 3	904
3. 15,036 ÷ 7	2148
4. 1,788 ÷ 8	223.5
5. 5,736 ÷ 12	478
6. 35,472 ÷ 16	2217
7. 13,384 ÷ 28	478
8. 31,317 ÷ 39	803
9. 1,113 ÷ 42	26.5
10. 4082 ÷ 52	78.5

Fluency work such as this exercise should take 5–12 minutes of class.

How to Conduct a White Board Exchange:

All students will need a personal white board, white board marker, and a means of erasing their work. An economical recommendation is to place card stock inside sheet protectors to use as the personal white boards and to cut sheets of felt into small squares to use as erasers.

It is best to prepare the problems in a way that allows you to reveal them to the class one at a time. For example, use a flip chart or PowerPoint presentation; write the problems on the board and cover with paper beforehand, allowing you to reveal one at a time; or, write only one problem on the board at a time. If the number of digits in the problem is very low (e.g., 12 divided by 3), it may also be appropriate to verbally call out the problem to the students.

The teacher reveals or says the first problem in the list and announces, "Go." Students work the problem on their personal white boards, holding their answers up for the teacher to see as soon as they have them ready. The teacher gives immediate feedback to each student, pointing and/or making eye contact with the student and responding with an affirmation for correct work such as, "Good job!", "Yes!", or "Correct!" For incorrect work, respond with guidance such as "Look again!", "Try again!", or "Check your work!"

If many students have struggled to get the answer correct, go through the solution of that problem as a class before moving on to the next problem in the sequence. Fluency in the skill has been established when the class is able to go through each problem in quick succession without pausing to go through the solution of each problem individually. If only one or two students have not been able to get a given problem correct when the rest of the students are finished, it is appropriate to move the class forward to the next problem without further delay; in this case, find a time to provide remediation to that student before the next fluency exercise on this skill is given.

Topic E:

Expressing Operations in Algebraic Form

6.EE.A.2b

Focus Standard:	6.EE.A.2b	Write, read, and evaluate expressions in which letters stand for numbers.
		b. Identify parts of an expression using mathematical terms (sum, term, product, factor, quotient, coefficient); view one or more parts of an expression as a single entity. *For example, describe the expression $2(8 + 7)$ as a product of two factors; view $(8 + 7)$ as both a single entity and a sum of two terms.*
Instructional Days:	3	
Lesson 15:		Read Expressions in Which Letters Stand for Numbers (P)[1]
Lessons 16–17:		Write Expressions in Which Letters Stand for Numbers (M, P)

In Topic E, students express mathematical terms in algebraic form. They read and write expressions in which letters stand for numbers. In Lesson 15, students provide word descriptions for operations in an algebraic expression. Given the expression $4b + c$, student assign the operation term "product" for multiplication and the term "sum" for addition. They verbalize the expression as "the sum of c and the product of 4 and b." However, in Lessons 16 and 17 students are given verbal expressions, and they write algebraic expressions to record operations with numbers and letters standing for numbers. Provided the verbal expression, "Devin quadrupled his money and deposited it with his mother's," students write the expression $4a + b$, where a represents the amount of money Devin originally had and b represents the amount of money his mother has. Or, provided the verbal expression, "Crayons and markers were put together and distributed equally to six tables," students create the algebraic expression $\frac{(a+b)}{6}$, where a represents the number of crayons and b represents the number of markers. Mastery of reading and writing expressions in this topic will lead to a fluent transition in the next topic where students will read, write, and evaluate expressions.

---

[1] Lesson Structure Key: **P**-Problem Set Lesson, **M**-Modeling Cycle Lesson, **E**-Exploration Lesson, **S**-Socratic Lesson

Lesson 15: Read Expressions in Which Letters Stand for Numbers

Student Outcomes

- Students read expressions in which letters stand for numbers. They assign operation terms to operations when reading.
- Students identify parts of an algebraic expression using mathematical terms for all operations.

Classwork

Opening Exercise (10 minutes)

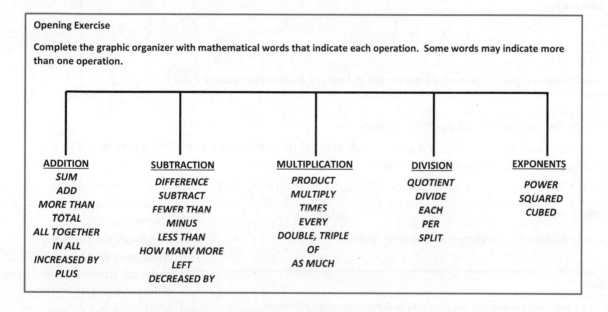

Opening Exercise

Complete the graphic organizer with mathematical words that indicate each operation. Some words may indicate more than one operation.

ADDITION	SUBTRACTION	MULTIPLICATION	DIVISION	EXPONENTS
SUM	DIFFERENCE	PRODUCT	QUOTIENT	POWER
ADD	SUBTRACT	MULTIPLY	DIVIDE	SQUARED
MORE THAN	FEWER THAN	TIMES	EACH	CUBED
TOTAL	MINUS	EVERY	PER	
ALL TOGETHER	LESS THAN	DOUBLE, TRIPLE	SPLIT	
IN ALL	HOW MANY MORE	OF		
INCREASED BY	LEFT	AS MUCH		
PLUS	DECREASED BY			

Have different students share the vocabulary words they wrote in each category. If students are missing vocabulary words in their graphic organizers, have them add the new words. At the end of the opening exercise, every student should have the same lists of vocabulary words for each operation.

Example 1 (13 minutes)

Have students write down an expression using words. Encourage students to refer back to the graphic organizer created during the opening exercise. After providing students time to write each expression, have different students read each expression out loud. Each student should use different mathematical vocabulary.

Example 1

a. $a - b$

Possible answers: a minus b; the difference of a and b; a decreased by b; b subtracted from a.

b. xy

Possible answers: the product of x and y; x multiplied by y; x times y.

c. $4f + u$

Possible answers: u added to the product of 4 and f; 4 times f plus u; the sum of 4 multiplied by f and u.

d. $d - b^3$

Possible answers: d minus b cubed; the difference of d and the quantity b to the third power.

e. $5(u - 10) + h$

Possible answers: add h to the product of 5 and the difference of u and 10; 5 times the quantity of u minus 10 added to h.

f. $\dfrac{3}{d+f}$

Possible answers: find the quotient of 3 and the sum of d and f; 3 divided by the quantity d plus f.

MP.6

- Why is 3 divided by d plus f not a correct answer?

  □ *Possible answer: 3 divided by d plus f would indicate that we divide 3 and d first and then add f, but this is not what the expression is showing.*

Exercises (12 minutes)

Students work with a partner to complete the following problems.

> *Scaffolding:*
>
> If students are using the vocabulary words well or finish early, ask students to write two different expressions for Exercises 1–4.

Exercises

Circle all the vocabulary words that could be used to describe the given expression.

1. $6h - 10$

   ADDITION   ~~SUBTRACTION~~   ~~MULTIPLICATION~~   DIVISION

2. $\dfrac{5d}{6}$

   SUM   DIFFERENCE   ~~PRODUCT~~   ~~QUOTIENT~~

3. $5(2 + d) - 8$

ADD   SUBTRACT   MULTIPLY   DIVIDE

4. abc

MORE THAN   LESS THAN   TIMES   EACH

Write an expression using vocabulary words to represent each given expression.

5. $8 - 2g$

Possible answers: 8 minus the product of 2 and g; 2 times g subtracted from 8; 8 decreased by g doubled.

6. $15(a + c)$

Possible answers: 15 times the quantity of a increased by c; the product of 15 and the sum of a and c; 15 multiplied by the total of a and c.

7. $\dfrac{m+n}{5}$

Possible answers: the sum of m and n divided by 5; the quotient of the total of m and n, and 5; m plus n split into 5 equal groups.

8. $b^3 - 18$

Possible answers: b cubed minus 18; b to the third power decreased by 18.

9. $f - \dfrac{d}{2}$

Possible answers: f minus the quotient of d and 2; d split into 2 groups then subtracted from f; d divided by 2 less than f.

10. $\dfrac{u}{x}$

Possible answers: u divided by x; the quotient of u and x; u divided into x parts

Closing (5 minutes)

▪ Peter says the expression $11 - 3c$ is three times c decreased by 11. Is he correct? Why or why not?

Exit Ticket (5 minutes)

Name _____   Date _____

Lesson 15: Read Expressions in Which Letters Stand for Numbers

Exit Ticket

1. Write two word expressions for each problem using different math vocabulary for each expression.

    a. $5d - 10$

    b. $\dfrac{a}{b+2}$

2. List five different math vocabulary words that could be used to describe each given expression.

    a. $3(d - 2) + 10$

    b. $\dfrac{ab}{c}$

Exit Ticket Sample Solutions

1. Write two word expressions for each problem, using different math vocabulary for each expression.

    a. $5d - 10$

    Possible answers: The product of 5 and d minus 10. 10 less than 5 times d.

    b. $\dfrac{a}{b+2}$

    Possible answers: The quotient of a and the quantity of b plus 2. a divided by the sum of b and 2.

2. List five different math vocabulary words that could be used to describe each given expression.

    a. $3(d - 2) + 10$

    Possible answers: difference, subtract, product, times, quantity, add, sum.

    b. $\dfrac{ab}{c}$

    Possible answers: quotient, divide, split, product, multiply, times, per, each.

Problem Set Sample Solutions

1. List five different vocabulary words that could be used to describe each given expression.

    a. $a - d + c$

    Possible answers: sum, add, total, more than, increase, decrease, difference, subtract, less than.

    b. $20 - 3c$

    Possible answers: difference, subtract, fewer than, triple, times, product.

    c. $\dfrac{b}{d+2}$

    Possible answers: quotient, divide, split, per, sum, add, increase, more than.

2. Write an expression using math vocabulary for each expression below.

    a. $5b - 18$

    Possible answers: The product of 5 and b minus 18. 18 less than 5 times b.

    b. $\dfrac{n}{2}$

    Possible answers: The quotient of n and 2. n split into 2 equal groups.

    c. $a + (d - 6)$

    Possible answers: a plus the quantity d minus 6. a increased by the difference of d and 6.

    d. $10 + 2b$

    Possible answers: 10 plus twice b. The total of 10 and the product of 2 and b.

Lesson 16: Write Expressions in Which Letters Stand for Numbers

Student Outcomes

- Students write algebraic expressions that record all operations with numbers and letters standing for the numbers.

Lesson Notes

In general, key word readings should be avoided. At this initial phase it is important for students to understand the direct relationship between words in a written phrase and their appearance in an algebraic expression.

Classwork

Opening Exercise (5 minutes)

Students underline the key math vocabulary words in each statement.

Opening Exercise

a. The sum of twice *b* and 5.

   The _sum_ of _twice_ *b* and 5.

b. The quotient of *c* and *d*.

   The _quotient_ of *c* and *d*.

c. *a* raised to the fifth power then increased by the product of 5 and *c*.

   a raised to the fifth _power_ then _increased by_ the _product_ of 5 and *c*.

d. The quantity of *a* plus *b* divided by 4.

   The _quantity_ of *a* _plus_ *b* _divided by_ 4.

e. 10 less than the product of 15 and *c*.

   10 _less than_ the _product_ of 15 and *c*.

f. 5 times *d* increased by 8.

   5 _times_ *d* _increased by_ 8.

	Lesson 16:	Write Expressions in Which Letters Stand for Numbers	
	Date:	12/11/13	152

Example 1 (10 minutes)

Model how to change the expressions given in the opening exercise from words to variables and numbers.

Example 1

   a.   **The sum of twice b and 5.**

- Underline key words: The <u>sum</u> of <u>twice</u> b and 5.
- Identify the operations each key word implies. "Sum" indicates addition and "twice" indicates multiplication by 2.
- Write an expression.

$2b + 5$

   b.   **The quotient of c and d.**

- Underline key words: The <u>quotient</u> of c and d.
- Identify the operation the key word implies: division.
- Write an expression.

$\dfrac{c}{d}$

   c.   **a raised to the fifth power, increased by the product of 5 and c.**

- Underline key words: a raised to the fifth <u>power, increased</u> by the <u>product</u> of 5 and c.
- Identify the operations each key word implies. "Power" indicates exponents, "increased" implies addition, and "product" implies multiplication.
- Write an expression.

$a^5 + 5c$

   d.   **The quantity of a plus b divided by 4.**

- Underline key words: The <u>quantity</u> of a <u>plus</u> b <u>divided by</u> 4.
- Identify the operations each key word implies. "Quantity" indicates parentheses, "plus" indicates addition, and "divided" by implies division.
- Write an expression.

$\dfrac{(a+b)}{4}$

   e.   **10 less than the product of 15 and c.**

P.6

- Underline key words: 10 <u>less than</u> the <u>product</u> of 15 and *c*.
- Identify the operations each key word implies. "Less than" indicates subtraction and "product" implies multiplication.
- Write an expression.

> $15c - 10$

MP.6

- Would $10 - 15c$ also be correct? Why or why not?
  - *This expression would not be correct. If the amount of money I have is* 10 *less than someone else, I would take the money the other person has and subtract the* 10.

> f.   **5 times *d* then increased by 8.**

- Underline key words: 5 <u>times</u> *d* then <u>increased</u> by 8.
- Identify the operations each key word implies. Times indicates multiplication and increased implies addition.
- Write an expression.

> $5d + 8$

Example 2 (10 minutes)

Model how to change each real world scenario to an expression using variables and numbers. Underline the text to show the key words before writing the expression.

> **Example 2**
>
> **Marcus has 4 more dollars than Yaseen. If *y* is the amount of money Yaseen has, write an expression to show how much money Marcus has.**

- Underline key words.
  - *Marcus has 4 <u>more dollars than</u> Yaseen.*
- If Yaseen had $7, how much money would Marcus have?
  - $11

MP.6

- How did you get that?
  - *Added* $7 + 4$
- Write an expression using *y* for the amount of money Yaseen has.
  - $y + 4$

> **Mario is missing half of his assignments. If *a* represents the number of assignments, write an expression to show how many assignments Mario is missing.**

- Underline key words.
  - *Mario is missing <u>half</u> of his assignments.*

- If Mario was assigned 10 assignments, how many is he missing?
  - 5
- How did you get that?
  - $10 \div 2$
- Write an expression using a for the number of assignments Mario was assigned.
  - $\dfrac{a}{2}$

Kamilah's weight has tripled since her first birthday. If w represents the amount Kamilah weighed on her first birthday, write an expression to show how much Kamilah weighs now.

- Underline key words.
  - *Kamilah's weight has <u>tripled</u> since her first birthday.*
- If Kamilah weighed 20 pounds on her first birthday, how much does she weight now?
  - 60 pounds
- How did you get that?
  - *Multiply 3 by 20.*
- Write an expression using w for Kamilah's weight on her first birthday.
  - $3w$

Nathan brings cupcakes to school and gives them to his five best friends who share them equally. If c represents the number of cupcakes Nathan brings to school, write an expression to show how many cupcakes each of his friends receive.

- Underline key words.
  - *Nathan brings cupcakes to school and gives them to his five best friends who <u>share</u> them <u>equally</u>.*
- If Nathan brings 15 cupcakes to school, how many will each friend receive?
  - 3
- How did you determine that?
  - $15 \div 5$
- Write an expression using c to represent the number of cupcakes Nathan brings to school.
  - $\dfrac{c}{5}$

Mrs. Marcus combines her atlases and dictionaries, and then divides them among 10 different tables. If a represents the number of atlases and d represents the number of dictionaries Mrs. Marcus has, write an expression to show how many books would be on each table.

- Underline key words.
  - *Mrs. Marcus <u>combines</u> her atlases and dictionaries, and then <u>divides</u> them among 10 different tables.*
- If Mrs. Marcus had 8 atlases and 12 dictionaries, how many books would be at each table?
  - 2

- How did you determine that?
  - *Added the atlases and dictionaries together, and then divided by 10.*
- Write an expression using a for atlases and d for dictionaries to represent how many books each table would receive.
  - $$\frac{a+d}{10}$$

> To improve in basketball, Ivan's coach told him that he needs to take four times as many free throws and four times as many jump shots every day. If f represents the number of free throws and j represents the number of jump shots Ivan shoots daily, write an expression to show how many shots he will need to take in order to improve in basketball.

MP.6

- Underline key words.
  - *To improve in basketball, Ivan needs to shoot 4 <u>times</u> more free throws <u>and</u> jump shots daily.*
- If Ivan shoots 5 free throws and 10 jump shots, how many will he need to shoot in order to improve in basketball?
  - 60
- How did you determine that?
  - *Added the free throws and jump shots together, and then multiplied by 4.*
- Write an expression using f for free throws and j for jump shots to represent how many shots Ivan will have to take in order to improve in basketball.
  - $4(f + j)$

Exercises (10 minutes)

Have students work individually on the following exercises.

> **Exercises**
>
> Mark the text by underlining key words, and then write an expression using variables and numbers for each statement below.
>
> 1. b decreased by c squared.
>
> b <u>decreased</u> by c <u>squared</u>.
>
> $b - c^2$
>
> 2.   24 divided by the product of 2 and a.
>
>   24 <u>divided</u> by the <u>product</u> of 2 and a.
>
> $$\frac{24}{2a}$$
>
> 3.   150 decreased by the quantity of 6 plus b.
>
>   150 <u>decreased</u> by the <u>quantity</u> of 6 <u>plus</u> b.
>
> $150 - (6 + b)$

4. The sum of twice c and 10.

   The <u>sum</u> of <u>twice</u> c and 10.

   $2c + 10$

5. Marlo had $35 but then spent $$m$.

   Mario had $35 but then <u>spent</u> $m.

   $35 - m$

6. Samantha saved her money and was able to quadruple the original amount, m.

   Samantha saved her money and was able to <u>quadruple</u> the original amount, m.

   $4m$

7. Veronica increased her grade, g, by 4 points, and then doubled it.

   Veronica <u>increased</u> her grade, g, by 4 points, and then <u>doubled</u> it.

   $2(g + 4)$

8. Adbell had m pieces of candy and ate 5 of them. Then he split the remaining candy equally among 4 friends.

   Adbell had m pieces of candy and <u>ate</u> 5 of them. Then he <u>split</u> the remaining candy equally among 4 friends.

   $\dfrac{m - 5}{4}$

9. To find out how much paint is needed, Mr. Jones must square the side length of the gate, and then subtract 15.

   To find out how much paint is needed, Mr. Jones must <u>square</u> the side length of the gate, and then <u>subtract</u> 15.

   $s^2 - 15$

10. Luis brought x cans of cola to the party, Faith brought d cans of cola, and De'Shawn brought h cans of cola. How many cans of cola did they bring all together?

    Luis <u>brought</u> x cans of cola to the party, Faith <u>brought</u> d cans of cola, <u>and</u> De'Shawn <u>brought</u> h cans of cola. How many cans of cola <u>did they bring all together?</u>

    $x + d + h$

Closing (5 minutes)

- How is writing expressions with variables and numbers similar to writing expressions using words?
  - *Possible answers: The same vocabulary words can be used; identifying parts of the expression before writing the expression is helpful.*
- How is writing expressions with variables and numbers different than writing expressions using words?
  - *Possible answers: When an expression with words is provided, it is possible that it might be represented mathematically in more than one way. However, when an algebraic expression is written, there can only be one correct answer.*

Exit Ticket (5 minutes)

| Lesson 16: | Write Expressions in Which Letters Stand for Numbers |
| Date: | 12/11/13 |

157

Name _____   Date _____

Lesson 16: Write Expressions in which Letters Stand for Numbers

Exit Ticket

Mark the text by underlining key words, and then write an expression using variables and numbers for each of the statements below.

1. Omaya picked x amount of apples, took a break, and then picked v more. Write the expression that models the total number of apples Omaya picked.

2. A number h is tripled and then decreased by 8.

3. Sidney brings s carrots to school and combines them with Jenan's j carrots. She then splits them equally between 8 friends.

4. 15 less than the quotient of e and d.

5. Marissa's hair was 10 inches long, and then she cut h inches.

Exit Ticket Sample Solutions

Mark the text by underlining key words, and then write an expression using variables and numbers for each of the statements below.

1. Omaya picked x amount of apples, took a break, and then picked v more. Write the expression that models the total number of apples Omaya picked.

    Omaya picked x amount of apples, took a break, and then picked v <u>more</u>.

    $x + v$

2. A number h is tripled, and then decreased by 8.

    A number h is <u>tripled,</u> and then <u>decreased</u> by 8.

    $3h - 8$

3. Sidney brought s carrots to school and combined them with Jenan's j carrots. She then split them equally between 8 friends.

    Sidney brought s carrots to school and <u>combined</u> them with Jenan's j carrots. She then <u>split</u> them equally between 8 friends.

    $\dfrac{s + j}{8}$

4. 15 less than the quotient of e and d.

    15 <u>less than</u> the <u>quotient</u> of e and d.

    $\dfrac{e}{d} - 15$

5. Marissa's hair was 10 inches long, and then she cut h inches.

    Marissa's hair was 10 inches long, and then she <u>cut</u> h inches.

    $10 - h$

Problem Set Sample Solutions

Mark the text by underlining key words, and then write an expression using variables and numbers for each of the statements below.

1. Justin can type w words per minute. Melvin can type 4 times as many words as Justin. Write an expression that represents the rate at which Melvin can type.

    Justin can type w words per minute. Melvin can type 4 <u>times</u> as many words as Justin. Write an expression that represents the rate at which Melvin can type.

    $4w$

2. Yohanna swam y yards yesterday. Sheylin swam 5 yards less than half the amount of yards as Yohanna. Write an expression that represents the number of yards Sheylin swam yesterday.

    Yohanna swam y yards yesterday. Sheylin swam 5 yards <u>less than half</u> the amount of yards as Yohanna. Write an expression that represents the number of yards Sheylin swam yesterday.

    $\dfrac{y}{2} - 5$

3. A number d decreased by 5 and then doubled.

    A number d __decreased by__ 5 and then __doubled__.

    $2(d - 5)$

4. Nahom and Semir combined their baseball cards, and then sold 10 of them.

    Nahom and Semir __combined__ their baseball cards, and then __sold__ 10 of them.

    $n + s - 10$

5. The sum of 25 and h is divided by f cubed.

    The __sum__ of 25 and h is __divided__ by f __cubed__.

    $$\frac{25 + h}{f^3}$$

Lesson 17: Write Expressions in Which Letters Stand for Numbers

Student Outcomes

- Students write algebraic expressions that record all operations with numbers and letters standing for the numbers.

Lesson Notes

Large paper is needed to complete this lesson.

Fluency Exercise (5 minutes)

Addition of Decimals Sprint

Classwork

Opening (5 minutes)

Discuss the exit ticket from Lesson 16. Students will be continuing to work on writing expressions, so discuss any common mistakes from the previous lesson.

Exercises (25 minutes)

Students work in groups of two or three to complete the stations. At each station, students write down the problem and the expression with variables and numbers. Encourage students to underline key words in each problem.

Exercises

Station One:

1. The sum of a and b.

    $a + b$

2. Five more than twice a number c.

    $5 + 2c \ or \ 2c + 5$

3. Martha bought d number of apples and then ate 6 of them.

    $d - 6$

> *Scaffolding:*
>
> If students struggled during Lesson 16, complete some examples with students before moving into the exercises.

Station Two:

1.   14 decreased by p.

    $14 - p$

2.   The total of d and f, divided by 8.

    $\dfrac{d + f}{8}$

3.   Rashod scored 6 less than 3 times as many baskets as Mike. Mike scores b baskets.

    $3b - 6$

Station Three:

1.   The quotient of c and 6.

    $\dfrac{c}{6}$

2.   Triple the sum of x and 17.

    $3(x + 17)$

3.   Gabrielle has b buttons but then lost 6. Gabrielle took the remaining buttons and split them equally among her 5 friends.

    $\dfrac{b - 6}{5}$

Station Four:

1. d doubled.

    $2d$

2.   Three more than 4 times a number x.

    $4x + 3$

3.   Mali has c pieces of candy. She doubles the amount of candy she has then gives away 15 pieces.

    $2c - 15$

Station Five:

1. f cubed.

    f^3

2.   The quantity of 4 increased by a, and then the sum is divided by 9.

    $\dfrac{4 + a}{9}$

3.   Tai earned 4 points fewer than double Oden's points. Oden earned p points.

    $2p - 4$

Station Six:

1. **The difference between d and 8.**

   $d - 8$

2. **6 less than the sum of d and 9.**

   $(d + 9) - 6$

3. **Adalyn has x pants and s shirts. She combined them and sold half of them. How many items did Adalyn sell?**

   $\dfrac{x+s}{2}$ or $\dfrac{1}{2}(x + s)$

When students reach the final station, they complete the station on larger paper. Students should put all of their work on the top half of the paper.

After all students have completed every station, they travel through the stations again to look at the answers provided on the larger paper. Students compare their answers with the answers at the stations and leave feedback on the bottom half of the paper. This may be positive feedback ("I agree with all of your answers" or "great job") or critiques ("I think your subtraction is in the incorrect order," or "Why did you write your answer in that order?").

Closing (5 minutes)

- Discuss feedback that was left on the larger sheets of paper. This will answer any questions and will provide an opportunity to discuss common mistakes.

- Is it possible to have more than one correct answer? Why or why not?

Exit Ticket (5 minutes)

Name _____   Date _____

Lesson 17: Write Expressions in which Letters Stand for Numbers

Exit Ticket

Write an expression using letters and numbers for each problem below.

1. d squared.

2. A number x increased by 6 and then the sum is doubled.

3. The total of h and b is split into 5 equal groups.

4. Jazmin has increased her $45 by m dollars and then spends a third of the entire amount.

5. Bill has d more than 3 times the number of baseball cards as Frank. Frank has f baseball cards.

Exit Ticket Sample Solutions

> Write an expression using letters and numbers for each problem below.
>
> 1. d squared.
>
> d^2
>
> 2. A number x increased by 6 and then the sum is doubled.
>
> $2(x + 6)$
>
> 3. The total of h and b is split into 5 equal groups.
>
> $\dfrac{h + b}{5}$
>
> 4. Jazmin has increased her \$45 by m dollars and then spends a third of the entire amount.
>
> $\dfrac{45 + m}{3}$ or $\dfrac{1}{3}(45 + m)$
>
> 5. Bill has d more than 3 times the number of baseball cards as Frank. Frank has f baseball cards.
>
> $3f + d$

Problem Set Sample Solutions

> Write an expression using letters and numbers for each problem below.
>
> 1. 4 less than the quantity of 8 times n.
>
> $8n - 4$
>
> 2. 6 times the sum of y and 11.
>
> $6(y + 11)$
>
> 3. The square of m reduced by 49.
>
> $m^2 - 49$
>
> 4. The quotient when the quantity of 17 plus p is divided by 8.
>
> $\dfrac{(17 + p)}{8}$
>
> 5. Jim earned j in tips, and Steve earned s in tips. They combine their tips then split them equally.
>
> $\dfrac{j + s}{2}$

	Lesson 17:	Write Expressions in Which Letters Stand for Numbers		
	Date:	12/11/13		**Lesson 17** 6•4

6. Owen has c collector cards. He quadruples the number of cards he had, and then combines them with Ian, who has i collector cards.

$4c + i$

7. Rae runs 4 times as many miles as Madison and Aaliyah combined. Madison runs m miles and Aaliyah runs a miles.

$4(m + a)$

8. By using coupons, Mary Jo is able to decrease the retail price of her groceries, g, by \$125.

$g - 125$

9. To calculate the area of a triangle, you find the product of the base and height and then divide by 2.

$\dfrac{bh}{2}$

10. The temperature today was 10 degrees colder than twice yesterday's temperature, t.

$2t - 10$

Addition of Decimals – Round 1

Number Correct: _____

Directions: Determine the sum of the decimals.

1.	1.3 + 2.1		18.	14.08 + 34.27	
2.	3.6 + 2.2		19.	24.98 + 32.05	
3.	8.3 + 4.6		20.	76.67 + 40.33	
4.	14.3 + 12.6		21.	46.14 + 32.86	
5.	21.2 + 34.5		22.	475.34 + 125.88	
6.	14.81 + 13.05		23.	561.09 + 356.24	
7.	32.34 + 16.52		24.	872.78 + 135.86	
8.	56.56 + 12.12		25.	788.04 + 324.69	
9.	78.03 + 21.95		26.	467 + 32.78	
10.	32.14 + 45.32		27.	583.84 + 356	
11.	14.7 + 32.8		28.	549.2 + 678.09	
12.	24.5 + 42.9		29.	497.74 + 32.1	
13.	45.8 + 32.4		30.	741.9 + 826.14	
14.	71.7 + 32.6		31.	524.67 + 764	
15.	102.5 + 213.7		32.	821.3 + 106.87	
16.	365.8 + 127.4		33.	548 + 327.43	
17.	493.4 + 194.8		34.	108.97 + 268.03	

Addition of Decimals – Round 1 [KEY]

Directions: Determine the sum of the decimals.

1.	$1.3 + 2.1$	**3.4**	18.	$14.08 + 34.27$	**48.35**
2.	$3.6 + 2.2$	**5.8**	19.	$24.98 + 32.05$	**57.03**
3.	$8.3 + 4.6$	**12.9**	20.	$76.67 + 40.33$	**117**
4.	$14.3 + 12.6$	**26.9**	21.	$46.14 + 32.86$	**79**
5.	$21.2 + 34.5$	**55.7**	22.	$475.34 + 125.88$	**601.22**
6.	$14.81 + 13.05$	**27.86**	23.	$561.09 + 356.24$	**917.33**
7.	$32.34 + 16.52$	**48.86**	24.	$872.78 + 135.86$	**1008.64**
8.	$56.56 + 12.12$	**68.68**	25.	$788.04 + 324.69$	**1112.73**
9.	$78.03 + 21.95$	**99.98**	26.	$467 + 32.78$	**499.78**
10.	$32.14 + 45.32$	**77.46**	27.	$583.84 + 356$	**939.84**
11.	$14.7 + 32.8$	**47.5**	28.	$549.2 + 678.09$	**1227.29**
12.	$24.5 + 42.9$	**67.4**	29.	$497.74 + 32.1$	**529.84**
13.	$45.8 + 32.4$	**78.2**	30.	$741.9 + 826.14$	**1568.04**
14.	$71.7 + 32.6$	**104.3**	31.	$524.67 + 764$	**1288.67**
15.	$102.5 + 213.7$	**316.2**	32.	$821.3 + 106.87$	**928.17**
16.	$365.8 + 127.4$	**493.2**	33.	$548 + 327.43$	**875.43**
17.	$493.4 + 194.8$	**688.2**	34.	$108.97 + 268.03$	**377**

Addition of Decimals – Round 2

Number Correct: _____

Improvement: _____

Directions: Determine the sum of the decimals.

1.	3.4 + 1.2	
2.	5.6 + 3.1	
3.	12.4 + 17.5	
4.	10.6 + 11.3	
5.	4.8 + 3.9	
6.	4.56 + 1.23	
7.	32.3 + 14.92	
8.	23.87 + 16.34	
9.	102.08 + 34.52	
10.	35.91 + 23.8	
11.	62.7 + 34.89	
12.	14.76 + 98.1	
13.	29.32 + 31.06	
14.	103.3 + 32.67	
15.	217.4 + 87.79	
16.	22.02 + 45.8	
17.	168.3 + 89.12	

18.	67.82 + 37.9	
19.	423.85 + 47.5	
20.	148.9 + 329.18	
21.	4 + 3.25	
22.	103.45 + 6	
23.	32.32 + 101.8	
24.	62.1 + 0.89	
25.	105 + 1.45	
26.	235.91 + 12	
27.	567.01 + 432.99	
28.	101 + 52.3	
29.	324.69 + 567.31	
30.	245 + 0.987	
31.	191.67 + 3.4	
32.	347.1 + 12.89	
33.	627 + 4.56	
34.	0.157 + 4.56	

Addition of Decimals – Round 2 [KEY]

Directions: Determine the sum of the decimals.

1.	3.4 + 1.2	**4.6**	18.	67.82 + 37.9	**105.72**
2.	5.6 + 3.1	**8.7**	19.	423.85 + 47.5	**471.35**
3.	12.4 + 17.5	**29.9**	20.	148.9 + 329.18	**478.08**
4.	10.6 + 11.3	**21.9**	21.	4 + 3.25	**7.25**
5.	4.8 + 3.9	**8.7**	22.	103.45 + 6	**109.45**
6.	4.56 + 1.23	**5.79**	23.	32.32 + 101.8	**134.12**
7.	32.3 + 14.92	**47.22**	24.	62.1 + 0.89	**62.99**
8.	23.87 + 16.34	**40.21**	25.	105 + 1.45	**106.45**
9.	102.08 + 34.52	**136.6**	26.	235.91 + 12	**247.91**
10.	35.91 + 23.8	**59.71**	27.	567.01 + 432.99	**1000**
11.	62.7 + 34.89	**97.59**	28.	101 + 52.3	**153.3**
12.	14.76 + 98.1	**112.86**	29.	324.69 + 567.31	**892**
13.	29.32 + 31.06	**60.38**	30.	245 + 0.987	**245.987**
14.	103.3 + 32.67	**135.97**	31.	191.67 + 3.4	**195.07**
15.	217.4 + 87.79	**305.19**	32.	347.1 + 12.89	**359.99**
16.	22.02 + 45.8	**67.82**	33.	627 + 4.56	**631.56**
17.	168.3 + 89.12	**257.42**	34.	0.157 + 4.56	**4.717**

Name _____   Date _____

1. Yolanda is planning out her vegetable garden. She decides that her garden will be square. Below are possible sizes of the garden she will create.

    a. Complete the table by continuing the pattern.

Side length	1 foot	2 feet	3 feet	4 feet	5 feet	x feet
Notation	$1^2 = 1 \cdot 1 = 1$					
Formula	$A = l \cdot w$ $A = 1 \cdot 1$ $A = 1^2 \text{ ft}^2$ $A = 1 \text{ ft}^2$					
Representation	□	⊞				

    b. Yolanda decides the length of her square vegetable garden will be 17 ft. She calculates that the area of the garden is 34 ft². Determine if Yolanda's calculation is correct. Explain.

2. Yolanda creates garden cubes to plant flowers. She will fill the cubes with soil and needs to know the amount of soil that will fill each garden cube. Volume is determined by the following formula: $V = s^3$, where s represents the side length.

32 inches

    a.   Represent the volume of the garden cube above using a numerical expression.

    b.   Evaluate the expression to determine the volume of the garden cube, and the amount of soil she will need for each cube.

3. Explain why $\left(\dfrac{1}{2}\right)^4 = \dfrac{1}{16}$.

4. Yolanda is building a patio in her back yard. She is interested in using both brick and wood for the flooring of the patio. Below is the plan she has created for the patio. All measurements are in feet.

    a. Create an expression to represent the area of the patio.

    b. Yolanda's husband develops another plan for the patio because he prefers the patio to be much wider than Yolanda's plan. Determine the length of the brick section and the length of the wood section. Then use the dimensions to write an expression that represent the area of the entire patio.

5. The landscaper hired for Yolanda's lawn suggests a patio that has the same measure of wood as it has brick.

    a. Express the perimeter of the patio in terms of x first using addition, and then using multiplication.

    b. Use substitution to determine if your expressions are equivalent. Explain.

6. Elena and Jorge have similar problems and find the same answer. Each determines that the solution to their problem is 24.

Elena: $(14 + 42) \div 7 + 4^2$ Jorge: $14 + (42 \div 7) + 4^2$

    a.   Evaluate each expression to determine if both Elena and Jorge are correct.

    b.   Why would each find the solution of 24? What mistakes were made, if any?

7. Jackson gave Lena this expression to evaluate: $14(8 + 12)$. Lena said that to evaluate the expression was simple; just multiply the factors 14 and 20. Jackson told Lena she was wrong. He solved it by finding the product of 14 and 8, then adding that to the product of 14 and 12.

    a.   Evaluate the expression using each student's method.

Lena's Method	Jackson's Method

    b.   Who was right in this discussion? Why?

A Progression Toward Mastery

Assessment Task Item		STEP 1 Missing or incorrect answer and little evidence of reasoning or application of mathematics to solve the problem.	STEP 2 Missing or incorrect answer but evidence of some reasoning or application of mathematics to solve the problem.	STEP 3 A correct answer with some evidence of reasoning or application of mathematics to solve the problem, or an incorrect answer with substantial evidence of solid reasoning or application of mathematics to solve the problem.	STEP 4 A correct answer supported by substantial evidence of solid reasoning or application of mathematics to solve the problem.
1	a 6.EE.A.1 6.EE.A.2c	Student completes the table with less than 10 cells correct. An entire row may be incorrect, indicating that incomplete understanding is still present.	Student completes the table with at least 10 of the 15 cells correct. One or more of the three rows in the last column are incorrect, indicating the student does not understand the general form of the notation, formula, and representation.	Student completes the table with at least 13 of the 15 cells correct. All three rows in the last column are correct, indicating the student understands the general form of the notation, formula, and representation.	Student completes the table without error. All notations, formulas and representations are correct. Please note student exemplar below.

Side length	1 foot	2 feet	3 feet	4 feet	5 feet	x feet
Notation	$1^2 = 1 \cdot 1 = 1$	$2^2 = 2 \cdot 2 = 4$	$3^2 = 3 \cdot 3 = 9$	$4^2 = 4 \cdot 4 = 16$	$5^2 = 5 \cdot 5 = 25$	$x^2 = x \cdot x = x^2$
Formula	$A = l \cdot w$ $A = 1 \cdot 1$ $A = 1\ ft^2$	$A = l \cdot w$ $A = 2 \cdot 2$ $A = 2^2 ft^2$ $A = 4 ft^2$	$A = l \cdot w$ $A = 3 \cdot 3$ $A = 3^2 ft^2$ $A = 9 ft^2$	$A = l \cdot w$ $A = 4 \cdot 4$ $A = 4^2 ft^2$ $A = 16 ft^2$	$A = l \cdot w$ $A = 5 \cdot 5$ $A = 5^2 ft^2$ $A = 25 ft^2$	$A = l \cdot w$ $A = x \cdot x$ $A = x^2 ft^2$
Representation	☐	⊞	(grid)	(grid)	(grid)	(square labeled x)

	b 6.EE.A.1 6.EE.A.2c	Student states that Yolanda was correct in her calculation or states that Yolanda was incorrect, but offers no explanation.	Student states that Yolanda was incorrect, but offers an incomplete analysis of the error.	Student states that Yolanda was incorrect and that Yolanda calculated $17 \cdot 2$.	Student states that Yolanda was incorrect and that Yolanda found $17 \cdot 2$, the base times the exponent. <u>AND</u> Student calculates the correct area: $17^2 = 289\ ft^2$.

2	a 6.EE.A.2c	Student does not write a numerical expression or writes an expression unrelated to the problem.	Student writes an expression that relates the volume and side length, but contains an error, such as using 2 as an exponent.	Student correctly represents the data, but writes an equation instead of expression: $V = 32^3$, or $V = 32 \cdot 32 \cdot 32$.	Student correctly represents the numerical expression for the volume of the cube: 32^3, or $32 \cdot 32 \cdot 32$.
	b 6.EE.A.1	Student does not attempt to evaluate the expression or has no expression from part (a) to evaluate.	Student attempts to evaluate the expression, but makes an arithmetic error.	Student correctly evaluates the expression and finds $V = 32{,}768$. The unit of volume, in^3, is missing. OR Student correctly evaluates an incorrect expression from part (a).	Student correctly evaluates the expression AND uses the correct units. Student gives the answer $V = 32{,}768\ in^3$.
3	6.EE.A.1	Student does not demonstrate understanding of exponentiation. One example would be adding $\frac{1}{2}$ four times.	Student makes a common error, such as $\left(\frac{1}{2}\right)^4 = \frac{4}{2}$ or $\left(\frac{1}{2}\right)^4 = \frac{1}{8}$.	Student shows that $\left(\frac{1}{2}\right)^4 = \frac{1}{2} \cdot \frac{1}{2} \cdot \frac{1}{2} \cdot \frac{1}{2}$, but makes an arithmetic error and arrives at an answer other than $\frac{1}{16}$.	Student shows that $\left(\frac{1}{2}\right)^4 = \frac{1}{2} \cdot \frac{1}{2} \cdot \frac{1}{2} \cdot \frac{1}{2} = \frac{1}{16}$.
4	a 6.EE.A.3	Student does not write an expression or does not indicate an understanding of $A = l \cdot w$.	Student writes an expression relating the width (12.5) to only one part of the length (3 or x).	Student writes the expressions incorrectly, without parentheses: $12.5 \cdot 3 + x$, but includes each term needed to find the area.	Student writes the correct expression: $12.5\,(3 + x)$ or $37.5 + 12.5\,x$.
	b 6.EE.A.3	Student does not write an expression or does not indicate an understanding of $A = l \cdot w$.	Student writes an expression using the width, 24 feet, but does not calculate the length, $2x + 4$, correctly.	Student writes the correct expression, $24\,(2x + 4)$.	Student writes the correct expression, $24\,(2x + 4)$ AND identifies the width, 24 feet, and the length, $2x + 4$ feet.
5	a 6.EE.A.3	Student does not express the perimeter of the figure in terms of x, using neither addition nor multiplication.	Student expresses the perimeter of the figure in terms of x, using either addition or multiplication, but not both.	Student expresses the perimeter of the figure in terms of x, using addition and multiplication, but makes an error in one of the expressions.	Student writes the expression $x + x + x + 2x + 2x + x + x + x$, or any other order of addends that is equivalent, AND the expression $10x$.
	b 6.EE.A.4	Student answers that the expressions are not equivalent, does not use substitution, and offers no explanation.	Student answers the expressions are equivalent, but does not use substitution and offers no explanation.	Student substitutes a value for x in both equations, but makes one or more arithmetic mistakes, and claims the two expressions are not equivalent.	Student substitutes any value for x into both the addition and multiplication expression, calculates them accurately, and finds them equivalent.

6	a 6.EE.A.1 6.EE.A.2c	Student evaluates both expressions incorrectly. Errors are both in Order of Operations and arithmetic.	Student evaluates one expression correctly, and one incorrectly. Errors are due to lack of application of Order of Operation rules.	Student follows the correct order of operations on both expressions, but fails to compute the exponents correctly on one or both expressions.	Student evaluates both expressions accurately, applying the rules of Order of Operations correctly. Elena's answer is 24 and Jorge's answer is 36.
	b 6.EE.A.1 6.EE.A.2c	Student offers no credible reason why both Elena and Jorge would both arrive at the answer 24. Jorge's mistakes are not identified.	Student shows partial understanding of Order of Operations, but is unable to find or describe Jorge's mistake. The student may have incomplete understanding of exponents.	Student finds that Elena followed the Order of Operation rules correctly. Jorge's mistake is noted, but is not described in detail.	Student finds that Elena followed the Order of Operation rules correctly. Also, Jorge's mistake is identified: Jorge did not evaluate the operation inside the parentheses first. Instead, he added $14 + 42$ first, arriving at a sum of 56. He then divided 56 by 7 to get 8, and added 4^2 to 8, for a final answer of 24.
7	a 6.EE.A.3	Student evaluates neither Lena's nor Jackson's methods accurately.	Student evaluates both expressions using the same method.	Student evaluates either Lena's or Jackson's methods accurately. The other is evaluated inaccurately.	Student evaluates both Lena's and Jackson's methods accurately.
	b 6.EE.A.2c 6.EE.A.3	Student claims both Lena and Jackson are incorrect. Evidence is missing or lacking.	Student chooses either Lena or Jackson as being correct, implying that the other is wrong. Evidence is not fully articulated.	Student indicates that methods used by both Lena and Jackson are correct. Both methods are described. No mention of the distributive property is made.	Student indicates that methods used by both Lena and Jackson are correct. The student claims Lena followed the Order of Operations by adding $8 + 12$ first because they were contained in parentheses, and then Lena multiplied the sum (20) by 14 to arrive at a product of 280. The student also identified Jackson's method as an application of the distributive property. Partial products of $14(8) = 112$ and $14(12) = 168$ are found first, and then added to arrive at 280.

Name _____ Date _____

1. Yolanda is planning out her vegetable garden. She decides that her garden will be square. Below are possible sizes of the garden she will create.

   a. Complete the table by continuing the pattern.

Side length	1 foot	2 feet	3 feet	4 feet	5 feet	x feet
Notation	$1^2 = 1 \cdot 1 = 1$	$2^2 = 2 \cdot 2 = 4$	$3^2 = 3 \cdot 3 = 9$	$4^2 = 4 \cdot 4 = 16$	$5^2 = 5 \cdot 5 = 25$	$x^2 = x \cdot x = x^2$
Formula	$A = l \cdot w$ $A = 1 \cdot 1$ $A = 1 \text{ ft}^2$	$A = l \cdot w$ $A = 2 \cdot 2$ $A = 2^2 \text{ ft}^2$ $A = 4 \text{ ft}^2$	$A = l \cdot w$ $A = 3 \cdot 3$ $A = 3^2 \text{ ft}^2$ $A = 9 \text{ ft}^2$	$A = l \cdot w$ $A = 4 \cdot 4$ $A = 4^2 \text{ ft}^2$ $A = 16 \text{ ft}^2$	$A = l \cdot w$ $A = 5 \cdot 5$ $A = 5^2 \text{ ft}^2$ $A = 25 \text{ ft}^2$	$A = l \cdot w$ $A = x \cdot x$ $A = x^2 \text{ ft}^2$
Representation						

   b. Yolanda decides the length of her square vegetable garden will be 17 ft. She calculates that the area of the garden is 34 ft². Determine if Yolanda's calculation is correct. Explain.

   $A = l \cdot w$
   $A = 17 \cdot 17$
   $A = 17^2 \text{ ft}^2$
   $A = 289 \text{ ft}^2$

   Yolanda is incorrect. Instead of finding 17^2 (or $17 \cdot 17$) she multiplied $17 \cdot 2$, the base · the exponent.

2. Yolanda creates garden cubes to plant flowers. She will fill the cubes with soil and needs to know the amount of soil that will fill each garden cube. Volume is determined by the following formula: $V = s^3$, where s equals the side length.

32 inches

a. Represent the volume of the garden cube above using a numerical expression.

$$32^3 \text{ or } 32 \cdot 32 \cdot 32$$

b. Evaluate the expression to determine the volume of the garden cube, and the amount of soil she will need for each cube.

$$32^3 =$$
$$32 \cdot 32 \cdot 32 =$$
$$32{,}768 \text{ in}^3$$

3. Explain why $\left(\frac{1}{2}\right)^4 = \frac{1}{16}$.

$$\left(\frac{1}{2}\right)^4 = \frac{1}{2} \cdot \frac{1}{2} \cdot \frac{1}{2} \cdot \frac{1}{2} = \frac{1}{16}$$
$$\underset{4}{\vee} \; \underset{8}{\vee} \; \underset{16}{\vee}$$

4. Yolanda is building a patio in her back yard. She is interested in using both brick and wood for the flooring of the patio. Below is the plan she has created for the patio. All measurements are in feet.

    a. Create an expression to represent the area of the patio.

$12.5(3+x)$ or

$37.5 + 12.5x$

    b. Yolanda's husband develops another plan for the patio because he prefers the patio to be much wider than Yolanda's plan. Determine the length of the brick section and the length of the wood section. Then use the dimensions to write an expression that represents the area of the entire patio.

$24(2x+4)$

5. The landscaper hired for Yolanda's lawn suggests a patio that has the same measure of wood as it has brick.

    a. Express the perimeter of the patio in terms of x first using addition, and then using multiplication.

$$x + x + x + 2x + 2x + x + x + x$$
$$10x$$

    b. Use substitution to determine if your expressions are equivalent. Explain.

These expressions are equivalent. Let $x = 2$

$x + x + x + 2x + 2x + x + x + x$
$2 + 2 + 2 + 4 + 4 + 2 + 2 + 2 = 20$

or

$10x$
$10(2) = 20$

6. Elena and Jorge have similar problems and find the same answer. Each determines that the solution to their problem is 24.

Elena: $(14 + 12) \div 7 + 4^2$ 　　　　　　　　　　Jorge: $14 + (42 \div 7) + 4^2$

$56 \div 7 + 4^2 =$
$56 \div 7 + 16 =$
$\quad 8 + 16 =$
$\qquad 24$

$14 + 6 + 4^2 =$
$14 + 6 + 16 =$
$\quad 20 + 16 =$
$\qquad 36$

a. Evaluate each expression to determine if both Elena and Jorge are correct.

b. Why would each find the solution of 24? What mistakes were made, if any?

> Elena followed the order of operations correctly.
> Jorge made a mistake. He
> added 14 + 42 first, and then divided
> the sum by 7 to get 8. He did not
> follow the correct order of operations.
> He should have evaluated the
> parentheses first.

7. Jackson gave Lena this expression to evaluate: $14(8 + 12)$. Lena said that to evaluate the expression was simple; just multiply the factors 14 and 20. Jackson told Lena she was wrong. He solved it by finding the product of 14 and 8, then adding that to the product of 14 and 12.

a. Evaluate the expression using each student's method.

Lena's Method	Jackson's Method
$14(8+12) =$ $14(20) =$ 280	$14(8+12)$ $112 + 168 =$ 280

b. Who was right in this discussion? Why?

> They were both correct. Lena used the order of operations
> correctly to determine 280. Jackson used the distributive
> property correctly to determine 280.

Topic F:

Writing and Evaluating Expressions and Formulas

6.EE.A.2c, 6.EE.B.5

Focus Standard:	6.EE.A.2c	Write, read, and evaluate expressions in which letters stand for numbers
	c.	Evaluate expressions at specific values of their variables. Include expressions that arise from formulas used in real-world problems. Perform arithmetic operations, including those involving whole-number exponents, in the conventional order when there are no parentheses to specify a particular order (Order of Operations). *For example, use the formulas $V = s^3$ and $A = 6s^2$ to find the volume and surface area of a cube with sides of length $s = 1/2$.*
	6.EE.B.5	Understand solving an equation or inequality as a process of answering a question; which values from a specified set, if any, make the equation or inequality true? Use substitution to determine whether a given number in a specified set makes an equation or inequality true.
Instructional Days:	5	
Lesson 18:	Writing and Evaluating Expressions—Addition and Subtraction (P)[1]	
Lesson 19:	Substituting to Evaluate Addition and Subtraction Expressions (P)	
Lesson 20:	Writing and Evaluating Expressions—Multiplication and Division (P)	
Lesson 21:	Writing and Evaluating Expressions—Multiplication and Addition (P)	
Lesson 22:	Writing and Evaluating Expressions—Exponents (P)	

In Topic F, students demonstrate their knowledge of expressions from previous topics in order to write and evaluate expressions and formulas. Students bridge their understanding of reading and writing expressions to substituting values in order to evaluate expressions. In Lesson 18, students use variables to write expressions involving addition and subtraction from real-world problems. They evaluate those expressions when they are given the value of the variable. For example, given the problem "Quentin has two more

---

[1] Lesson Structure Key: **P**-Problem Set Lesson, **M**-Modeling Cycle Lesson, **E**-Exploration Lesson, **S**-Socratic Lesson

dollars than his sister, Juanita," students determine the variable to represent the unknown. In this case, students let $x =$ Juanita's money, in dollars. Since Quentin has two more dollars than Juanita, students represent his quantity as $x + 2$. Now, students can substitute given values for the variable to determine the amount of money Quentin and Juanita have. If Juanita has fourteen dollars, students substitute the x with the amount, 14, and evaluate the expression: $x + 2$

$$14 + 2$$
$$16$$

Here, students determine that the amount of money Quentin has is 16 dollars because 16 is two more than the 14 dollars Juanita has.

In Lesson 19, students develop expressions involving addition and subtraction from real-world problems. They use tables to organize the information provided and evaluate expressions for given values. They continue to Lesson 20 where they develop expressions again, this time focusing on multiplication and division from real-world problems. Students bridge their study of the relationships between operations from Topic A to further develop and evaluate expressions in Lesson 21, focusing on multiplication and addition in real-world contexts.

Building from their previous experiences in this topic, students create formulas in Lesson 22 by setting expressions equal to another variable. Students assume, for example, that there are p peanuts in a bag. There are three bags and four extra peanuts all together. Students express the total number of peanuts in terms of p: $3p + 4$. Students let t be the total number of peanuts and determine a formula that expresses the relationship between the number of peanuts in a bag and the total number of peanuts, $t = 3p + 4$. From there, students are provided a value for p, which they substitute into the formula: if $p = 10$, they determine that $3(10) + 4 = 30 + 4 = 34$ peanuts.

In the final lesson of the topic, students evaluate formulas involving exponents for given values in real-world problems.

Lesson 18: Writing and Evaluating Expressions—Addition and Subtraction

Student Outcomes

- Students use variables to write expressions involving addition and subtraction from real-world problems.
- Students evaluate these expressions when given the value of the variable.

Lesson Notes

When students write expressions, make sure they are as specific as possible. Students should understand the importance of specifying units when defining letters. For example, students should say, "Let K = Karolyn's weight in pounds" instead of "Let K = Karolyn's weight" because weight is not a number until it is specified by pounds, ounces, grams, etc. They also must be taught that it is inaccurate to define K as Karolyn because Karolyn is not a number. Students conclude that in word problems, each letter represents a number, and its meaning must be clearly stated.

Classwork

Opening Exercise (2 minutes)

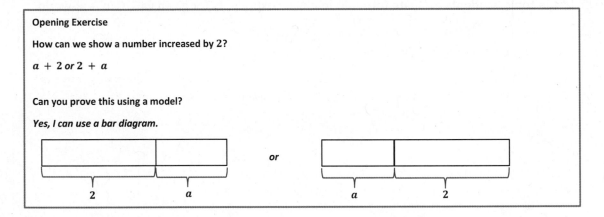

Opening Exercise

How can we show a number increased by 2?

$a + 2$ or $2 + a$

Can you prove this using a model?

Yes, I can use a bar diagram.

Discussion (5 minutes)

- In this lesson, you will connect real-world problems to addition and subtraction expressions. What story problem could you make up to go along with the expression $a + 2$?

Allow a few moments for students to form realistic scenarios. As students share these, critique them.

  - *Ronnie has some apples, but Gayle has two more than Ronnie. How many apples does Gayle have?*

Example 1 (10 minutes): The Importance of Being Specific in Naming Variables

> **Example 1: The Importance of Being Specific in Naming Variables**
>
> When naming variables in expressions, it is important to be very clear about what they stand for. The units of measure must be included if something is measured.

Exercise 1 (5 minutes)

Ask students to read the variables listed in the table and correct them for specificity.

> **Exercises**
>
> 1. Read the variable in the table and improve the description given, making it more specific.
>
> | Variable | Incomplete Description | Complete Description with Units |
> |---|---|---|
> | Joshua's speed (J) | Let J = Joshua's speed | Let J = Joshua's speed in meters per second |
> | Rufus's height (R) | Let R = Rufus's height | Let R = Rufus's height in centimeters |
> | Milk sold (M) | Let M = the amount of milk sold | Let M = the amount of milk sold in gallons |
> | Colleen's time in the 40 meter hurdles (C) | Let C = Colleen's time | Let C = Colleen's time in seconds |
> | Sean's age (S) | Let S = Sean's age | Let S = Sean's age in years |

Again, when naming variables in expressions, it is important to be very clear about what they represent. When a variable represents a quantity of items, this too must be specified.

Review the concept of speed from the above table. Recall from Module 1 that speed is a rate. Emphasize that there are two different units needed to express speed (meters per second in the above example).

Exercise 2 (5 minutes)

> 2. Read each variable in the table and improve the description given, making it more specific.
>
> | Variable | Incomplete Description | Complete Description with Units |
> |---|---|---|
> | Karolyn's CDs (K) | Let K = Karolyn's CDs | Let K = the number of CDs Karolyn has |
> | Joshua's merit badges (J) | Let J = Joshua's merit badges | Let J = the number of merit badges Joshua has earned |
> | Rufus's trading cards (R) | Let R = Rufus's trading cards | Let R = the number of trading cards in Rufus's collection |
> | Milk money (M) | Let M = the amount of milk money | Let M = the amount of milk money collected in dollars |

Example 2 (20 minutes): Writing and Evaluating Addition and Subtraction Expressions

- Read the following story descriptions and write an addition or subtraction expression for each one in the table.

Example 2: Writing and Evaluating Addition and Subtraction Expressions

Read each story problem. Identify the unknown quantity, and write the addition or subtraction expression that is described. Finally, evaluate your expression using the information given in column four.

Story Problem	Description with Units	Expression	Evaluate the Expression if:	Show your Work and Evaluate
Gregg has two more dollars than his brother Jeff. Write an expression for the amount of money Gregg has.	Let j = Jeff's money in dollars	$j + 2$	Jeff has $12.	$j + 2$ $12 + 2$ 14 Gregg has $14.
Gregg has two more dollars than his brother Jeff. Write an expression for the amount of money Jeff has.	Let g = Gregg's money in dollars	$g - 2$	Gregg has $14.	$g - 2$ $14 - 2$ 12 Jeff has $12.
Abby read 8 more books than Kristen in the first marking period. Write an expression for the number of books Abby read.	Let k = the number of books Kristen read in the first marking period	$k + 8$	Kristen read 9 books in the first making period.	$k + 8$ $9 + 8$ 17 Abby read 17 books in the first marking period.
Abby read 6 more books than Kristen in the second marking period. Write an expression for the number of books Kristen read.	Let a = the number of books Abby read in the second marking period	$a - 6$	Abby read 20 books in the second marking period.	$a - 6$ $20 - 6$ 14 Kristen read 14 books in the second marking period.
Daryl has been teaching for one year longer than Julie. Write an expression for the number of years that Daryl has been teaching.	Let j = the number of years Julie has been teaching	$j + 1$	Julie has been teaching for 28 years.	$j + 1$ $28 + 1$ 29 Daryl has been teaching for 29 years.
Ian scored 4 fewer goals than Julia in the first half of the season. Write an expression for the number of goals Ian scored.	Let j = the number of goals scored by Julia	$j - 4$	Julia scored 13 goals.	$j - 4$ $13 - 4$ 9 Ian scored 9 goals in the first half of the season.
Ian scored 3 fewer goals than Julia in the second half of the season. Write an expression for the number of goals Julia scored.	Let i = the number of goals scored by Ian	$i + 3$	Ian scored 8 goals.	$i + 3$ $8 + 3$ 11 Julia scored 11 goals in the second half of the season.
Johann visited Niagara Falls 3 times fewer than Arthur. Write an expression for the number of times Johann visited Niagara Falls.	Let f = the number of times Arthur visited Niagara Falls	$f - 3$	Arthur visited Niagara Falls 5 times.	$f - 3$ $5 - 3$ 2 Johann visited Niagara Falls twice.

Closing (4 minutes)

- Why is it important to describe the variable in an expression?
    - *The biggest reason to define the variable is to know what the expression represents.*
    - *If something is measured, include units. If something is counted, include that it is a number of items.*
- How do you determine if an expression will be an addition expression or a subtraction expression?
    - *In the first problem above, if we define x as the amount of money that Jeff has, then we would write an expression for the amount of money that Gregg has as $x + 2$. However, if we define the variable to be the amount of money that Gregg has, then we would write an expression to represent the amount of money that Jeff has as $x - 2$. Since the story problem represents a relationship between two quantities, both expressions are equally relevant.*

Exit Ticket (5 minutes)

Name _____   Date _____

Lesson 18: Writing and Evaluating Expressions—Addition and Subtraction

Exit Ticket

1. Kathleen lost a tooth today. Now she has lost 4 more than her sister Cara lost.
    Write an expression to represent the number of teeth Cara has lost. Let K = the number of teeth Kathleen lost.

    Expression:

2. Write an expression to represent the number of teeth Kathleen has lost. Let C = the number of teeth Cara lost.

    Expression:

3. If Cara lost 3 teeth, how many teeth has Kathleen lost?

Exit Ticket Sample Solutions

1. Kathleen lost a tooth today. Now she has lost 4 more than her sister Cara lost.

   Write an expression to represent the number of teeth Cara has lost. Let K = the number of teeth Kathleen lost.

   Expression: $K - 4$

2. Write an expression to represent the number of teeth Kathleen lost. Let C = the number of teeth Cara lost.

   Expression: $C + 4$

3. If Cara lost 3 teeth, how many teeth has Kathleen lost?

   $C + 4$; $3 + 4$; Kathleen has lost 7 teeth.

Problem Set Sample Solutions

1. Read each story problem. Identify the unknown quantity, and write an addition or subtraction expression that is described. Finally, evaluate your expression using the information given in column four.

   Sample answers are shown. An additional expression can be written for each.

Story Problem	Description with Units	Expression	Evaluate the Expression if:	Show your Work and Answer
Sammy has two more baseballs than his brother Ethan.	Let e = the number of balls Ethan has	$e + 2$	Ethan has 7 baseballs.	$e + 2$ $7 + 2$ 9 Sammy has 9 baseballs.
Ella wrote 8 more stories than Anna in the fifth grade.	Let s = the number of stories Anna wrote in fifth grade	$s + 8$	Anna wrote 10 stories in the fifth grade.	$s + 8$ $10 + 8$ 18 *Ella wrote 18 stories in fifth grade.*
Lisa has been dancing for 3 more years than Danika.	Let y = the number of years Danika has been dancing	$y + 3$	Danika has been dancing for 6 years.	$y + 3$ $6 + 3$ 9 *Lisa has been dancing for 9 years.*
The New York Rangers scored 2 fewer goals than the Buffalo Sabres last night.	Let g = the number of goals scored by the Rangers	$g + 2$	The Rangers scored 3 goals last night.	$g + 2$ $3 + 2$ 5 *The Buffalo Sabres scored 5 goals last night.*
George has gone camping 3 times fewer than Dave.	Let c = the number of times George has gone camping	$c + 3$	George has gone camping 8 times.	$c + 3$ $8 + 3$ 11 *Dave has gone camping 11 times.*

2. If George went camping 15 times, how could you figure out how many times Dave went camping?

   Adding 3 to George's camping trip total (15) would yield an answer of 18 trips for Dave.

Lesson 18:   Writing and Evaluating Expressions—Addition and Subtraction
Date: 12/15/13

Lesson 19: Substituting to Evaluate Addition and Subtraction Expressions

Student Outcomes

- Students develop expressions involving addition and subtraction from real-world problems.
- Students evaluate these expressions for given values.

Lesson Notes

In this lesson, students begin by filling in data tables to help them organize data and see patterns; then, they move to drawing their own tables. Encourage students to label the columns completely.

Fluency Exercise (10 minutes)

Subtraction of Decimals Sprint

Classwork

Opening Exercise (3 minutes)

> **Opening Exercise**
>
> My older sister is exactly two years older than I am. Sharing a birthday is both fun and annoying. Every year on our birthday we have a party, which is fun, but she always brags that she is two years older than I am, which is annoying. Shown below is a table of our ages, starting when I was born:
>
> | My Age (in years) | My Sister's Age (in years) |
> |---|---|
> | 0 | 2 |
> | 1 | 3 |
> | 2 | 4 |
> | 3 | 5 |
> | 4 | 6 |

Scaffolding:
Some students will benefit from having blank tables prepared ahead of time.

Make sure students understand the context of the story problem. It should be clear that the day I was born was my sister's second birthday. My first birthday was her third birthday; my second birthday was her fourth birthday; etc.

Discussion (5 minutes)

- Today in class we will use data tables. They help us organize data and see patterns. We can use variables to make generalizations about the patterns we see.

---

1. **Looking at the table, what patterns do you see? Tell a partner.**

   My sister's age is always two years more than my age.

2. **On the day I turned 8 years old, how old was my sister?**

   10 *years old*

3. **How do you know?**

   Since my sister's age is always two years more than my age, we just add 2. $8 + 2 = 10$

4. **On the day I turned 16 years old, how old was my sister?**

   18 *years old*

5. **How do you know?**

   Since my sister's age is always two years more than my age, we just add 2. $16 + 2 = 18.$

6. **Do we need to extend the table to calculate these answers?**

   No; the pattern is to add 2 *to your age to calculate your sister's age.*

Example 1 (10 minutes)

Example 1

My Age (in years)	My Sister's Age (in years)
0	2
1	3
2	4
3	5
4	6
Y	$Y + 2$

> **Scaffolding:**
>
> A number line in the classroom can provide an additional reference for students. A cardboard sheet with two windows cut to reveal Y and $Y + 2$ works with Examples 1 and 2.

a. **What if you don't know how old I am? Let's use a variable for my age. Let Y = my age in years. Can you develop an expression to describe how old my sister is?**

   Your sister is $Y + 2$ years old.

b. **Please add that to the last row of the table.**

- My age is Y years. My sister is $Y + 2$ years old. So, no matter what my age is, or was, my sister's age in years will always be two greater than mine.

Lesson 19:	Substituting to Evaluate Addition and Subtraction Expressions
Date:	12/15/13

191

Example 2 (5 minutes)

Example 2

My Age (in years)	My Sister's Age (in years)
0	2
1	3
2	4
3	5
4	6
$G - 2$	G

a. How old was I when my sister was 6 years old?

4 years old

b. How old was I when my sister was 15 years old?

13 years old

c. How do you know?

My age is always 2 years less than my sister's age.

d. Look at the table in Example 2. If you know my sister's age, can you determine my age?

We can subtract two from your sister's age, and that will equal your age.

e. If we use the variable G for my sister's age in years, what expression would describe my age in years?

$G - 2$

f. Fill in the last row of the table with the expressions.

My age is $G - 2$ years. My sister is G years old.

g. With a partner, calculate how old I was when my sister was 22, 23, and 24 years old.

You were 20, 21, and 22 years old, respectively.

Exercise 1–3 (15 minutes)

Exercises 1–3

1. Noah and Carter are collecting box tops for their school. They each bring in 1 per day starting on the first day of school. However, Carter had a head start because his aunt sent him 15 box tops before school began. Noah's grandma saved 10 box tops, and Noah added those on his first day.

    a. Fill in the missing values that indicate the total number of box tops each boy brought to school.

School Day	Number of Box Tops Noah Has	Number of Box Tops Carter Has
1	11	16
2	12	17
3	13	18
4	14	19
5	15	20

    b. If we let D be the number of days since the new school year began, on day D of school, how many box tops will Noah have brought to school?

    $D + 10$ *box tops*

    c. On day D of school, how many box tops will Carter have brought to school?

    $D + 15$ *box tops*

    d. On day 10 of school, how many box tops will Noah have brought to school?

    20 *box tops*

    e. On day 10 of school, how many box tops will Carter have brought to school?

    25 *box tops*

2. Each week the Primary School recycles 200 pounds of paper. The Intermediate School also recycles the same amount but had another 300 pounds left over from summer school. The Intermediate School custodian added this extra 300 pounds to the first recycle week.

    a. Number the weeks and record the amount of paper recycled by both schools.

Week	Total Amount of Paper Recycled by the Primary School This School Year in Pounds	Total Amount of Paper Recycled by the Intermediate School This School Year in Pounds
1	200	500
2	400	700
3	600	900
4	800	1,100
5	1,000	1,300

    b. If this trend continues, what will be the total amount collected for each school on Week 10?

    The Primary School will have collected 2,000 *pounds. The Intermediate School will have collected* 2,300 *pounds.*

3. Shelly and Kristen share a birthday, but Shelly is 5 years older.

    a. Make a table showing their ages every year, beginning when Kristen was born.

Kristen's Age (in years)	Shelly's Age (in years)
0	5
1	6
2	7
3	8

    b. If Kristen is 16 years old, how old is Shelly?

        If Kristen is 16 years old, Shelly is 21 years old.

    c. If Kristen is K years old, how old is Shelly?

        If Kristen is K years old, Shelly is K + 5 years old.

    d. If Shelly is S years old, how old is Kristen?

        If Shelly is S years old, Kristen is S − 5 years old.

Closing (2 minutes)

- Why were we able to write these expressions?
    - *There was a relationship between the two quantities that we could identify.*
- What is important to remember about labeling columns in a table?
    - *The label should be complete, with units, so the reader understands precisely what is meant.*
- How are addition and subtraction expression related to one another?
    - *They are inverse operations. One undoes the other.*

Exit Ticket (5 minutes)

	Lesson 19:	Substituting to Evaluate Addition and Subtraction Expressions
	Date:	12/15/13

194

Name _____   Date _____

Lesson 19: Substituting to Evaluate Addition and Subtraction Expressions

Exit Ticket

1. Jenna and Allie work together at a piano factory. They both were hired on January 3, but Jenna was hired in 2005, and Allie was hired in 2009.

    a. Fill in the table below to summarize the two workers' experience totals.

Year	Allie's Years of Experience	Jenna's Years of Experience
2010		
2011		
2012		
2013		
2014		

    b. If both workers continue working at the piano factory, when Allie has A years of experience on the job, how many years of experience will Jenna have on the job?

    c. If both workers continue working at the piano factory, when Allie has 20 years of experience on the job, how many years of experience will Jenna have on the job?

Exit Ticket Sample Solutions

1. Jenna and Allie work together at a piano factory. They both were hired on January 3, but Jenna was hired in 2005, and Allie was hired in 2009.

   a. Fill in the table below to summarize the two workers' experience totals.

Year	Allie's Years of Experience	Jenna's Years of Experience
2010	1	5
2011	2	6
2012	3	7
2013	4	8
2014	5	9

   b. If both workers continue working at the piano factory, when Allie has A years of experience on the job, how many years of experience will Jenna have on the job?

   Jenna will have been on the job for $A + 4$ years.

   c. If both workers continue working at the piano factory, when Allie has 20 years of experience on the job, how many years of experience will Jenna have on the job?

   Jenna will have been on the job for 24 years.

Problem Set Sample Solutions

1. Suellen and Tara are in 6th grade, and both take dance lessons at Twinkle Toes Dance Studio. This is Suellen's first year, while this is Tara's fifth year. Both girls plan to continue taking lessons throughout high school.

   a. Complete the table showing the number of years the girls will have danced at the studio.

Grade	Suellen's Years of Experience Dancing	Tara's Years of Experience Dancing
Sixth	1	5
Seventh	2	6
Eighth	3	7
Ninth	4	8
Tenth	5	9
Eleventh	6	10
Twelfth	7	11

   b. If Suellen has been taking dance lessons for Y years, how many years has Tara been taking lessons?

   Tara has been taking dance lessons for $Y + 4$ years.

2. Daejoy and Damian collect fossils. Before they went on a fossil-hunting trip, Daejoy had 25 fossils in her collection, and Damian had 16 fossils in his collection. On a 10-day fossil hunting trip, they each collected 2 new fossils each day.

    a. Make a table showing how many fossils each person had at the end of each day.

Day	Number of Fossils in Daejoy's Collection	Number of Fossils in Damian's Collection
1	27	18
2	29	20
3	31	22
4	33	24
5	35	26
6	37	28
7	39	30
8	41	32
9	43	34
10	45	36

    b. If this pattern of fossil-finding continues, how many fossils will Damian have when Daejoy has F fossils?

        When Daejoy has F fossils, Damian will have $F - 9$ fossils.

    c. If this pattern of fossil-finding continues, how many fossils will Damian have when Daejoy has 55 fossils?

        When Daejoy has 55 fossils, Damian will have 46 fossils.

3. A train consists of three types of cars: box cars, an engine, and a caboose.

Number of Box Cars	Number of Cars in the Train
0	2
1	3
2	4
10	12
100	102

    a. Tom wrote an expression for the relationship depicted in the table as $B + 2$. Theresa wrote an expression for the same relationship as $C - 2$. Is it possible to have two different expressions to represent one relationship? Explain.

        Both expressions can represent the same relationship, depending on the point of view. The expression $B + 2$ represents the number of box cars plus an engine and a caboose. The expression $C - 2$ represents the whole car length of the train, less the engine and caboose.

    b. What do you think the variable in each student's expression represents? How would you define them?

        The variable C would represent the total cars in the train. The variable B would represent the number of box cars.

Lesson 19:   Substituting to Evaluate Addition and Subtraction Expressions
Date: 12/15/13

4. David was 3 when Marieka was born. Complete the table.

Marieka's Age in Years	David's Age in Years
5	8
6	9
7	10
8	11
10	13
17	20
32	35
M	$M + 3$
$D - 3$	D

5. Caitlin and Michael are playing a card game. In the first round, Caitlin scored 200 points, and Michael scored 175 points. In each of the next few rounds, they each scored 50 points. Their score sheet is below.

Caitlin's points	Michael's points
200	175
250	225
300	275
350	325

a. If this trend continues, how many points will Michael have when Caitlin has 600 points?

Michael will have 575 points.

b. If this trend continues, how many points will Michael have when Caitlin has C points?

Michael will have $C - 25$ points.

c. If this trend continues, how many points will Caitlin have when Michael has 975 points?

Caitlin will have 1,000 points.

d. If this trend continues, how many points will Caitlin have when Michael has M points?

Caitlin will have $M + 25$ points.

6. The high school marching band has 15 drummers this year. The band director insists that there are to be 5 more trumpet players than drummers at all times.

a. How many trumpet players are in the marching band this year?

$15 + 5 = 20$. *There are 20 trumpet players this year.*

b. Write an expression that describes the relationship of the number of trumpet players (T) and the number of drummers (D).

$T = D + 5$ *or* $D = T - 5$

c. If there are only 14 trumpet players interested in joining the marching band next year, how many drummers will the band director want in the band?

The band director will want 9 drummers.

Subtraction of Decimals – Round 1

Number Correct: _____

Directions: Subtract the decimals to determine the difference.

1.	9.4 − 4.1	
2.	7.4 − 3.2	
3.	49.5 − 32.1	
4.	20.9 − 17.2	
5.	9.2 − 6.8	
6.	7.48 − 2.26	
7.	58.8 − 43.72	
8.	38.99 − 24.74	
9.	116.32 − 42.07	
10.	46.83 − 35.6	
11.	54.8 − 43.66	
12.	128.43 − 87.3	
13.	144.54 − 42.09	
14.	105.4 − 68.22	
15.	239.5 − 102.37	

16.	41.72 − 33.9	
17.	354.65 − 67.5	
18.	448.9 − 329.18	
19.	8 − 5.38	
20.	94.21 − 8	
21.	134.25 − 103.17	
22.	25.8 − 0.42	
23.	115 − 1.65	
24.	187.49 − 21	
25.	345.77 − 248.69	
26.	108 − 54.7	
27.	336.91 − 243.38	
28.	264 − 0.742	
29.	174.38 − 5.9	
30.	323.2 − 38.74	

Subtraction of Decimals – Round 1 **[KEY]**

Directions: Subtract the decimals to determine the difference.

1.	9.4 − 4.1	**5.3**	16.	41.72 − 33.9	**7.82**
2.	7.4 − 3.2	**4.2**	17.	354.65 − 67.5	**287.15**
3.	49.5 − 32.1	**17.4**	18.	448.9 − 329.18	**119.72**
4.	20.9 − 17.2	**3.7**	19.	8 − 5.38	**2.62**
5.	9.2 − 6.8	**2.4**	20.	94.21 − 8	**86.21**
6.	7.48 − 2.26	**5.22**	21.	134.25 − 103.17	**31.08**
7.	58.8 − 43.72	**15.08**	22.	25.8 − 0.42	**25.38**
8.	38.99 − 24.74	**14.25**	23.	115 − 1.65	**113.35**
9.	116.32 − 42.07	**74.25**	24.	187.49 − 21	**166.49**
10.	46.83 − 35.6	**11.23**	25.	345.77 − 248.69	**97.08**
11.	54.8 − 43.66	**11.14**	26.	108 − 54.7	**53.3**
12.	128.43 − 87.3	**41.13**	27.	336.91 − 243.38	**93.53**
13.	144.54 − 42.09	**102.45**	28.	264 − 0.742	**263.258**
14.	105.4 − 68.22	**37.18**	29.	174.38 − 5.9	**168.48**
15.	239.5 − 102.37	**137.13**	30.	323.2 − 38.74	**284.46**

Subtraction of Decimals – Round 2

Number Correct: _____

Improvement: _____

Directions: Subtract the decimals to determine the difference.

1.	8.4 − 5.4		16.	14 − 10.32	
2.	5.6 − 3.1		17.	43.37 − 28	
3.	9.7 − 7.2		18.	24.56 − 18.88	
4.	14.3 − 12.1		19.	33.55 − 11.66	
5.	34.5 − 13.2		20.	329.56 − 284.49	
6.	14.86 − 13.85		21	574.3 − 342.18	
7.	43.27 − 32.14		22.	154 − 128.63	
8.	48.48 − 27.27		23.	247.1 − 138.57	
9.	64.74 − 31.03		24.	12 − 3.547	
10.	98.36 − 24.09		25.	1.415 − 0.877	
11.	33.54 − 24.4		26.	185.774 − 154.86	
12.	114.7 − 73.42		27.	65.251 − 36.9	
13.	45.2 − 32.7		28.	144.2 − 95.471	
14.	74.8 − 53.9		29.	2.11 − 1.949	
15.	238.4 − 114.36		30.	100 − 34.746	

Subtraction of Decimals – Round 2 [KEY]

Directions: Subtract the decimals to determine the difference.

1.	8.4 − 5.4	**3.0**	16.	14 − 10.32	**3.68**
2.	5.6 − 3.1	**2.5**	17.	43.37 − 28	**15.37**
3.	9.7 − 7.2	**2.5**	18.	24.56 − 18.88	**5.68**
4.	14.3 − 12.1	**2.2**	19.	33.55 − 11.66	**21.89**
5.	34.5 − 13.2	**21.3**	20.	329.56 − 284.49	**45.07**
6.	14.86 − 13.85	**1.01**	21.	574.3 − 342.18	**232.12**
7.	43.27 − 32.14	**11.13**	22.	154 − 128.63	**25.37**
8.	48.48 − 27.27	**21.21**	23.	247.1 − 138.57	**108.53**
9.	64.74 − 31.03	**33.71**	24.	12 − 3.547	**8.453**
10.	98.36 − 24.09	**74.27**	25.	1.415 − 0.877	**0.538**
11.	33.54 − 24.4	**9.14**	26.	185.774 − 154.86	**30.914**
12.	114.7 − 73.42	**41.28**	27.	65.251 − 36.9	**28.351**
13.	45.2 − 32.7	**12.5**	28.	144.2 − 95.471	**48.729**
14.	74.8 − 53.9	**20.9**	29.	2.11 − 1.949	**0.161**
15.	238.4 − 114.36	**124.04**	30.	100 − 34.746	**65.254**

Lesson 20: Writing and Evaluating Expressions—Multiplication and Division

Student Outcomes

- Students develop expressions involving multiplication and division from real-world problems.
- Students evaluate these expressions for given values.

Lesson Notes

This lesson builds on Lesson 19, extending the concepts using multiplication and division expressions.

Classwork

Opening (3 minutes)

Use a short time to make sure the answers to the problem set from the previous lesson are clear. The labels on the tables should be complete.

Discussion (3 minutes)

- In the previous lesson, we created expressions that used addition and subtraction to describe the relationship between two quantities. How did using tables help your understanding?

  □ *Patterns were easy to see. Looking down the columns revealed a number pattern. Looking across the rows revealed a constant difference between columns.*

- In this lesson, we are going to develop expressions involving multiplication and division, much like the last lesson. We will also evaluate these expressions for given values.

Example 1 (5 minutes)

- The farmers' market is selling bags of apples. In every bag, there are 3 apples. If I buy one bag, how many apples will I have?

  □ *Three.*

- If I buy two bags, how many apples will I have?

  □ Since $2 \cdot 3 = 6$, *you will have 6 apples.*

- If I buy three bags, how many apples will I have?

  □ Since $3 \cdot 3 = 9$, *you will have 9 apples.*

- Fill in the table for a purchase of 4 bags of apples. Check your answer with a partner.

> *Scaffolding:*
>
> Having interlocking cubes ready in groups of three will make a concrete visual for students to see and hold for Example 1. Put these in clear plastic bags, if desired.

- What if I bought some other number of bags? If I told you how many bags, could you calculate the number of apples I would have altogether?

  □ *Yes, multiply the number of bags by 3 to find the total number of apples.*

- What if I bought B bags of apples? Can you write an expression in the table that describes the total number of apples I have purchased?

  □ *$3B$ or $3(B)$ or $3 \cdot B$*

Take a moment to review the different notations used for multiplication. Students should be comfortable reading and writing the expressions in all three forms.

- What if the market had 25 bags of apples to sell? How many apples is that in all?

  □ *If $B = 25$, then $3B = 3 \cdot 25 = 75$ apples.*

Exercise 1 (5 minutes)

> **Exercises 1–4**
>
> 1. The farmers' market is selling bags of apples. In every bag, there are 3 apples.
>
>   a. Complete the table.
>
> | Number of Bags | Total Number of Apples |
> |:---:|:---:|
> | 1 | 3 |
> | 2 | 6 |
> | 3 | 9 |
> | 4 | 12 |
> | B | $3B$ |
>
>   b. What if the market had 25 bags of apples to sell? How many apples is that in all?
>
>   *If $B = 25$, then $3B = 3 \cdot 25 = 75$ apples.*
>
>   c. If a truck arrived that had some number, a, more apples on it, then how many bags would the clerks use to bag up the apples?
>
>   *$a \div 3$ bags are needed. If there are 1 or 2 apples left over, an extra bag will be needed (although not full).*
>
>   d. If a truck arrived that had 600 more apples on it, how many bags would the clerks use to bag up the apples?
>
>   *$600\ apples \div \dfrac{3\ apples}{1\ bag} = 200\ bags.$*
>
>   e. How is part (d) different from part (b)?
>
>   *Part (d) gives the number of apples and asks for the number of bags. Therefore, we needed to divide the number of apples by 3. Part (b) gives the number of bags and asks for the number of apples. Therefore, we needed to multiply the number of bags by 3.*

Exercise 2 (5 minutes)

Students work on Exercise 2 independently.

---

2. In New York State, there is a five cent deposit on all carbonated beverage cans and bottles. When you return the empty can or bottle, you get the five cents back.

    a. Complete the table.

Number of Containers Returned	Refund in Dollars
1	0.05
2	0.10
3	0.15
4	0.20
10	0.50
50	2.50
100	5.00
C	$0.05C$

    b. If we let C represent the number of cans, what is the expression that shows how much money is returned?

       $0.05C$

    c. Use the expression to find out how much money Brett would receive if he returned 222 cans.

       If $C = 222$, then $0.05C = 0.05 \cdot 222 = \$11.10$.

    d. If Gavin needs to earn $4.50 for returning cans, how many cans does he need to collect and return?

       $\$4.50 \div 0.05 = 90$ cans.

    e. How is part (d) different from part (c)?

       Part (d) gives the amount of money and asks for the number of cans. Therefore, we needed to divide the amount of money by 0.05. Part (c) gives the number of cans and asks for the amount of money. Therefore, we needed to multiply the number of cans by 0.05.

Discuss the similarities and differences between Examples 1 and 2. In both examples, the second quantity is a multiple of the first. Multiplication by the constant term is used to show the relationship between the quantities in the first column and the quantities in the second column. Division is used to show the relationship between the quantities in the second column and the quantities in the first column.

Lesson 20:	Writing and Evaluating Expressions—Multiplication and Division
Date:	12/15/13

Exercise 3 (10 minutes)

Students work on Exercise 3 independently.

---

3. The fare for a subway or a local bus ride is $2.50.
   a. Complete the table.

Number of Rides	Cost of Rides in Dollars
1	2.50
2	5.00
3	7.50
4	10.00
5	12.50
10	25.00
30	75.00
R	$2.50R$ or $2.5R$

   b. If we let R represent the number of rides, what is the expression that shows the cost of the rides?

   $2.50R$ or $2.5R$

   c. Use the expression to find out how much money 60 rides would cost.

   If $R = 60$, then $2.50R = 2.50 \cdot 60 = \$150.00$.

   d. If a commuter spends $175.00 on subway or bus rides, how many trips did the commuter take?

   $\$175.00 \div \$2.50 = 70$ *trips.*

   e. How is part (d) different from part (c)?

   Part (d) gives the amount of money and asks for the number of rides. Therefore, we needed to divide the amount of money by the cost of each ride (2.50). Part (c) gives the number of rides and asks for the amount of money. Therefore, we needed to multiply the number of rides by $\$2.50$.

Exercise 4 (10 minutes): Challenge Problem

---

4. A pendulum swings though a certain number of cycles in a given time. Owen made a pendulum that swings 12 times every 15 seconds.
   a. Construct a table showing the number of cycles through which a pendulum swings. Include data for up to one minute. Use the last row for C cycles, and write an expression for the time it takes for the pendulum to make C cycles.

Number of Cycles	Time in Seconds
12	15
24	30
36	45
48	60
C	$\dfrac{15C}{12}$

---

b.   Owen and his pendulum team set their pendulum in motion and counted 16 cycles. What was the elapsed time?

   20 seconds

c.   Write an expression for the number of cycles a pendulum swings in S seconds.

   $\dfrac{12}{15} S$ *or* $\dfrac{4}{5} S$ *or* $0.8 \cdot S$

d.   In a different experiment, Owen and his pendulum team counted the cycles of the pendulum for 35 seconds. How many cycles did they count?

   28 cycles

Closing (2 minutes)

- In Example 1 and Exercise 1, we looked at the relationship between the number of bags purchased at the farmers' market and the total number of apples purchased. We created two different expressions: $3B$ and $a \div 3$. What does each variable represent, and why did we multiply by 3 in the first expression and divide by 3 in the second?

  - *The variable B represented the number of bags. We had to multiply by 3 because there were 3 apples packaged in each bag. The variable a represented the number of apples. These were grouped 3 per bag, so we divided by 3.*

- What would the expressions be if the farmers' market sold bags that contained 5 apples instead of 3?

  - *$5B$ and $a \div 5$, respectively.*

Exit Ticket (3 minutes)

Name _____   Date _____

Lesson 20: Writing and Evaluating Expressions—Multiplication and Division

Exit Ticket

1. Anna charges $8.50 per hour to babysit. Complete the table and answer the questions below.

Number of Hours	Amount Anna Charges in Dollars
1	
2	
5	
8	
H	

    a. Write an expression describing her earnings for working H hours.

    b. How much will she earn if she works for $3\frac{1}{2}$ hours?

    c. How long will it take Anna to earn $51.00?

Exit Ticket Sample Solutions

1.   Anna charges $8.50 per hour to babysit. Complete the table and answer the questions below.

Number of Hours	Amount Anna Charges in Dollars
1	8.50
2	17.00
5	42.50
8	68
H	$8.50H$ or $8.5H$

    a.   Write an expression describing her earnings for working H hours.

        $8.50H$ *or* $8.5H$

    b.   How much will she earn if she works for $3\frac{1}{2}$ hours?

        If $H = 3.5$, *then* $8.5H = 8.5 \cdot 3.5 = 29.75$. *She earned* $29.75.

    c.   How long will it take Anna to earn $51.00?

        $51 \div 8.5 = 6$. *It takes Anna 6 hours to earn* $51.00.

Problem Set Sample Solutions

1.   A radio station plays 12 songs each hour. They never stop for commercials, news, weather, or traffic reports.

    a.   Write an expression describing how many songs are played by the radio station in H hours.

        $12H$

    b.   How many songs will be played in an entire day (24 hours)?

        $12 \cdot 24 = 288$. *There will be* 288 *songs played.*

    c.   How long does it take the radio station to play 60 consecutive songs?

        $60 \text{ songs} \div \dfrac{12 \text{ songs}}{1 \text{ hour}} = 5 \text{ hours}$.

2.   A ski area has a high speed lift that can move 2,400 skiers to the top of the mountain each hour.

    a.   Write an expression describing how many skiers can be lifted each hour.

        $2,400H$

    b.   How many skiers can be moved to the top of the mountain in 14 hours?

        $14 \cdot 2,400 = 33,600$. 33,600 *skiers can be moved.*

    c.   How long will it take to move $3,600$ skiers to the top of the mountain?

$3,600 \div 2,400 = 1.5$; *it will take an hour and a half.*

3.   Polly writes a magazine column, for which she earns $35 per hour.   Create a table of values that shows the relationship between the number of hours that Polly works, H, and the amount of money Polly earns in dollars, E.

Answers will vary. Sample answers are shown.

Hours Polly Works (H)	Polly's Earnings in Dollars (E)
1	35
2	70
3	105
4	140

    a.   If you know how many hours Polly works, can you determine how much money she earned? Write the corresponding expression.

Multiplying the number of hours that Polly works by her rate ($35 per hour) will calculate her pay. $35H$ is the expression for her pay in dollars.

    b.   Use your expression to determine how much Polly earned after working for $3\frac{1}{2}$ hours.

$35H = 35 \cdot 3.5 = 122.5$. *Polly makes $122.50 for working $3\frac{1}{2}$ hours.*

    c.   If you know how much money Polly earned, can you determine how long she worked? Write the corresponding expression.

Dividing Polly's pay by 35 will calculate the number of hours she worked. $E \div 35$ is the expression for the number of hours she worked.

    d.   Use your expression to determine how long Polly worked if she earned $52.50.

$52.50 \div 35 = 1.5$; *Polly worked an hour and a half for $52.50.*

4.   Mitchell delivers newspapers after school, for which he earns $0.09 per paper.   Create a table of values that shows the relationship between the number of papers that Mitchell delivers, P, and the amount of money Mitchell earns in dollars, E.

Answers will vary. Sample answers are shown.

Number of Papers Delivered (P)	Mitchell's Earnings in Dollars (E)
1	0.09
10	0.90
100	9.00
1000	90.00

    a.   If you know how many papers Mitchell delivers, can you determine how much money he earned? Write the corresponding expression.

Multiplying the number of papers that Mitchell delivers by his rate ($0.09 per paper) will calculate his pay. $0.09P$ is the expression for his pay in dollars.

Lesson 20:   Writing and Evaluating Expressions—Multiplication and Division
Date: 12/15/13

b. Use your expression to determine how much Mitchell earned by delivering 300 newspapers.

$0.09P = 0.09 \cdot 300 = 27$. *Mitchell earned* $27.00 *for delivering* 300 *newspapers.*

c. If you know how much money Mitchell earned, can you determine how many papers he delivered? Write the corresponding expression.

Dividing Mitchell's pay by $0.09 *will calculate the number of papers he delivered.* $E \div 0.09$ *is the expression for the number of papers he delivered.*

d. Use your expression to determine how many papers Mitchell delivered if he earned $58.50 last week.

$58.50 \div 0.09 = 650$; *therefore, Mitchell delivered* 650 *newspapers last week.*

5. Randy is an art dealer who sells reproductions of famous paintings. Copies of the *Mona Lisa* sell for $475.

a. Last year Randy sold $9,975.00 worth of *Mona Lisa* reproductions. How many did he sell?

$9,975 \div 475 = 21$. *He sold* 21 *copies of the painting.*

b. If Randy wants to increase his sales to at least $15,000 this year, how many copies will he need to sell (without changing the price per painting)?

$15,000 \div 475$ *is about* 31.6; *therefore, he will have to sell* 32 *paintings.*

Lesson 21: Writing and Evaluating Expressions—

Multiplication and Addition

Student Outcomes

- Students develop formulas involving multiplication and addition from real-world problems.
- Students evaluate these formulas for given values.

Lesson Notes

This lesson begins with students making a model of a real-world problem they most likely have already encountered: moving enough tables together so that a large group of people can sit together. After the problem is posed, students use square tiles to model the problem. Using this data and looking for patterns, they make generalizations about the expression that describes the problem.

It will be necessary to prepare bags of five square tiles before class and to group students thoughtfully.

Classwork

Opening (2 minutes)

Move students into groups of two or three and distribute the bags of tiles and student materials.

Discussion (3 minutes)

- Today we will model a problem that happens in restaurants every day: moving tables together so that everyone in a group can sit together. Use the square tiles to represent square tables. One person can sit along each edge of a table side. (No crowding!) Our first goal is to find how many people can sit at tables made of various numbers of square tables pushed together end-to-end.

- Use the table in your student materials to record your findings.

Example 1 (10 minutes)

- How many chairs can fit around one square table? What is the perimeter of the square if the edge length is one yard?

  - 4; 4 yards

- If two square tables are pushed together to form a longer rectangular table, how many chairs will fit around the new table? What is the perimeter of the rectangle?

  - 6; 6 yards

Make sure that each student can connect the square model on the desk to the picture on the classwork sheet.

- If there are twice as many square tables in the new rectangular table, why can't twice as many chairs fit around it?

  □ *No chairs will fit right where the tables come together.*

- Make a record of the number of chairs that will fit around longer rectangular tables when 3, 4, and 5 square tables are pushed together to form long rectangular tables.

Exercise 1 (10 minutes)

Exercise 1

The Italian Villa Restaurant has square tables that the servers can push together to accommodate the customers. Only one chair fits along the side of the square table. Make a model of each situation to determine how many seats will fit around various rectangular tables.

Number of square tables	Number of seats at the table
1	4
2	6
3	8
4	10
5	12
50	102
200	402
T	$2T + 2$ or $2(T + 1)$

Are there any other ways to think about solutions to this problem?

Regardless of the number of tables, there is one chair on each end, and each table has two chairs opposite one another.

It is impractical to make a model of pushing 50 tables together to make a long rectangle. If we did have a rectangle that long, how many chairs would fit on the long sides of the table?

50 on each side, for a total of 100.

How many chairs fit on the ends of the long table?

2 chairs, one on each end

How many chairs fit in all? Record it.

102 chairs in all

Work with your group to determine how many chairs would fit around a very long rectangular table if 200 square tables were pushed together.

200 chairs on each side, totaling 400, plus one on each end; grand total 402.

If we let T represent the number of square tables that make one long rectangular table, what is the expression for the number of chairs that will fit around it?

$2T + 2$

Example 2 (10 minutes)

Example 2

Look at Example 2 with your group. Determine the cost for various numbers of pizzas, and also determine the expression that describes the cost of having P pizzas delivered.

a. Pizza Queen has a special offer on lunch pizzas: $4.00 each. They charge $2.00 to deliver, regardless of how many pizzas are ordered. Determine the cost for various numbers of pizzas, and also determine the expression that describes the cost of having P pizzas delivered.

Number of Pizzas Delivered	Total Cost in Dollars
1	6
2	10
3	14
4	18
10	42
50	202
P	$4P + 2$

Allow the groups to discover patterns and share them.

> What mathematical operations did you need to perform to find the total cost?
>
> *Multiplication and addition. We multiplied the number of pizzas by $4, and then added the $2 delivery fee.*
>
> Suppose our principal wanted to buy a pizza for everyone in our class? Determine how much this would cost.
>
> *Answers will vary depending on the number of students in your class.*

b. If the booster club had $400 to spend on pizza, what is the greatest number of pizzas they could order?

Students can use the "guess and check" method for answering this question. A scaffold question might be: "Could they order 100 pizzas at this price?"

> *The greatest number of pizzas they could order would be 99. The pizzas themselves would cost $99 \times \$4 =$ $396, and then add $2.00 for delivery. The total bill is $398.*

c. If the pizza price was raised to $5.00 and the delivery price was raised to $3.00, create a table that shows the total cost (pizza plus delivery) of 1, 2, 3, 4, and 5 pizzas. Include the expression that describes the new cost of ordering P pizzas.

Number of Pizzas Delivered	Total Cost in Dollars
1	8
2	13
3	18
4	23
5	28
P	$5P + 3$

Closing (5 minutes)

- Some mathematical expressions use both multiplication and addition. With your partner, make up a new example of a problem that uses both multiplication and addition.

Allow a short time for groups to make up a situation. Share these as a group. Ensure that there is both a coefficient and a constant in each problem. Naming these terms is not important for this lesson.

Exit Ticket (5 minutes)

Name _____   Date _____

Lesson 21: Writing and Evaluating Expressions—Multiplication and Addition

Exit Ticket

1. Krystal Klear Cell Phone Company charges $5.00 per month for service. The company also charges $0.10 for each text message sent.

    a. Complete the table below to calculate the monthly charges for various numbers of text messages sent.

Number of Text Messages Sent (T)	Total Monthly Bill in Dollars
0	
10	
20	
30	
T	

    b. If Suzannah's budget limit is $10 per month, how many text messages can she send in one month?

COMMON CORE™ | **Lesson 21:** | Writing and Evaluating Expressions—Multiplication and Addition
                   | **Date:** | 12/15/13

216

Exit Ticket Sample Solutions

1. Krystal Klear Cell Phone Company charges $5.00 per month for service. The company also charges $0.10 for each text message sent.

   a. Complete the table below to calculate the monthly charges for various number of text messages sent.

Number of Text Messages Sent (T)	Total Monthly Bill in Dollars
0	5
10	6
20	7
30	8
T	$0.1T + 5$

   b. If Suzannah's budget limit is $10 per month, how many text messages can she send in one month?

   Suzannah can send 50 *text messages for* $10.

Problem Set Sample Solutions

1. Compact discs cost $12 each at the Music Emporium. The company charges $4.50 for shipping and handling, regardless of how many compact discs are purchased.

   a. Create a table of values that shows the relationship between the number of compact discs that Mickey buys, D, and the amount of money Mickey spends, C, in dollars.

Number of CDs Mickey Buys (D)	Total Cost in Dollars (C)
1	$16.50
2	$28.50
3	$40.50

   b. If you know how many CDs Mickey orders, can you determine how much money he spends? Write the corresponding expression.

   $12D + 4.5$

   c. Use your expression to determine how much Mickey spent buying 8 CDs.

   $8(12) + 4.50 = 100.50$. *Mickey spent* $100.50.

2. Mr. Gee's class orders paperback books from a book club. The books cost $2.95 each. Shipping charges are set at $4.00, regardless of the number of books purchased.

   a. Create a table of values that shows the relationship between the number of books that Mr. Gee's class buys, B, and the amount of money they spend, C, in dollars.

Number of Books Ordered (B)	Amount of Money Spent in Dollars (C)
1	6.95
2	9.90
3	12.85

   b. If you know how many books Mr. Gee's class orders, can you determine how much money they spend? Write the corresponding expression.

   $2.95B + 4$

    c.　Use your expression to determine how much Mr. Gee's class spent buying 24 books.

$$24(2.95) + 4 = 74.8;\ \textit{Mr. Gee's class spent } \$74.80.$$

3.　Sarah is saving money to take a trip to Oregon.　She received $450 in graduation gifts and saves $120 per week working.

    a.　Write an expression that shows how much money Sarah has after working W weeks.

$$450 + 120\,W$$

    b.　Create a table that shows the relationship between the amount of money Sarah has (M) and the number of weeks she works (W).

Amount of Money Sarah Has (M)	Number of Weeks Worked (W)
570	1
690	2
810	3
930	4
1050	5
1170	6
1290	7
1410	8

    c.　The trip will cost $1,200.　How many weeks will Sarah have to work to earn enough for the trip?

    Sarah will have to work 7 *weeks to earn enough for the trip.*

4.　Mr. Gee's English Language Arts class keeps track of how many words per minute are read aloud by each of the students.　They collect this Oral Reading Fluency data each month.　Below is the data they collected for one student in the first four months of school.

    a.　Assume this increase in Oral Reading Fluency continues throughout the rest of the school year.　Complete the table to project the reading rate for this student for the rest of the year.

Month	Number of Words Read Aloud in One Minute
September	126
October	131
November	136
December	141
January	146
February	151
March	156
April	161
May	166
June	171

b.   If this increase in Oral Reading Fluency continues throughout the rest of the school year, when would this student achieve the goal of reading 165 words per minute?

The student will meet the goal in May.

c.   The expression for this student's Oral Reading Fluency is $121 + 5m$, where m represents the number of months during the school year. Use this expression to determine how many words per minute the student would read after 12 months of instructions.

The student would read 181 *words per minute:* $121 + 5 \times 12$.

5.   When corn seeds germinate, they tend to grow 5 inches in the first week, then 3 inches per week for the remainder of the season. The relationship between height (H) and number of weeks since germination (W) is shown below.

a.   Complete the missing values in the table.

Number of Weeks Since Germination (W)	Height of Corn Plant (H)
1	5
2	8
3	11
4	14
5	17
6	20

b.   The expression for this height is $2 + 3W$. How tall will the corn plant be after 15 weeks of growth?

$2 + 3 (15) = 47$. *The plant will be 47 inches tall.*

6.   The Honeymoon Charter Fishing Boat Company only allows newlywed couples on their sunrise trips. There is a captain, a first mate, and a deck hand manning the boat on these trips.

a.   Write an expression that shows the number of people on the boat when there are C couples booked for the trip.

$3 + 2C$

b.   If the boat can hold a maximum of 20 people, how many couples can go on the sunrise fishing trip?

Eight couples (16 passengers) can fit along with the 3 crew members, totaling 19 *people on the boat. A ninth couple would overload the boat.*

Lesson 22: Writing and Evaluating Expressions—Exponents

Student Outcomes

- Students evaluate and write formulas involving exponents for given values in real-world problems.

Lesson Notes

Exponents are used in calculations of both area and volume. Other examples of exponential applications involve bacterial growth (powers of 2) and compound interest.

Students will need a full size sheet of paper ($8\frac{1}{2} \times 11$ inches) for the first example. Teachers should try the folding activity ahead of time to anticipate outcomes. If time permits at the end of the lesson, a larger sheet of paper can be used to experiment further.

Fluency Exercise (10 minutes)

Multiplication of Decimals White Board Exchange

Classwork

Example 1 (10 minutes): Folding paper

Ask students to predict how many times they can fold a piece of paper in half. Allow a short discussion before allowing students to try it.

- Let's try an experiment: How many times do you think you would be able to fold a piece of paper in half? The folds must be as close to a half as possible.

Students will repeatedly fold a piece of paper until it is impossible, about seven folds. Remind students they must fold the paper the same way each time.

- Fold the paper once. Record the number of layers of paper that result.
  - 2

- Fold again. Record the number of layers of paper that result.
  - 4

> **Scaffolding:**
> Some students will benefit from unfolding and counting rectangles on the paper throughout Example 1. This provides a concrete representation of the exponential relationship at the heart of this lesson.

Ensure that students see that doubling the two sheets results in four sheets. At this stage, they can be counted. During subsequent stages, it will be impractical to do so. Focus the count on the corner that has four loose pieces.

- Fold again. Count and record the number of layers you have now.
  - 8

The number of layers is doubling from one stage to the next; so, the pattern is modeled by multiplying by 2, not adding 2. It is critical that students find that there are eight layers here, not six.

- Continue folding and recording the number of layers you make. Use a calculator if desired. Record your answers as both numbers in standard form and using exponents, as powers of 2.

Exercises 1–3

1. Predict how many times you can fold a piece of paper in half.

    My Prediction: _____

2. Before any folding (zero folds), there is only one layer of paper. This is recorded in the first row of the table.

    Fold your paper in half. Record the number of layers of paper that result. Continue as long as possible.

Number of Folds	Number of Paper Layers that Result	Number of Paper Layers Written as a Power of 2
0	1	2^0
1	2	2^1
2	4	2^2
3	8	2^3
4	16	2^4
5	32	2^5
6	64	2^6
7	128	2^7
8	256	2^8

a. Are you able to continue folding the paper indefinitely? Why or why not?

    No. The stack got too thick on one corner. It kept doubling each time.

b. How could you use a calculator to find the next number in the series?

    I could multiply the number by 2 to find the next number.

c. What is the relationship between the number of folds and the number of layers?

    As the number of folds increases by one, the number of layers doubles.

d. How is this relationship represented in the exponential form of the numerical expression?

    I could use 2 as a base and the number of folds as the exponent.

e. If you fold a paper f times, write an expression to show the number of paper layers.

    There would be 2^f layers of paper.

3. If the paper were to be cut instead of folded, the height of the stack would double at each successive stage, and it would be possible to continue.

    a. Write an expression that describes how many layers of paper result from 16 cuts.

        2^{16}

    b. Evaluate this expression by writing it in standard form.

        $2^{16} = 65,536$

Example 2 (10 minutes): Bacterial Infection

- Modeling of exponents in real life leads to our next example of the power of doubling. Think about the last time you had a cut or a wound that became infected. What caused the infection?
    - *Bacteria growing in the wound.*
- When colonies of certain types of bacteria are allowed to grow unchecked, serious illness can result.

Example 2: Bacterial Infection

Bacteria are microscopic one-celled organisms that reproduce in a couple of different ways, one of which is called binary fission. In binary fission, a bacterium increases its size until it is large enough to split into two parts that are identical. These two grow until they are both large enough to split into two individual bacteria. This continues as long as growing conditions are favorable.

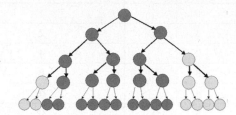

a.   Record the number of bacteria that result from each generation.

Generation	Number of Bacteria	Number of Bacteria Written as a Power of 2
1	2	2^1
2	4	2^2
3	8	2^3
4	16	2^4
5	32	2^5
6	64	2^6
7	128	2^7
8	256	2^8
9	512	2^9
10	1,024	2^{10}
11	2,048	2^{11}
12	4,096	2^{12}
13	8,192	2^{13}
14	16,384	2^{14}

b.   How many generations would it take until there were over one million bacteria present?

20 generations will produce more than one million bacteria. $2^{20} = 1,048,576$

c.   Under the right growing conditions, many bacteria can reproduce every 15 minutes. Under these conditions, how long would it take for one bacterium to reproduce itself into more than one million bacteria?

It would take 20 fifteen-minute periods, or 5 hours.

d.   Write an expression for how many bacteria would be present after g generations.

There will be 2^g bacteria present after g generations.

Example 3 (10 minutes): Volume of a Rectangular Solid

- Exponents are used when we calculate the volume of rectangular solids.

Example 3: Volume of a Rectangular Solid

This box has a width, w. The height of the box, h, is twice the width. The length of the box, l, is three times the width. That is, the width, height, and length of a rectangular prism are in the ratio of $1:2:3$.

For rectangular solids like this, the volume is calculated by multiplying length times width times height.

$$V = l \cdot w \cdot h$$
$$V = 3w \cdot w \cdot 2w$$
$$V = 3 \cdot 2 \cdot w \cdot w \cdot w$$
$$V = 6\,w^3$$

Follow the above example to calculate the volume of these rectangular solids, given the width, w.

Width in centimeters (cm)	Volume in cubic centimeters (cm^3)
1	$1\ cm \times 2\ cm \times 3\ cm = 6\ cm^3$
2	$2\ cm \times 4\ cm \times 6\ cm = 48\ cm^3$
3	$3\ cm \times 6\ cm \times 9\ cm = 162\ cm^3$
4	$4\ cm \times 8\ cm \times 12\ cm = 384\ cm^3$
w	$w \times 2w \times 3w = 6\,w^3\ cm^3$

Closing (2 minutes)

- Why is 5^3 different from 5×3?
    - 5^3 *means* $5 \times 5 \times 5$. *Five is the factor that will be multiplied by itself* 3 *times. That equals* 125.
    - *On the other hand,* 5×3 *means* $5 + 5 + 5$. *Five is the addend that will be added to itself* 3 *times. This equals* 15.

Exit Ticket (3 minutes)

Name _____   Date _____

Lesson 22: Writing and Evaluating Expressions—Exponents

Exit Ticket

1. Naomi's allowance is $2.00 per week. If she convinces her parents to double her allowance each week for two months, what will her weekly allowance be at the end of the second month (week 8)?

Week Number	Allowance
1	$2.00
2	
3	
4	
5	
6	
7	
8	
w	

2. Write the expression that describes Naomi's allowance during week w, in dollars.

Exit Ticket Sample Solutions

1. Naomi's allowance is $2.00 per week. If she convinces her parents to double her allowance each week for two months, what will her weekly allowance be at the end of the second month (week 8)?

Week Number	Allowance
1	$2.00
2	$4.00
3	$8.00
4	$16.00
5	$32.00
6	$64.00
7	$128.00
8	$256.00
w	$\$2^w$

2. Write the expression that describes Naomi's allowance during week w, in dollars.

$\$2^w$

Problem Set Sample Solutions

1. A checkerboard has 64 squares on it.

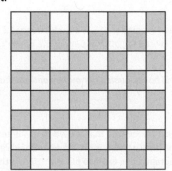

a. If a grain of rice is put on the first square, 2 grains of rice on the second square, 4 grains of rice on the third square, 8 grains of rice on the fourth square, etc. (doubling each time), how many grains of rice would be on the last square? Represent your answer first in exponential form. Use the table below to help solve the problem.

There would be $2^{63} = 9,223,372,036,854,775,808$ *grains of rice.*

Checkerboard Square	Grains of Rice	Checkerboard Square	Grains of Rice	Checkerboard Square	Grains of Rice	Checkerboard Square	Grains of Rice
1		17		33		49	
2		18		34		50	
3		19		35		51	
4		20		36		52	
5		21		37		53	
6		22		38		54	
7		23		39		55	
8		24		40		56	
9		25		41		57	
10		26		42		58	
11		27		43		59	
12		28		44		60	
13		29		45		61	
14		30		46		62	
15		31		47		63	
16		32		48		64	

b.   Would it have been easier to write your answer to part (a) in exponential form or standard form?

Answers will vary. Exponential form is more concise: 2^{63}. Standard form is longer and more complicated to calculate: $9,223,372,036,854,775,808$. (In word form: nine quintillion, two hundred twenty-three quadrillion, three hundred seventy-two trillion, thirty-six billion, eight hundred fifty-four million, seven hundred seventy-five thousand, eight hundred eight.)

2.   If an amount of money is invested at an annual interest rate of 6%, it doubles every 12 years. If Alejandra invests $\$500$, how long will it take for her investment to exceed $\$2,000$ (assuming she doesn't contribute any additional funds)?

It will take 24 years. After 12 years, Alejandra will have doubled her money and will have $\$1000$. If she waits an additional 12 years, she will have $\$2,000$.

3.   The athletics director at Peter's school has created a phone tree that is used to notify team players in the event that all games have to be canceled or rescheduled. The phone tree is initiated when the director calls two captains. During the second stage of the phone tree, the captains each call two players. During the third stage of the phone tree, these players each call two other players. The phone tree continues until all players have been notified. If there are 50 players on the teams, how many stages will it take to notify all of the players?

It will take five stages. After the first stage, two players have been called, and 48 will not have been called. After the second stage, four more players will have been called, for a total of six; 44 will remain uncalled. After the third stage, 2^3 players (eight) more will have been called, totaling 14; 36 remain uncalled. After the 4th stage, 2^4 more players (16) will have gotten a call, for a total of 30 players notified. Twenty remain uncalled at this stage. The 5th round of calls will cover all of them.

White Board Exchange: Multiplication of Decimals

Progression of Exercises:	**Answers:**
1. 0.5×0.5	0.25
2. 0.6×0.6	0.36
3. 0.7×0.7	0.49
4. 0.5×0.6	0.3
5. 1.5×1.5	2.25
6. 2.5×2.5	6.25
7. 0.25×0.25	0.0625
8. 0.1×0.1	0.01
9. 0.1×123.4	12.34
10. 0.01×123.4	1.234

Fluency work such as this exercise should take 5–12 minutes of class.

How to Conduct a White Board Exchange:

All students will need a personal white board, white board marker, and a means of erasing their work. An economical recommendation is to place card stock inside sheet protectors to use as the personal white boards and to cut sheets of felt into small squares to use as erasers.

It is best to prepare the problems in a way that allows you to reveal them to the class one at a time. For example, use a flip chart or PowerPoint presentation; write the problems on the board and cover with paper beforehand, allowing you to reveal one at a time; or, write only one problem on the board at a time. If the number of digits in the problem is very low (e.g., 12 divided by 3), it may also be appropriate to verbally call out the problem to the students.

The teacher reveals or says the first problem in the list and announces, "Go." Students work the problem on their personal white boards, holding their answers up for the teacher to see as soon as they have them ready. The teacher gives immediate feedback to each student, pointing and/or making eye contact with the student and responding with an affirmation for correct work such as, "Good job!", "Yes!", or "Correct!" For incorrect work, respond with guidance such as "Look again!", "Try again!", or "Check your work!"

If many students have struggled to get the answer correct, go through the solution of that problem as a class before moving on to the next problem in the sequence. Fluency in the skill has been established when the class is able to go through each problem in quick succession without pausing to go through the solution of each problem individually. If only one or two students have not been able to get a given problem correct when the rest of the students are finished, it is appropriate to move the class forward to the next problem without further delay; in this case, find a time to provide remediation to that student before the next fluency exercise on this skill is given.

Lesson 22:	Writing and Evaluating Expressions—Exponents
Date:	12/15/13

227

Mathematics Curriculum

Topic G:

Solving Equations

6.EE.5, 6.EE.6, 6.EE.7

Focus Standard:	6.EE.5	Understand solving an equation or inequality as a process of answering a question; which values from a specified set, if any, make the equation or inequality true? Use substitution to determine whether a given number in a specified set makes an equation or inequality true.
	6.EE.6	Use variables to represent numbers and write expressions when solving a real-world or mathematical problem; understand that a variable can represent an unknown number, or, depending on the purpose at hand, any number in a specified set.
	6.EE.7	Solve real-world and mathematical problems by writing and solving equations in the form $x + p = q$ and $px = q$ for cases in which p, q and x are all nonnegative rational numbers.
Instructional Days:	7	
Lessons 23–24:	True and False Number Sentences (P, P)[1]	
Lesson 25:	Finding Solutions to Make Equations True (P)	
Lesson 26:	One-Step Equations—Addition and Subtraction (M)	
Lesson 27:	One-Step Equations—Multiplication and Division (E)	
Lesson 28:	Two-Step Problems—All Operations (M)	
Lesson 29:	Multi-Step Problems—All Operations (P)	

In Topic G, students move from identifying true and false number sentences to making true number sentences false and false number sentences true. In Lesson 23, students explain what equality and inequality symbols represent. They determine if a number sentence is true or false based on the equality or inequality symbol.

---

[1] Lesson Structure Key: **P**-Problem Set Lesson, **M**-Modeling Cycle Lesson, **E**-Exploration Lesson, **S**-Socratic Lesson

Symbol	Meaning	Example
=	Is equal to	$1.8 + 3 = 4.8$
≠	Is not equal to	$6 \div \frac{1}{2} \neq 3$
>	Is greater than	$1 > 0.9$
<	Is less than	$\frac{1}{4} < \frac{1}{2}$

In Lesson 24, students move to identifying a value or a set of values that make number sentences true. They identify values that make a true sentence false. For example, students substitute 4 for the variable in $x + 12 = 14$ to determine if the sentence is true or false. They note that when 4 is substituted for x, the sum of $x + 12$ is 16, which makes the sentence false because $16 \neq 14$. They change course in the lesson to find what they can do to make the sentence true. They ask themselves, "What number must we add to 12 to find the sum of 14?" By substituting 2 for x, the sentence becomes true because $x + 12 = 14$, $2 + 12 = 14$, and $14 = 14$. They bridge this discovery to Lesson 25 where students understand that the solution of an equation is the value or values of the variable that makes the equation true.

Students begin solving equations in Lesson 26. They use bar models or tape diagrams to depict an equation and apply previously learned properties of equality for addition and subtraction to solve the equation. Students check to determine if their solution makes the equation true. Given the equation $1 + a = 6$, students represent the equation with the following model:

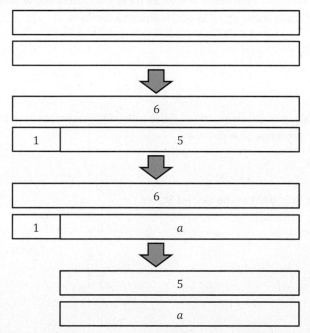

Students recognize that the solution can also be found using properties of operations. They make connections to the model and determine that $1 + a - 1 = 6 - 1$ and, ultimately, that $a = 5$. Students represent two step and multi-step equations involving all operations with bar models or tape diagrams while continuing to apply properties of operations and the order of operations to solve equations in the remaining lessons in this topic.

Lesson 23: True and False Number Sentences

Student Outcomes

- Students explain what the equality and inequality symbols including $=$, $<$, $>$, $\leq$, and $\geq$ stand for. They determine if a number sentence is true or false based on the given symbol.

Lesson Notes

For students to be prepared to solve equations later in this module, it is important that they understand truth values in number sentences and in equations. In the next three lessons, students will learn to differentiate between number sentences and generic equations. Later, in Lesson 26, students will learn why number sentences play a fundamental role in understanding both equations with unknown numbers and solution sets of equations that contain variables. Number sentences are special among types of equations because they have truth values. A number sentence is the most concrete version of an equation. It has the very important property that it is always true or always false, and it is this property that distinguishes it from a generic equation. Examples include $2 + 3 = 5$ (true) and $2 + 2 = 5$ (false). The property guarantees the ability to check whether or not a number is a solution to an equation with a variable. Just substitute the number into the variable; then, check to see if the resulting *number sentence* is either true or false. If the number sentence is true, the number is a solution. For that reason, number sentences are the first and most important type of equation that students need to understand. We begin Lesson 23 by first determining what is true and false and then moving to true and false number sentences using equality and inequality symbols.

Classwork

Opening (4 minutes)

Discuss the meaning of *true* and *false* by calling on students to tell if the following statements are true or false. Conclude with a discussion of what makes a number sentence true or false.

- The sun rises each day.
    - *True.*

- George Washington was the first President of the United States.
    - *True.*

- There are 25 hours in a day.
    - *False.*

- $3 + 3 = 6$.
    - *True.*

- $2 + 2 = 5$.
    - *False.*

- Why is $2 + 2 = 5$ a false number sentence?
    - *Answers will vary but should include the idea that the expressions on both sides of the equal sign should evaluate to the same number; so, for this number sentence to be true, either the first or second addend should be three, resulting in the sum of five.*

Opening Exercise/Discussion (8 minutes)

Discuss what each symbol below stands for and provide students with an example. Students can complete the table in their student materials.

Have one student come up to the front of the room and stand against the wall or board. Mark the student's height with a piece of masking tape. (It is important to pick a student who is about average height.) Measure the height of the tape mark using a tape measure, and record it as a mixed number in feet, along with the student's name, on the piece of masking tape. Next, start the following table on the board/screen:

Opening Exercise

Determine what each symbol stands for and provide an example.

Symbol	What the Symbol Stands For	Example
=	*is equal to*	$4\frac{7}{8} = 4.875$

- What is another example of a number sentence that includes an equal symbol?
  - *Answers will vary. You may ask more than one student.*

The student's height is the height marked by the tape on the wall. Have students stand next to their marked heights. Discuss how their height compares to the height of the tape. Are there other students in the room who have the same height?

>	*is greater than*	$5\frac{1}{4} > 4\frac{7}{8}$

- Use the student's height measurement in the example (our example uses a student $4\frac{7}{8}$ ft. in height).
- What is another example of a number sentence that includes a greater than symbol?
  - *Answers will vary. You may ask more than one student.*

Have students taller than the tape on the wall stand near the tape. Discuss how more than one student has a height that is greater than the tape, so there could be more than one number we could insert into the inequality: _____ $> 4\frac{7}{8}$.

<	*is less than*	$4\frac{1}{2} < 4\frac{7}{8}$

- What is another example of a number sentence that includes a less than symbol?
  - *Answers will vary. You may ask more than one student.*

Have students shorter than the tape on the wall stand near the tape. Discuss how more than one student has a height that is less than the tape, so there could be more than one number we could insert into the inequality: _____ $< 4\frac{7}{8}$.

≤	*is less than or equal to*	$4\frac{7}{8} \leq 4\frac{7}{8}$

Lesson 23:	True and False Number Sentences
Date:	12/16/13

231

- What is another example of a number sentence that includes a less than or equal to symbol?
  - □ *Answers will vary. You may ask more than one student.*

Ask students who are the exact height as the tape and students who are shorter than the tape to stand near the tape. Discuss how this symbol is different than the previous symbol.

$\geq$	*is greater than or equal to*	$5\frac{1}{4} \geq 4\frac{7}{8}$

- What is another example of a number sentence that includes a greater than or equal to symbol?

Answers will vary. You may ask more than one student.

- Which students would stand near the tape to demonstrate this symbol?
  - □ *Students who are the same height as or taller than the tape.*

Example 1 (5 minutes)

Display each of the equations and inequalities one by one with the students.

> **Example 1**
>
> For each inequality or equation your teacher displays, write the equation or inequality, then substitute 3 for every x. Determine if the equation or inequality results in a true number sentence or a false number sentence.

Display $5 + x = 8$.

- Substitute 3 for x and evaluate. Does this result in a true number sentence or a false number sentence?
  - □ *True.*
- Why is the number sentence a true number sentence?
  - □ *Each expression on either side of the equal sign evaluates to* 8. $8 = 8$.

Display $5x = 8$.

- Substitute 3 for x and evaluate. Does this result in a true number sentence or a false number sentence?
  - □ *False.*
- Why is the number sentence a false number sentence?
  - □ *Five times three equals fifteen. Fifteen does not equal eight, so the number sentence* $5(3) = 8$ *is false.*

Display $5 + x > 8$.

- Substitute 3 for x and evaluate. Does this result in a true number sentence or a false number sentence?
  - □ *False.*
- Why is the number sentence a false number sentence?
  - □ *Each expression on either side of the inequality sign evaluates to* 8. *However, the inequality sign states that eight is greater than eight, which is not true. We have already shown that* $8 = 8$.

Display $5x > 8$.

- Substitute 3 for x and evaluate. Does this result in a true number sentence or a false number sentence?
  - *True.*
- Why is the number sentence a true number sentence?
  - *When three is substituted, the left side of the inequality evaluates to fifteen. Fifteen is greater than eight. So, the sentence is true.*

Display $5 + x \geq 8$.

- Substitute 3 for x and evaluate. Does this result in a true number sentence or a false number sentence?
  - *True.*
- Why is the number sentence a true number sentence?
  - *Each expression on either side of the inequality sign evaluates to 8. Because the inequality sign states that the expression on the left side can be greater than or equal to the expression on the right side, it is true because we have already shown that $8 = 8$.*
- Can you find a number other than three that we can substitute for x that will result in a false number sentence?
  - *Answers will vary, but any number less than three will result in a false number sentence.*

Exercises (13 minutes)

Students work on the following exercises independently. Note that students are writing complete sentences to describe what happens when a variable is substituted with a number and if it turns the equation into a true number sentence or a false number sentence.

Exercises

Substitute the value into the variable and state (in a complete sentence) whether the resulting number sentence is true or false. If true, find a value that would result in a false number sentence. If false, find a value that would result in a true number sentence.

1. $4 + x = 12$. Substitute 8 for x.

    When 8 is substituted for x, the number sentence is true.

    Answers will vary on values to make the sentence false; any number other than 8 will make the sentence false.

2. $3g > 15$. Substitute $4\frac{1}{2}$ for g.

    When $4\frac{1}{2}$ is substituted for g, the number sentence is false.

    Answers will vary on values that make the sentence true; any number greater than 5 will make the sentence true.

3. $\frac{f}{4} < 2$. Substitute 8 for f.

    When 8 is substituted for f, the number sentence is false.

    Answers will vary on values to make the sentence true; any number less than 8 will make the sentence true.

---

4. $14.2 \leq h - 10.3$. Substitute 25.8 for h.

   When 25.8 is substituted for h, the number sentence is true.

   Answers will vary on values to make the sentence false; any number less than 24.5 will make the sentence false.

5. $4 = \frac{8}{d}$. Substitute 6 for h.

   When 6 is substituted for h, the number sentence is false.

   2 is the only value that will make the sentence true.

6. $3 > k + \frac{1}{4}$. Substitute $1\frac{1}{2}$ for k.

   When $1\frac{1}{2}$ is substituted for k, the number sentence is true.

   Answers will vary on values to make the sentence false; the number $2\frac{3}{4}$ or any number greater than $2\frac{3}{4}$ will make the sentence false.

MP.6

7. $4.5 - d > 2.5$. Substitute 2.5 for d.

   When 2.5 is substituted for d, the number sentence is false.

   Answers will vary on values to make the sentence true; any number less than 2 will make the number sentence true.

8. $8 \geq 32p$. Substitute $\frac{1}{2}$ for p.

   When $\frac{1}{2}$ is substituted for p, the number sentence is false.

   Answers will vary on values to make the sentence true; the number $\frac{1}{4}$ or any number less than $\frac{1}{4}$ will make the sentence true.

9. $\frac{w}{2} < 32$. Substitute 16 for w.

   When 16 is substituted for p, the number sentence is true.

   Answers will vary on values to make the sentence false; the number 64 or any other number greater than 64 will make the sentence false.

10. $18 \leq 32 - b$. Substitute 14 for b.

    When 14 is substituted for b, the number sentence is true.

    Answers will vary on values to make the sentence false; any number greater than 14 will make the sentence false.

COMMON CORE™

Lesson 23:	True and False Number Sentences
Date:	12/16/13

234

Closing (10 minutes)

Take 3 minutes to discuss the answers from the exercises. From the exercises, continue the discussion from the lesson.

- Let's take a look at Exercise 1: $4 + x = 12$. We substituted 8 for x. What did we determine?
  - *When we substituted 8 for x, the number sentence was true.*
- And then we tried to find values to substitute for x to make the number sentence false. What number did you substitute for x to make this number sentence false?

Elicit responses from the class. Answers will vary, but collect all that make the number sentence false and record on the board. Elicit responses for the next set of questions:

- Did anyone substitute with zero? A thousand? A trillion? How about a fraction? A decimal?
- If all of these responses result in a false number sentence, what can you conclude?
  - *Only one number can be substituted to make the two expressions equal, and that number is 8.*
- Look at all of the numbers that will make this number sentence false, and then look at the one number that will make this number sentence true. Why do you think the number 8 is important compared to all the others that make the number sentence false?

Elicit various responses. The goal is for students to understand that since all numbers other than 8 results in false statements, those numbers do not contribute valuable information about the equation in the same way that the number 8 does.

- What about inequalities? Let's take another look at Exercise 2: $3g > 15$. We substituted $4\frac{1}{2}$ for g and determined, after we evaluated the inequality, that it created a false number sentence because $13\frac{1}{2}$ is not greater than 15. What number did you substitute for g to make this number sentence true?

Elicit responses from the class. Answers will vary, but collect all that make the number sentence true and record on the board. Elicit responses for the next set of questions:

- What about 14, 16, 18, or 20? 100? 200? How about 5.1? 5.01? 5.001? 5.0000000000000001?
- What can you conclude about the substituted numbers that will make this number sentence true?
  - *To make this number sentence true, any number greater than five can be substituted for the variable, whether it is a whole number, fraction, or decimal.*
- Which substituted numbers made this number sentence false?
  - *Answers will vary but must be five or any number less than five.*
- Visualize a number line in your mind. If we can only substitute numbers greater than five on the number line to make this number sentence true, what would that number line look like?

Answers will vary. The goal is for students to visualize that only part of the number line works for the inequality in order to create a true number sentence, while the other part does not work and makes the number sentence false.

Lesson Summary

Number Sentence: A *number sentence* is a statement of equality (or inequality) between two numerical expressions.

Truth Values of a Number Sentence: A number sentence that is an equation is said to be *true* if both numerical expressions evaluate to the same number; it is said to be *false* otherwise. True and false are called *truth values*.

Number sentences that are inequalities also have truth values. For example, $3 < 4$, $6 + 8 > 15 - 12$, and $(15 + 3)^2 < 1000 - 32$ are all true number sentences, while the sentence $9 > 3(4)$ is false.

Exit Ticket (5 minutes)

Name _____   Date _____

Lesson 23: True and False Number Sentences

Exit Ticket

Substitute the value for the variable and state (in a complete sentence) whether the resulting number sentence is true or false. If true, find a value that would result in a false number sentence. If false, find a value that would result in a true number sentence.

1. $15a \geq 75$. Substitute 5 for a.

2. $23 + b = 30$. Substitute 10 for b.

3. $20 > 86 - h$. Substitute 45 for h.

4. $32 \geq 8m$. Substitute 5 for m.

Exit Ticket Sample Solutions

> Substitute the value for the variable and state (in a complete sentence) whether the resulting number sentence is true or false. If true, find a value that would result in a false number sentence. If false, find a value that would result in a true number sentence.
>
> 1. $15a \geq 75$. Substitute 5 for a.
>
>   *True – Answers will vary. Any value less than 5 will result in a false number sentence.*
>
> 2. $23 + b = 30$. Substitute 10 for b.
>
>   *False – The only value that will result in a true number sentence is 7.*
>
> 3. $20 > 86 - h$. Substitute 46 for h.
>
>   *False – Answers will vary. Any value greater than 66 will result in a true number sentence.*
>
> 4. $32 \geq 8m$. Substitute 5 for m.
>
>   *False – Answers will vary. The value of 4 and any value less than 4 will result in a true number sentence.*

Problem Set Sample Solutions

> Substitute the value for the variable and state (in a complete sentence) whether the resulting number sentence is true or false. If true, find a value that would result in a false number sentence. If false, find a value that would result in a true number sentence.
>
> 1. $3\frac{5}{6} = 1\frac{2}{3} + h$. Substitute $2\frac{1}{6}$ for h.
>
>   *True – Any number other than $2\frac{1}{6}$ will result in a false number sentence.*
>
> 2. $39 > 156g$. Substitute $\frac{1}{4}$ for g.
>
>   *False – Answers will vary. Any value less than $\frac{1}{4}$ will result in a true number sentence.*
>
> 3. $\frac{f}{4} \leq 3$. Substitute 12 for f.
>
>   *True – Answers will vary. Any value greater than 12 will result in a false number sentence.*
>
> 4. $121 - 98 \geq r$. Substitute 23 for r.
>
>   *True – Answers will vary. Any value greater than 23 will result in a false number sentence.*
>
> 5. $\frac{54}{q} = 6$. Substitute 10 for q.
>
>   *False – The number 9 is the only value that will result in a true number sentence.*

Lesson 23:   True and False Number Sentences
Date: 12/16/13

238

Create a number sentence using the given variable and symbol. The number sentence you write must be true for the given value of the variable.

6. Variable: d Symbol: $\geq$ The sentence is true when 5 is substituted for d.

7. Variable: y Symbol: $\neq$ The sentence is true when 10 is substituted for y.

8. Variable: k Symbol: $<$ The sentence is true when 8 is substituted for k.

9. Variable: a Symbol: $\leq$ The sentence is true when 9 is substituted for a.

Answers will vary for Problems 6–9.

Lesson 24: True and False Number Sentences

Student Outcomes

- Students identify values for the variable in an equation and inequality that result in true number sentences.
- Students identify values for the variable in an equation and inequality that result in false number sentences.

Lesson Notes

Beginning in the previous lesson and continuing here, the language used in answering questions has been carefully chosen. We have purposefully elicited responses from students in the form of numbers, quantities, or sentences. Soon, students will see that another way to report an answer to an equation or inequality *is another equation or inequality*. For example, the solution to $3x \geq 15$ can be reported as $x \geq 5$.

During this lesson, students will discover that solutions and solution sets can be represented by a sentence description, leading to (or followed by) the use of equations or inequalities. This discussion will provide students with knowledge to systemically solve and check one-step equations later in the module. For example, in this lesson, students transition from,

> "The inequality is true for any value of x that is greater than or equal to five," to
> "The inequality is true when $x \geq 5$."

This transition is preparing students to understand why they rewrite complicated-looking equations and inequalities as simpler ones (such as $x = 5$ or $x \geq 5$) to describe solutions. This is an important goal in the solution process.

The $\neq$ symbol has purposefully been omitted in these lessons because it does not satisfy all of the properties listed in Tables 4 and 5 of the Common Core State Standards. However, it is a symbol that is useful and easy to understand. Its absence from the lessons does not mean that you cannot use it in your class, nor should it be forgotten.

Classwork

Opening Exercise (3 minutes)

Opening Exercise

State whether each number sentence is true or false. If the number sentence is false, explain why.

1. $4 + 5 > 9$

   False. $4 + 5$ is not greater than 9.

2. $3 \cdot 6 = 18$

   True.

3. $32 > \dfrac{64}{4}$

   True.

---

4. $78 - 15 < 68$

    True.

5. $22 \geq 11 + 12$

    False. 22 is not greater than or equal to 23.

Students share their answers and defend their decision for each problem.

Example 1 (10 minutes)

Teacher leads the following discussion after students complete the table below. Have students work on the first two columns alone or in groups of two, writing true or false if the number substituted for g results in a true or false number sentence.

Example 1

Write true or false if the number substituted for g results in a true or false number sentence.

Substitute g with	$4g = 32$	$g = 8$	$3g \geq 30$	$g \geq 10$	$\dfrac{g}{2} > 2$	$g > 4$	$30 \geq 38 - g$	$g \geq 8$
8	True	True	False	False	True	True	True	True
4	False	False	False	False	False	False	False	False
2	False	False	False	False	False	False	False	False
0	False	False	False	False	False	False	False	False
10	False	False	True	True	True	True	True	True

- Let's look at $4g = 32$ and $g = 8$. What do you notice happens when eight is substituted for g in both of the equations?
    - *Eight makes both of the equations result in true number sentences.*
- What do you notice about the substitutions with 4, 2, 0, and 10?
    - *Each of those substituted values makes the equations result in false number sentences.*
- Why do you think that happened?
    - *Because they are both equations, we expect only one number can be substituted for g to result in a true number sentence. In this case, eight is the only number that can be substituted to make both equations true.*
- How are $4g = 32$ and $g = 8$ related?
    - *You can get from $4g = 32$ to $g = 8$ by dividing both sides of $4g = 32$ by 4. You can get from $g = 8$ to $4g = 32$ by multiplying both sides of $g = 8$ by 4.*
- In which equation is it easier to observe the value of g that makes the number sentence true?
    - *The second! It is certainly easier to recognize the value in the second equation.*
- Let's look at the next set of inequalities: $3g \geq 30$ and $g \geq 10$. (Let students fill out the table for these two columns.) What do you notice happens when ten is substituted for g in both of the inequalities?
    - *Ten makes both of the inequalities result in true number sentences.*

Lesson 24:	True and False Number Sentences
Date:	12/16/13

241

- Let's substitute some numbers into each inequality to test. For the second inequality, as long as the number is greater than or equal to ten, the inequality will result in a true number sentence. Let's read the inequality aloud together.

  □ *Chorally: g is greater than or equal to 10.*

- Let's try eleven. Eleven is greater than or equal to ten. Substitute eleven for g in $3g \geq 30$. Does this result in a true number sentence?

  □ *Yes.*

- How are $3g \geq 30$ and $g \geq 10$ related?

  □ *You can get from $3g \geq 30$ to $g \geq 10$ by dividing both sides of $3g \geq 30$ by 3. You can get from $g \geq 10$ to $3g \geq 30$ by multiplying both sides of $g \geq 10$ by 3.*

- In which inequality is it easier to observe the value of g that makes the number sentence true?

  □ *The second, which is similar to the first example.*

Continue testing the substitutions, and continue the discussion for the remaining sets of inequalities (but don't ask how the last two inequalities are related). The goal is to have students discover that for each set of equations and inequalities, the second in the set represents a *much clearer* way to represent the solutions. Point out to them that the second equation or inequality will play an important role in the next few lessons. Please note that it is not necessary that students fully understand a process for solving equations from these examples.

Example 2 (10 minutes)

Guide students in how to use mental math to answer the questions. Students do not know how to solve one-step equations using a formal method; therefore, they will need guidance in solving these problems. Please note that the second problem includes the use of subtraction to get a negative value. While operations with integers is a seventh grade topic, this example should be accessible using a visual model.

State when the following equations/inequalities will be true and when they will be false.

a. $r + 15 = 25$

- Can you think of a number that will make this equation true?

  □ *Yes, substituting 10 for r will make a true number sentence.*

- Is 10 the only number that results in a true number sentence? Why?

  □ *Yes, there is only one value that, if substituted, will result in a true number sentence. There is only one number that can be added to 15 to get 25.*

- What will make the number sentence false?

  □ *Any number that is not 10 will result in a false number sentence.*

- If we look back to the original questions, how can we state when the equation will be true? False?

  □ *The equation is true when the value substituted for r is 10 and false when the value is any other number.*

MP.6

b. $6 - d > 0$

- If we wanted $6 - d$ to equal 0, what would the value of d have to be? Why?

  □ *The value of d would have to be 6 because $6 - 6 = 0$.*

- Will substituting 6 for d result in a true number sentence? Why or why not?

  □ *If d has a value of 6, then the resulting number sentence would not be true because the left side has to be greater than 0, not equal to 0.*

- How about substituting 5 for d? 4? 3? 2?

  □ *Yes, substituting any of these numbers for d into the inequality results in true number sentences.*

- What values can substitute for d in order for the resulting number sentence to be true?

  □ *The inequality is true for any value of d that is less than 6.*

- What values for d would make the resulting number sentence false?

  □ *The inequality is false for any value of d that is greater than or equal to 6.*

- Let's take a look at a number line and see why these statements make sense.

Display a number line on the board. Label the number line as shown below.

- Let's begin at six. If I were to subtract one from six, where would that place be on the number line?

  □ *Five.*

- So, if we substitute 1 for d, then $6 - 1 = 5$, and the resulting number sentence is true. How about if I subtracted two from six? Would our number sentence be true for the value 2?

  □ *Yes.*

- What if I subtracted six from the six on the number line? Where would that be on the number line?

  □ *Zero.*

- So if we substitute 6 for d, will the resulting number sentence be true or false?

  □ *False.*

- Let's try one more. We have already determined that any number greater than or equal to six will result in a false number sentence. Let's try a number greater than six. Let's try the number seven.

- Start with the six on the number line. If we were to subtract seven, in which direction on the number line would we move?

  □ *To the left.*

- And how many times will we move to the left?

  □ *Seven.*

Model beginning at six on the number line and move your finger, or draw the unit skips, as you continually move to the left on the number line seven times.

- So, it seems we've ended up at a place to the left of zero. What number is represented by this position?

  □ *−1*

Label the number line with -1.

- Using our knowledge of ordering rational numbers, is -1 greater than or less than zero?
  - *Less than.*
- So, we have shown: The inequality is true for any value of d that is less than 6 and is false when the value is greater than or equal to 6.

Continue to discuss how to answer each question below with students. As students gain more confidence, have them try to solve the problems individually; discuss the answers when students are finished.

c. $\frac{1}{2}f = 15$

   - *The equation is true when the value substituted for f is 30 and false when the value is any other number.*

d. $\frac{y}{3} < 10$

   - *The inequality is true for any value of y that is less than 30 and false when the value is greater than or equal to 30.*

e. $7g \geq 42$

   - *The inequality is true for any value of g that is greater than or equal to 6, but false when the value is less than 6.*

MP.6

f. $a - 8 \leq 15$

   - *The inequality is true for any value of a that is less than or equal to 23, but false when the value is greater than 23.*

Exercises (10 minutes)

Students complete the following problems in pairs.

Exercises

Complete the following problems in pairs. State when the following equations and inequalities will be true and when they will be false.

1. $15c > 45$

   The inequality is true for any value of c that is greater than 3 and false when the value is less than or equal to 3.

2. $25 = d - 10$

   The equation is true when the value of d is 35 and false when the value is any other number.

3. $56 \geq 2e$

   The inequality is true for any value of e that is less than or equal to 28 and false when the value is greater than 28.

---

4. $\dfrac{h}{5} \geq 12$

   The inequality is true for any value of h that is greater than or equal to 60 and false when the value is less than 60.

5. $45 > h + 29$

   The inequality is true for any value of h that is less than 16 and false when the value is greater than or equal to 16.

6. $4a \leq 16$

   The inequality is true for any value of a that is less than or equal to 4 and false when the value is greater than 4.

7. $3x = 24$

   The equation is true when the value of x is 8 and false when the value is any other number.

Identify all equality and inequality signs that can be placed into the blank to make a true number sentence.

8. $15 + 9$ _____ 24

   = or ≥ or ≤

9. $8 \cdot 7$ _____ 50

   > or ≥

10. $\dfrac{15}{2}$ _____ 10

    < or ≤

11. 34 _____ $17 \cdot 2$

    = or ≥ or ≤

12. 18 _____ $24. 5 - 6$

    < or ≤

Closing (7 minutes)

- For the past two lessons, we have been using sentences to describe when values substituted for variables in equations and inequalities result in true number sentences or false number sentences.

- Let's take a look at an example from each of the past two lessons.

Display the following equation on the board: $5 + x = 8$.

- Substituting 3 for x in the equation results in a true number sentence: $5 + 3 = 8$. Let's evaluate to be sure.

- What is $5 + 3$?
  - ▫ *8.*

- Does $8 = 8$?
  - ▫ *Yes.*

- So, when we substitute 3 for x, the equation results in a true number sentence. Let's try to substitute 3 for x in $x = 3$.

Display $x = 3$ on the board.

- If we substituted 3 for x, what would our number sentence look like?
  - $3 = 3$.
- Is this a true number sentence?
  - *Yes.*
- Previously, we described the values of x that would make the equation $5 + x = 8$ true in a sentence.

Display on the board: *The equation is true when the value of x is 3.*

- This is the same sentence we would write for the equation $x = 3$. Therefore, we can shorten this sentence and, instead, say: *The equation is true when $x = 3$.* Display on the board: *The equation is true when $x = 3$.*
- Let's look at an inequality from today:

Display $4a \leq 16$ on the board.

- What numbers did we determine would make this inequality result in a true number sentence?
  - *We determined that any number less than or equal to 4 would result in a true number sentence.*

Write this statement on the board: *The inequality is true for any value of a that is less than or equal to 4.*

- Is there any way we can abbreviate or shorten this statement using symbols instead of words?

Display $a \leq 4$ on the board.

- Let's read this aloud. a is less than or equal to four. We can use this equation to rewrite the sentence.

Display on the board: *The inequality is true when $a \leq 4$.*

- Either sentence is a correct way to state the values that make $4a \leq 16$ true.

Exit Ticket (5 minutes)

Name _____   Date _____

Lesson 24: True and False Number Sentences

Exit Ticket

State when the following equations and inequalities will be true and when they will be false.

1. $5g > 45$

2. $14 = 5 + k$

3. $26 - w < 12$

4. $32 \leq a + 8$

5. $2 \cdot h \leq 16$

Exit Ticket Sample Solutions

State when the following equations and inequalities will be true and when they will be false.

1. $5g > 45$

    The inequality is true for any value of g that is greater than 9 and false when the value is less than or equal to 9.

    OR

    The inequality is true when $g > 9$ and false when $g \leq 9$.

2. $14 = 5 + k$

    The equation is true when the value of k is 9 and false when the value is any other number.

    OR

    The equation is true when $k = 9$ and false when $k \neq 9$.

3. $26 - w < 12$

    The inequality is true for any value of w that is greater than 14 and false when the value is less than or equal to 14.

    OR

    The inequality is true when $w > 14$ and false when $w \leq 14$.

4. $32 \leq a + 8$

    The inequality is true for any value of a that is greater than or equal to 24 and false when the value is less than 24.

    OR

    The inequality is true when $a \geq 24$ and false when $a < 24$.

5. $2 \cdot h \leq 16$

    The inequality is true for any value of h that is less than or equal to 8 and false when the value is greater than 8.

    OR

    The inequality is true when $h \leq 8$ and false when $h > 8$.

Problem Set Sample Solutions

State when the following equations and inequalities will be true and when they will be false.

1. $36 = 9k$

    The equation is true when the value of k is 4 and false when the value is any number other than 4.

    OR

    The equation is true when $k = 4$ and false when $k \neq 4$.

2. $67 > f - 15$

    The inequality is true for any value of f that is less than 82 and false when the value is greater than or equal to 82.

    OR

    The inequality is true when $f < 82$ and false when $f \geq 82$.

3. $\frac{v}{9} = 3$

The equation is true when the value of v is 27 and false when the value is any number other than 27.

OR

The equation is true when $v = 27$ and false when $v \neq 27$.

4. $10 + b > 42$

The inequality is true for any value of b that is greater than 32 and false when the value is less than or equal to 32.

OR

The inequality is true when $b > 32$ and false when $b \leq 32$.

5. $d - 8 \geq 35$

The inequality is true for any value of d that is greater than or equal to 43 and false when the value is less than 43.

OR

The inequality is true when $d \geq 43$ and false when $d < 43$.

6. $32f < 64$

The inequality is true for any value of f that is less than 2 and false when the value is greater than or equal to 2.

OR

The inequality is true when $f < 2$ and false when $f \geq 2$.

7. $10 - h \leq 7$

The inequality is true for any value of h that is greater than or equal to 3 and false when the value is less than 3.

OR

The inequality is true when $h \geq 3$ and false when $h < 3$.

8. $42 + 8 \geq g$

The inequality is true for any value of g that is less than or equal to 50 and false when the value is greater than 50.

OR

The inequality is true when $g \leq 50$ and false when $g > 50$.

9. $\frac{m}{3} = 14$

The equation is true when the value of m is 42 and false when the value is any number other than 42.

OR

The equation is true when $m = 42$ and false when $m \neq 42$.

Lesson 25: Find Solutions to Make Equations True

Student Outcomes

- Students learn the definition of solution in the context of placing a value into a variable to see if it makes the equation true.

Lesson Notes

In previous lessons, students used sentences and symbols to describe the values that, when substituted for the variable in an equation, resulted in a true number sentence. In this lesson, students will make the transition from their previous learning (e.g., substituting numbers into equations, writing complete sentences to describe when an equation results in a true number sentence, and using symbols to reduce the wordiness of a description) to today's lesson where they identify the value that makes an equation true as a *solution*.

As they did in previous lessons, students test for solutions by substituting numbers into equations and checking whether the resulting number sentence is true. They have already seen how equations like $x = 3$ relate to the original equation, and that it is valuable to find ways to simplify equations until they are in the form of $x =$ "a number." In the next lesson, students begin to learn the formal process of "solving an equation," that is, the process of transforming the original equation to an equation of the form $x =$ "a number," where it is easy to identify the solution.

Materials: Students will complete a matching game that needs to be cut out and prepared before the class period begins. Ideally, there should be 20 sets prepared, each in a separate bag, so that students may work in pairs. Specific directions for the game are below.

Fluency Exercise (5 minutes)

Sprint – Division of Fractions

Classwork

Opening Exercise (5 minutes)

> **Opening Exercise**
>
> Identify a value for the variable that would make each equation or inequality into a true number sentence. Is this the only possible answer? State when the equation or inequality is true using equality and inequality symbols.
>
> 1. $3 + g = 15$
>
>   12. *The equation is true when* $g = 12$.
>
> 2. $30 > 2d$
>
>   *Answers will vary. The inequality is true when* $d < 15$.

3. $\dfrac{15}{f} > 5$

   Answers will vary. The inequality is true when $f < 3$.

4. $42 \le 50 - m$

   Answers will vary. The inequality is true when $m \le 8$.

Example 1 (5 minutes)

Example 1

Each of the following numbers, if substituted for the variable, makes one of the equations below into a true number sentence. Match the number to that equation: 3, 6, 15, 16, 44.

a. $n + 26 = 32$

   6

b. $n - 12 = 32$

   44

c. $17n = 51$

   3

d. $4^2 = n$

   16

e. $\dfrac{n}{3} = 5$

   15

Discussion (2 minutes)

In most of the equations we have looked at so far, the numbers we used to substitute in for the variable have resulted in true number sentences. A number or value for the variable that results in a true number sentence is special and is called a "*solution to the equation*." In the example above, 6 is a solution to $n + 26 = 32$, 44 is a solution to $n - 12 = 32$, and so on.

Exercises (15 minutes)

Students work with a partner to match the equation with its solution. Please note that below are the answers for the activity. The actual game cut-out pieces are at the end of the lesson.

$a + 14 = 36$	22	$3^3 = b$	27
$\dfrac{c}{5} = 3$	15	$d - 10 = 32$	42
$24 = e + 11$	13	$32 = 4 \cdot f$	8
$9 = \dfrac{45}{g}$	5	$43 = h - 17$	60
$1.5 + 0.5 = j$	2	$9 \cdot \dfrac{1}{3} = k$	3
$m = \dfrac{56}{8}$	7	$n = 35.5 - 9.5$	26
$p + 13\dfrac{3}{4} = 32\dfrac{3}{4}$	19	$4 = \dfrac{1}{4}q$	16
$\dfrac{63}{r} = 7$	9	$99 - u = 45$	54

Closing (8 minutes)

- Let's look at the equation $8n = 72$. We know that 9 is a value we can substitute for n that will result in a true number sentence. In previous lessons, we described this solution as "The equation is true when the value of n is 9," and noted that the equation is false when any number other than 9 is substituted for n, or when $n \neq 9$. Therefore, there is only one solution to $8n = 72$ and it is 9.

- We also saw that both statements (i.e., the numbers that make the equation true and the numbers that make it false) can be summarized with one sentence, "The equation is true when $n = 9$," because the values that make $n = 9$ true or false are the same as the values that make $8n = 72$ true or false. Thus, we can represent the solution as "the solution is 9," or $n = 9$.

- The next lesson shows the process for transforming an equation like $8n = 72$ until it is in the form $x = 9$. You have been doing this process for many years in tape diagrams and unknown angle problems, but now we will describe explicitly the steps you were following.

Note: The domain of the variable is just the set of numbers from which we are looking for solutions. For example, sometimes we only want to consider integers as solutions. In those cases, the domain of the variable would be the set of integer numbers.

Lesson Summary

<u>Variable</u>*: A *variable* is a symbol (such as a letter) that represents a number (i.e., it is a placeholder for a number).

A variable is a placeholder for "a" number that does not "vary."

<u>Expression</u>: An *expression* is a numerical expression, or a result of replacing some (or all) of the numbers in a numerical expression with variables.

<u>Equation</u>: An *equation* is a statement of equality between two expressions.

If A and B are two expressions in the variable x, then $A = B$ is an equation in the variable x.

Teacher notes:

*A common description of a variable in the U.S. is "a quantity that varies." Ask yourselves, how can "a quantity" vary? A less vague description of a variable is "a placeholder for a number;" better, because it denotes a single, non-varying number.

The upside of the description of *variable* (and this is a point that must be made explicit to students) is that it is the *user of the variable* who controls what number to insert into the placeholder. Hence, it is the student who has the power to change or vary the number, *as they so desire*. The power to vary rests with the student, not with the variable itself!

Exit Ticket (5 minutes)

Name _____ Date _____

Lesson 25: Finding Solutions to Make Equations True

Exit Ticket

Find the solution to each equation.

1. $7f = 49$

2. $1 = \dfrac{r}{12}$

3. $1.5 = d + 0.8$

4. $9^2 = h$

5. $q = 45 - 19$

6. $40 = \dfrac{1}{2}p$

Exit Ticket Sample Solutions

Find the solution to each equation.

1. $7f = 49$

    $f = 7$

2. $1 = \dfrac{r}{12}$

    $r = 12$

3. $1.5 = d + 0.8$

    $d = 0.7$

4. $9^2 = h$

    $h = 81$

5. $q = 45 - 19$

    $q = 26$

6. $40 = \dfrac{1}{2}p$

    $p = 80$

Problem Set Sample Solutions

Find the solution to each equation.

1. $4^3 = y$

    64

2. $8a = 24$

    3

3. $32 = g - 4$

    36

4. $56 = j + 29$

    27

5. $\dfrac{48}{r} = 12$

    4

Lesson 25:	Finding Solutions to Make Equations True
Date:	12/16/13

6. $k = 15 - 9$

      6

7. $x \cdot \frac{1}{5} = 60$

      300

8. $m + 3.45 = 12.8$

      9.35

9. $a = 1^5$

      1

$a + 14 = 36$	22	$3^3 = b$
27	$\dfrac{c}{5} = 3$	15
$d - 10 = 32$	42	$24 = e + 11$
13	$32 = 4 \cdot f$	8
$9 = \dfrac{45}{g}$	5	$43 = h - 17$

60	$1.5 + 0.5 = j$	2
$9 \cdot \dfrac{1}{3} = k$	3	$m = \dfrac{56}{8}$
7	$n = 35.5 - 9.5$	26
$p + 13\dfrac{3}{4} = 32\dfrac{3}{4}$	19	$4 = \dfrac{1}{4}q$
16	$\dfrac{63}{r} = 7$	9

| $99 - u = 45$ | 54 |

Division of Fractions – Round 1

Number Correct: _____

Directions: Determine the quotients of the fractions.

1.	$\dfrac{1}{2} \div \dfrac{3}{5}$	
2.	$\dfrac{5}{6} \div \dfrac{1}{5}$	
3.	$\dfrac{3}{7} \div \dfrac{6}{11}$	
4.	$\dfrac{2}{5} \div \dfrac{8}{9}$	
5.	$\dfrac{1}{6} \div \dfrac{9}{10}$	
6.	$\dfrac{11}{12} \div \dfrac{8}{9}$	
7.	$\dfrac{5}{6} \div \dfrac{10}{13}$	
8.	$\dfrac{7}{8} \div \dfrac{13}{15}$	
9.	$\dfrac{3}{5} \div \dfrac{7}{9}$	
10.	$\dfrac{14}{17} \div \dfrac{13}{20}$	
11.	$3\dfrac{1}{2} \div 4\dfrac{4}{5}$	
12.	$6\dfrac{1}{5} \div 6\dfrac{3}{4}$	
13.	$2\dfrac{1}{4} \div 3\dfrac{1}{8}$	
14.	$1\dfrac{3}{5} \div \dfrac{7}{8}$	
15.	$\dfrac{1}{5} \div 4\dfrac{1}{2}$	

16.	$6\dfrac{7}{8} \div 11\dfrac{2}{3}$	
17.	$5\dfrac{5}{6} \div 3\dfrac{1}{2}$	
18.	$10\dfrac{5}{8} \div 12\dfrac{3}{7}$	
19.	$9\dfrac{1}{3} \div 8\dfrac{2}{5}$	
20.	$\dfrac{3}{4} \div 6\dfrac{7}{10}$	
21.	$2\dfrac{1}{3} \div 3\dfrac{5}{6}$	
22.	$2\dfrac{4}{5} \div 7\dfrac{9}{10}$	
23.	$5\dfrac{8}{9} \div 3\dfrac{3}{5}$	
24.	$12\dfrac{5}{9} \div 5$	
25.	$1\dfrac{5}{6} \div 2\dfrac{6}{7}$	
26.	$10 \div 5\dfrac{8}{9}$	
27.	$14\dfrac{3}{5} \div 10$	
28.	$7\dfrac{9}{11} \div 1\dfrac{9}{10}$	
29.	$15\dfrac{2}{3} \div 24$	
30.	$32 \div 12\dfrac{6}{7}$	

Division of Fractions – Round 1 [KEY]

Directions: Determine the quotients of the fractions.

1.	$\dfrac{1}{2} \div \dfrac{3}{5}$	$\dfrac{5}{6}$	16.	$6\dfrac{7}{8} \div 11\dfrac{2}{3}$	$\dfrac{165}{280} = \dfrac{33}{56}$	
2.	$\dfrac{5}{6} \div \dfrac{1}{5}$	$\dfrac{25}{6} = 4\dfrac{1}{4}$	17.	$5\dfrac{5}{6} \div 3\dfrac{1}{2}$	$\dfrac{70}{42} = 1\dfrac{2}{3}$	
3.	$\dfrac{3}{7} \div \dfrac{6}{11}$	$\dfrac{33}{42} = \dfrac{11}{14}$	18.	$10\dfrac{5}{8} \div 12\dfrac{3}{7}$	$\dfrac{595}{696}$	
4.	$\dfrac{2}{5} \div \dfrac{8}{9}$	$\dfrac{18}{40} = \dfrac{9}{20}$	19.	$9\dfrac{1}{3} \div 8\dfrac{2}{5}$	$\dfrac{140}{126} = 1\dfrac{1}{9}$	
5.	$\dfrac{1}{6} \div \dfrac{9}{10}$	$\dfrac{10}{54} = \dfrac{5}{27}$	20.	$\dfrac{3}{4} \div 6\dfrac{7}{10}$	$\dfrac{30}{268} = \dfrac{15}{134}$	
6.	$\dfrac{11}{12} \div \dfrac{8}{9}$	$\dfrac{99}{96} = 1\dfrac{1}{32}$	21.	$2\dfrac{1}{3} \div 3\dfrac{5}{6}$	$\dfrac{42}{69} = \dfrac{14}{23}$	
7.	$\dfrac{5}{6} \div \dfrac{10}{13}$	$\dfrac{65}{60} = 1\dfrac{1}{12}$	22.	$2\dfrac{4}{5} \div 7\dfrac{9}{10}$	$\dfrac{140}{395} = \dfrac{28}{79}$	
8.	$\dfrac{7}{8} \div \dfrac{13}{15}$	$\dfrac{105}{104} = 1\dfrac{1}{104}$	23.	$5\dfrac{8}{9} \div 3\dfrac{3}{5}$	$\dfrac{265}{162} = 1\dfrac{103}{162}$	
9.	$\dfrac{3}{5} \div \dfrac{7}{9}$	$\dfrac{27}{35}$	24.	$12\dfrac{5}{9} \div 5$	$\dfrac{113}{45} = 2\dfrac{23}{45}$	
10.	$\dfrac{14}{17} \div \dfrac{13}{20}$	$\dfrac{280}{221} = 1\dfrac{59}{221}$	25.	$1\dfrac{5}{6} \div 2\dfrac{6}{7}$	$\dfrac{77}{120}$	
11.	$3\dfrac{1}{2} \div 4\dfrac{4}{5}$	$\dfrac{35}{48}$	26.	$10 \div 5\dfrac{8}{9}$	$\dfrac{90}{53} = 1\dfrac{37}{53}$	
12.	$6\dfrac{1}{5} \div 6\dfrac{3}{4}$	$\dfrac{124}{135}$	27.	$14\dfrac{3}{5} \div 10$	$\dfrac{73}{50} = 1\dfrac{23}{50}$	
13.	$2\dfrac{1}{4} \div 3\dfrac{1}{8}$	$\dfrac{72}{100} = \dfrac{18}{25}$	28.	$7\dfrac{9}{11} \div 1\dfrac{9}{10}$	$\dfrac{860}{209} = 4\dfrac{24}{209}$	
14.	$1\dfrac{3}{5} \div \dfrac{7}{8}$	$\dfrac{64}{35} = 1\dfrac{29}{35}$	29.	$15\dfrac{2}{3} \div 24$	$\dfrac{47}{72}$	
15.	$\dfrac{1}{5} \div 4\dfrac{1}{2}$	$\dfrac{2}{45}$	30.	$32 \div 12\dfrac{6}{7}$	$\dfrac{224}{90} = 2\dfrac{22}{45}$	

Division of Fractions – Round 2

Number Correct: _____

Improvement: _____

Directions: Determine the quotients of the fractions.

1.	$\frac{1}{2} \div \frac{3}{4}$	
2.	$\frac{3}{5} \div \frac{1}{7}$	
3.	$\frac{5}{6} \div \frac{1}{8}$	
4.	$\frac{3}{8} \div \frac{5}{9}$	
5.	$\frac{1}{4} \div \frac{2}{5}$	
6.	$\frac{7}{8} \div \frac{9}{10}$	
7.	$\frac{8}{11} \div \frac{4}{5}$	
8.	$\frac{5}{6} \div \frac{7}{12}$	
9.	$\frac{3}{4} \div \frac{8}{9}$	
10.	$\frac{7}{11} \div \frac{4}{7}$	
11.	$1\frac{3}{4} \div \frac{1}{2}$	
12.	$\frac{1}{10} \div 2\frac{3}{4}$	
13.	$5\frac{2}{3} \div \frac{7}{9}$	
14.	$\frac{5}{6} \div 6\frac{1}{2}$	
15.	$\frac{6}{7} \div 2\frac{1}{3}$	

16.	$\frac{7}{8} \div 2\frac{1}{4}$	
17.	$\frac{3}{4} \div 2\frac{3}{5}$	
18.	$4\frac{1}{5} \div 2\frac{1}{3}$	
19.	$4\frac{3}{8} \div \frac{2}{7}$	
20.	$\frac{4}{5} \div 2\frac{1}{8}$	
21.	$1\frac{1}{2} \div 3\frac{5}{6}$	
22.	$3\frac{2}{3} \div 2\frac{1}{4}$	
23.	$4\frac{3}{5} \div 1\frac{3}{4}$	
24.	$7\frac{1}{2} \div 6\frac{1}{3}$	
25.	$3\frac{4}{5} \div 2\frac{9}{10}$	
26.	$3\frac{5}{6} \div 2\frac{1}{2}$	
27.	$3\frac{3}{4} \div 4\frac{1}{8}$	
28.	$5 \div 4\frac{5}{6}$	
29.	$3\frac{1}{4} \div 2$	
30.	$8 \div 5\frac{1}{3}$	

Division of Fractions – Round 2 [KEY]

Directions: Determine the quotients of the fractions.

1.	$\dfrac{1}{2} \div \dfrac{3}{4}$	$\dfrac{4}{6} = \dfrac{2}{3}$	16.	$\dfrac{7}{8} \div 2\dfrac{1}{4}$	$\dfrac{28}{72} = \dfrac{7}{18}$
2.	$\dfrac{3}{5} \div \dfrac{1}{7}$	$\dfrac{21}{5} = 4\dfrac{1}{5}$	17.	$\dfrac{3}{4} \div 2\dfrac{3}{5}$	$\dfrac{15}{52}$
3.	$\dfrac{5}{6} \div \dfrac{1}{8}$	$\dfrac{40}{6} = 6\dfrac{2}{3}$	18.	$4\dfrac{1}{5} \div 2\dfrac{1}{3}$	$\dfrac{63}{35} = 1\dfrac{4}{5}$
4.	$\dfrac{3}{8} \div \dfrac{5}{9}$	$\dfrac{27}{40}$	19.	$4\dfrac{3}{8} \div \dfrac{2}{7}$	$\dfrac{245}{16} = 15\dfrac{5}{16}$
5.	$\dfrac{1}{4} \div \dfrac{2}{5}$	$\dfrac{5}{8}$	20.	$\dfrac{4}{5} \div 2\dfrac{1}{8}$	$\dfrac{32}{85}$
6.	$\dfrac{7}{8} \div \dfrac{9}{10}$	$\dfrac{70}{72} = \dfrac{35}{36}$	21.	$1\dfrac{1}{2} \div 3\dfrac{5}{6}$	$\dfrac{18}{46} = \dfrac{9}{23}$
7.	$\dfrac{8}{11} \div \dfrac{4}{5}$	$\dfrac{40}{44} = \dfrac{10}{11}$	22.	$3\dfrac{2}{3} \div 2\dfrac{1}{4}$	$\dfrac{44}{27} = 1\dfrac{17}{27}$
8.	$\dfrac{5}{6} \div \dfrac{7}{12}$	$\dfrac{60}{42} = 1\dfrac{3}{7}$	23.	$4\dfrac{3}{5} \div 1\dfrac{3}{4}$	$\dfrac{92}{35} = 2\dfrac{22}{35}$
9.	$\dfrac{3}{4} \div \dfrac{8}{9}$	$\dfrac{27}{32}$	24.	$7\dfrac{1}{2} \div 6\dfrac{1}{3}$	$\dfrac{45}{38} = 1\dfrac{7}{38}$
10.	$\dfrac{7}{11} \div \dfrac{4}{7}$	$\dfrac{49}{44} = 1\dfrac{5}{44}$	25.	$3\dfrac{4}{5} \div 2\dfrac{9}{10}$	$\dfrac{190}{145} = 1\dfrac{9}{29}$
11.	$1\dfrac{3}{4} \div \dfrac{1}{2}$	$\dfrac{14}{4} = 3\dfrac{1}{2}$	26.	$3\dfrac{5}{6} \div 2\dfrac{1}{2}$	$\dfrac{46}{30} = 1\dfrac{8}{15}$
12.	$\dfrac{1}{10} \div 2\dfrac{3}{4}$	$\dfrac{40}{110} = \dfrac{2}{55}$	27.	$3\dfrac{3}{4} \div 4\dfrac{1}{8}$	$\dfrac{120}{132} = \dfrac{10}{11}$
13.	$5\dfrac{2}{3} \div \dfrac{7}{9}$	$\dfrac{153}{21} = 7\dfrac{2}{7}$	28.	$5 \div 4\dfrac{5}{6}$	$\dfrac{30}{29} = 1\dfrac{1}{29}$
14.	$\dfrac{5}{6} \div 6\dfrac{1}{2}$	$\dfrac{10}{78} = \dfrac{5}{39}$	29.	$3\dfrac{1}{4} \div 2$	$\dfrac{13}{8} = 1\dfrac{5}{8}$
15.	$\dfrac{6}{7} \div 2\dfrac{1}{3}$	$\dfrac{18}{49}$	30.	$8 \div 5\dfrac{1}{3}$	$\dfrac{24}{16} = 1\dfrac{1}{2}$

Lesson 26: One-Step Equations—Addition and Subtraction

Student Outcomes

- Students solve one-step equations by relating an equation to a diagram.
- Students check to determine if their solution makes the equation true.

Lesson Notes

This lesson serves as a means for students to solve one-step equations through the use of tape diagrams. Through the construction of tape diagrams, students create algebraic equations and solve for one variable. In this lesson, students continue their study of the properties of operations and identity and develop intuition of the properties of equality. This lesson continues the informal study of the properties of equality students have practiced since first grade and also serves as a springboard to the formal study, use, and application of the properties of equality seen in seventh grade. While students will intuitively use the properties of equality, understand that diagrams are driving the meaning behind the content of this lesson. This lesson purposefully omits focus on the actual properties of equality, which is reserved for Grade 7. Students will relate an equation directly to diagrams and verbalize what they do with diagrams to construct and solve algebraic equations.

Classwork

Opening (3 minutes)

In order for students to learn how to solve multi-step equations (in future grades), they must first learn how to solve basic equations. Although a majority of students have the ability to find the solution to the equations using mental math, it is crucial they understand the importance of knowing and understanding the process so they can apply it to more complex equations in the future.

Mathematical Modeling Exercise (8 minutes)

Model the example to show students how to use tape diagrams to calculate solutions to one-step equations.

Calculate the solution: $a + 2 = 8$

- Draw two tape diagrams that are the same length.

MP.3 & MP.4

- Label the first tape diagram 8.

8

- Represent 2 on the second tape diagram. What must the remaining section of the tape diagram represent? How do you know?

	2

  - *The remaining part of the tape diagram represents 6 because the entire tape diagram is 8 and we know one section is 2. Therefore, we can compute the difference, 8 − 2, to determine the remaining part.*

- Label your tape diagram.

6	2

- Draw another set of tape diagrams to represent the given equation: $a + 2 = 8$

8

a	2

- Because both of the following tape diagrams represent the same value, what would the value of a be? Explain.

a	2

6	2

  - *Since both of the tape diagrams represent the same value, both parts that have a and 6 must represent the same value. Therefore, a must be 6.*

- Using this knowledge, try to show or explain how to solve equations without tape diagrams. What actually happened when constructing the tape diagrams?

Guide and promote this discussion with students:

  - *The first set of tape diagrams shows that the quantity of 6 + 2 is equal to 8. To write this algebraically, we can use the equal sign. $6 + 2 = 8$.*

  - *The second set of tape diagrams shows two things: first, that a + 2 is equal to 8, and also that $a + 2 = 8$ is equal to $6 + 2 = 8$.*

  - *We found that the only number that a can represent in the equation is 6. Therefore, when $a + 2 = 8$, the only solution for a is 6.*

- In previous lessons we discussed identity properties. How can we explain why $a + 2 - 2 = a$ using the identity properties?

  - *We know that when we add a number, then subtract the same number, the result is the original number. Previously, we demonstrated this identity with $a + b - b = a$.*

- How can we check our answer?

  - *Substitute 6 in for a to determine if the number sentence is true. $6 + 2 = 8$ is a true number sentence, because $6 + 2 - 2 = 8 - 2$, resulting in $6 = 6$. So, our answer is correct.*

Exercise 1 (8 minutes)

Students work with partners to complete the following problems. They will show how to solve each equation using tape diagrams and algebraically. Then, students will use substitution to check their answers after each problem.

Exercise 1

Solve each equation. Use both tape diagrams and algebraic methods for each problem. Use substitution to check your answers.

a. $b + 9 = 15$

Algebraically:

$$b + 9 = 15$$
$$b + 9 - 9 = 15 - 9$$
$$b = 6$$

Check: $6 + 9 - 9 = 15 - 9; 6 = 6.$ *This is a true number sentence, so 6 is the correct solution.*

b. $12 = 8 + c$

12

8	4

12

8	c

8	4

8	c

4

c

Algebraically:

$$12 = 8 + c$$
$$12 - 8 = 8 + c - 8$$
$$4 = c$$

Check: $12 - 8 = 8 + 4 - 8$; $4 = 4$. *This is a true number sentence, so 4 is the correct solution.*

Exercise 2 (8 minutes)

Students use the knowledge gained in the first part of the lesson to determine how to solve an equation with subtraction.

MP.4

> **Exercise 2**
>
> Given the equation $d - 5 = 7$:
>
> a. Demonstrate how to solve the equation using tape diagrams.
>
>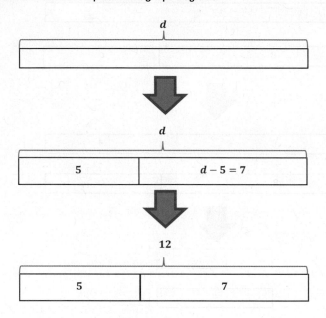
>
> b. Demonstrate how to solve the equation algebraically.
>
> $$d - 5 = 7$$
> $$d - 5 + 5 = 7 + 5$$
> $$d = 12$$
>
> c. Check your answer.
>
> $12 - 5 + 5 = 7 + 5$; $12 = 12$. *This is a true number sentence, so our solution is correct.*

Provide students time to work and then show some examples that show how to solve the equation using both methods. At this time, remind students of the identity with subtraction to explain why $d - 5 + 5 = d$.

Exercise 3 (8 minutes)

Students solve each problem using the method of their choice, but they must show their work. Have students check their answers.

Example 3

Solve each problem and show your work. You may choose which method (tape diagrams or algebraically) you prefer. Check your answers after solving each problem.

a. $e + 12 = 20$

Tape Diagram:

20

8	12

20

e	12

8	12

e	12

8

e

Algebraically:

$$e + 12 = 20$$
$$e + 12 - 12 = 20 - 12$$
$$e = 8$$

Check: $8 + 12 - 12 = 20 - 12$; $8 = 8$. *This is a true number sentence so our answer is correct.*

b. $f - 10 = 15$

$$f$$

$$f$$

10	$f - 10 = 15$

$$25$$

10	15

Algebraically:

$$f - 10 = 15$$
$$f - 10 + 10 = 15 + 10$$
$$f = 25$$

Check: $25 - 10 + 10 = 15 + 10$; $25 = 25$. *This is a true number sentence, so our solution is correct.*

c. $g - 8 = 9$

$$g$$

$$g$$

8	9

$$17$$

8	9

Algebraically:

$$g - 8 = 9$$
$$g - 8 + 8 = 9 + 8$$
$$g = 17$$

Check: $17 - 8 + 8 = 9 + 8$; $17 = 17$. *This number sentence is true, so our solution is correct.*

Closing (5 minutes)

- John checked his answer and found that it was incorrect. John's work is below. What did he do incorrectly?

$$h + 10 = 25$$
$$h + 10 + 10 = 25 + 10$$
$$h = 35$$

- Use a tape diagram to show why John's method does not lead to the correct answer.

- Why do you do the inverse operation to calculate the solution of the equation? Include a tape diagram as part of your explanation.

Exit Ticket (5 minutes)

Name _____ Date _____

Lesson 26: One-Step Equations—Addition and Subtraction

Exit Ticket

1. If you know the answer, state it. Then use a tape diagram to demonstrate why this is the correct answer. If you do not know the answer, find the solution using a tape diagram.

$$j + 12 = 25$$

2. Find the solution to the equation algebraically. Check your answer.

$$k - 16 = 4$$

Exit Ticket Sample Solutions

1. If you know the answer, state it. Then use a tape diagram to demonstrate why this is the correct answers. If you do not know the answer, find the solution using a tape diagram.

$$j + 12 = 25$$

25

13	12

25

j	12

13	12

j	12

13

j

j is equal to 13; *j* = 13

Check: $13 + 12 = 25$; $25 = 25$. *This is a true number sentence, so the solution is correct.*

2. Find the solution to the equation algebraically. Check your answer.

$$k - 16 = 4$$
$$k - 16 + 16 = 4 + 16$$
$$k = 20$$

Check: $20 - 16 = 4$; $4 = 4$. *This is a true number sentence, so the solution is correct.*

Problem Set Sample Solutions

1. Find the solution to the equation below using tape diagrams. Check your answer.

$$m - 7 = 17$$

m is equal to 24; m = 24

Check: $24 - 7 = 17$; $17 = 17$. *This number sentence is true, so the solution is correct.*

2. Find the solution of the equation below algebraically. Check your answer.

$$n + 14 = 25$$
$$n + 14 - 14 = 25 - 14$$
$$n = 11$$

Check: $11 + 14 = 25$; $25 = 25$. *This number sentence is true, so the solution is correct.*

3. Find the solution of the equation below using tape diagrams. Check your answer.

$p + 8 = 18$ $p = 10$

Check: $10 + 8 = 18$; $18 = 18$. *This number sentence is true, so the solution is correct.*

---

4. Find the solution to the equation algebraically. Check your answer.

$$g - 62 = 14$$
$$g - 62 + 62 = 14 + 62$$
$$g = 76$$

Check: $76 - 62 = 14$;　$14 = 14$.　*This number sentence is true, so the solution is correct.*

5. Find the solution to the equation using the method of your choice. Check your answer.

$$m + 108 = 243$$

Tape Diagrams:

243

135	108

243

m	108

135	108

m	108

135

m

Algebraically:

$$m + 108 = 243$$
$$m + 108 - 108 = 243 - 108$$
$$m = 135$$

Check: $135 + 108 = 243$;　$243 = 243$.　*This number sentence is true, so the solution is correct.*

6. Identify the mistake in the problem below. Then, correct the mistake.

$$p - 21 = 34$$
$$p - 21 - 21 = 34 - 21$$
$$p = 13$$

The mistake is subtracting rather than adding 21. This is incorrect because $p - 21 - 21$ would not equal p.

$$p - 21 = 34$$
$$p - 21 + 21 = 34 + 21$$
$$p = 55$$

7. Identify the mistake in the problem below. Then, correct the mistake.

$$q + 18 = 22$$
$$q + 18 - 18 = 22 + 18$$
$$q = 40$$

The mistake is adding 18 on the right side of the equation instead of subtracting it from both sides.

$$q + 18 = 22$$
$$q + 18 - 18 = 22 - 18$$
$$q = 4$$

8. Match the equation with the correct solution on the right.

$r + 10 = 22$ $r = 10$
$r - 15 = 5$ $r = 20$
$r - 18 = 14$ $r = 12$
$r + 5 = 15$ $r = 32$

Lesson 27: One-Step Equations—Multiplication and Division

Student Outcomes

- Students solve one-step equations by relating an equation to a diagram.
- Students check to determine if their solution makes the equation true.

Lesson Notes

This lesson teaches students to solve one-step equations using tape diagrams. Through the construction of tape diagrams, students will create algebraic equations and solve for one variable. This lesson not only allows students to continue studying the properties of operations and identity, but also allows students to develop intuition of the properties of equality. This lesson continues the informal study of the properties of equality students have practiced since first grade, and also serves as a springboard to the formal study, use, and application of the properties of equality seen in Grade 7. Understand that, while students will intuitively use the properties of equality, diagrams are the focus of this lesson. This lesson purposefully omits focusing on the actual properties of equality, which will be covered in Grade 7. Students will relate an equation directly to diagrams and verbalize what they do with diagrams to construct and solve algebraic equations.

Poster paper is needed for this lesson. Posters need to be prepared ahead of time, one set of questions per poster.

Classwork

Example 1 (5 minutes)

Example 1

Solve $3z = 9$ using tape diagrams and algebraically. Then, check your answer.

First, draw two tape diagrams, one to represent each side of the equation.

9

z	z	z

If 9 had to be split into three groups, how big would each group be?

3

Demonstrate the value of z using tape diagrams.

3	3	3

z

> How can we demonstrate this algebraically?
>
> *We know we have to split 9 into three equal groups, so we have to divide by 3 to show this algebraically.*
>
> $3z \div 3 = 9 \div 3$
>
> How does this get us the value of z?
>
> *The left side of the equation will equal z, because we know the identity property, where $a \cdot b \div b = a$, so we can use this identity here.*
>
> *The right side of the equation will be 3 because $9 \div 3 = 3$.*
>
> *Therefore, the value of z is 3.*
>
> How can we check our answer?
>
> *We can substitute the value of z into the original equation to see if the number sentence is true.*
>
> $3(3) = 9; 9 = 9.$ *This number sentence is true, so our answer is correct.*

Example 2 (5 minutes)

> **Example 2**
>
> Solve $\frac{y}{4} = 2$ using tape diagrams and algebraically. Then, check your answer.
>
> First, draw two tape diagrams, one to represent each side of the equation.
>
> | $y \div 4$ |
> |---|
>
> | 2 |
> |---|
>
> If the first tape diagram shows the size of $y \div 4$, how can we draw a tape diagram to represent y?
>
> *The tape diagram to represent y should be four sections of the size $y \div 4$.*
>
> Draw this tape diagram.
>
> | y | | | |
> |---|---|---|---|
> | $y \div 4$ | $y \div 4$ | $y \div 4$ | $y \div 4$ |
>
> What value does each $y \div 4$ section represent? How do you know?
>
> *Each $y \div 4$ section represents a value of 2, we knows this from our original tape diagram.*
>
> How can you use a tape diagram to show the value of y?
>
> *Draw four equal sections of 2, which will give y the value of 8.*
>
> | 2 | 2 | 2 | 2 |
> |---|---|---|---|

How can we demonstrate this algebraically?

$\frac{y}{4} \cdot 4 = 2 \cdot 4$. *Because we multiplied the number of sections in the original equation by 4, we know the identity*

$\frac{a}{b} \cdot b = a$ *and can use this identity here.*

How does this help us find the value of y?

The left side of the equation will equal y, and the right side will equal 8. Therefore, the value of y is 8.

How can we check our answer?

Substitute 8 into the equation for y, then check to see if the number sentence is true.

$\frac{8}{4} = 2$. *This is a true number sentence, so 8 is the correct answer.*

Exploratory Challenge (15 minutes)

Each group (two or three) of students receives one set of problems. Have students solve both problems on poster paper with tape diagrams and algebraically. Students should also check their answers on the poster paper. More than one group may have each set of problems.

> *Scaffolding:*
>
> If students are struggling, model one set of problems before continuing with the Exploratory Challenge.

Set 1

On poster paper, solve each problem below algebraically and using tape diagrams. Check each answer to show that you solved the equation correctly.

1. $2a = 16$

   Tape Diagrams:

   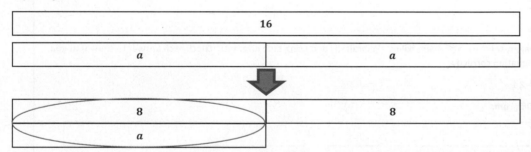

   Algebraically:
   $$2a = 16$$
   $$2a \div 2 = 16 \div 2$$
   $$a = 8$$

   Check:
   $2 \cdot 8 = 16; \ 16 = 16$. *This is a true number sentence, so 8 is the correct solution.*

---

2. $\frac{b}{3} = 4$

   Tape Diagrams:

$b \div 3$

4

b

$b \div 3$	$b \div 3$	$b \div 3$

4	4	4

b

12

   Algebraically:

   $$\frac{b}{3} = 4$$
   $$\frac{b}{3} \cdot 3 = 4 \cdot 3$$
   $$b = 12$$

   Check: $\frac{12}{3} = 4$; $4 = 4$. *This number sentence is true, so 12 is the correct solution.*

MP.1

Set 2

On poster paper, solve each problem below algebraically and using tape diagrams. Check each answer to show that you solved the equation correctly.

1. $4 \cdot c = 24$

   Tape Diagram:

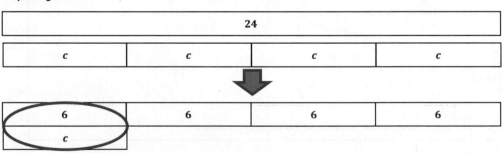

24

c	c	c	c

6	6	6	6
c			

   Algebraically:

   $$4 \cdot c = 24$$
   $$4 \cdot c \div 4 = 24 \div 4$$
   $$c = 6$$

   Check: $4 \cdot 6 = 24$; $24 = 24$. *This number sentence is true, so 6 is the correct solution.*

COMMON CORE™   Lesson 27:   One-Step Equations—Multiplication and Division
Date: 12/16/13

280

2. $\dfrac{d}{7} = 1$

Tape Diagrams:

$d \div 7$
1

d

$d \div 7$	$d \div 7$	$d \div 7$	$d \div 7$	$d \div 7$	$d \div 7$	$d \div 7$
1	1	1	1	1	1	1

d

7

Algebraically:

$$\dfrac{d}{7} = 1$$
$$\dfrac{d}{7} \cdot 7 = 1 \cdot 7$$
$$d = 7$$

Check: $\dfrac{7}{7} = 1$; $1 = 1$. *This number sentence is true, so 7 is the correct solution.*

Set 3

On poster paper, solve each problem below algebraically and using tape diagrams. Check each answer to show that you solved the equation correctly.

1. $5e = 45$

Tape Diagram:

45

e	e	e	e	e

9	9	9	9	9
e				

Algebraically:

$$5e = 45$$
$$5e \div 5 = 45 \div 5$$
$$e = 9$$

Check: $5(9) = 45$; $45 = 45$. *This number sentence is true, so 9 is the correct solution.*

2. $\frac{f}{3} = 10$

Tape Diagrams:

$f \div 3$

10

f

$f \div 3$	$f \div 3$	$f \div 3$

10	10	10

f

30

Algebraically:

$$\frac{f}{3} = 10$$

$$\frac{f}{3} \cdot 3 = 10 \cdot 3$$

$$f = 30$$

Check: $\frac{30}{3} = 10;\ 10 = 10.$ *This number sentence is true, so 30 is the correct solution.*

Set 4

On poster paper, solve each problem below algebraically and using tape diagrams. Check each answer to show that you solved the equation correctly.

1. $9 \cdot g = 54$

Tape Diagrams:

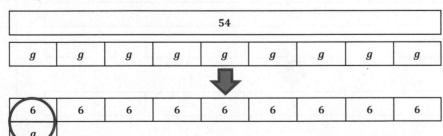

Algebraically:

$$9 \cdot g = 54$$

$$9 \cdot g \div 9 = 54 \div 9$$

$$g = 6$$

Check: $9 \cdot 6 = 54;\ 54 = 54.$ *This number sentence is true, so 6 is the correct solution.*

Lesson 27: One-Step Equations—Multiplication and Division
Date: 12/16/13

282

2. $2 = \dfrac{h}{7}$

Tape Diagrams:

| $h \div 7$ |
| 2 |

⬇

| h |

| $h \div 7$ | $h \div 7$ | $h \div 7$ | $h \div 7$ | $h \div 7$ | $h \div 7$ | $h \div 7$ |
| 2 | 2 | 2 | 2 | 2 | 2 | 2 |

⬇

| h |

| 14 |

Algebraically:

$$2 = \frac{h}{7}$$
$$2 \cdot 7 = \frac{h}{7} \cdot 7$$
$$14 = h$$

Check: $2 = \dfrac{14}{7}$; $2/2$. *This number sentence is true, so 14 is the correct solution.*

Set 5

On poster paper, solve each problem below algebraically and using tape diagrams. Check each answer to show that you solved the equation correctly.

1. $50 = 10j$

Tape Diagrams:

| 50 |

| j | j | j | j | j | j | j | j | j | j |

⬇

| 5 | 5 | 5 | 5 | 5 | 5 | 5 | 5 | 5 | 5 |

Algebraically:
$$50 = 10j$$
$$50 \div 10 = 10j \div 10$$
$$5 = j$$

Check: $50 = 10(5)$; $50 = 50$. *This number sentence is true, so 5 is the correct solution.*

2. $\dfrac{k}{8} = 3$

Tape Diagrams:

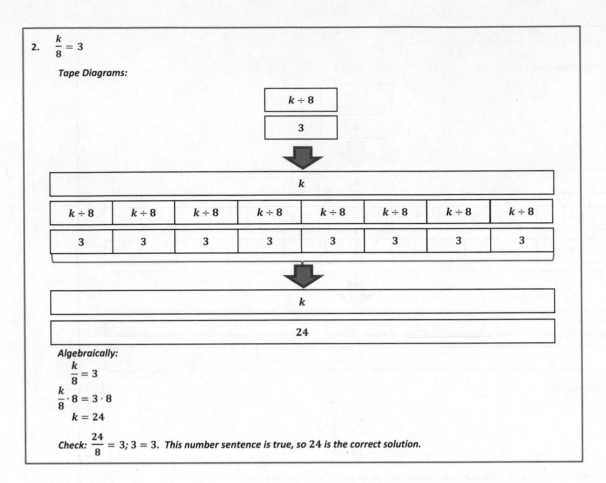

Algebraically:

$$\frac{k}{8} = 3$$
$$\frac{k}{8} \cdot 8 = 3 \cdot 8$$
$$k = 24$$

Check: $\dfrac{24}{8} = 3$; $3 = 3$. **This number sentence is true, so 24 is the correct solution.**

MP.1

MP.3
Hang completed posters around the room. Students walk around to examine other groups' posters. Students may either write on a piece of paper or write on the posters any questions or comments they may have. Answer students' questions after providing time for students to examine posters.

Exercises (10 minutes)

Students complete the following problems individually. Remind students to check their solutions.

Exercises

1. Use tape diagrams to solve the following problem: $3m = 21$.

Check: $3(7) = 21$; $21 = 21$. **This number sentence is true, so 7 is the correct solution.**

2. Solve the following problem algebraically: $15 = \frac{n}{5}$.

$$15 = \frac{n}{5}$$
$$15 \cdot 5 = \frac{n}{5} \cdot 5$$
$$75 = n$$

Check: $15 = \frac{75}{5}$; $15 = 15$.

This number sentence is true, so 75 *is the correct solution.*

3. Calculate the solution of the equation using the method of your choice: $4p = 36$.

Tape Diagrams:

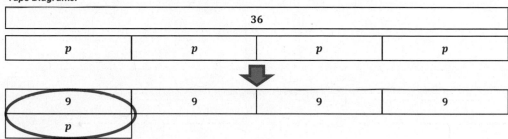

Algebraically:
$$4p = 36$$
$$4p \div 4 = 36 \div 4$$
$$p = 9$$

Check: $4(9) = 36$; $36 = 36$. *This number sentence is true, so* 9 *is the correct solution.*

4. Examine the tape diagram below and write an equation it represents. Then, calculate the solution to the equation using the method of your choice.

70						
q	q	q	q	q	q	q

$7q = 70$ or $70 = 7q$

Tape Diagram:

Algebraically:

$$7q = 70 \qquad\qquad 70 = 7q$$
$$7q \div 7 = 70 \div 7 \qquad 70 \div 7 = 7q \div 7$$
$$q = 10 \qquad\qquad q = 10$$

Check: $7(10) = 70$, $70 = 7(10)$; $70 = 70$. *This number sentence is true, so* 10 *is the correct answer.*

5. Write a multiplication equation that has a solution of 12. Use tape diagrams to prove that your equation has a solution of 12.

Answers will vary.

6. Write a division equation that has a solution of 12. Prove that your equation has a solution of 12 using algebraic methods.

Answers will vary.

Closing (5 minutes)

- How is solving addition and subtraction equations similar and different to solving multiplication and division equations?
- What do you know about the pattern in the operations you used to solve the equations today?
  - *We used inverse operations to solve the equations today. Division was used to solve multiplication equations, and multiplication was used to solve division equations.*

Exit Ticket (5 minutes)

Name _____   Date _____

Lesson 27: One-Step Equations—Multiplication and Division

Exit Ticket

Calculate the solution to each equation below using the indicated method. Remember to check your answers.

1. Use tape diagrams to find the solution of $\dfrac{r}{10} = 4$.

2. Find the solution of $64 = 16u$ algebraically.

3. Use the method of your choice to find the solution of $12 = 3v$.

Exit Ticket Sample Solutions

Calculate the solution to each equation below using the indicated method. Remember to check your answers.

1. Use tape diagrams to find the solution of $\frac{r}{10} = 4$.

$r \div 10$

4

r

$r \div 10$	$r \div 10$	$r \div 10$	$r \div 10$	$r \div 10$	$r \div 10$	$r \div 10$	$r \div 10$	$r \div 10$	$r \div 10$

4	4	4	4	4	4	4	4	4	4

r

40

Check: $\frac{40}{10} = 4$; $4 = 4$. *This number sentence is true, so 40 is the correct solution.*

2. Find the solution of $64 = 16u$ algebraically.

$$64 = 16u$$
$$64 \div 16 = 16u \div 16$$
$$4 = u$$

Check: $64 = 16(4)$; $64 = 64$. *This number sentence is true, so 4 is the correct solution.*

3. Use the method of your choice to find the solution of $12 = 3v$.

Tape Diagrams:

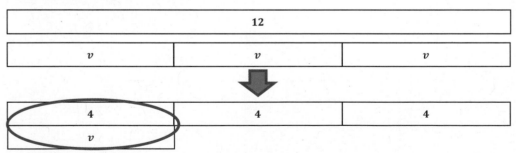

Algebraically:

$$12 = 3v$$
$$12 \div 3 = 3v \div 3$$
$$4 = v$$

Check: $12 = 3(4)$; $12 = 12$. *This number sentence is true, so 4 is the correct solution.*

Lesson 27: One-Step Equations—Multiplication and Division
Date: 12/16/13

288

Problem Set Sample Solutions

1. Use tape diagrams to calculate the solution of $30 = 5w$. Then, check your answer.

30				

w	w	w	w	w

6	6	6	6	6
w				

Check: $30 = 5(6)$; $30 = 30$. *This number sentence is true, so 6 is the correct solution.*

2. Solve $12 = \frac{x}{4}$ algebraically. Then, check your answer.

$$12 = \frac{x}{4}$$
$$12 \cdot 4 = \frac{x}{4} \cdot 4$$
$$48 = x$$

Check: $12 = \frac{48}{4}$; $12 = 12$. *This number sentence is true, so 48 is the correct solution.*

3. Use tape diagrams to calculate the solution of $\frac{y}{5} = 15$. Then, check your answer.

$y \div 5$

15

y

$y \div 5$	$y \div 5$	$y \div 5$	$y \div 5$	$y \div 5$

15	15	15	15	15

y

75

Check: $\frac{75}{5} = 15$; $15 = 15$. *This number sentence is true, so the solution is correct.*

4. Solve $18z = 72$ algebraically. Then, check your solution.

$$18z = 72$$
$$18z \div 18 = 72 \div 18$$
$$z = 4$$

Check: $18(4) = 72$; $72 = 72$. *This number sentence is true, so the solution is correct.*

5. Write a division equation that has a solution of 8. Prove that your solution is correct by using tape diagrams.

Answers will vary.

6. Write a multiplication equation that has a solution of 8. Solve the equation algebraically to prove that your solution is correct.

Answers will vary.

7. When solving equations algebraically, Meghan and Meredith each got a different solution. Who is correct? Why did the other person not get the correct answer?

Meghan	Meredith
$\dfrac{y}{2} = 4$	$\dfrac{y}{2} = 4$
$\dfrac{y}{2} \cdot 2 = 4 \cdot 2$	$\dfrac{y}{2} \div 2 = 4 \div 2$
$y = 8$	$y = 2$

Meghan is correct. Meredith divided by 2 to solve the equation, which is not correct because she would end up with $\dfrac{y}{4} = 2$. To solve a division equation, Meredith must multiply by 2 to end up with $1y$, which is the same as y.

Lesson 28: Two-Step Problems—All Operations

Student Outcomes

- Students calculate the solution of one-step equations by using their knowledge of order of operations and the properties of equality for addition, subtraction, multiplication, and division. Students employ tape diagrams to determine their answer.
- Students check to determine if their solution makes the equation true.

Fluency Exercise (5 minutes)

Addition of Decimals Sprint

Classwork

Mathematical Modeling Exercise (6 minutes)

Model the problems while students follow along.

Mathematical Modeling Exercise

Juan has gained 20 lb. since last year. He now weighs 120 lb. Rashod is 15 lb. heavier than Diego. If Rashod and Juan weighed the same amount last year, how much does Diego weigh? Allow j to be Juan's weight last year (in lb.) and d to be Diego's weight (in lb.).

Draw a tape diagram to represent Juan's weight.

120

| j | 20 |

Draw a tape diagram to represent Rashod's weight.

| d | 15 |

Draw a tape diagram to represent Diego's weight.

| d |

What would combining all three tape diagrams look like?

Write an equation to represent Juan's tape diagram.

$$j + 20 = 120$$

Write an equation to represent Rashod's tape diagram.

$$d + 15 + 20 = 120$$

How can we use the final tape diagram or the equations above to answer the question presented?

By combining 15 and 20 from Rashod's equation, we can use our knowledge of addition identities to determine Diego's weight.

The final tape diagram can be used to write a third equation $d + 35 = 120$. We can use our knowledge of addition identities to determine Diego's weight.

Calculate Diego's weight.

$$d + 35 - 35 = 120 - 35$$
$$d = 85$$

We can use identities to defend our thought that $d + 35 - 35 = d$.

Does your answer make sense?

Yes, if Diego weighs 85 lb., and Rashod weighs 15 lb. more than Deigo, then Rashod weighs 100 lb., which is what Juan weighed before he gained 20 lb.

Example 1 (5 minutes)

Assist students in solving the problem by providing step-by-step guidance.

Example 1

Marissa has twice as much money as Frank. Christina has $20 more than Marissa. If Christina has $100, how much money does Frank have? Let f represent the amount of money Frank has in dollars and m represent the amount of money Marissa has in dollars.

Draw a tape diagram to represent the amount of money Frank has.

f

Draw a tape diagram to represent the amount of money Marissa has.

f	f

Draw a tape diagram to represent the amount of money Christina has.

100

m	20

Which tape diagram provides enough information to determine the value of the variable m?

The tape diagram that represents the amount of money Christina has.

Write and solve the equation.

$$m + 20 = 100$$
$$m + 20 - 20 = 100 - 20$$
$$m = 80$$

The identities we have discussed throughout the module solidify that $m + 20 - 20 = m$.

What does the 80 represent?

80 is the amount of money, in dollars, that Marissa has.

Now that we know Marissa has $80, how can we use this information to find out how much money Frank has?

We can write an equation to represent Marissa's tape diagram since we now know the length is 80.

Write an equation.

$2f = 80$

Solve the equation.

$2f \div 2 = 80 \div 2$
$f = 40$

Once again, the identities we have used throughout the module can solidify that $2f \div 2 = f$.

What does the 40 represent?

The 40 represents the amount of money Frank has, in dollars.

Does 40 make sense in the problem?

Yes, because if Frank has $40, then Marissa has twice this, which is $80. Then, Christina has $100 because she has $20 more than Marissa, which is what the problem stated.

Exercises (20 minutes: 5 minutes per station)

Students work in small groups to complete the following stations.

Station One: Use tape diagrams to solve the problem.

Raeana is twice as old as Madeline and Laura is 10 years older than Raeana. If Laura is 50 years old, how old is Madeline? Let m represent Madeline's age in years and let r represent Raeana's age in years.

Raeana's Tape Diagram:

m	m

Madeline's Tape Diagram:

m

Laura's Tape Diagram:

50

r	10

Equation for Laura's Tape Diagram:

$$r + 10 = 50$$
$$r + 10 - 10 = 50 - 10$$
$$r = 40$$

We now know that Raeana is 40 years old, we can use this and Raeana's tape diagram to determine the age of Madeline.

$$2m = 40$$
$$2m \div 2 = 40 \div 2$$
$$m = 20$$

Therefore, Madeline is 20 years old.

Station Two: Use tape diagrams to solve the problem.

Carli has 90 apps on her phone. Braylen has half the amount of apps as Theiss. If Carli has three times the amount of apps as Theiss, how many apps does Braylen have? Let b represent the number of Braylen's apps and t represent the number of Theiss' apps.

Theiss' Tape Diagram:

t

Braylen's Tape Diagram:

b	b

Carli's Tape Diagram:

90

t	t	t

Equation for Carli's Tape Diagram:

$$3t = 90$$
$$3t \div 3 = 90 \div 3$$
$$t = 30$$

We now know that Theiss has 30 apps on his phone. We can use this information to write an equation for Braylen's tape diagram and determine how many apps are on Braylen's phone.

$$2b = 30$$
$$2b \div 2 = 30 \div 2$$
$$b = 15$$

Therefore, Braylen has 15 apps on his phone.

MP.1

Station Three: Use tape diagrams to solve the problem.

Reggie ran for 180 yards during the last football game, which is 40 more yards than his previous personal best. Monte ran 50 more yards than Adrian during the same game. If Monte ran the same amount of yards Reggie ran for his previous personal best, how many yards did Adrian run? Let r represent the number yards Reggie ran during his previous personal best and a represent the number of yards Adrian ran.

Reggie's Tape Diagram:

180	
r	40

Monte's Tape Diagram:

a	50

Adrian's Tape Diagram:

a

Combining all 3 tape diagrams:

	180		
Reggie	r		40
Monte	a	50	40
	a	90	

Equation for Reggie's Tape Diagram: $r + 40 = 180$

Equation for Monte's Tape Diagram:

$$a + 50 + 40 = 180$$
$$a + 90 = 180$$
$$a + 90 - 90 = 180 - 90$$
$$a = 90$$

Therefore, Adrian ran 90 yards during the football game.

<u>Station Four:</u> Use tape diagrams to solve the problem.

Lance rides his bike at a pace of 60 miles per hour down hills. When Lance is riding uphill, he rides 8 miles per hour slower than on flat roads. If Lance's downhill speed is 4 times faster than his flat road speed, how fast does he travel uphill? Let f represent Lance's pace on flat roads in miles per hour and u represent Lance's pace uphill in miles per hour.

Tape Diagram for Uphill Pace:

Tape Diagram for Downhill:

Equation for Downhill Pace:

$$4f = 60$$
$$4f \div 4 = 60 \div 4$$
$$f = 15$$

Equation for Uphill Pace:

$$u + 8 = 15$$
$$u + 8 - 8 = 15 - 8$$
$$u = 7$$

Therefore, Lance travels at a pace of 7 miles per hour uphill.

Closing (4 minutes)

- Use this time to go over the solutions to the stations and answer student questions.
- How did the tape diagrams help you create the expressions and equations that you used to solve the problems?

Exit Ticket (5 minutes)

Name _____   Date _____

Lesson 28: Two-Step Problems—All Operations

Exit Ticket

Use tape diagrams and equations to solve the problem with visual models and algebraic methods.

Alyssa is twice as old as Brittany, and Jazmyn is 15 years older than Alyssa. If Jazmyn is 35 years old, how old is Brittany? Let a represent Alyssa's age in years and b repreent Brittany's age in years.

Exit Ticket Sample Solutions

Use tape diagrams and equations to solve the problem with visual models and algebraic methods.

Alyssa is twice as old as Brittany, and Jazmyn is 15 years older than Alyssa. If Jazmyn is 35 years old, how old is Brittany? Let a represent Alyssa's age in years and b represent Brittany's age in years.

Brittany's Tape Diagram:

b

Alyssa's Tape Diagram:

b	b

Jazmyn's Tape Diagram:

35

a	15

Equation for Jazmyn's Tape Diagram:

$$a + 15 = 35$$
$$a + 15 - 15 = 35 - 15$$
$$a = 20$$

Now that we know Alyssa is 20 years old, we can use this information and Alyssa's tape diagram to determine Brittany's age.

$$2b = 20$$
$$2b \div 2 = 20 \div 2$$
$$b = 10$$

Therefore, Brittany is 10 years old.

Problem Set Sample Solutions

Use tape diagrams to solve each problem.

1. Dwayne scored 55 points in the last basketball game, which is 10 points more than his personal best. Lebron scored 15 points more than Chris in the same game. Lebron scored the same number of points as Dwayne's personal best. Let d represent the number of points Dwayne scored during his personal best and c represent the number of Chris' points.

   a. How many points did Chris score during the game?

   Equation for Dwayne's Tape Diagram: $d + 10 = 55$

   Equation for Lebron's Tape Diagram:

   $$c + 15 + 10 = 55$$
   $$c + 25 = 55$$
   $$c + 25 - 25 = 55 - 25$$
   $$c = 30$$

   Therefore, Chris scored 30 points in the game.

Lesson 28: Two-Step Problems—All Operations
Date: 12/16/13

298

b.   If these are the only three players who scored, what was the team's total number of points at the end of the game?

Dwayne scored 55 points. Chris scored 30 points. Lebron scored 45 points (answer to Dwayne's equation). Therefore, the total number of points scored is $55 + 30 + 45 = 130$.

2.   The number of customers at Yummy Smoothies varies throughout the day. During the lunch rush on Saturday, there were 120 customers at Yummy Smoothies. The number of customers at Yummy Smoothies during dinner time was 10 customers less than the number during breakfast. The number of customers at Yummy Smoothies during lunch was 3 times more than during breakfast. How many people were at Yummy Smoothies during breakfast? How many people were at Yummy Smoothies during dinner? Let d represent the number of customers at Yummy Smoothies during dinner and b represent the number of customers at Yummy Smoothies during breakfast.

Tape Diagrams for Lunch:

Tape Diagram for Dinner:

Equation for Lunch's Tape Diagram:

$$3b = 120$$
$$3b \div 3 = 120 \div 3$$
$$b = 40$$

Now that we know 40 customers were at Yummy Smoothies for breakfast, we can use this information and the tape diagram for dinner to determine how many customers were at Yummy Smoothies during dinner.

$$d + 10 = 40$$
$$d + 10 - 10 = 40 - 10$$
$$d = 30$$

Therefore, 30 customers were at Yummy Smoothies during dinner and 40 customers during breakfast.

3. Karter has 24 t-shirts. The number of pairs of shoes Karter has is 8 less than the number of pants he has. If the number of shirts Karter has is double the number of pants he has, how many pairs of shoes does Karter have? Let p represent the number of pants Karter has and s represent the number of pairs of shoes he has.

Tape Diagram for T-Shirts:

24

| p | p |

Tape Diagram for Shoes:
p

| s | 8 |

Equation for T-Shirts Tape Diagram:

$$2p = 24$$
$$2p \div 2 = 24 \div 2$$
$$p = 12$$

Equation for Shoes Tape Diagram:

$$s + 8 = 12$$
$$s + 8 - 8 = 12 - 8$$
$$s = 4$$

Karter has 4 pairs of shoes.

4. Darnell completed 35 push-ups in one minute, which is 8 more than his previous personal best. Mia completed 6 more push-ups than Katie. If Mia completed the same amount of push-ups as Darnell completed during his previous personal best, how many push-ups did Katie complete? Let d represent the number of push-ups Darnell completed during his previous personal best and k represent the number of push-ups Katie completed.

35

d		8
k	6	8
k	14	

$$d + 8 = 35$$
$$k + 6 + 8 = 35$$
$$k + 14 = 35$$
$$k + 14 - 14 = 35 - 14$$
$$k = 21$$

Katie completed 21 push-ups.

5. Justine swims freestyle at a pace of 150 laps per hour. Justine swims breaststroke 20 laps per hour slower than she swims butterfly. If Justine's freestyle speed is three times faster than her butterfly speed, how fast does she swim breaststroke? Let b represent Justine's butterfly speed and r represent Justine's breaststroke speed.

Tape Diagram for Breaststroke:

Tape Diagram for Freestyle:

$$3b = 150$$
$$3b \div 3 = 150 \div 3$$
$$b = 50$$

Therefore, Justine swims butterfly at a pace of 50 laps per hour.

$$r + 20 = 50$$
$$r + 20 - 20 = 50 - 20$$
$$r = 30$$

Therefore, Justine swims breaststroke at a pace of 30 laps per hour.

Addition of Decimals – Round 1

Number Correct: _____

Directions: Determine the sum of the decimals.

1.	1.3 + 2.1	
2.	3.6 + 2.2	
3.	8.3 + 4.6	
4.	14.3 + 12.6	
5.	21.2 + 34.5	
6.	14.81 + 13.05	
7.	32.34 + 16.52	
8.	56.56 + 12.12	
9.	78.03 + 21.95	
10.	32.14 + 45.32	
11.	14.7 + 32.8	
12.	24.5 + 42.9	
13.	45.8 + 32.4	
14.	71.7 + 32.6	
15.	102.5 + 213.7	
16.	365.8 + 127.4	
17.	493.4 + 194.8	

18.	14.08 + 34.27	
19.	24.98 + 32.05	
20.	76.67 + 40.33	
21.	46.14 + 32.86	
22.	475.34 + 125.88	
23.	561.09 + 356.24	
24.	872.78 + 135.86	
25.	788.04 + 324.69	
26.	467 + 32.78	
27.	583.84 + 356	
28.	549.2 + 678.09	
29.	497.74 + 32.1	
30.	741.9 + 826.14	
31.	524.67 + 764	
32.	821.3 + 106.87	
33.	548 + 327.43	
34.	108.97 + 268.03	

Addition of Decimals – Round 1 [KEY]

Directions: Determine the sum of the decimals.

1.	1.3 + 2.1	**3.4**	18.	14.08 + 34.27	**48.35**
2.	3.6 + 2.2	**5.8**	19.	24.98 + 32.05	**57.03**
3.	8.3 + 4.6	**12.9**	20.	76.67 + 40.33	**117**
4.	14.3 + 12.6	**26.9**	21.	46.14 + 32.86	**79**
5.	21.2 + 34.5	**55.7**	22.	475.34 + 125.88	**601.22**
6.	14.81 + 13.05	**27.86**	23.	561.09 + 356.24	**917.33**
7.	32.34 + 16.52	**48.86**	24.	872.78 + 135.86	**1,008.64**
8.	56.56 + 12.12	**68.68**	25.	788.04 + 324.69	**1,112.73**
9.	78.03 + 21.95	**99.98**	26.	467 + 32.78	**499.78**
10.	32.14 + 45.32	**77.46**	27.	583.84 + 356	**939.84**
11.	14.7 + 32.8	**47.5**	28.	549.2 + 678.09	**1,227.29**
12.	24.5 + 42.9	**67.4**	29.	497.74 + 32.1	**529.84**
13.	45.8 + 32.4	**78.2**	30.	741.9 + 826.14	**1,568.04**
14.	71.7 + 32.6	**104.3**	31.	524.67 + 764	**1,288.67**
15.	102.5 + 213.7	**316.2**	32.	821.3 + 106.87	**928.17**
16.	365.8 + 127.4	**493.2**	33.	548 + 327.43	**875.43**
17.	493.4 + 194.8	**688.2**	34.	108.97 + 268.03	**377**

Addition of Decimals – Round 2

Number Correct: _____

Improvement: _____

Directions: Determine the sum of the decimals.

1.	3.4 + 1.2		18.	67.82 + 37.9	
2.	5.6 + 3.1		19.	423.85 + 47.5	
3.	12.4 + 17.5		20.	148.9 + 329.18	
4.	10.6 + 11.3		21.	4 + 3.25	
5.	4.8 + 3.9		22.	103.45 + 6	
6.	4.56 + 1.23		23.	32.32 + 101.8	
7.	32.3 + 14.92		24.	62.1 + 0.89	
8.	23.87 + 16.34		25.	105 + 1.45	
9.	102.08 + 34.52		26.	235.91 + 12	
10.	35.91 + 23.8		27.	567.01 + 432.99	
11.	62.7 + 34.89		28.	101 + 52.3	
12.	14.76 + 98.1		29.	324.69 + 567.31	
13.	29.32 + 31.06		30.	245 + 0.987	
14.	103.3 + 32.67		31.	191.67 + 3.4	
15.	217.4 + 87.79		32.	347.1 + 12.89	
16.	22.02 + 45.8		33.	627 + 4.56	
17.	168.3 + 89.12		34.	0.157 + 4.56	

Addition of Decimals – Round 2 [KEY]

Directions: Determine the sum of the decimals.

1.	3.4 + 1.2	**4.6**	18.	67.82 + 37.9	**105.72**
2.	5.6 + 3.1	**8.7**	19.	423.85 + 47.5	**471.35**
3.	12.4 + 17.5	**29.9**	20.	148.9 + 329.18	**478.08**
4.	10.6 + 11.3	**21.9**	21.	4 + 3.25	**7.25**
5.	4.8 + 3.9	**8.7**	22.	103.45 + 6	**109.45**
6.	4.56 + 1.23	**5.79**	23.	32.32 + 101.8	**134.12**
7.	32.3 + 14.92	**47.22**	24.	62.1 + 0.89	**62.99**
8.	23.87 + 16.34	**40.21**	25.	105 + 1.45	**106.45**
9.	102.08 + 34.52	**136.6**	26.	235.91 + 12	**247.91**
10.	35.91 + 23.8	**59.71**	27.	567.01 + 432.99	**1000**
11.	62.7 + 34.89	**97.59**	28.	101 + 52.3	**153.3**
12.	14.76 + 98.1	**112.86**	29.	324.69 + 567.31	**892**
13.	29.32 + 31.06	**60.38**	30.	245 + 0.987	**245.987**
14.	103.3 + 32.67	**135.97**	31.	191.67 + 3.4	**195.07**
15.	217.4 + 87.79	**305.19**	32.	347.1 + 12.89	**359.99**
16.	22.02 + 45.8	**67.82**	33.	627 + 4.56	**631.56**
17.	168.3 + 89.12	**257.42**	34.	0.157 + 4.56	**4.717**

Lesson 29: Multi-Step Problems—All Operations

Student Outcomes

- Students use their knowledge of simplifying expressions, order of operations and properties of equality to calculate the solution of multi-step equations. Students use tables to determine their answer.
- Students check to determine if their solution makes the equation true.

Classwork

Example 1 (20 minutes)

Students participate in the discussion by answering the teacher's questions and following along in their student materials.

Example 1

The school librarian, Mr. Marker, knows the library has $1,400$ books, but wants to reorganize how the books are displayed on the shelves. Mr. Marker needs to know how many fiction, nonfiction, and resource books are in the library. He knows that the library has four times as many fiction books as resource books and half as many nonfiction books as fiction books. If these are the only types of books in the library, how many of each type of book are in the library?

 Give students time to work individually or with a partner in order to attempt to make sense of the problem. Students may attempt to solve the problem on their own prior to the following discussion.

Draw a tape diagram to represent the total number of books in the library.

1,400

Draw two more tape diagrams, one to represent the number of fictions books in the library and one to represent the number of resource books in the library.

Resource Books:

Fiction Books:

What variable should we use throughout the problem?

We should use r to represent the number of resource books in the library because it represents the fewest books. Choosing the variable to represent a different type of book we would create fractions throughout the problem.

Write the relationship between resource books and fiction books algebraically.

If we let r represent the number of resource books, then 4r represents the number of fiction books.

Draw a tape diagram to represent the number of nonfiction books.

Nonfiction Books:

How did you decide how many sections this tape diagram would have?

There are half as many nonfiction books as fictions books, since the fiction book tape diagram has four sections, nonfiction books should have two.

Represent the number of nonfiction books in the library algebraically.

$2r$ because that is half as many as fiction books ($4r$).

Use the tape diagrams we drew to solve the problem.

We know that combining the tape diagrams for each type of book will leave us with $1,400$ total books.

1,400		
r	$4r$	$2r$

Write an equation that represents the tape diagram.

$4r + 2r + r = 1,400$

Determine the value of r.

We can gather like terms, and then solve the equation.

$$7r = 1,400$$
$$7r \div 7 = 1,400 \div 7$$
$$r = 200$$

- What does this 200 mean?
  - *There are 200 resource books in the library.*

How many fiction books are in the library?

There are 800 fiction books in the library because $4(200) = 800$.

How many nonfiction books are in the library?

There are 400 nonfiction books in the library because $2(200) = 400$.

- We can use a different math tool to solve the problem as well. If we were to make a table, how many columns would we need?
  - 4

- Why do we need four columns?
  - *We need to keep track of the number of fiction, nonfiction, and resource books that are in the library, but we also need to keep track of the total number of books.*

Set up a table with four columns and label each column.

Fiction	Nonfiction	Resource	Total

- Highlight the important information from the word problem that will help us fill out the second row in our table.

  □ *The school librarian, Mr. Marker, **knows the library has** 1,400 **books**, but wants to reorganize how the books are displayed on the shelves. Mr. Marker needs to know how many fiction, nonfiction, and resource books are in the library. He knows that the library has **four times as many fiction books as resource books and half as many nonfiction books as fiction books**. If these are the only types of books in the library, how many of each type of book are in the library?*

- Fill out the second row of the table using the algebraic representations.

Fiction	Nonfiction	Resource	Total
$4r$	$2r$	r	$7r$

- If $r = 1$, how many of each type of book would be in the library?

Fiction	Nonfiction	Resource	Total
$4r$	$2r$	r	$7r$
4	2	1	7

- How can we fill out another row of the table?

  □ *Substitute different values in for r.*

- Substitute 5 in for r, how many of each type of book would be in the library then?

Fiction	Nonfiction	Resource	Total
4	2	1	7
20	10	5	35

- Does the library have four times as many fiction books as resource books?

  □ *Yes, because $5 \cdot 4 = 20$*

- Does the library have half as many nonfiction books as fiction books?

  □ *Yes, because half of 20 is 10.*

- How do we determine how many of each type of book is in the library when there are 1,400 books in the library?

  □ *Continue to multiply the rows by the same value, until the total column has 1,400 books.*

At this point, allow the students to work individually to determine how many fiction, nonfiction, and resource books are in the library if there are 1,400 total books. Each table may look different because students may choose different values to multiply by. A sample answer is shown below.

Fiction	Nonfiction	Resource	Total
4	2	1	7
20	10	5	35
200	100	50	350
800	400	200	1,400

How many fiction books are in the library?

800

How many nonfiction books are in the library?

400

How many resource books are in the library?

200

- Let us check and make sure that our answers fit the relationship described in the word problem.

Does the library have four times as many fiction books as resource books?

Yes, because $200 \cdot 4 = 800$.

Does the library have half as many nonfiction books as fiction books?

Yes, because half of 800 *is* 400.

Does the library have 1400 books?

Yes, because $800 + 400 + 200 = 1,400$.

Exercises (15 minutes)

Students work in small groups to answer the following problems using tables and algebraically.

Exercises

Solve each problem below. Then check your answer with the word problem.

1. Indian Ridge Middle School wanted to add a new school sport, so they surveyed the students to determine which sport is most popular. Students were able to choose between soccer, football, lacrosse, or swimming. The same number of students chose lacrosse and swimming. The number of students who chose soccer was double the number of students who chose lacrosse. The number of students who chose football was triple the number of students who chose swimming. If 434 students completed the survey, how many students chose each sport?

Soccer	Football	Lacrosse	Swimming	Total
2	3	1	1	7

The rest of the table will vary.

Soccer	Football	Lacrosse	Swimming	Total
2	3	1	1	7
124	186	62	62	434

124 *students chose soccer,* 186 *students chose football,* 62 *students chose lacrosse and* 62 *students chose swimming.*

We can confirm that these numbers satisfy the conditions of the word problem because lacrosse and swimming were chosen by the same number of students. 124 *is double* 62*, so soccer was chosen by double the number of students as lacrosse and* 186 *is triple* 62*, so football was chosen by 3 times as many students as swimming. Also,* $124 + 186 + 62 + 62 = 434$.

Algebraically: Let s represent the number of students who chose swimming. Then, $2s$ *is the number of students who chose soccer,* $3s$ *is the number of students who chose football and* s *is the number of students who chose lacrosse.*

$$2s + 3s + s + s = 434$$
$$7s = 434$$
$$7s \div 7 = 434 \div 7$$
$$s = 62$$

Therefore, 62 *students chose swimming and* 62 *students chose lacrosse.* 124 *students chose soccer because* $2(62) = 124$*, and* 186 *students chose football because* $3(62) = 186$.

2. At Prairie Elementary School, students are asked to pick their lunch ahead of time so the kitchen staff will know what to prepare. On Monday, 6 times as many students chose hamburgers as chose salads. The number of students who chose lasagna was one third the number of students who chose hamburgers. If 225 students ordered lunch, how many students chose each option if hamburger, salad, and lasagna were the only three options?

Hamburger	Salad	Lasagna	Total
6	1	2	9

The rest of the table will vary.

Hamburger	Salad	Lasagna	Total
6	1	2	9
150	25	50	225

150 *students chose a hamburger for lunch,* 25 *students chose a salad and* 50 *students chose lasagna.*

We can confirm that these numbers satisfy the conditions of the word problem because $25 \cdot 6 = 150$, *so hamburgers were chosen by 6 times more students than salads. Also,* $\frac{1}{3} \cdot 150 = 50$, *which means lasagna was chosen by one third of the number of students who chose hamburgers. Finally,* $150 + 25 + 50 = 225$, *which means* 225 *students completed the survey.*

Algebraically: Let s represent the number of students who chose a salad. Then 6s *represents the number of students who chose hamburgers and* 2s *represents the number of students who chose lasagna.*

$$6s + s + 2s = 225$$
$$9s = 225$$
$$9s \div 9 = 225 \div 9$$
$$s = 25$$

This means that 25 *students chose salad,* 150 *students chose hamburgers because* $6(25) = 150$, *and* 50 *students chose lasagna because* $2(25) = 50$.

MP.1

3. The art teacher, Mr. Gonzalez, is preparing for a project. In order for students to have the correct supplies, Mr. Gonzalez needs 10 times more markers than pieces of construction paper. He needs the same number of bottles of glue as pieces of construction paper. The number of scissors required for the project is half the number of piece of construction paper. If Mr. Gonzalez collected 400 items for the project, how many of each supply did he collect?

Markers	Construction Paper	Glue Bottles	Scissors	Total
20	2	2	1	25

The rest of the table will vary.

Markers	Construction Paper	Glue Bottles	Scissors	Total
20	2	2	1	25
320	32	32	16	400

Mr. Gonzalez collected 320 *markers,* 32 *pieces of construction paper,* 32 *glue bottles, and* 16 *scissors for the project.*

We can confirm that these numbers satisfy the conditions of the word problem because Mr. Gonzalez collected the same number of pieces of construction paper and glue bottles. Also, $32 \cdot 10 = 320$, *so Mr. Gonzalez collected* 10 *times more markers than pieces of construction paper and glue bottles. Mr. Gonzalez only collected* 16 *pairs of scissors which is half of the number of pieces of construction paper. The supplies collected add up to* 400 *supplies, which is the number of supplies indicated in the word problem.*

Algebraically: Let s represent the number of scissors needed for the project. Which means 20s *represents the number of markers needed,* 2s *represents the number of construction paper needed and* 2s *represents the number of glue bottles needed.*

$$20s + 2s + 2s + s = 400$$
$$25s = 400$$
$$25s \div 25 = 400 \div 25$$
$$s = 16$$

This means that 16 *pairs of scissors,* 320 *markers,* 32 *pieces of construction paper, and* 32 *glue bottles are required for the project.*

 Lesson 29:   Multi-Step Problems—All Operations
Date: 12/16/13

4. The math teacher, Ms. Zentz, is buying appropriate math tools to use throughout the year. She is planning on buying twice as many rulers as protractors. The number of calculators Ms. Zentz is planning on buying is one quarter of the number of protractors. If Ms. Zentz buys 65 items, how many protractors does Ms. Zentz buy?

Rulers	Protractors	Calculators	Total
8	4	1	13

The rest of the table will vary.

Rulers	Protractors	Calculators	Total
8	4	1	13
40	20	5	65

Ms. Zentz will buy 20 protractors.

We can confirm that these numbers satisfy the conditions of the word problem, because the number of protractors is half of the number of rulers and the number of calculators is one fourth of the number of protractors. Also $40 + 20 + 5 = 65$, so my total matches the total supplies that Ms. Zentz bought.

Algebraically: Let c represent the number of calculators Ms. Zentz needs for the year. Then $8c$ represents the number of rulers and $4c$ represents the number of protractors Ms. Zentz will need throughout the year.

$$8c + 4c + c = 65$$
$$13c = 65$$
$$13c \div 13 = 65 \div 13$$
$$c = 5$$

Therefore, Ms. Zentz will need 5 calculators, 40 rulers, and 20 protractors throughout the year.

Allow time to answer student questions and discuss answers. In particular, encourage students to compare solution methods with one another, commenting on the accuracy and efficiency of each.

Closing (5 minutes)

- Pam says she only needed two rows to solve each of the problems. How was she able to do this?
- Is there a more efficient way to get to the answer than choosing random values by which to multiply each row?
  - *Find out how many groups of one set of materials it will take to obtain the total amount desired. Then, multiply the entire row by this number.*
  - *Students may need to see a demonstration to fully understand the reasoning. Use the exercises to further explain.*
  - *Relate this problem-solving strategy to the ratio tables discussed throughout Module 1.*

Exit Ticket (5 minutes)

Name _____   Date _____

Lesson 29: Multi-Step Problems—All Operations

Exit Ticket

Solve the problem using tables and equations and then check your answer with the word problem. Try to find the answer only using two rows of numbers on your table.

A pet store owner, Byron, needs to determine how much food he needs to feed the animals. Byron knows that he needs to order the same amount of bird food as hamster food. He needs four times as much dog food as bird food, and needs half the amount of cat food as dog food. If Byron orders 600 packages of animal food, how much dog food does he buy? Let b represent the amount of bird food.

Exit Ticket Sample Solutions

Solve the problem using tables and equations, and then check your answer with the word problem. Try to find the answer only using two rows of numbers on your table.

A pet store owner, Byron, needs to determine how much food he needs to feed the animals. Byron knows that he needs to order the same amount of bird food as hamster food. He needs four times as much dog food as bird food, and needs half the amount of cat food as dog food. If Byron orders 600 packages of animal food, how much dog food does he buy? Let b represent the amount of bird food.

Bird Food	Hamster Food	Dog Food	Cat Food	Total
1	1	4	2	8

The rest of the table will vary (unless they follow suggestions from the closing).

Bird Food	Hamster Food	Dog Food	Cat Food	Total
1	1	4	2	8
75	75	300	150	600

Byron would need to order 300 packages of dog food.

The answer makes sense because Byron ordered the same amount of bird food and hamster food. The table also shows that Byron order four times as much dog food as bird food, and the amount of cat food he ordered is half the amount of dog food. The total amount of pet food Byron ordered was 600 packages, which matches the word problem.

Algebraically: Let b represent the amount of bird food the pet store needs. Therefore, b also represents the amount of hamster food, 4b represents the amount of dog food and 2b represents the amount of cat food required by the pet store.

$$b + b + 4b + 2b = 600$$
$$8b = 600$$
$$8b \div 8 = 600 \div 8$$
$$b = 75$$

Therefore, Byron will order 75 pounds of bird food, which results in 300 pounds of dog food because $4(75) = 300$.

Problem Set Sample Solutions

Solve the problems and then check your answers with the word problem.

1. On average, a baby uses three times the number of large diapers as small diapers, and double the number of medium diapers as small diapers.

   a. If the average baby uses 2,940 diapers size large and smaller, how many of each size would be used?

Small	Medium	Large	Total
1	2	3	6
490	980	1470	2,940

   An average baby would use 490 small diapers, 980 medium diapers, and 1,470 large diapers.

   The answer makes sense because the number of large diapers is 3 times more than small diapers. The number of medium diapers is double the number of small diapers and the total number of diapers is 2,940.

b.   Support your answer with equations.

Let s represent the number of small diapers a baby needs. Therefore, 2s represents the number of medium diapers, and 3s represents the amount of large diapers a baby needs.

$$s + 2s + 3s = 2,940$$
$$6s = 2,940$$
$$6s \div 6 = 2,940 \div 6$$
$$s = 490$$

Therefore, a baby requires 490 small diapers, 980 medium diapers (because 2(490) = 980), and 1,470 large diapers (because 3(490) = 1,470), which matches the answer in part (a).

2.   Tom has three times as many pencils as pens, but has a total of 100 writing utensils.

a.   How many pencils does Tom have?

Pencils	Pens	Total
3	1	4
75	25	100

b.   How many more pencils than pens does Tom have?

75 − 25 = 50. Tom has 50 more pencils than pens.

3.   Serena's mom is planning her birthday party. She bought balloons, plates, and cups. Serena's mom bought twice as many plates as cups. The number of balloons Serena's mom bought was half the number of cups.

a.   If Serena's mom bought 84 items, how many of each item did she buy?

Balloons	Plates	Cups	Total
1	4	2	7
12	48	24	84

Serena's mom bought 12 balloons, 48 plates, and 24 cups.

b.   Tammy brought 12 balloons to the party. How many total balloons were at Serena's birthday party?

12 + 12 = 24. There were 24 totals balloons at the party.

c.   If half the plates and all but four cups were used during the party, how many plates and cups were used?

$\frac{1}{2} \cdot 48 = 24.$ *Twenty-four plates were used during the party.*

24 − 4 = 20. Twenty cups were used during the party.

4.   Elizabeth has a lot of jewelry. She has four times as many earrings as watches, but half the number of necklaces as earrings. Elizabeth has the same number of necklaces as bracelets.

a.   If Elizabeth has 117 pieces of jewelry, how many earrings does she have?

Earrings	Watches	Necklaces	Bracelets	Total
4	1	2	2	9
52	13	26	26	117

Elizabeth has 52 earrings, 13 watches, 26 necklaces, and 26 bracelets.

b.   Support your answers with an equation.

Let w represent the number of watches Elizabeth has. Therefore, 4w represents the number of earrings Elizabeth has, and 2w represents both the number of necklaces and bracelets she has.

$$4w + w + 2w + 2w = 117$$
$$9w = 117$$
$$9w \div 9 = 117 \div 9$$
$$w = 13$$

Therefore, Elizabeth has 13 watches and 52 earrings because 4(13) = 52, and 26 necklaces and bracelets each because 2(13) = 26.

5.   Claudia was cooking breakfast for her entire family. She made double the amount of chocolate chip pancakes as she did regular pancakes. She only made half as many blueberry pancakes as she did regular pancakes. Claudia also knows her family loves sausage, so she made triple the amount of sausage as blueberry pancakes.

   a.   How many of each breakfast item did Claudia make if she cooked 90 items in total?

Chocolate Chip Pancakes	Regular Pancakes	Blueberry Pancakes	Sausage	Total
4	2	1	3	10
36	18	9	27	90

   b.   After everyone ate breakfast, there were 4 chocolate chip pancakes, 5 regular pancakes, 1 blueberry pancake, and no sausage left. How many of each item did the family eat?

   The family ate 32 chocolate chip pancakes, 13 regular pancakes, 8 blueberry pancakes, and 27 pieces of sausage during breakfast.

6.   During a basketball game, Jeremy scored triple the number of points as Donovan. Kolby scored double the number of points as Donovan.

   a.   If the three boys scored 36 points, how many points did each boy score?

Jeremy	Donovan	Kolby	Total
3	1	2	6
18	6	12	36

   Jeremy scored 18 points, Donovan scored 6 points, and Kolby scored 12 points.

   b.   Support your answer with an equation.

   Let d represent the number of points Donovan scored, which means 3d represents the number of points Jeremy scored, and 2d represents the number of points Kolby scored.

$$3d + d + 2d = 36$$
$$6d = 36$$
$$6d \div 6 = 36 \div 6$$
$$d = 6$$

   Therefore, Donovan scored 6 points and Jeremy scored 18 points because 3(6) = 18 and Kolby scored 12 points because 2(6) = 12.

Topic H:

Applications of Equations

6.EE.5, 6.EE.6, 6.EE.7, 6.EE.8, 6.EE.9

Focus Standard:	6.EE.5	Understand solving an equation or inequality as a process of answering a question; which values from a specified set, if any, make the equation or inequality true? Use substitution to determine whether a given number in a specified set makes an equation or inequality true.
	6.EE.6	Use variables to represent numbers and write expressions when solving a real-world or mathematical problem; understand that a variable can represent an unknown number, or, depending on the purpose at hand, any number in a specified set.
	6.EE.7	Solve real-world and mathematical problems by writing and solving equations in the form $x + p = q$ and $px = q$ for cases in which p, q and x are all nonnegative rational numbers.
	6.EE.8	Write an inequality of the form $x > c$ or $x < c$ to represent a constraint or condition in a real-world mathematical problem. Recognize that inequalities of the form $x > c$ or $x < c$ have infinitely many solutions; represent solutions of such inequalities on number line diagrams.
	6.EE.9	Use variables to represent two quantities in a real-world problem that change in relationship to one another; write an equation to express one quantity, thought of as the dependent variable, in terms of the other quantity, thought of as the independent variable. Analyze the relationship between the dependent and independent variables using graphs and tables, and relate these to the equation. *For example, in a problem involving motion at constant speed, list and graph ordered pairs of distances and times, and write the equation $d = 65t$ to represent the relationship between distance and time.*

Instructional Days:	5
Lesson 30:	One-Step Problems in the Real World (P)[1]
Lesson 31:	Problems in Mathematical Terms (P)
Lesson 32:	Multi-Step Problems in the Real World (P)
Lesson 33:	From Equations to Inequalities (P)
Lesson 34:	Writing and Graphing Inequalities in Real-World Problems (P)

In Topic H, students apply their knowledge from the entire module to solve equations in real-world, contextual problems. In Lesson 30, students use prior knowledge from Grade 4 to solve missing angle problems. Students write and solve one step equations in order to determine a missing angle. Lesson 31 involves students using their prior knowledge from Module 1 to contruct tables of independent and dependent values in order to analyze equations with two variables from real-life contexts. They represent equations by plotting values from the tables on a coordinate grid in Lesson 32. The module concludes with Lessons 33 and 34, where students refer to true and false number sentences in order to move from solving equations to writing inequalities that represent a constraint or condition in real-life or mathematical problems. Students understand that inequalities have infinitely many solutions and represent those solutions on number line diagrams.

---

[1] 1 Lesson Structure Key: **P**-Problem Set Lesson, **M**-Modeling Cycle Lesson, **E**-Exploration Lesson, **S**-Socratic Lesson

Topic H:	Applications of Equations	
Date:	12/16/13	

317

Lesson 30: One-Step Problems in the Real World

Student Outcomes

- Students calculate missing angle measures by writing and solving equations.

Lesson Notes

This is an application lesson based on understandings developed in Grade 4. The three standards applied in this lesson include:

4.MD.C.5   Recognize angles as geometric shapes that are formed wherever two rays share a common endpoint, and understand concepts of angle measurement:

    a.   An angle is measured with reference to a circle with its center at the common endpoint of the rays, by considering the fraction of the circular arc between the points where the two rays intersect the circle. An angle that turns through 1/360 of a circle is called a "one-degree angle," and can be used to measure angles.

    b.   An angle that turns through n one-degree angles is said to have an angle measure of n degrees.

4.MD.C.6   Measure angles in whole-number degrees using a protractor. Sketch angles of specified measure.

4.MD.C.7   Recognize angle measure as additive. When an angle is decomposed into non-overlapping parts, the angle measure of the whole is the sum of the angle measures of the parts. Solve addition and subtraction problems to find unknown angles on a diagram in real-world and mathematical problems, e.g., by using an equation with a symbol for the unknown angle measure.

This lesson focuses, in particular, on 4.MD.C.7.

Fluency Exercise (5 minutes)

Subtraction of Decimals Sprint

Classwork

Opening Exercise (3 minutes)

Students start the lesson with a review of key angle terms from Grade 4.

Opening Exercise

Draw an example of each term and write a brief description.

Acute

    Less than $90°$

Obtuse	*Between 90° and 180°*	
Right	*Exactly 90°*	
Straight	*Exactly 180°*	
Reflex	*Between 180° and 360°*	

Example 1 (3 minutes)

Example 1

$\angle ABC$ measures 90°. The angle has been separated into two angles. If one angle measures 57°, what is the measure of the other angle?

- In this lesson we will be using algebra to help us determine unknown measures of angles.

How are these two angles related?

The two angles have a sum of 90°.

What equation could we use to solve for x.

$x° + 57° = 90°$

Now let's solve.

$x° + 57° - 57° = 90° - 57°$

$x° = 33°$

The unknown angle is 33°

Example 2 (3 minutes)

Example 2

Michelle is designing a parking lot. She has determined that one of the angles should be 115°. What is the measure of angle x and angle y?

How is angle x related to the 115° angle?

The two angles form a straight line. Therefore they should add up to 180°.

What equation would we use to show this?

$x° + 115° = 180°$

How would you solve this equation?

115 was added to the x, so I will take away 115 to get back to just x.

$x° + 115° - 115° = 180° - 115°$
$x° = 65°$

The angle next to 115°, labeled with an x is equal to 65°.

How is angle y related the angle that measures 115°?

These two angles also form a straight line and must add up to 180°.

Therefore, x and y must both be equal to 65°.

MP.4

Example 3 (3 minutes)

Example 3

A beam of light is reflected off of a mirror. Below is a diagram of the reflected beam. Determine the missing angle measure.

How are the angles in this question related?

There are three angles that when all placed together form a straight line. This means that the three angles have a sum of 180°.

What equation could we write to represent the situation?

$55° + x° + 55° = 180°$

How would you solve an equation like this?

We can combine the two angles that we do know.

$$55° + 55° + x° = 180°$$
$$110° + x° = 180°$$
$$110° - 110° + x° = 180° - 110°$$
$$x° = 70°$$

The angle of the bounce is 70°.

Exercises 1–5 (20 minutes)

Students will work independently.

Exercises 1–5

Write and solve an equation in each of the problems.

1. $\angle ABC$ measures 90°. It has been split into two angles, $\angle ABD$ and $\angle DBC$. The measure of the two angles is in a ratio of $2:1$. What are the measures of each angle?

$$x° + 2x° = 90°$$
$$3x° = 90°$$
$$\frac{3x°}{3} = \frac{90°}{3}$$
$$x° = 30°$$

One of the angles measures 30°, and the other measures 60°.

2. Solve for x.

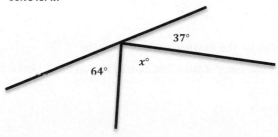

$$x° + 64° + 37° = 180°$$
$$x° + 101° = 180°$$
$$x° + 101° - 101° = 180° - 101°$$
$$x° = 79°$$

3. Candice is building a rectangular piece of a fence according to the plans her boss gave her. One of the angles is not labeled. Write an equation and use it to determine the measure of the unknown angle.

$$x° + 49° = 90°$$
$$x° + 49° - 49° = 90° - 49°$$
$$x° = 41°$$

4. Rashid hit a hockey puck against the wall at a 38° angle. The puck hit the wall and traveled in a new direction. Determine the missing angle in the diagram.

$$38° + x° + 38° = 180°$$
$$76° + x = 180°$$
$$76° - 76° + x = 180° - 76°$$
$$x = 104°$$

5. Jaxon is creating a mosaic design on a rectangular table. He has added two pieces to one of the corners. The first piece has an angle measuring 38° that is placed in the corner. A second piece has an angle measuring 27° that is also placed in the corner. Draw a diagram to model the situation. Then, write an equation and use it to determine the measure of the unknown angle in a third piece that could be added to the corner of the table.

$$x° + 38° + 27° = 90°$$
$$x° + 65° = 90°$$
$$x° + 65° - 65° = 90° - 65°$$
$$x° = 25°$$

Closing (3 minutes)

- Explain how you determined the equation you used to solve for the missing angle or variable.

  □ *I used the descriptions in the word problems. For example, if it said "the sum of the angles," I knew to add the measures together.*

Exit Ticket (7 minutes)

Name _____   Date _____

Lesson 30: One-Step Problems in the Real World

Write an equation and solve for the missing angle in each question.

1. Alejandro is repairing a stained glass window. He needs to take it apart to repair it. Before taking it apart he makes a sketch with angle measures to put it back together.

    Write an equation and use it to determine the measure of the unknown angle.

2. Hannah is putting in a tile floor. She needs to determine the angles that should be cut in the tiles to fit in the corner. The angle in the corner measures 90°. One piece of the tile will have a measure of 38°. Write an equation and use it to determine the measure of the unknown angle.

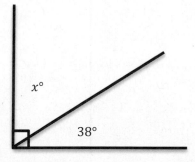

Exit Ticket Sample Solutions

1. Alejandro is repairing a stained glass window. He needs to take it apart to repair it. Before taking it apart he makes a sketch with angle measures to put it back together.

   Write an equation and use it to determine the measure of the unknown angle.

   $$40° + x° + 30° = 180°$$
   $$x° + 40° + 30° = 180°$$
   $$x° + 70° = 180°$$
   $$x° + 70° - 70° = 180° - 70°$$
   $$x° = 110°$$

   The missing angle measures 110°.

2. Hannah is putting in a tile floor. She needs to determine the angles that should be cut in the tiles to fit in the corner. The angle in the corner measures 90°. One piece of the tile will have a measure of 38°. Write an equation and use it to determine the measure of the unknown angle.

   $$x° + 38° = 90°$$
   $$x° + 38° - 38° = 90° - 38°$$
   $$x° = 52°$$

   The unknown angle is 52°.

Problem Set Sample Solutions

Write and solve an equation for each problem.

1. Solve for x.

   $$x° + 52° = 90°$$
   $$x° + 52° - 52° = 90° - 52°$$
   $$x° = 38°$$

2. $\angle BAE$ measures 90°. Solve for x.

   $$15° + x° + 25° = 90°$$
   $$15° + 25° + x° = 90°$$
   $$40° + x° = 90°$$
   $$40° - 40° + x° = 90° - 40°$$
   $$x° = 50°$$

3. Thomas is putting in a tile floor. He needs to determine the angles that should be cut in the tiles to fit in the corner. The angle in the corner measures $90°$. One piece of the tile will have a measure of $24°$. Write an equation and use it to determine the measure of the unknown angle.

$$x° + 24° = 90°$$
$$x° + 24° - 24° = 90° - 24°$$
$$x° = 66°$$

The unknown angle is $66°$.

4. Solve for x.

$$x° + 105° + 62° = 180°$$
$$x° + 167° = 180°$$
$$x° + 167° - 167° = 180° - 167°$$
$$x° = 13°$$

5. Aram has been studying the mathematics behind pinball machines. He made the following diagram of one of his observations. Determine the measure of the missing angle.

$$52° + x° + 68° = 180°$$
$$x° + 52° + 68° = 180°$$
$$x° + 120° = 180°$$
$$x° + 120° - 120° = 180° - 120°$$
$$x° = 60°$$

6. The measures of two angles have a sum of $90°$. The measures of the angles are in a ratio of $2:1$. Determine the measures of both angles.

$$2x° + x° = 90°$$
$$3x° = 90°$$
$$\frac{3x°}{3} = \frac{90}{3}$$
$$x° = 30°$$

The angles measure $30°$ and $60°$.

7. The measures of two angles have a sum of $180°$. The measures of the angles are in a ratio of $5:1$. Determine the measures of both angles.

$$5x° + x° = 180°$$
$$6x° = 180°$$
$$\frac{6x°}{6} = \frac{180}{6}$$
$$x° = 30°$$

The angles measure $30°$ and $150°$.

Subtraction of Decimals – Round 1

Number Correct: _____

Directions: Subtract the decimals to determine the difference.

1.	9.4 − 4.1		16.	41.72 − 33.9	
2.	7.4 − 3.2		17.	354.65 − 67.5	
3.	49.5 − 32.1		18.	448.9 − 329.18	
4.	20.9 − 17.2		19.	8 − 5.38	
5.	9.2 − 6.8		20.	94.21 − 8	
6.	7.48 − 2.26		21.	134.25 − 103.17	
7.	58.8 − 43.72		22.	25.8 − 0.42	
8.	38.99 − 24.74		23.	115 − 1.65	
9.	116.32 − 42.07		24.	187.49 − 21	
10.	46.83 − 35.6		25.	345.77 − 248.69	
11.	54.8 − 43.66		26.	108 − 54.7	
12.	128.43 − 87.3		27.	336.91 − 243.38	
13.	144.54 − 42.09		28.	264 − 0.742	
14.	105.4 − 68.22		29.	174.38 − 5.9	
15.	239.5 − 102.37		30.	323.2 − 38.74	

Subtraction of Decimals – Round 1 [KEY]

Directions: Subtract the decimals to determine the difference.

1.	9.4 − 4.1	**5.3**	16.	41.72 − 33.9	**7.82**
2.	7.4 − 3.2	**4.2**	17.	354.65 − 67.5	**287.15**
3.	49.5 − 32.1	**17.4**	18.	448.9 − 329.18	**119.72**
4.	20.9 − 17.2	**3.7**	19.	8 − 5.38	**2.62**
5.	9.2 − 6.8	**2.4**	20.	94.21 − 8	**86.21**
6.	7.48 − 2.26	**5.22**	21.	134.25 − 103.17	**31.08**
7.	58.8 − 43.72	**15.08**	22.	25.8 − 0.42	**25.38**
8.	38.99 − 24.74	**14.25**	23.	115 − 1.65	**113.35**
9.	116.32 − 42.07	**74.25**	24.	187.49 − 21	**166.49**
10.	46.83 − 35.6	**11.23**	25.	345.77 − 248.69	**97.08**
11.	54.8 − 43.66	**11.14**	26.	108 − 54.7	**53.3**
12.	128.43 − 87.3	**41.13**	27.	336.91 − 243.38	**93.53**
13.	144.54 − 42.09	**102.45**	28.	264 − 0.742	**263.258**
14.	105.4 − 68.22	**37.18**	29.	174.38 − 5.9	**168.48**
15.	239.5 − 102.37	**137.13**	30.	323.2 − 38.74	**284.46**

Subtraction of Decimals – Round 2

Number Correct: _____

Improvement: _____

Directions: Subtract the decimals to determine the difference.

1.	$8.4 - 5.4$		16.	$14 - 10.32$	
2.	$5.6 - 3.1$		17.	$43.37 - 28$	
3.	$9.7 - 7.2$		18.	$24.56 - 18.88$	
4.	$14.3 - 12.1$		19.	$33.55 - 11.66$	
5.	$34.5 - 13.2$		20.	$329.56 - 284.49$	
6.	$14.86 - 13.85$		21.	$574.3 - 342.18$	
7.	$43.27 - 32.14$		22.	$154 - 128.63$	
8.	$48.48 - 27.27$		23.	$247.1 - 138.57$	
9.	$64.74 - 31.03$		24.	$12 - 3.547$	
10.	$98.36 - 24.09$		25.	$1.415 - 0.877$	
11.	$33.54 - 24.4$		26.	$185.774 - 154.86$	
12.	$114.7 - 73.42$		27.	$65.251 - 36.9$	
13.	$45.2 - 32.7$		28.	$144.2 - 95.471$	
14.	$74.8 - 53.9$		29.	$2.11 - 1.949$	
15.	$238.4 - 114.36$		30.	$100 - 34.746$	

Subtraction of Decimals – Round 2 **[KEY]**

Directions: Subtract the decimals to determine the difference.

1.	8.4 – 5.4	**3.0**	16.	14 – 10.32	**3.68**
2.	5.6 – 3.1	**2.5**	17.	43.37 – 28	**15.37**
3.	9.7 – 7.2	**2.5**	18.	24.56 – 18.88	**5.68**
4.	14.3 – 12.1	**2.2**	19.	33.55 – 11.66	**21.89**
5.	34.5 – 13.2	**21.3**	20.	329.56 – 284.49	**45.07**
6.	14.86 – 13.85	**1.01**	21.	574.3 – 342.18	**232.12**
7.	43.27 – 32.14	**11.13**	22.	154 – 128.63	**25.37**
8.	48.48 – 27.27	**21.21**	23.	247.1 – 138.57	**108.53**
9.	64.74 – 31.03	**33.71**	24.	12 – 3.547	**8.453**
10.	98.36 – 24.09	**74.27**	25.	1.415 – 0.877	**0.538**
11.	33.54 – 24.4	**9.14**	26.	185.774 – 154.86	**30.914**
12.	114.7 – 73.42	**41.28**	27.	65.251 – 36.9	**28.351**
13.	45.2 – 32.7	**12.5**	28.	144.2 – 95.471	**48.729**
14.	74.8 – 53.9	**20.9**	29.	2.11 – 1.949	**0.161**
15.	238.4 – 114.36	**124.04**	30.	100 – 34.746	**65.254**

Lesson 31: Problems in Mathematical Terms

Student Outcomes

- Students analyze an equation in two variables to choose an independent variable and dependent variable. Students determine whether or not the equation is solved for the second variable in terms of the first variable or vice versa. They then use this information to determine which variable is the independent variable and which is the dependent variable.
- Students create a table by placing the independent variable in the first row or column and the dependent variable in the second row or column. They compute entries in the table by choosing arbitrary values for the independent variable (no constraints) and then determine what the dependent variable must be.

Classwork

Example 1 (10 minutes)

> **Example 1**
>
> Marcus reads for 30 minutes each night. He wants to determine the total number of minutes he will read over the course of a month. He wrote the equation $t = 30d$ to represent the total amount of time that he has spent reading, where t represents the total number of minutes read and d represents the number of days that he read during the month. Determine which variable is independent and which is dependent. Then create a table to show how many minutes he has read in the first seven days.
>
> | Number of Days (d) | Total Minutes Read (30d) |
> |---|---|
> | 1 | 30 |
> | 2 | 60 |
> | 3 | 90 |
> | 4 | 120 |
> | 5 | 150 |
> | 6 | 180 |
> | 7 | 210 |
>
> Independent variable   _Number of Days_
>
> Dependent variable   _Total Minutes Read_

MP.1

- When setting up a table, we want the independent variable in the first column and the dependent variable in the second column.

- What do independent and dependent mean?

  □ *The independent variable changes, and when it does, it affects the dependent variable. So, the dependent variable "depends" on the independent variable.*

- In this example, which would be the independent variable and which would be the dependent variable?

  □ *The dependent variable is the total number of minutes read because it depends on how many days Marcus reads. The independent variable is the number of days that Marcus reads.*

- How could you use the table of values to determine the equation if it had not been given?

  □ *The number of minutes read shown in the table is always 30 times the number of days. So, the equation would need to show that the total number of minutes is equal to the number of days times 30.*

Example 2 (5 minutes)

Example 2

Kira designs websites. She can create three different websites each week. Kira wants to create an equation that will give her the total number of websites she can design given the number of weeks she works. Determine the independent and dependent variables. Create a table to show the number of websites she can design over the first 5 weeks. Finally, write an equation to represent the number of websites she can design when given any number of weeks.

Independent variable____# of weeks worked____

Dependent variable____# of websites designed____

# of Weeks Worked (w)	# of Websites Designed (d)
1	5
2	10
3	15
4	20
5	25

Equation____$d = 5w$, where w is the number of weeks worked and d is the number of websites designed____

- How did you determine which is the dependent variable and which is the independent variable?
    - *Because the number of websites she can make depends on how many weeks she works, I determined that the number of weeks was the independent variable and the number of websites designed was the dependent variable.*

- Does knowing which one is independent and which one is dependent help you write the equation?
    - *I can write the equation and solve for the dependent variable by knowing how the independent variable will affect the dependent variable. In this case, I knew that every week 5 more websites could be completed, so then I multiplied the number of weeks by 5.*

.1

Example 3 (5 minutes)

Example 3

Priya streams movies through a company that charges her a $5 monthly fee plus $1.50 per movie. Determine the independent and dependent variables, write an equation to model the situation, and create a table to show the total cost per month given that she might stream between 4 and 10 movies in a month.

Independent variable____# of movies watched per month____

Dependent variable____Total cost per month____

Equation____$c = 1.5m + 5$ or $c = 1.50m + 5$____

# of Movies (m)	Total Cost Per Month (c)
4	11
5	12.50
6	14
7	15.50
8	17
9	18.50
10	20

- Is the flat fee an independent variable, a dependent variable, or neither?
    - *The $5 flat fee is neither. It is not causing the change in the dependent value, and it is not changing. Instead, the $5 flat fee is a constant that is added on each month.*

- Why isn't the equation $c = 5m + 1.50$?
    - *The $5 fee is only paid once a month. m is the number of movies watched per month, so it needs to be multiplied by the price per movie, which is $1.50.*

Lesson 31: Problems in Mathematical Terms
Date: 12/16/13

Exercises 1–4 (15 minutes)

Students work in pairs or independently.

Exercises 1–4

1. Sarah is purchasing pencils to share. Each package has 12 pencils. The equation $n = 12p$, where n is the number of pencils and p is the number of packages can be used to determine the total number of pencils Sarah purchased. Determine which variable is dependent and which is independent. Then make a table showing the number of pencils purchased for 3–7 packages.

   p, the number of packages, is the independent variable.

   n, the total number of pencils, is the dependent variable.

# of Packages (p)	Total # of Pencils (n = 12p)
3	36
4	48
5	60
6	72
7	84

2. Charlotte reads 4 books each week. Let b be the number of books she reads each week and let w be the number of weeks that she reads. Determine which variable is dependent and which is independent. Then write an equation to model the situation, and make a graph that shows the number of books read in under 6 weeks.

   The number of weeks, w, is the independent variable.

   The number of books, b, is the dependent variable.

   $b = 4w$

# of Weeks (w)	# of Books (b = 4w)
1	4
2	8
3	12
4	16
5	20

3. A miniature golf course has a special group rate. You can pay $20 plus $3 per person when you have a group of 5 or more friends. Let f be the number of friends and c be the total cost. Determine which variable is independent and which is dependent, and write an equation that models the situation. Then make a table to show the cost for 5 to 12 friends.

   The number of friends, f, is the independent variable.

   The total cost, c, is the dependent variable.

   $c = 3f + 20$

# of Friends (f)	Total Cost (c = 3f + 20)
5	35
6	38
7	41
8	44
9	47
10	50
11	53
12	56

---

4. Carlos is shopping for school supplies. He bought a pencil box for $3, and he also needs to buy notebooks. Each notebook is $2. Let t = the total cost of the supplies and n be the number of notebooks. Determine which variable is independent and which is dependent, and write an equation that models the situation. Then make a table to show the cost for 1 to 5 notebooks.

The total number of notebooks, n, is the independent variable. $t = 2n + 3$

The total cost, t, is the dependent variable.

# of Notebooks (n)	Total Cost ($t = 2n + 3$)
1	5
2	7
3	9
4	11
5	13

Closing (5 minutes)

- Use this time for partners to share their tables with another set of partners.
- End class with a quick discussion of how the students determined which variable is independent and which is dependent.
  - *The dependent variable is affected by changes in the independent variable.*
  - *I can write a sentence that one variable depends on another. For example, the amount of money earned depends on the number of hours worked. So, the money earned is dependent and the number of hours worked is independent.*

Exit Ticket (5 minutes)

Name _____   Date _____

Lesson 31: Problems in Mathematical Terms

Exit Ticket

For each problem, determine the independent and dependent variables, write an equation to represent the situation, and then make a table with at least 5 values that models the situation.

1. Kyla spends 60 minutes of each day exercising. Let d be the number of days, and let m represent the total minutes of exercise in a given time frame. Show the relationship between the number of days and the total minutes of exercise.

Independent Variable _____

Dependent Variable _____

Equation _____

2. A taxi cab service charges a flat fee of $8 plus an additional $1.50 per mile. Show the relationship between the total cost and the number of miles driven.

Independent Variable _____

Dependent Variable _____

Equation _____

Exit Ticket Sample Solutions

For each problem, determine the independent and dependent variables, write an equation to represent the situation, and then make a table with at least 5 values that models the situation.

1. Kyla spends 60 minutes of each day exercising. Let d be the number of days, and let m represent the total minutes of exercise in a given time frame. Show the relationship between the number of days and the total number of minutes.

   Tables may vary.

# of Days	# of Minutes
0	0
1	60
2	120
3	180
4	240

   Independent Variable ___*Number of Days*___

   Dependent Variable ___*Total Number of Minutes*___

   Equation ___$m = 60d$___

2. A taxi cab service charges a flat fee of $8 plus an additional $1.50 per mile. Show the relationship between the total cost and the number of miles driven.

   Tables may vary.

# of Miles	Total Cost
0	8.00
1	9.50
2	11.00
3	12.50
4	14.00

   Independent Variable ___*Number of Miles*___

   Dependent Variable ___*Total Cost*___

   Equation ___$c = 1.50m + 8$___

Problem Set Sample Solutions

1. Jaziyah sells 3 houses each month. To determine the number of houses she can sell in any given number of months she uses the equation $t = 3m$, where t is the total number of houses sold and m is the number of months. Name the independent and dependent variables. Then create a table to show how many houses she sells in less than 6 months.

   The independent variable is the number of months. The dependent variable is the total number of houses sold.

# of Months	Total Number of Houses
1	3
2	6
3	9
4	12
5	15

2.   Joshua spends 25 minutes of each day reading. Let d be the number of days that he reads, and let m represent the total minutes of reading. Determine which variable is independent and which is dependent. Then write an equation that will model the situation. Make a table showing the number of minutes spent reading over 7 days.

The number of days (d) is the independent variable.

The total number of minutes of reading (m) is the dependent variable.

$m = 25d$

# of Days	# of Minutes
1	25
2	50
3	75
4	100
5	125
6	150
7	175

3.   Each package of hot dog buns contains 8 buns. Let p be the number of packages and b be the total number of buns. Determine which variable is independent and which is dependent. Then write an equation that will model the situation and make a table showing the number of hot dog buns in 3 to 8 packages.

The number of packages (p) is the independent variable.

The total number of hot dog buns (b) is the dependent variable.

$b = 8p$

# of Packages	Total # of Hot Dog Buns
3	24
4	32
5	40
6	48
7	56
8	64

4.   Emma was given 5 sea shells. Each week she collected 3 more. Let w be the number of weeks and s be the number of sea shells she has total. Which variable is independent and which is dependent? Write an equation to model the relationship, and make a table to show how many shells she has from week 4 to week 10.

The number of weeks (w) is the independent variable.

The total number of sea shells (s) is the dependent variable.

$S = 3w + 5$

# of Weeks	Total # of Sea Shells
4	17
5	20
6	23
7	26
8	29
9	32
10	35

5. Emilia is shopping for fresh produce at a farmer's market. She bought a watermelon for $5, and she also wants to buy peppers. Each pepper is $0.75. Let t = the total cost of the produce and n be the number of peppers bought. Determine which variable is independent and which is dependent, and write an equation that models the situation. Then make a table to show the cost for 1 to 5 peppers.

The number of peppers, n, is the independent variable. $t = 0.75n + 5$

The total cost, t, is the dependent variable.

# of Peppers (n)	Total Cost
1	5.75
2	6.50
3	7.25
4	8.00
5	8.75

6. A taxi cab service charges a flat fee of $7 plus an additional $1.25 per mile. Show the relationship between the total cost and the number of miles. Which variable is independent and which is dependent? Write an equation to model the relationship, and make a table to show the cost of 4 to 10 miles.

The number of miles, m, is the independent variable.

The cost, c, is the dependent variable.

$c = \$1.25m + 7$

# of Miles	Total Cost
4	$12
5	$13.25
6	$14.50
7	$15.75
8	$17
9	$18.25
10	$19.50

Lesson 32: Multi-Step Problems in the Real World

Student Outcomes

- Students analyze an equation in two variables, choose an independent variable and a dependent variable, make a table and make a graph for the equation by plotting the points in the table. For the graph, the independent variable is usually represented by the horizontal axis and the dependent variable is usually represented by the vertical axis.

Classwork

Opening Exercise (5 minutes)

Opening Exercise

Xin is buying beverages for a party which are individually packaged and come in packs of 8. Let p be the number of packages Xin buys and t be the total number of beverages. The equation $t = 8p$ can be used to calculate the total number of beverages when the number of packages is known. Determine the independent and dependent variable in this scenario. Then make a table using whole number values of p less than 6.

The independent variable is the number of packages. I know this because I can use the equation to determine the number of beverages. Therefore, the number of individual beverages depends on the number of packages purchased.

The dependent variable is the total number of beverages because this is affected by the number of packages changing.

# of Packages (p)	Total Number of Beverages ($t = 8p$)
0	0
1	8
2	16
3	24
4	32
5	40

Example 1 (7 minutes)

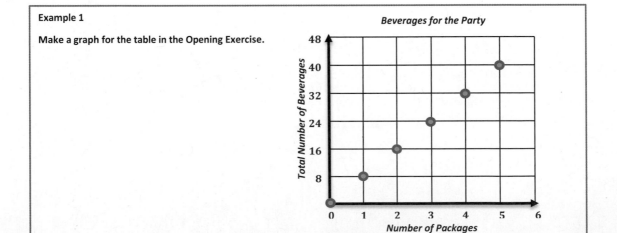

Example 1

Make a graph for the table in the Opening Exercise.

Beverages for the Party

- To make a graph, we must determine which variable is measured along the horizontal axis and which variable is measured along the vertical axis.
- Generally, the independent variable is measured along the x-axis. Which axis is the x-axis?
  - *The x-axis is the horizontal axis.*
- Where would you put the dependent variable?
  - *On the y-axis, it travels vertically, or up and down.*
- We want to show how the number of beverages changes when the number of packages changes. To check that you have set up your graph correctly, try making a sentence out of the labels on the axis. Write your sentence using the label from the y-axis first followed by the label from the x-axis. "The number of beverages depends on the number of packages purchased."

Example 2 (3 minutes)

Example 2

Use the graph to determine which variable is the independent variable and which is the dependent variable. Then state the relationship between the quantities represented by the variables.

The number of miles driven depends on how many hours they drive. Therefore, the number of miles is the dependent variable and the number of hours is the independent variable. This graph shows that they can travel 50 miles every hour. So, the total number of miles driven increases by 50 every time the number of hours increases by 1.

Exercises (20 minutes)

Students work individually.

Exercises

1. Each week Quentin earns $30. If he saves this money, create a graph that shows the total amount of money Quentin has saved from week 1 through week 8. Write an equation that represents the relationship between the number of weeks that Quentin has saved his money (w) and the total amount of money he has saved (s). Then name the independent and dependent variable. Write a sentence that shows this relationship.

$s = 30w$

s is the dependent variable and w is the independent variable.

# of Weeks	Total Saved ($)
1	30
2	60
3	90
4	120
5	150
6	180
7	210
8	240

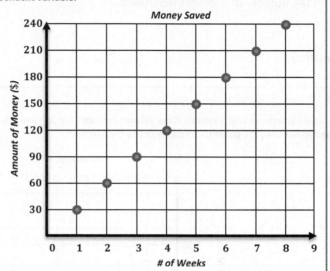

2. Zoe is collecting books to donate. She started with 3 and collects two more each week. She is using the equation $b = 2w + 3$, where b is the total number of books collected and w is the number of weeks she has been collecting. Name the independent and dependent variables. Then create a graph to represent how many books Zoe has collected when w is 5 or less.

The number of weeks is independent. The number of books collected is dependent.

# of Weeks	# of Books Collected
0	3
1	5
2	7
3	9
4	11
5	13

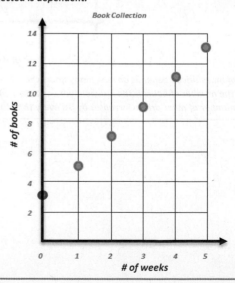

3. Eliana plans to visit the fair. She must pay $5 to enter the fair grounds and an additional $3 per ride. Write an equation to show the relationship between r, the number of rides, and t, the total cost. State which variable is dependent and which is independent. Then create a graph that models the equation.

$t = 3r + 5$

The number of rides is the independent variable and the total cost is the dependent variable.

# of Rides	Total Cost (in dollars)
0	5
1	8
2	11
3	14
4	17

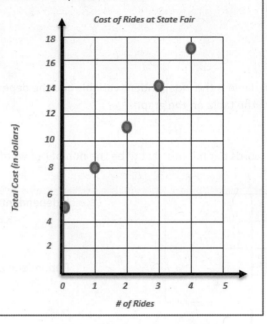

Closing (5 minutes)

- Imagine that you are helping a friend with his math work. Here is the problem he was solving:

Henry is taking a taxi cab home. The cab company charges an initial fee of $5 plus $2 for each additional mile. Henry uses the equation $t = 2m + 5$ to calculate the cost of the ride, where t is the total cost and m is the number of miles.

Your friend states that t is the dependent variable and m is the independent variable. Then the friend starts to sketch a graph.

- What would you tell your friend when looking over his/her work?

  □ *I would tell my friend that the dependent variable should go on the vertical axis. Then your graph will show that the total cost of the ride depends on how many miles you travel in the taxi cab.*

Exit Ticket (5 minutes)

Name _____   Date _____

Lesson 32: Multistep Problems in the Real World

Exit Ticket

Determine which variable is the independent variable and the dependent variable. Write an equation, make a table and plot the points from the table on the graph.

Enoch can type 40 words per minute. Let w be the number of words and m be the number of minutes.

Independent variable _____

Dependent variable _____

Equation _____

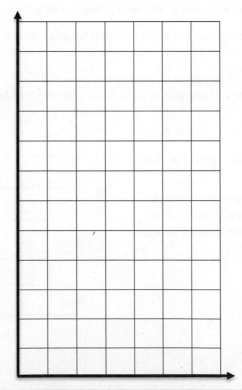

Exit Ticket Sample Solutions

Determine which variable is the independent variable and the dependent variable. Write an equation, make a table and plot the points from the table on the graph.

Enoch can type 40 words per minutes. Let w be the number of words and m be the number of minutes.

The independent variable is the number of minutes. The dependent variable is the number of words.

The equation is $w = 40m$.

# of Minutes	# of Words
0	0
1	40
2	80
3	120
4	160
5	200

Words typed per Minute

Problem Set Sample Solutions

1. Caleb started saving money in a cookie jar. He started with $\$25$. He adds $\$10$ to the account each week. Write an equation where w is the number of weeks and t is the total amount in the account. Determine which variable is independent and which is dependent. Then graph the total amount in the account for w being less than 6 weeks.

    $t = 10w + 25$

    t is the dependent variable.

    w is the independent variable.

# of Weeks	Total Amount in Account (in dollars)
0	25
1	35
2	45
3	55
4	65
5	75

Money in Savings Account

2. Kevin is taking a taxi from the airport to his home. There is a $6 flat fee for riding in the taxi. In addition, Kevin must also pay $1 per mile. Write an equation where m is the number of miles and t is the total cost of the taxi ride. Determine which variable is independent and which is dependent. Then graph the total cost for m being less than 6 miles.

$$t = 1m + 6$$

t is the dependent variable.

m is the independent variable.

# of Miles	Total Cost
0	6
1	7
2	8
3	9
4	10
5	11

Total Cost of a Taxi Ride

3. Anna started with $10. She saved an additional $5 each week. Write an equation that can be used to determine the total amount saved, t, after a given number of weeks, w. Determine which variable is independent and which is dependent. Then graph the total amount saved for first 8 weeks.

$$t = 5w + 10$$

t is the dependent variable.

w is the independent variable.

# of Weeks	Total Amount ($)
0	10
1	15
2	20
3	25
4	30
5	35
6	40
7	45
8	50

Total Amount Saved

4. Aliyah is purchasing produce at the farmers' market. She plans to buy $10 worth of potatoes and some apples. The apples cost $1.50 per pound. Write an equation to show the total cost of the produce, where T is the total cost and a is the number of pounds of apples. Determine which variable is dependent and independent. Then graph the equation on the coordinate plane.

$T = 1.50a + 10$

The total cost is the dependent variable. The number of pounds of apples is the independent variable.

# of Pounds of Apples	Total Cost ($)
0	10
1	11.50
2	13
3	14.50
4	16
5	17.50

Total Cost at the Farmers' Market

# of lb. of apples

Lesson 33: From Equations to Inequalities

Student Outcomes

- Students understand that an inequality with numerical expressions is either true or false. It is true if the numbers calculated on each side of the inequality sign result in a correct statement and false otherwise.
- Students understand solving an inequality is answering the question of which values from a specified set, if any, make the inequality true.

Classwork

Example 1 (8 minutes)

Students will review their work from Lesson 23 and use this throughout the lesson.

Example 1

What value(s) does the variable have to represent for the number sentence to be a true statement? What value(s) does the variable have to represent for the number sentence to be a false statement?

a. $y + 6 = 16$

   The number sentence is true when y is 10. The sentence is false when y is any number other than 10.

b. $y + 6 > 16$

   The number sentence is true when y is any number greater than 10. The sentence is false when y is 10 or any number less than 10.

c. $y + 6 \geq 16$

   The number sentence is true when y is 10 or any number greater than 10. The sentence is false when y is a number less than 10.

d. $3g = 15$

   The number sentence is true when g is 5. The number sentence is false when g is any number other than 5.

e. $3g < 15$

   The number sentence is true when g is any number less than 5. The number sentence is false when g is 5 or any number greater than 5.

f. $3g \leq 15$

   The number sentence is true when g is 5 or any number less than 5. The number sentence is false when g is any number greater than 5.

Example 2 (12 minutes)

Students move from naming the values that make the sentence true or false to using a set of numbers and determining whether or not the numbers in the set make the equation or inequality true or false.

Example 2

Which of the following numbers make the equation true? $\{0, 3, 5, 8, 10, 14\}$

    a. $m + 4 = 12$

         $m = 8$ *or* $\{8\}$

    b. $m + 4 < 12$

         $\{0, 3, 5\}$

- How does the answer to part (a) compare to the answer to part (b)?
  - *In part (a), 8 is the only number that will make the statement true. But in part (b), any number in the set that is less than 8 will make the statement true.*

---

    c. $f - 4 = 2$

        None of the numbers in the set will make a true sentence.

    d. $f - 4 > 2$

        $\{8, 10, 14\}$

- Is there a number that we could include in the set so that part (c) will have a solution?
  - *Yes, the number 6 will make the equation in part (c) true.*
- Would 6 be part of the solution set in part (d)?
  - *No, the 6 would not make part (d) a true statement because $6 - 4$ is not greater than 2.*
- How could we change part (d) so that 6 would be part of the solution?
  - *Answers will vary; If the $>$ was changed to a $\geq$, we could include 6 in the solution set.*

---

    e. $\frac{1}{2}h = 8$

        None of the numbers in the set will make the statement true.

    f. $\frac{1}{2}h \geq 8$

        None of the numbers in the set will make the statement true.

- Which whole numbers, if any, make the inequality true?
  - *Answers will vary; 16 and any number greater than 16 will make the number sentence true.*

Lesson 33:	From Equations to Inequalities
Date:	12/16/13

Exercises (16 minutes)

Students will practice either individually or in pairs.

Exercises

Choose the numbers that make the equation or inequality true from the following set of numbers: $\{0, 1, 5, 8, 11, 17\}$.

1. $m + 5 = 6$

    $m = 1 \text{ or } \{1\}$

2. $m + 5 \leq 6$

    $\{0, 1\}$

3. $5h = 40$

    $h = 8 \text{ or } \{8\}$

4. $5h > 40$

    $\{11, 17\}$

5. $\frac{1}{2}y = 5$

    There is no solution in the set.

6. $\frac{1}{2}y \leq 5$

    $\{0, 1, 5, 8\}$

7. $k - 3 = 20$

    There is no solution in the set.

8. $k - 3 > 20$

    There is no solution in the set.

Closing (3 minutes)

▪ In some of the equations and inequalities we worked within this lesson none of the numbers in the given set were solutions. What does this mean? Are there numbers that will make the statements true that are not in the set?

  □ *None of the numbers in the set made a true statement. There are numbers that could make the statement true. For example, in Exercise 5, $y = 10$ would make a true statement.*

▪ Is it possible for every number in a set to make a true statement?

  □ *Yes it is possible. For example, if the inequality says $x > 5$ and all the numbers in the set are greater than 5, then all the numbers in the set will make a true statement.*

Lesson 33:	From Equations to Inequalities
Date:	12/16/13

348

- Consider the equation $y + 3 = 11$ and the inequality $y + 3 < 11$. How does the solution to the equation help you determine the solution set to the inequality?

  □ *In the equation $y + 3 = 11$, $y = 8$ will make the statement true. In the inequality, we want $y + 3$ to be a value less than 11. So the numbers that will make it true must be less than 8.*

Exit Ticket (6 minutes)

Name _____   Date _____

Lesson 33: From Equations to Inequalities

Exit Ticket

Choose the numbers that make the equation or inequality true from the following set of numbers: $\{3, 4, 7, 9, 12, 18, 32\}$.

1. $\frac{1}{3}f = 4$

2. $\frac{1}{3}f < 4$

3. $m + 7 = 20$

4. $m + 7 \geq 20$

Exit Ticket Sample Solutions

Choose the numbers that make the equation or inequality true from the following set of numbers: $\{3, 4, 7, 9, 12, 18, 32\}$.

1. $\frac{1}{3}f = 4$

   $f = 12$ or $\{12\}$

2. $\frac{1}{3}f < 4$

   $\{3, 4, 7, 9\}$

3. $m + 7 = 20$

   There is no number in the set that will make this equation true.

4. $m + 7 \geq 20$

   $\{18, 32\}$

Problem Set Sample Solutions

Choose the numbers that make the equation or inequality true from the following set of numbers:
$\{0, 3, 4, 5, 9, 13, 18, 24\}$.

1. $h - 8 = 5$

   $h = 13$ or $\{13\}$

2. $h - 8 < 5$

   $\{0, 3, 4, 5, 9\}$

3. $4g = 36$

   $g - 9$ or $\{9\}$

4. $4g \geq 36$

   $\{9, 13, 18, 24\}$

5. $\frac{1}{4}y = 7$

   There is no number in the set that will make this equation true.

6. $\frac{1}{4}y > 7$

   There is no number in the set that will make this inequality true.

7. $m - 3 = 10$

   $m = 13$ or $\{13\}$

8. $m - 3 \leq 10$

   $\{0, 3, 4, 5, 9, 13\}$

Lesson 34: Writing and Graphing Inequalities in Real-World Problems

Student Outcomes

- Students recognize that inequalities of the form $x < c$ and $x > c$, where x is a variable and c is a fixed number have infinitely many solutions when the values of x come from a set of rational numbers.

Classwork

Example 1 (10 minutes)

Begin with a discussion of what each of these statements means. Have students share possible amounts of money that could fit the given statement to build towards a graph and an inequality.

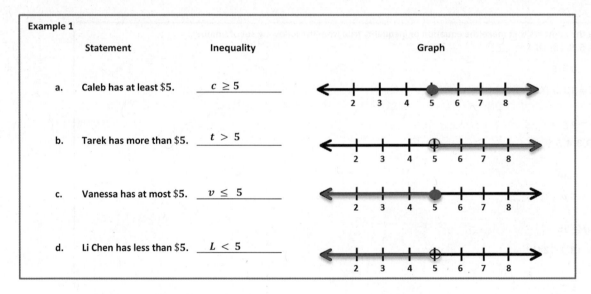

MP.4

- How much money could Caleb have?
  - □ *He could have $5, $5.01, $5.90, $6, $7, $8, $9.... More simply, he could have $5 or any number greater than 5.*
- How would we show this as an inequality?
  - □ $c \geq 5$, *where c is the amount of money that Caleb has in dollars.*
- What numbers on the graph do we need to show as a solution?
  - □ 5 *is a solution and everything to the right.*
- Because we want to include 5 in the solution we will draw a solid circle over the 5 and then an arrow to the right to show that all the numbers 5 and greater are part of the solution.

- How does the statement about Tarek differ from the statement about Caleb?
  - *Tarek has more than $5, but he can't have exactly 5, where Caleb might have had exactly 5.*
- So, how would we show this as an inequality?
  - *$t > 5$, where t is the amount of money Tarek has in dollars.*
- When we graph the inequality for Tarek, we still want a circle on the 5, but this time it won't be solid to show that 5 is not included in the solution.
- What does "at most" mean in Vanessa's example?
  - *Vanessa could have $5, but no more than 5. So, she could have less than 5, including 4, 3, 2, 1, 0 or even a negative amount if she owes someone money.*
- How would we write this as an inequality?
  - *$v \leq 5$, where v is the amount of money Vanessa has in dollars.*
- How would you show this on the graph?
  - *We would put a circle on the 5 and then an arrow towards the smaller numbers.*
- Would we have a solid or open circle?
  - *It would be solid to show that 5 is part of the solution.*
- Would the inequality and graph for Li Chen be the same as Vanessa's solution?
  - *No, they would be similar but not exactly the same. Li Chen cannot have $5 exactly. So the circle in the graph would be open and the inequality would be $L < 5$, where L represents the amount of money Li Chen has in dollars.*

Example 2 (5 minutes)

Example 2

Kelly works for Quick Oil Change. If customers have to wait longer than 20 minutes for the oil change, the company does not charge for the service. The fastest oil change that Kelly has ever done took 6 minutes. Show the possible customer wait times in which the company charges the customer.

$6 \leq x \leq 20$

- How is this example different than the problems in Example 1?
  - *This one is giving a range of possible values. The number of minutes he takes to change the oil should be somewhere between two values instead of greater than just one or less than just one.*
- Let's start with the first bit of information. What does the second sentence of the problem tell us about the wait times for paying customers?
  - *The oil change must take 20 minutes or less.*
- How would we show this on a number line?
  - *Because 20 minutes is part of the acceptable time limit, we will use a solid circle and shade to the left.*

- Now, let's look at the other piece of information. The fastest Kelly has ever completed the oil change is 6 minutes. What does this mean about the amount of time it will take?
  - □ *This means that it will take 6 minutes or more to complete an oil change.*
- How would we show this on a number line?
  - □ *Because 6 minutes is a possible amount of time, we will use a solid circle. Then we will shade to the right.*

- Now, we need to put both of these pieces of information together to make one model of the inequality.
- How could we show both of these on one number line?
  - □ *Instead of an arrow, we would have two circles and we would shade in between.*
- Should the circles be open or closed?
  - □ *Because he has to change the oil in 20 minutes or less, the 20 is part of the solution and the circle will be closed. The 6 minutes is also part of the solution because it is an actual time that Kelly has completed the work. The circle at 6 should also be closed.*

Example 3 (5 minutes)

MP.4

Example 3

Gurnaz has been mowing lawns to save money for a concert. Gurnaz will need to work for at least six hours to save enough money, but he must work less than 16 hours this week. Write an inequality to represent this situation, and then graph the solution.

$6 \le x < 16$

- How would we represent Gurnaz working at least six hours?
  - □ *"At least" tells us that Gurnaz must work 6 hours or more.*
  - □ $x \ge 6$

- What inequality would we use to show that he must work less than 16 hours?
  - □ *Less than means that Gurnaz cannot actually work 16 hours. So, we will use $x < 16$.*

Exercises 1–5 (15 minutes)

Students work individually.

Exercises 1–5

Write an inequality to represent each situation. Then graph the solution.

1. Blayton is at most 2 meters above sea level.

   $b \leq 2$, where b is Blayton's position in relationship to sea level in meters.

2. Edith must read for a minimum of 20 minutes.

   $E \geq 20$, where E is the number of minutes Edith reads.

3. Travis milks his cows each morning. He has never gotten less than 3 gallons of milk; however, he always gets less than 9 gallons of milk.

   $3 \leq x < 9$

4. Rita can make 8 cakes for a bakery each day. So far she has orders for more than 32 cakes. Right now, Rita needs more than four days to make all 32 cakes.

   $x > 4$, where x is the number of days Rita has to bake the cakes.

5. Rita must have all the orders placed right now done in 7 days or less. How will this change your inequality and your graph?

   $4 < x \leq 7$

Possible Extension

The following problems combine the skills used to solve equations in previous lessons within this module and inequalities.

---

6. Kasey has been mowing lawns to save up money for a concert. He earns $15 per hour and needs at least $90 to go to the concert. How many hours should he mow?

   $$15x \geq 90$$
   $$\frac{15x}{15} \geq \frac{90}{15}$$
   $$x \geq 6$$

   Kasey will need to mow for 6 or more hours.

---

7. Rachel can make 8 cakes for a bakery each day. So far she has orders for more than 32 cakes. How many days will it take her to complete the orders?

$8x > 32$
$\dfrac{8x}{8} > \dfrac{32}{8}$
$x > 4$

Rachel will need to work more than 4 days.

3. Ranger saves $70 each week. He needs to save at least $2,800 to go on a trip to Europe. How many weeks will he need to save?

$70x \geq 2,800$
$\dfrac{70x}{70} \geq \dfrac{2,800}{70}$
$x \geq 40$

Ranger needs to save for at least 40 weeks.

4. Clara has less than $75. She wants to buy 3 pairs of shoes. What price shoes can Clara afford if all the shoes are the same price?

$3x < 75$
$\dfrac{3x}{3} < \dfrac{75}{3}$
$x < 25$

Clara can afford shoes that are greater than $0 and less than $25.

5. A gym charges $25 per month plus $4 extra to swim in the pool for an hour. If a member only has $45 to spend each month, at most how many hours can the member swim?

$4x + 25 \leq 45$
$4x + 25 - 25 \leq 45 - 25$
$4x \leq 20$
$\dfrac{4x}{4} \leq \dfrac{20}{4}$
$x \leq 5$

The member can swim in the pool for 5 hours. However, we also know that the total amount of time the member spends in the pool must be greater than or equal to 0 hours.

$0 \leq x \leq 5$

Closing (5 minutes)

▪ How are inequalities different from equations?

☐ *Inequalities can have a range of possible values that make the statement true, where equations do not.*

▪ Does the phrase "at most" refer to being less than or greater than something? Give an example to support your answer.

☐ *At most means that you can have that amount or less than that amount. You cannot go over. My mom says that I can watch at most 1 TV show after I do my homework. This means that I can watch 1 or less than 1 TV show.*

Exit Ticket (5 minutes)

Name _____ Date _____

Lesson 34: Writing and Graphing Inequalities in Real-World Problems

Exit Ticket

For each question, write an inequality. Then graph your solution.

1. Keisha needs to make at least 28 costumes for the school play. Since she can make four costumes each week, Keisha plans on working on the costumes for at least 7 weeks.

2. If Keisha has to have the costumes complete in 10 weeks or less, how will our solution change?

Exit Ticket Sample Solutions

1. Keisha needs to make at least 28 costumes for the school play. Since she can make four costumes each week, Keisha plans on working on the costumes for at least 7 weeks.

   $x \geq 7$

   Keisha should plan on working on the costumes for 7 or more weeks.

2. If Keisha has to have the costumes complete in 10 weeks or less, how will our solution change?

   Keisha had 7 or more weeks in problem 1. It will still take her at least 7 weeks, but she cannot have more than 10 weeks.

   $7 \leq x \leq 10$

Problem Set Sample Solutions

Write and graph an inequality for each problem.

1. At least 13.

   $x \geq 13$

2. Less than 7.

   $x < 7$

3. Chad will need at least 24 minutes to complete the 5K race. However, he wants to finish in under 30 minutes.

   $24 \leq x < 30$

4. Eva saves \$60 each week. Since she needs to save at least \$2,400 to go on a trip to Europe, she will need to save for at least 40 weeks.

   $x \geq 40$

5.   Clara has $100. She wants to buy 4 pairs of the same pants. Due to tax, Clara can afford pants that are less than $25.

     $0 < x < 25$

6.   A gym charges $30 per month plus $4 extra to swim in the pool for an hour. Because a member has just $50 to spend at the gym each month, the member can swim 5 hours at most.

     The member can swim in the pool for 5 hours. However, we also know that the total amount of time the member spends in the pool must be greater than or equal to 0 hours.

     $0 \leq x \leq 5$

Name _____   Date _____

1. Gertrude is deciding which cell phone plan is the best deal for her to buy. Super Cell charges a monthly fee of $10 and also charges $0.15 per call. She makes a note that the equation is $M = 0.15\,C + 10$, where M is the monthly charge and C is the number of calls placed. Global Cellular has a plan with no monthly fee, but charges $0.25 per call. She makes a note that the equation is $M = 0.25\,C$, where M is the monthly charge and C is the number of calls placed. Both companies offer unlimited text messages.

   a. Make a table for both companies showing the cost of service, M, for making from 0 to 200 calls per month. Use multiples of 20.

Number of Calls, C	Super Cell $M = 0.15C + 10$	Global Cellular $M = 0.25C$

   b. Construct a graph for the two equations on the same graph. Use the number of calls, C, as the independent variable, and the monthly charge, M, as the dependent variable.

    c.   Which cell phone plan is the best deal for Gertrude? Defend your answer with specific examples.

2.   Sadie is saving her money to buy a new pony, which costs \$600. She has already saved \$75. She earns \$50 per week working at the stables and wonders how many weeks it will take to earn enough for a pony of her own.

    a.   Make a table showing the week number, W, and total savings, S, in Sadie's savings account.

Number of Weeks												
Total Savings												

    b.   Show the relationship between the number of weeks and Sadie's savings using an expression.

    c.   How many weeks will Sadie have to work to earn enough to buy the pony?

3. The elevator at the local mall has a weight limit of 1,800 pounds and requires that the maximum person allowance be no more than nine people.

    a.   Let x represent the number of people. Write an inequality to describe the maximum allowance of people allowed in the elevator at one time.

    b.   Draw a number line diagram to represent all possible solutions to part (a).

    c.   Let w represent the amount of weight. Write an inequality to describe the maximum weight allowance in the elevator at one time.

    d.   Draw a number line diagram to represent all possible solutions to part (c).

4. Devin's football team carpools for practice every week. This week is his parents' turn to pick up team members and take them to the football field. While still staying on the roads, Devin's parents always take the shortest route in order to save gasoline. Below is a map of their travels. Each gridline represents a street and the same distance.

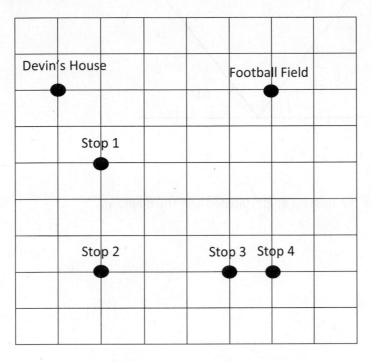

Devin's father checks his mileage and notices that he drove 18 miles between his house and Stop 3.

a. Create an equation and determine the amount of miles each gridline represents.

b. Using this information, determine how many total miles Devin's father will travel from home to the football field, assuming he made every stop. Explain how you determined the answer.

c. At the end of practice, Devin's father dropped off team members at each stop and went back home. How many miles did Devin's father travel altogether?

5. For a science experiment, Kenneth reflects a beam off a mirror. He is measuring the missing angle created when the light reflects off the mirror. (Note: figure is not drawn to scale.)

Use an equation to determine the missing angle, labeled x in the diagram.

A Progression Toward Mastery

Assessment Task Item		STEP 1 Missing or incorrect answer and little evidence of reasoning or application of mathematics to solve the problem.	STEP 2 Missing or incorrect answer but evidence of some reasoning or application of mathematics to solve the problem.	STEP 3 A correct answer with some evidence of reasoning or application of mathematics to solve the problem, <u>or</u> an incorrect answer with substantial evidence of solid reasoning or application of mathematics to solve the problem.	STEP 4 A correct answer supported by substantial evidence of solid reasoning or application of mathematics to solve the problem.
1	a 6.EE.9	Student is not able to make a table with multiples of 20 calls or cannot calculate monthly charge based on number of calls.	A table is drawn showing the number of calls and company/equation, but neither column is accurately calculated.	A table is drawn showing the number of calls and company/equation. One column is accurately calculated, but the other has errors.	Both tables are calculated accurately. Columns (or rows) are labeled clearly, including the equation.
	b 6.EE.9	Student is not able to draw a graph from the data in the table.	An attempt is made to graph the points from the table. Several mistakes or omissions are present.	A graph is drawn with minor mistakes or omissions. It includes at least three of the four criteria of a perfect graph.	The graph is drawn without error (i.e., graph is titled, axes labeled, units included on axes, and points plotted accurately).
	c 6.EE.9	Student cannot conclude which plan is better or chooses a plan without evidentiary support.	Student chooses one plan or the other, showing support for that plan. Student does not recognize that the best deal depends on the number of calls placed.	Student concludes that the best deal depends on the number of calls placed in a month. Complete analysis is not described.	Student concludes that the best deal depends on the number of calls placed in a month. The break-even point, 100 calls costing $25, is identified. Answer specifically states that Super Cell is the better deal if the number of calls per month is < 100, and Global Cellular is a better deal if the number of calls per month is > 100.

2	**a** **6.EE.9**	Student is not able to make a table or attempts to make the table but has many errors.	Student is able to make the table and calculate most rows accurately. Compounding errors may be present. Titles or variables might be missing.	Student accurately makes the table and accurately computes the total savings for each week. Titles or variables might be missing. OR Student begins with 50 and 75 every week.	Student accurately makes the table and accurately computes the total savings for each week. Titles and variables are present.
	b **6.EE.9**	Student is not able to write the expression.	Student attempts to write the expression, but is inaccurate (perhaps writing $75W + 50$).	Student writes the expression $50W + 75$.	Student accurately writes the expression $50W + 75$ and includes a description of what the variable represents.
	c **6.EE.9**	Student cannot make a conclusion about how many weeks are needed for the purchase or an answer is provided that is not supported by the student's table.	Student concludes that some number of weeks other than 11 weeks will be needed for the purchase.	Student concludes that 11 weeks of work will be needed for the purchase.	Student concludes that 11 weeks of work will be needed for the purchase and that Sadie will have $625, which is $25 more than the cost of the pony.
3	**a** **6.EE.8**	Student does not write an inequality or tries writing the inequality with incorrect information (e.g., 1,800).	Student writes the inequality $x \geq 9$ or $x > 9$.	Student writes the inequality $x < 9$ because student does not realize there can be nine people on the elevator.	Student writes the inequality $0 \leq x \leq 9$.
	b **6.EE.9**	Student does not draw a number line or draws a line but does not indicate $0 \leq x \leq 9$.	Student draws an accurate number line and uses either a line segment or discrete symbols, but does not include 0 and/or 9 in the solution set.	Student draws a number line but uses a line segment to indicate continuous points $0 \leq x \leq 9$.	Student draws an accurate number line, using discrete symbols indicating whole numbers from 0 to 9.
	c **6.EE.8**	Student does not write an inequality or tries writing the inequality with incorrect information (e.g., 9).	Student writes the inequality $W \geq 1,800$, or $W > 1,800$.	Student writes the inequality $W < 1,800$ because student does not realize there can be 1,800 pounds on the elevator.	Student writes the inequality $0 \leq W \leq 1,800$.
	d **6.EE.9**	Student does not draw a number line or draws a line but does not indicate $0 \leq W \leq 1,800$.	Student draws an accurate number line and uses either a line segment or discrete symbols, but does not include 0 and/or 1,800 in the solution set.	Student draws a number line but uses discrete symbols indicating whole numbers from 0 to 1,800 are in the solution set $0 \leq W \leq 1,800$.	Student draws an accurate number line, using a line segment indicating all numbers from 0 to 1,800 are in the solution set $0 \leq W \leq 1,800$.

4	**a** **6.EE.7** **6.EE.9**	Student is unable to create an equation and is unable to determine the amount of miles Devin's father traveled between their house and Stop 3.	Student is able to determine the amount of miles Devin's father traveled between their house and Stop 3, but does not write an equation.	Student creates an equation, $9G = 18$ miles, but does not use the equation to determine the amount of miles Devin's father traveled between their house and Stop 3.	Student creates an equation and uses it to determine the amount of miles Devin's father traveled between their house and Stop 3. Let $G =$ the number of gridlines passed on the map. $$9G = 18 \; miles$$ $$\frac{G}{9} = \frac{18 \; miles}{9}$$ $$G = 2 \; miles$$
	b **6.EE.2.c**	Student does not describe how the answer was derived or leaves the answer blank.	Student determines the correct distance (30 miles), but does not explain how the answer was determined or offers an incomplete explanation.	Student counts some number other than 15, but accurately applies the equation with the incorrect count. Explanation is correct and clear.	Student answer includes accurately counting the intersections passed (15) and applies that to the correct equation: $15 \cdot 2 \; miles = 30 \; miles.$
	c **6.EE.9**	Student answer does not indicate a concept of round-trip distance being double that of a one-way trip.	Student does not double the answer for part (b) or doubles the number incorrectly.	Student does not use the information from part (b), but counts the blocks for the round-trip.	Student correctly uses the expression to double the correct one-way trip distance (30 miles) to arrive at the correct round-trip distance (60 miles).
5	**6.EE.9**	Student does not show any of the steps necessary to solve the problem or simply answered 51°.	Student adds ° + 51° to arrive at 102°, but does not subtract this from 180°.	Student correctly finds the missing angle, 78°, showing clearly the steps involved, but does not use an equation. <u>OR</u> Student makes an arithmetic error, but clear evidence of conceptual understanding is evident.	Student correctly finds the missing angle, 78°, by using an equation and showing clearly the steps involved. The student might reference the term "supplementary angles," or start with $51° + 51° + x° = 180°$ before solving it correctly.

Name _____   Date _____

1. Gertrude is deciding which cell phone plan is the best deal for her to buy. Super Cell charges a monthly fee of $10 and also charges $0.15 per call. She makes a note that the equation is $M = 0.15C + 10$, where M is the monthly charge and C is the number of calls placed. Global Cellular has a plan with no monthly fee, but charges $0.25 per call. She makes a note that the equation is $M = 0.25C$, where M is the monthly charge and C is the number of calls placed. Both companies offer unlimited text messages.

    a. Make a table for both companies showing the cost of service, M, for making from 0 to 200 calls per month. Use multiples of 20.

Number of calls, C	Super Cell M=0.15C+10	Global Cellular M=0.25C
0	$10.00	$0.00
20	$13.00	$5.00
40	$16.00	$10.00
60	$19.00	$15.00
80	$22.00	$20.00
100	$25.00	$25.00
120	$28.00	$30.00
140	$31.00	$35.00
160	$34.00	$40.00
180	$37.00	$45.00
200	$40.00	$50.00

    b. Construct a graph for the two equations on the same graph. Use the number of calls, C, as the independent variable and the monthly charge, M, as the dependent variable.

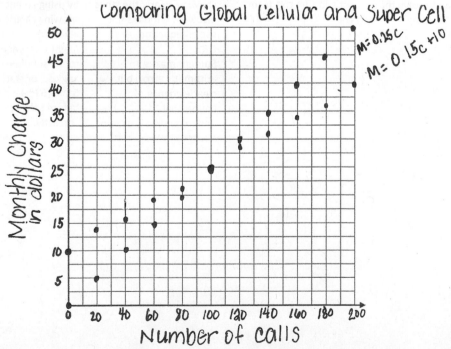

c.   Which cell phone plan is the best deal for Gertrude? Defend your answer with specific examples.

The best deal depends on the number of calls placed in a month. The break even point is 100 calls per month. Super Cell is a better deal if the number of monthly calls is less than 100. Global Cellular is a better deal if the number of monthly calls is greater than 100.

2.   Sadie is saving her money to buy a new pony, which costs $600. She has already saved $75. She earns $50 per week working at the stables and wonders how many weeks it will take to earn enough for a pony of her own.

a.   Make a table showing the week number, W, and total savings, S, in Sadie's savings account.

Number of Weeks	1	2	3	4	5	6	7	8	9	10	11	12
Total Savings	125	175	225	275	325	375	425	475	525	575	625	675

b.   Show the relationship between the number of weeks and Sadie's savings using an expression.

$$50w + 75$$

c.   How many weeks will Sadie have to work to earn enough to buy the pony?

If Sadie works 11 weeks, she will earn $625, which is $25 more than the cost of the pony.

3. The elevator at the local mall has a weight limit of 1,800 pounds and requires that the maximum person allowance be no more than nine people.

   a. Let x represent the number of people. Write an inequality to describe the maximum allowance of people allowed in the elevator at one time.

$$0 \leq x \leq 9$$

   b. Draw a number line diagram to represent all possible solutions to part (a).

   c. Let w represent the amount of weight. Write an inequality to describe the maximum weight allowance in the elevator at one time.

$$0 \leq w \leq 1,800$$

   d. Draw a number line diagram to represent all possible solutions to part (c).

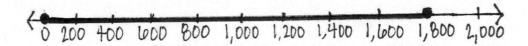

4. Devin's football team carpools for practice every week. This week is his parents' turn to pick up team members and take them to the football field. While still staying on the roads, Devin's parents always take the shortest route in order to save gasoline. Below is a map of their travels. Each gridline represents a street and the same distance.

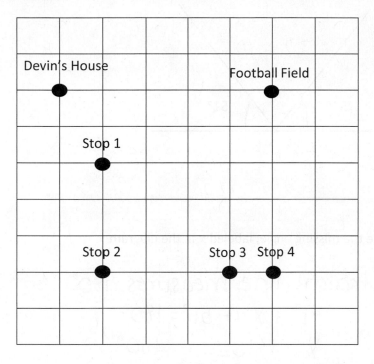

Devin's father checks his mileage and notices that he drove 18 miles between his house and Stop 3.

a. Create an equation and determine the amount of miles each gridline represents.

   Let C represent the number of gridlines passed on the map. $9G = 18$ $\dfrac{9G}{9} = \dfrac{18}{9}$ $G = 2\ miles.$

b. Using this information, determine how many total miles Devin's father will travel from home to the football field, assuming he made every stop. Explain how you determined the answer.

   $15\,G = miles$
   $15\,(2\,miles) = 30\,miles$

c. At the end of practice, Devin's father dropped off team members at each stop and went back home. How many miles did Devin's father travel altogether?

   $30\,G = miles$
   $30\,(2\,miles) = 60\,miles$

5. For a science experiment, Kenneth reflects a beam off a mirror. He is measuring the missing angle created when the light reflects off the mirror. (Note: figure is not drawn to scale.)

Use an equation to determine the missing angle, labeled x in the diagram.

A straight line measures 180°.

$$51° + x° + 51° = 180°$$

$$x° + 102° = 180°$$

$$x° + 102° - 102° = 180° - 102°$$

$$x° = 78°$$

Student Materials

Lesson 1: The Relationship of Addition and Subtraction

Classwork

Opening Exercise

a. Draw a tape diagram to represent the following expression: $5 + 4$.

b. Write an expression for each tape diagram.

    i.

    ii.

Exercises

1. Predict what will happen when a tape diagram has a large number of squares, some squares are removed, but then the same amount of squares are added back on.

2. Build a tape diagram with 10 squares.

    a. Remove 6 of them. Write an expression to represent the tape diagram.

    b. Add 6 squares onto the tape diagram. Alter the original expression to represent the current tape diagram.

    c. Evaluate the expression.

	Lesson 1:	The Relationship of Addition and Subtraction
	Date:	12/11/13

S.1

3. Write a number sentence, using variables, to represent the identities we demonstrated with tape diagrams.

4. Using your knowledge of identities, fill in each of the blanks.

    a. $4 + 5 -$ _____ $= 4$

    b. $25 -$ _____ $+ 10 = 25$

    c. _____ $+16 - 16 = 45$

    d. $56 - 20 + 20 =$ _____

5. Using your knowledge of identities, fill in each of the blanks.

    a. $a + b -$ _____ $= a$

    b. $c - d + d =$ _____

    c. $e +$ _____ $-f = e$

    d. _____ $-h + h = g$

Problem Set

1. Fill in each blank

   a. _____ $+ 15 - 15 = 21$

   b. $450 - 230 + 230 =$_____

   c. $1289 -$ _____ $+ 856 = 1289$

2. Why are the number sentences $w - x + x = w$ and $w + x - x = w$ called identities?

COMMON CORE™

Lesson 1:   The Relationship of Addition and Subtraction
Date: 12/11/13

S.3

Lesson 2: The Relationship of Multiplication and Division

Classwork

Opening Exercise

Draw a pictorial representation of the division and multiplication problems using a tape diagram.

a. $8 \div 2$

b. 3×2

Exploratory Challenge

Work in pairs or small groups to determine number sentences to show the relationship between multiplication and division. Use tape diagrams to provide support for your findings.

1. Create two number sentences to show the relationship between multiplication and division. These number sentences should be identities and include variables. Use the squares to develop these number sentences.

2. Write your number sentences on large paper. Show a series of tape diagrams to defend each of your number sentences.

Use the following rubric to critique other posters.

1. Name of group you are critiquing.

2. Number sentence you are critiquing.

3. Whether or not you believe their number sentences are true and reasons why.

Problem Set

1. Fill in each blank.

    a. $132 \div 3 \times 3 = \underline{\hspace{2em}}$

    b. $\underline{\hspace{2em}} \div 25 \times 25 = 225$

    c. $56 \times \underline{\hspace{2em}} \div 8 = 56$

    d. $452 \times 12 \div \underline{\hspace{2em}} = 452$

2. How are the relationships of addition and subtraction similar to the relationship of multiplication and division?

Lesson 3: The Relationship of Multiplication and Addition

Classwork

Opening Exercise

Write two different expressions that can be depicted by the tape diagram shown. One expression should include addition, while the other should include multiplication.

a.

b.

c.

Exercises

1. Write the addition sentence that describes the model and the multiplication sentence that describes the model.

COMMON CORE™

Lesson 3:
Date:

The Relationship of Multiplication and Addition
12/11/13

S.6

2. Write an equivalent expression to demonstrate the relationship of multiplication and addition.

    a. $6 + 6$

    b. $3 + 3 + 3 + 3 + 3 + 3$

    c. $4 + 4 + 4 + 4 + 4$

    d. 6×2

    e. 4×6

    f. 3×9

    g. $h + h + h + h + h$

    h. $6y$

3. Roberto is not familiar with tape diagrams and believes that he can show the relationship of multiplication and addition on a number line. Help Roberto demonstrate that the expression 3×2 is equivalent to $2 + 2 + 2$ on a number line.

4. Tell whether the following number sentences are true or false. Then explain your reasoning.

   a. $x + 6g - 6g = x$

   b. $2f - 4e + 4e = 2f$

5. Write an equivalent expression to demonstrate the relationship between addition and multiplication.

   a. $6 + 6 + 6 + 6 + 4 + 4 + 4$

   b. $d + d + d + w + w + w + w + w$

   c. $a + a + b + b + b + c + c + c + c$

Problem Set

Write an equivalent expression to show the relationship of multiplication and addition.

1. $10 + 10 + 10$

2. $4 + 4 + 4 + 4 + 4 + 4 + 4$

3. 8×2

4. 3×9

5. $6m$

6. $d + d + d + d + d$

Lesson 4: The Relationship of Division and Subtraction

Classwork

Exercise 1

Build subtraction expressions using the indicated equations. The first example has been completed for you.

Division Equation	Divisor Indicates the Size of the Unit	Tape Diagram	What is x, y, z?
$12 \div x = 4$	$12 - x - x - x - x = 0$	$12 - 3 - 3 - 3 - 3 = 0; x = 3$ *units in each group*	$x = 3$
$18 \div x = 3$			
$35 \div y = 5$			
$42 \div z = 6$			

Division Equation	Divisor Indicates the Number of Units	Tape Diagram	What is x, y, z?
$12 \div x = 4$	$12 - 4 - 4 - 4 = 0$	$12 - 4 - 4 - 4 = 0; x = 3$ *groups*	$x = 3$
$18 \div x = 3$			
$35 \div y = 5$			
$42 \div z = 6$			

Exercise 2

Answer each question using what you have learned about the relationship of division and subtraction.

a.   If $12 \div x = 3$, how many times would x have to be subtracted from 12 in order for the answer to be zero? What is the value of x?

b. $36 - f - f - f - f = 0$. Write a division sentence for this repeated subtraction sentence. What is the value of f?

c.   If $24 \div b = 12$, which number is being subtracted twelve times in order for the answer to be zero?

Problem Set

Build subtraction expressions using the indicated equations.

	Division Equation	Divisor Indicates the Size of the Unit	Tape Diagram	What is x, y, z?
1.	$24 \div x = 4$			
2.	$36 \div x = 6$			
3.	$28 \div y = 7$			
4.	$30 \div y = 5$			
5.	$16 \div z = 4$			

	Division Equation	Divisor Indicates the Number of Units	Tape Diagram	What is x, y, z?
1.	$24 \div x = 4$			
2.	$36 \div x = 6$			
3.	$28 \div y = 7$			
4.	$30 \div y = 5$			
5.	$16 \div z = 4$			

Lesson 5: Exponents

Opening Exercise

As you evaluate these expressions, pay attention to how you arrived at your answers.

$4 + 4 + 4 + 4 + 4 + 4 + 4 + 4 + 4 + 4$

$9 + 9 + 9 + 9 + 9$

$10 + 10 + 10 + 10 + 10$

Examples 1–5

1. $5 \times 5 \times 5 \times 5 \times 5 =$

2. $2 \times 2 \times 2 \times 2 =$

3. $8^3 =$

4. $10^6 =$

5. $g^3 =$

Go back to Examples 1 – 4 and use a calculator to evaluate the expressions.

What is the difference between $3g$ and g^3?

Examples 6–8

6. $3.8^4 =$

7. $2.1 \times 2.1 =$

8. $0.75 \times 0.75 \times 0.75 =$

The base number can also be a fraction. Convert the decimals to fractions in Examples 7 and 8 and evaluate. Leave your answer as a fraction. Remember how to multiply fractions!

Examples 9–10

9. $\frac{1}{2} \times \frac{1}{2} \times \frac{1}{2} =$

10. $\left(\frac{2}{3}\right)^2 =$

Exercises

Fill in the chart, supplying the missing expression.

1. Fill in the missing expression for each row. For whole number and decimal bases, use a calculator to find the standard form of the number. For fraction bases, leave your answer as a fraction.

Exponential Form	Written as a Multiplication Expression Having Repeated Factors	Standard Form
3^2	3×3	9
	$2 \times 2 \times 2 \times 2 \times 2 \times 2$	
4^5		
	$\dfrac{3}{4} \times \dfrac{3}{4}$	
	1.5×1.5	

2. Write "five cubed" in all three forms (exponential form, written as a series of products, standard form)

3. Write "fourteen and seven tenths squared" in all three forms.

4. One student thought two to the third power was equal to six. What mistake do you think they made and how would you help them fix their mistake?

Lesson Summary

Exponential Notation for Whole Number Exponents: Let m be a non-zero whole number. For any number a, the expression a^m is the product of m factors of a, i.e.,

$$a^m = \underbrace{a \cdot a \cdots \cdot a}_{m\ times}.$$

The number a is called the *base*, and m is called the *exponent* or *power* of a.

When m is 1, "the product of one factor of a" just means a, i.e., $a^1 = a$. Raising any non-zero number a to the power of 0 is defined to be 1, i.e., $a^0 = 1$ for all $a \neq 0$.

Problem Set

1. Complete the table by filling in the blank cells. Use a calculator when needed.

Exponential Form	Written as a Series of Products	Standard Form
3^5		
	$4 \times 4 \times 4$	
1.9^2		
$\left(\dfrac{1}{2}\right)^5$		

2. Why do whole numbers raised to an exponent get greater while fractions raised to an exponent get smaller?

3. The powers of 2 that are in the range 2 through 1,000 are 2, 4, 8, 16, 32, 64, 128, 256, and 512. Find all the powers of 3 that are in the range 3 through 1,000.

4. Find all the powers of 4 in the range 4 through 1,000.

5. Write an equivalent expression for $n \times a$ using only addition.

6. Write an equivalent expression for w^b using only multiplication.

    a. Explain what w is in this new expression.

    b. Explain what b is in this new expression.

7. What are the advantages to using exponential notation?

8. What is the difference between $4x$ and x^4? Evaluate both of these expressions when $x = 2$.

COMMON CORE™ | Lesson 5:   Exponents
Date: 12/11/13

S.16

Lesson 6: Order of Operations

Classwork

Example 1: Expressions with Only Addition, Subtraction, Multiplication, and Division

What operations are evaluated first?

What operations are always evaluated last?

Exercises

1. $4 + 2 \times 7$

2. $36 \div 3 \times 4$

3. $20 - 5 \times 2$

Example 2: Expressions with Four Operations and Exponents

$$4 + 9^2 \div 3 \times 2 - 2$$

What operation is evaluated first?

What operations are evaluated next?

What operations are always evaluated last?

What is the final answer?

Exercises

4. $90 - 5^2 \times 3$

5. $4^3 + 2 \times 8$

Example 3: Expressions with Parentheses

Consider a family of 4 that goes to a soccer game. Tickets are $5.00 each. The mom also buys a soft drink for $2.00. How would you write this expression?

How much will this outing cost?

Consider a different scenario: the family goes to the game like before, but each of the family members wants a drink. How would you write this expression?

Why would you add the 5 and 2 first?

How much will this outing cost?

How many groups are there?

What is each group comprised of?

Exercises

6. $2 + (9^2 - 4)$

7. $2 \cdot \left(13 + 5 - 14 \div (3 + 4)\right)$

Example 4: Expressions with Parentheses and Exponents

$$2 \times (3 + 4^2)$$

Which value will we evaluate first within the parentheses? Evaluate.

Evaluate the rest of the expression.

What do you think will happen when the exponent in this expression is outside of the parentheses?

$$2 \times (3 + 4)^2$$

Will the answer be the same?

Which should we evaluate first? Evaluate.

What happens differently here than in our last example?

What should our next step be?

Evaluate to find the final answer.

What do you notice about the two answers?

What was different between the two expressions?

What conclusions can you draw about evaluating expressions with parentheses and exponents?

Exercises

8. $7 + (12 - 3^2)$

9. $7 + (12 - 3)^2$

Lesson Summary

Numerical Expression: A *numerical expression* is a number, or it is any combination of sums, differences, products or divisions of numbers that evaluates to a number.

Statements like, "3 +" or "3 ÷ 0," are not numerical expressions because neither represents a point on the number line. Note: raising numbers to whole number powers are considered numerical expressions as well, since the operation is just an abbreviated form of multiplication: $2^3 = 2 \cdot 2 \cdot 2$.

Value of a Numerical Expression: The *value* of a numerical expression is the number found by evaluating the expression.

For example: $\frac{1}{3} \cdot (2 + 4) + 7$ is a numerical expression and its value is 9.

Problem Set

Evaluate each expression.

1. $3 \times 5 + 2 \times 8 + 2$

2. $(\$1.75 + 2 \times \$0.25 + 5 \times \$0.05) \times 24$

3. $(2 \times 6) + (8 \times 4) + 1$

4. $\big((8 \times 1.95) + (3 \times 2.95) + 10.95\big) \times 1.06$

5. $\big((12 \div 3)^2 - (18 \div 3^2)\big) \times (4 \div 2)$

Lesson 7: Replacing Letters with Numbers

Classwork

Example 1

What is the length of one side of this square?

What is the formula for the area of a square?

What is the square's area as a multiplication expression?

What is the square's area?

We can count the units. However, look at this other square. Its side length is 23 cm. That is just too many tiny units to draw. What expression can we build to find this square's area?

23 cm

What is the area of the square? Use a calculator if you need to.

Exercise 1

Complete the table below for both squares. Note: These drawings are not to scale.

$s = 4$

$s = 25$ in.

Length of One Side of the Square	Square's Area Written as an Expression	Square's Area Written as a Number

Example 2

b cm   8 cm

x cm

4 cm

What does the letter b represent in this blue rectangle?

With a partner, answer the following question: Given that the second rectangle is divided into four equal parts, what number does the x represent?

How did you arrive at this answer?

What is the total length of the second rectangle? Tell a partner how you know.

If the two large rectangles have equal lengths and widths, find the area of each rectangle.

Discuss with your partner how the formulas for the area of squares and rectangles can be used to evaluate area for a particular figure.

Exercise 2

Complete the table below for both rectangles. Note: These drawings are not to scale. Using a calculator is appropriate.

32 m

46 m

Length of Rectangle	Width of Rectangle	Rectangle's Area Written as an Expression	Rectangle's Area Written as a Number

Example 3

What does the l represent in the first diagram?

What does the w represent in the first diagram?

What does the h represent in the first diagram?

Since we know the formula to find the volume is $V = l \times w \times h$, what number can we substitute for the l in the formula? Why?

What other number can we substitute for the l?

What number can we substitute for the w in the formula? Why?

What number can substitute for the h in the formula?

Determine the volume of the second right rectangular prism by substituting the letters in the formula with their appropriate numbers.

Exercise 3

Complete the table for both figures. Using a calculator is appropriate.

15 units

5 units

12 units

7 cm

4 cm

23 cm

Length of Rectangular Prism	Width of Rectangular Prism	Height of Rectangular Prism	Rectangular Prism's Volume Written as an Expression	Rectangular Prism's Volume Written as a Number

Lesson Summary

Expression: An *expression* is a numerical expression, or it is the result of replacing some (or all) of the numbers in a numerical expression with variables

There are two ways to build expressions:

1. We can start out with a numerical expression, like $\frac{1}{3} \cdot (2 + 4) + 7$, and replace some of the numbers with letters to get $\frac{1}{3} \cdot (x + y) + z$.

2. We can build such expressions from scratch, as in $x + x(y - z)$, and note that if numbers were placed in the expression for the variables x, y, and z, the result would be a numerical expression.

Problem Set

1. Replace the side length of this square with 4 in. and find the area.

    s

2. Complete the table for each of the given figures.

23 m
36 m
14 yd
3.5 yd

Length of Rectangle	Width of Rectangle	Rectangle's Area Written as an Expression	Rectangle's Area as a Number

3. Find the perimeter of each quadrilateral in Problems 1 and 2.

4. Using the formula $V = l \times w \times h$, find the volume of a right rectangular prism when the length of the prism is 45 cm, the width is 12 cm, and the height is 10 cm.

Lesson 8: Replacing Numbers with Letters

Classwork

Opening Exercise

$$4 + 0 = 4$$

$$4 \times 1 = 4$$

$$4 \div 1 = 4$$

$$4 \times 0 = 0$$

$$1 \div 4 = \frac{1}{4}$$

How many of these statements are true?

How many of those statements would be true if the number 4 was replaced with the number 7 in each of the number sentences?

Would the number sentences be true if we were to replace the number 4 with any other number?

What if we replaced the number 4 with the number 0? Would each of the number sentences be true?

What if we replace the number 4 with a letter g? Please write all 4 expressions below, replacing each 4 with a g.

Are these all true (except for $g = 0$) when dividing?

Example 1: Additive Identity Property of Zero

$$g + 0 = g$$

Remember a letter in a mathematical expression represents a number. Can we replace g with any number?

Choose a value for g and replace g with that number in the number sentence. What do you observe?

Repeat this process several times, each time choosing a different number for g.

Is the number sentence true for all values of g?

Write the mathematical language for this property below:

Example 2: Multiplicative Identity Property of One

$$g \times 1 = g$$

Remember a letter in a mathematical expression represents a number. Can we replace g with any number?

Choose a value for g and replace g with that number in the number sentence. What do you observe?

Is the number sentence true for all values of g? Experiment with different values before making your claim.

Write the mathematical language for this property below:

Example 3: Commutative Property of Addition and Multiplication

$$3 + 4 = 4 + 3$$
$$3 \times 4 = 4 \times 3$$
$$3 + 3 + 3 + 3 = 4 \times 3$$
$$3 \div 4 = \frac{3}{4}$$

Replace the 3 in these equations with the letter a.

Choose a value for a and replace a with that number in each of the number sentences. What do you observe?

Are the number sentences true for all values of a? Experiment with different values before making your claim.

Now write the number sentences again, this time replacing the number 4 with a variable, b.

Are the first two number sentences true for all values of a and b? Experiment with different values before making your claim.

Write the mathematical language for this property below:

Problem Set

1. State the commutative property of addition using the variables a and b.

2. State the commutative property of multiplication using the variables a and b.

3. State the additive property of zero using the variable b.

4. State the multiplicative identity property of one using the variable b.

5. Demonstrate the property listed in the first column by filling in the third column of the table.

Commutative Property of Addition	$25 + c =$	
Commutative Property of Multiplication	$l \times w =$	
Additive Property of Zero	$h + 0 =$	
Multiplicative Identity Property of One	$v \times 1 =$	

6. Why is there no commutative property for subtraction or division? Show examples.

Lesson 9: Writing Addition and Subtraction Expressions

Classwork

Example 1

Create a bar diagram to show 3 plus 5.

How would this look if you were asked to show 5 plus 3?

Are these two expressions equivalent?

Example 2

How can we show a number increased by 2?

Can you prove this using a model?

Example 3

Write an expression to show the sum of m and k.

Which property can be used in Examples 1–3 to show that both expressions given are equivalent?

Example 4

How can we show 10 minus 6?

- Draw a bar diagram to model this expression.

- What expression would represent this model?

- Could we also use $6 - 10$?

Example 5

How can we write an expression to show 3 less than a number?

- Start by drawing a diagram to model the subtraction. Are we taking away from the 3 or the unknown?

- What expression would represent this model?

Example 6

How would we write an expression to show the number c being subtracted from the sum of a and b?

- Start by writing an expression for "the sum of a and b."

- Now show c being subtracted from the sum.

Example 7

Write an expression to show the number c minus the sum of a and b.

Why are the parentheses necessary in this example and not the others?

Replace the variables with numbers to see if $c - (a + b)$ is the same as $c - a + b$.

Exercises

1. Write an expression to show the sum of 7 and 1.5.

2. Write two expressions to show w increased by 4. Then draw models to prove that both expressions represent the same thing.

3. Write an expression to show the sum of a, b, and c.

4. Write an expression and a model showing 3 less than p.

5. Write an expression to show the difference of 3 and p.

6. Write an expression to show 4 less than the sum of g and 5.

7. Write an expression to show 4 decreased by the sum of g and 5.

8. Should Exercises 6 and 7 have different expressions? Why or why not?

Problem Set

1. Write two expressions to show a number decreased by 11. Then draw models to prove that both expressions represent the same thing.

2. Write an expression to show the sum of x and y.

3. Write an expression to show h decreased by 13.

4. Write an expression to show k less than 3.5.

5. Write an expression to show the sum of g and h reduced by 11.

6. Write an expression to show 5 less than y, plus g.

7. Write an expression to show 5 less than the sum of y and g.

Lesson 10: Writing and Expanding Multiplication Expressions

Classwork

Example 1

Write each expression using the fewest number of symbols and characters. Use math terms to describe the expressions and parts of the expression.

a. $6 \times b$

b. $4 \cdot 3 \cdot h$

c. $2 \times 2 \times 2 \times a \times b$

d. $5 \times m \times 3 \times p$

e. $1 \times g \times w$

Example 2

To expand multiplication expressions we will rewrite the expressions by including the "•" back into the expressions.

a. $5g$

b. $7abc$

c. $12g$

d. $3h \cdot 8$

e. $7g \cdot 9h$

Example 3

a.   Find the product of $4f \cdot 7g$.

b.   Multiply $3de \cdot 9yz$.

c.   Double the product of $6y$ and $3bc$.

> **Lesson Summary**
>
> **An Expression in Expanded Form:** An expression that is written as sums (and/or differences) of products whose factors are numbers, variables, or variables raised to whole number powers is said to be in *expanded form*. A single number, variable, or a single product of numbers and/or variables is also considered to be in expanded form.

Problem Set

1. Rewrite the expression using the fewest number of symbols and characters possible.

    a. $5 \cdot y$

    b. $7 \cdot d \cdot e$

    c. $5 \cdot 2 \cdot 2 \cdot y \cdot z$

    d. $3 \cdot 3 \cdot 2 \cdot 5 \cdot d$

2. Expand the following expressions.

    a. $3g$

    b. $11mp$

    c. $20yz$

    d. $15abc$

3. Find the product.

    a. $5d \cdot 7g$

    b. $12ab \cdot 3cd$

Lesson 11: Factoring Expressions

Classwork

Example 1

a.   Use the model to answer the following questions.

How many fives are in the model?

How many threes are in the model?

What does the expression represent in words?

What expression could we write to represent the model?

b.   Use the new model and the previous model to answer the next set of questions.

How many fives are in the model?

How many threes are in the model?

What does the expression represent in words?

What expression could we write to represent the model?

| Lesson 11: | Factoring Expressions |
| Date: | 12/15/13 |

c.   Is the model in part (a) equivalent to the model in part (b)?

d.   What relationship do we see happening on either side of the equal sign?

e.   In 5th grade and in Module 2 of this year, you have used similar reasoning to solve problems. What is the name of the property that is used to say that $2(5 + 3)$ is the same as $2 \times 5 + 2 \times 3$?

Example 2

Now, we will take a look at an example with variables. Discuss the questions with your partner.

What does the model represent in words?

What does $2a$ mean?

How many a's are in the model?

How many $b's$ are in the model?

Lesson 11:   Factoring Expressions
Date: 12/15/13

What expression could we write to represent the model?

How many $a's$ are in the expression?

How many $b's$ are in the expression?

What expression could we write the represent the model?

Are the two expressions equivalent?

Example 3

Use GCF and the distributive property to write equivalent expressions.

1. $3f + 3g =$ _____

    What is the question asking us to do?

    How would Problem 1 look if we expanded each term?

    What is the GCF in Problem 1?

    How can we use the GCF to rewrite this?

2. $6x + 9y = $ _____

What is the question asking us to do?

How would Problem 2 look if we expanded each term?

What is the GCF in Problem 2?

How can we use the GCF to rewrite this?

3. $3c + 11c = $ _____

Is there a greatest common factor in Problem 3?

Rewrite the expression using the distributive property.

4. $24b + 8 = $ _____

Explain how you used GCF and the distributive property to rewrite the expression in Problem 4.

Why is there a 1 in the parentheses?

How is this related to the first two examples?

Exercises

1. Apply the distributive property to write equivalent expressions.

   a. $7x + 7y$

   b. $15g + 20h$

   c. $18m + 42n$

   d. $30a + 39b$

   e. $11f + 15f$

   f. $18h + 13h$

   g. $55m + 11$

   h. $7 + 56y$

2. Evaluate each of the expressions below.

   a. $6x + 21y$ and $3(2x + 7y)$ $x = 3$ and $y = 4$

   b. $5g + 7g$ and $g(5 + 7)$ $g = 6$

    c. $14x + 2$ and $2(7x + 1)$ $x = 10$

    d.   Explain any patterns that you notice in the results to parts (a)–(c).

    e.   What would happen if other values were given for the variables?

Closing

How can use you use your knowledge of GCF and the distributive property to write equivalent expressions?

Find the missing value that makes the two expressions equivalent.

$14x + 12y$ _____$(x + 3y)$

$35x + 50y$ _____$(7x + 10y)$

$18x + 9y$ _____$(2x + y)$

$32x + 8y$ _____$(4x + y)$

$100x + 700y$ _____$(x + 7y)$

Explain how you determine the missing number.

Lesson Summary

An Expression in Factored Form: An expression that is a product of two or more expressions is said to be in *factored form*.

Problem Set

1. Use models to prove that $3(a + b)$ is equivalent to $3a + 3b$.

2. Use greatest common factor and the distributive property to write equivalent expressions for the following expressions.

   a. $4d + 12e$

   b. $18x + 30y$

   c. $21a + 28y$

   d. $24f + 56g$

Lesson 12: Distributing Expressions

Classwork

Opening Exercise

a.   Create a model to show 2×5.

b.   Create a model to show $2 \times b$, or $2b$.

Example 1

Write an expression that is equivalent to $2(a + b)$.

Create a model to represent $(a + b)$.

The expression $2(a + b)$ tells us that we have 2 of the $(a + b)$'s. Create a model that shows 2 groups of $(a + b)$.

How many a's and how many b's do you see in the diagram?

How would the model look if we grouped together the a's and then grouped together the b's?

What expression could we write to represent the new diagram?

What conclusion can we draw from the models about equivalent expressions?

Let $a = 3$ and $b = 4$.

What happens when we double $(a + b)$?

Example 2

Write an expression that is equivalent to double $(3x + 4y)$.

How can we rewrite double $(3x + 4y)$?

Is this expression in factored form, expanded form, or neither?

Let's start this problem the same way that we started the first example. What should we do?

How can we change the model to show $2(3x + 4y)$?

Are there terms that we can combine in this example?

What is an equivalent expression that we can use to represent $2(3x + 4y)$?

Summarize how you would solve this question without the model.

Example 3

Write an expression in expanded form that is equivalent to the model below.

$$4x \quad + \quad 5$$

What factored expression is represented in the model?

How can we rewrite this expression?

Example 4

Write an expression that is equivalent to $3(7d + 4e)$.

Exercises

Create a model for each expression below. Then write another equivalent expression using the distributive property.

1. $3(x + y)$

2. $4(2h + g)$

Apply the distributive property to write an equivalent expression.

3. $8(h + 3)$

4. $3(2h + 7)$

5. $5(3x + 9y)$

6. $4(11h + 3g)$

7.

$7k$	$12m$	
		j

8. $a(9b + 13)$

Problem Set

1. Use the distributive property to expand the following expressions.

    a. $4(x + y)$

    b. $8(a + 3b)$

    c. $3(2x + 11y)$

    d. $9(7a + 6b)$

    e. $c(3a + b)$

    f. $y(2x + 11z)$

2. Create a model to show that $2(2x + 3y) = 4x + 6y$.

Lesson 13: Writing Division Expressions

Classwork

Example 1

Write an expression showing $1 \div 2$ without the use of the division symbol.

From the model what can we determine?

Example 2

Write an expression showing $a \div 2$ without the use of the division symbol.

From the model what can we determine?

When we write division expressions using the division symbol we represent _____ .

How would this look when we write division expressions using a fraction?

Example 3

a. Write an expression showing $a \div b$ without the use of the division symbol.

b. Write an expression for g divided by the quantity h plus 3.

c. Write an expression for the quotient of the quantity m reduced by 3 and 5.

Exercises

Write each expression two ways: using the division symbol and as a fraction.

1. 12 divided by 4.

2. 3 divided by 5.

3. a divided by 4.

4. The quotient of 6 and m.

5. Seven divided by the quantity x plus y.

$7(x+y)$

6. y divided by the quantity x minus 11.

7. The sum of the quantity h and 3 divided by 4.

8. The quotient of the quantity k minus 10 and m.

Problem Set

1. Rewrite the expressions using the division symbol and as a fraction.

    a. Three divided by 4.

    b. The quotient of m and 11.

    c. 4 divided by the sum of h and 7.

    d. The quantity x minus 3 divided by y.

2. Draw a model to show that $x \div 3$ is the same as $\dfrac{x}{3}$.

Lesson 14: Writing Division Expressions

Classwork

Example 1

Fill in the three remaining squares so that all the squares contain equivalent expressions.

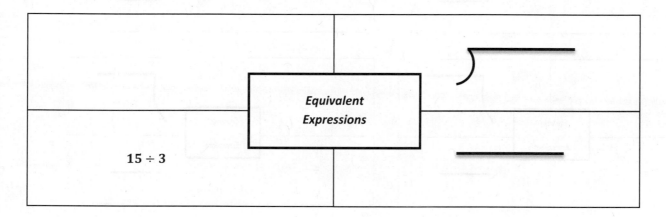

Example 2

Fill in a blank copy of the four boxes using the words *dividend* and *divisor* so that it is set up for any example.

Exercises

Complete the missing spaces in each rectangle set.

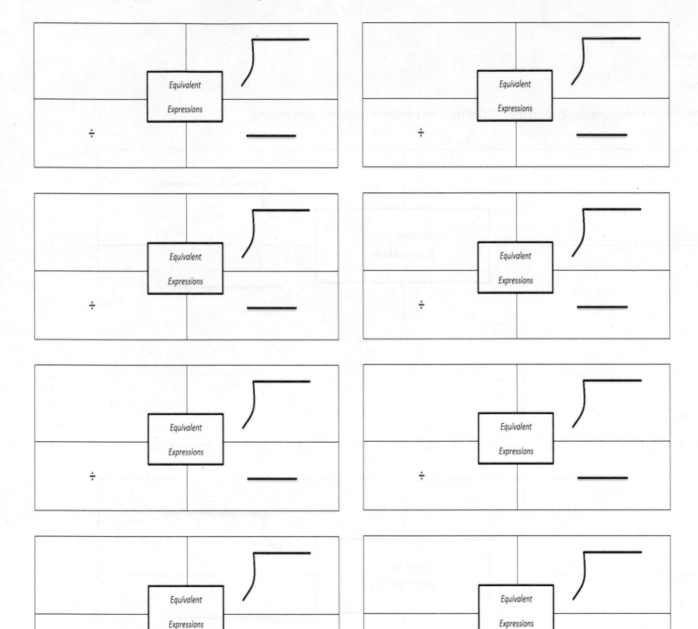

Problem Set

Complete the missing spaces in each rectangle set.

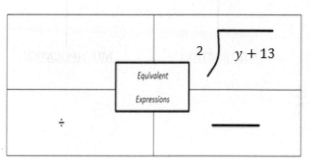

Lesson 15: Read Expressions in Which Letters Stand for Numbers

Classwork

Opening Exercise

Complete the graphic organizer with mathematical words that indicate each operation. Some words may not indicate only one operation.

ADDITION   SUBTRACTION   MULTIPLICATION   DIVISION   EXPONENTS

Example 1

Write an expression using words.

a. $a - b$

b. xy

c. $4f + u$

d. $d - b^3$

e. $5(u - 10) + h$

f. $\dfrac{3}{d+f}$

Exercises

Circle all the vocabulary words that could be used to describe the given expression.

1. $6h - 10$

   ADDITION   SUBTRACTION   MULTIPLICATION   DIVISION

2. $\dfrac{5d}{6}$

   SUM   DIFFERENCE   PRODUCT   QUOTIENT

3. $5(2 + d) - 8$

   ADD   SUBTRACT   MULTIPLY   DIVIDE

4. abc

   MORE THAN   LESS THAN   TIMES   EACH

Write an expression using vocabulary to represent each given expression.

5. $8 - 2g$

6. $15(a + c)$

7. $\dfrac{m+n}{5}$

8. $b^3 - 18$

9. $f - \dfrac{d}{2}$

10. $\dfrac{u}{x}$

Problem Set

1. List five different vocabulary words that could be used to describe each given expression.

   a. $a - d + c$

   b. $20 - 3c$

   c. $\dfrac{b}{d+2}$

2. Write an expression using math vocabulary for each expression below.

   a. $5b - 18$

   b. $\dfrac{n}{2}$

   c. $a + (d - 6)$

   d. $10 + 2b$

Lesson 16: Write Expressions in Which Letters Stand for Numbers

Classwork

Opening Exercise

Underline the key words in each statement.

a.   The sum of twice b and 5.

b.   The quotient of c and d.

c. a raised to the fifth power then increased by the product of 5 and c.

d.   The quantity of a plus b divided by 4.

e.   10 less than the product of 15 and c.

f.   5 times d increased by 8.

Example 1

a.   The sum of twice b and 5.

b.   The quotient of c and d.

c. a raised to the fifth power, increased by the product of 5 and c.

d.   The quantity of a plus b divided by 4.

e.   10 less than the product of 15 and c.

f.   5 times d then increased by 8.

Example 2

Marcus has 4 more dollars than Yaseen. If y is the amount of money Yaseen has, write an expression to show how much money Marcus has.

Mario is missing half of his assignments. If a represents the number of assignments, write an expression to show how many assignments Mario is missing.

Kamilah's weight has tripled since her first birthday. If w represents the amount Kamilah weighed on her first birthday, write an expression to show how much Kamilah weighs now.

Nathan brings cupcakes to school and gives them to his five best friends who share them equally. If c represents the number of cupcakes Nathan brings to school, write an expression to show how many cupcakes each of his friends receive.

Mrs. Marcus combines her atlases and dictionaries and then divides them among 10 different tables. If a represents the number of atlases and d represents the number of dictionaries Mrs. Marcus has, write an expression to show how many books would be on each table.

To improve in basketball, Ivan's coach told him that he needs to take four times as many free throws and four times as many jump shots every day. If f represents the number of free throws and j represents the number of jump shots Ivan shoots daily, write an expression to show how many shots he will need to take in order to improve in basketball.

Exercises

Mark the text by underlining key words, and then write an expression using variables and numbers for each statement below.

1. b decreased by c squared.

2. 24 divided by the product of 2 and a.

3. 150 decreased by the quantity of 6 plus b.

4. The sum of twice c and 10.

5. Marlo had $35 but then spent $$m$.

6. Samantha saved her money and was able to quadruple the original amount, m.

7. Veronica increased her grade, g, by 4 points, and then doubled it.

8. Adbell had m pieces of candy and ate 5 of them. Then he split the remaining candy equally among 4 friends.

9. To find out how much paint is needed, Mr. Jones must square the side length of the gate, and then subtract 15.

10. Luis brought x cans of cola to the party, Faith brought d cans of cola, and De'Shawn brought h cans of cola. How many cans of cola did they bring all together?

Problem Set

Mark the text by underlining key words, and then write an expression using variables and numbers for each of the statements below.

1. Justin can type w words per minute. Melvin can type 4 times as many words as Justin. Write an expression that represents the rate at which Melvin can type.

2. Yohanna swam y yards yesterday. Sheylin swam 5 yards less than half the amount of yards as Yohanna. Write an expression that represents the number of yards Sheylin swam yesterday.

3. A number d decreased by 5 and then doubled.

4. Nahom and Semir combined their baseball cards, and then sold 10 of them.

5. The sum of 25 and h is divided by f cubed.

Lesson 17: Write Expressions in Which Letters Stand for Numbers

Classwork

Exercises

Station One	1.
	2.
	3.
Station Two	1.
	2.
	3.
Station Three	1.
	2.
	3.

Station Four	1.
	2.
	3.
Station Five	1.
	2.
	3.
Station Six	1.
	2.
	3.

Problem Set

Write an expression using letters and numbers for each problem below.

1. 4 less than the quantity of 8 times n.

2. 6 times the sum of y and 11.

3. The square of m reduced by 49.

4. The quotient when the quantity of 17 plus p is divided by 8.

5. Jim earned j in tips, and Steve earned s in tips. They combine their tips then split them equally.

6. Owen has c collector cards. He quadruples the number of cards he had, and then combines them with Ian, who has i collector cards.

7. Rae ran 4 times as many miles as Madison and Aaliyah combined. Madison ran m miles and Aaliyah ran a miles.

8. By using coupons, Mary Jo was able to decrease the retail price of her groceries, g, by \$125.

9. To calculate the area of a triangle, you find the product of the base and height and then divide by 2.

10. The temperature today was 10 degrees colder than twice yesterday's temperature, t.

Lesson 18: Writing and Evaluating Expressions—Addition and Subtraction

Classwork

Opening Exercise

How can we show a number increased by 2?

Can you prove this using a model?

Example 1: The Importance of Being Specific in Naming Variables

When naming variables in expressions, it is important to be very clear about what they stand for. The units of measure must be included if something is measured.

Exercises

1. Read the variable in the table and improve the description given, making it more specific.

Variable	Incomplete Description	Complete Description with Units
Joshua's speed (J)	Let J = Joshua's speed	
Rufus's height (R)	Let R = Rufus's height	
Milk sold (M)	Let M = the amount of milk sold	
Colleen's time in the 40 meter hurdles (C)	Let C = Colleen's time	
Sean's age (S)	Let S = Sean's age	

2. Read each variable in the table and improve the description given, making it more specific.

Variable	Incomplete Description	Complete Description with Units
Karolyn's CDs (K)	Let K = Karolyn's CDs	Let K = the number of CDs Karolyn has
Joshua's merit badges (J)	Let J = Joshua's merit badges	
Rufus's trading cards (R)	Let R = Rufus's trading cards	
Milk money (M)	Let M = the amount of milk money	

Example 2 (20 minutes): Writing and Evaluating Addition and Subtraction Expressions

Read each story problem. Identify the unknown quantity, and write an addition or subtraction expressions that is described. Finally, evaluate your expression using the information given in column four.

Story Problem	Description with Units	Expression	Evaluate the Expression if:	Show your Work and Evaluate
Gregg has two more dollars than his brother Jeff. Write an expression for the amount of money Gregg has.	Let j = Jeff's money in dollars	$j + 2$	Jeff has $12.	$j + 2$ $12 + 2$ 14 Gregg has $14.
Gregg has two more dollars than his brother Jeff. Write an expression for the amount of money Jeff has.	Let g = Gregg's money in dollars	$g - 2$	Gregg has $14.	$g - 2$ $14 - 2$ 12 Jeff has $12.
Abby read 8 more books than Kristen in the first marking period. Write an expression for the number of books Abby read.			Kristen read 9 books in the first making period.	

Abby read 6 more books than Kristen in the second marking period. Write an expression for the number of books Kristen read.			Abby read 20 books in the second marking period.	
Daryl has been teaching for one year longer than Julie. Write an expression for the number of years that Daryl has been teaching.			Julie has been teaching for 28 years.	
Ian scored 4 fewer goals than Julia in the first half of the season. Write an expression for the number of goals Ian scored.			Julia scored 13 goals.	
Ian scored 3 fewer goals than Julia in the second half of the season. Write an expression for the number of goals Julia scored.			Ian scored 8 goals.	
Johann visited Niagara Falls 3 times fewer than Arthur. Write an expression for the number of times Johann visited Niagara Falls.			Arthur visited Niagara Falls 5 times.	

Problem Set

1. Read the story problem. Identify the unknown quantity and write an addition or subtraction expression that is described. Then evaluate your expression given the further information.

Story Problem	Description with Units	Expression	Evaluate the Expression if:	Show your Work and Answer
Sammy has two more baseballs than his brother Ethan.	Let e = the number of balls Ethan has	$e + 2$	Ethan has 7 baseballs.	$e + 2$ $7 + 2$ 9 Sammy has 9 baseballs.
Ella wrote 8 more stories than Anna in the fifth grade.			Anna wrote 10 stories in the fifth grade.	
Lisa has been dancing for 3 more years than Danika.			Danika has been dancing for 6 years.	
The New York Rangers scored 2 fewer goals than the Buffalo Sabres last night.			The Rangers scored 3 goals last night.	
George has gone camping 3 times fewer than Dave.			George has gone camping 8 times.	

2. If George went camping 15 times, how could you figure out how many times Dave went camping?

Lesson 18:   Writing and Evaluating Expressions—Addition and Subtraction
Date: 12/15/13

Lesson 19: Substituting to Evaluate Addition and Subtraction Expressions

Classwork

Opening Exercise

My older sister is exactly two years older than I am. Sharing a birthday is both fun and annoying. Every year on our birthday we have a party, which is fun, but she always brags that she is two years older than I am, which is annoying. Shown below is a table of our ages, starting when I was born:

My Age (in years)	My Sister's Age (in years)
0	2
1	3
2	4
3	5
4	6

1. Looking at the table, what patterns do you see? Tell a partner.

2. On the day I turned 8 years old, how old was my sister?

3. How do you know?

4. On the day I turned 16 years old, how old was my sister?

5. How do you know?

6. Do we need to extend the table to calculate these answers?

Example 1

My Age (in years)	My Sister's Age (in years)
0	2
1	3
2	4
3	5
4	6

a. What if you don't know how old I am? Let's use a variable for my age. Let Y = my age in years. Can you develop an expression to describe how old my sister is?

b. Please add that to the last row of the table.

Example 2

My Age (in years)	My Sister's Age (in years)
0	2
1	3
2	4
3	5
4	6

a. How old was I when my sister was 6 years old?

b. How old was I when my sister was 15 years old?

c. How do you know?

d.   Look at the table in Example 2. If you know my sister's age, can you determine my age?

e.   If we use the variable G for my sister's age in years, what expression would describe my age in years?

f.   Fill in the last row of the table with the expressions.

g.   With a partner, calculate how old I was when my sister was 22, 23, and 24 years old.

Exercises

1.   Noah and Carter are collecting box tops for their school. They each bring in 1 per day starting on the first day of school. However, Carter had a head start because his aunt sent him 15 box tops before school began. Noah's grandma saved 10 box tops, and Noah added those on his first day.

   a.   Fill in the missing values that indicate the total number of box tops each boy brought to school.

School Day	Number of Box Tops Noah Has	Number of Box Tops Carter Has
1	11	16
2		
3		
4		
5		

   b.   If we let D be the number of days since the new school year began, on day D of school, how many box tops will Noah have brought to school?

   c.   On day D of school, how many box tops will Carter have brought to school?

   d.   On day 10 of school, how many box tops will Noah have brought to school?

   e.   On day 10 of school, how many box tops will Carter have brought to school?

2. Each week the Primary School recycles 200 pounds of paper. The Intermediate School also recycles the same amount but had another 300 pounds left over from summer school. The Intermediate School custodian added this extra 300 pounds to the first recycle week.

   a. Number the weeks and record the amount of paper recycled by both schools.

Week	Total Amount of Paper Recycled by the Primary School This School Year in Pounds	Total Amount of Paper Recycled by the Intermediate School This School Year in Pounds

   b. If this trend continues, what will be the total amount collected for each school on Week 10?

3. Shelly and Kristen share a birthday, but Shelly is 5 years older.

   a. Make a table showing their ages every year, beginning when Kristen was born.

   b. If Kristen is 16 years old, how old is Shelly?

   c. If Kristen is K years old, how old is Shelly?

   d. If Shelly is S years old, how old is Kristen?

Problem Set

1. Suellen and Tara are in 6th grade and both take dance lessons at Twinkle Toes Dance Studio. This is Suellen's first year, while this is Tara's fifth year. Both girls plan to continue taking lessons throughout high school.

    a. Complete the table showing the number of years the girls will have danced at the studio.

Grade	Suellen's Years of Experience Dancing	Tara's Years of Experience Dancing
Sixth		
Seventh		
Eighth		
Ninth		
Tenth		
Eleventh		
Twelfth		

    b. If Suellen has been taking dance lessons for Y years, how many years has Tara been taking lessons?

2. Daejoy and Damian collect fossils. Before they went on a fossil-hunting trip, Daejoy had 25 fossils in her collection, and Damian had 16 fossils in his collection. On a 10-day fossil hunting trip, they each collected 2 new fossils each day.

    a. Make a table showing how many fossils each person had in their collection at the end of each day.

    b. If this pattern of fossil finding continues, how many fossils will Damian have when Daejoy has F fossils?

    c. If this pattern of fossil finding continues, how many fossils will Damian have when Daejoy has 55 fossils?

3. A train consists of three types of cars: box cars, an engine, and a caboose.

Number of Box Cars	Number of Cars in the Train
0	2
1	3
2	4
10	12
100	102

   a. Tom wrote an expression for the relationship depicted in the table as $B + 2$. Theresa wrote an expression for the same relationship as $C - 2$. Is it possible to have two different expressions to represent one relationship? Explain.

   b. What do you think the variable in each students expression represent? How would you define them?

4. David was 3 when Marieka was born. Complete the table.

Marieka's Age in Years	David's Age in Years
5	8
6	9
7	10
8	11
10	
	20
32	
M	
	D

5. Caitlin and Michael are playing a card game. In the first round, Caitlin scored 200 points and Michael scored 175 points. In each of the next few rounds, they each scored 50 points. Their score sheet is below.

Caitlin's points	Michael's points
200	175
250	225
300	275
350	325

   a. If this trend continues, how many points will Michael have when Caitlin has 600 points?

   b. If this trend continues, how many points will Michael have when Caitlin has C points?

   c. If this trend continues, how many points will Caitlin have when Michael has 975 points?

   d. If this trend continues, how many points will Caitlin have when Michael has M points?

6. The high school marching band has 15 drummers this year. The band director insists that there are to be 5 more trumpet players than drummers at all times.

   a. How many trumpet players are in the marching band this year?

   b. Write an expression that describes the relationship of the number of trumpet players (T) and the number of drummers (D).

   c. If there are only 14 trumpet players interested in joining the marching band next year, how many drummers will the band director want in the band?

Lesson 20: Writing and Evaluating Expressions—Multiplication and Division

Classwork

Exercises

1. The farmers' market is selling bags of apples. In every bag, there are 3 apples.

    a.   Complete the table.

Number of Bags	Total Number of Apples
1	3
2	
3	
4	
B	

    b.   What if the market had 25 bags of apples to sell? How many apples is that in all?

    c.   If a truck arrived that had some number, a, more apples on it, then how many bags would the clerks use to bag up the apples?

    d.   If a truck arrived that had 600 more apples on it, how many bags would the clerks use to bag up the apples?

    e.   How is part (d) different from part (b)?

2. In New York State, there is a five-cent deposit on all carbonated beverage cans and bottles. When you return the empty can or bottle, you get the five cents back.

    a. Complete the table.

Number of Containers Returned	Refund in Dollars
1	
2	
3	
4	
10	
50	
100	
C	

    b. If we let C represent the number of cans, what is the expression that shows how much money is returned?

    c. Use the expression to find out how much money Brett would receive if he returned 222 cans.

    d. If Gavin needs to earn $4.50 for returning cans, how many cans does he need to collect and return?

    e. How is part (d) different from part (c)?

3. The fare for a subway or a local bus ride is $2.50.

   a. Complete the table.

Number of Rides	Cost of Rides in Dollars
1	
2	
3	
4	
5	
10	
30	
R	

   b. If we let R represent the number of rides, what is the expression that shows the cost of the rides?

   c. Use the expression to find out how much money 60 rides would cost.

   d. If a commuter spends $175.00 on subway or bus rides, how many trips did the commuter take?

   e. How is part (d) different from part (c)?

COMMON CORE™ | **Lesson 20:** Writing and Evaluating Expressions—Multiplication and Division | **Date:** 12/15/13 | S.86

© 2013 Common Core, Inc. All rights reserved. commoncore.org

4. A pendulum swings though a certain number of cycles in a given time. Owen made a pendulum that swings 12 times every 15 seconds.

    a. Construct a table showing the number of cycles through which a pendulum swings. Include data for up to one minute. Use the last row for C cycles, and write an expression for the time it takes for the pendulum to make C cycles.

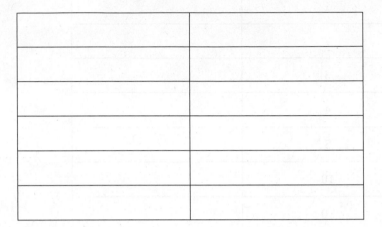

    b. Owen and his pendulum team set their pendulum in motion and counted 16 cycles. What was the elapsed time?

    c. Write an expression for the number of cycles a pendulum swings in S seconds.

    d. In a different experiment, Owen and his pendulum team counted the cycles of the pendulum for 35 seconds. How many cycles did they count?

Problem Set

1. A radio station plays 12 songs each hour. They never stop for commercials, news, weather, or traffic reports.

    a. Write an expression describing how many songs are played by the radio station in H hours.

    b. How many songs will be played in an entire day (24 hours)?

    c. How long does it take the radio station to play 60 consecutive songs?

2. A ski area has a high speed lift that can move 2,400 skiers to the top of the mountain each hour.

    a. Write an expression describing how many skiers can be lifted each hour.

    b. How many skiers can be moved to the top of the mountain in 14 hours?

    c. How long will it take to move 3,600 skiers to the top of the mountain?

3. Polly writes a magazine column, for which she earns $35 per hour.   Create a table of values that shows the relationship between the number of hours that Polly works, H, and the amount of money Polly earns in dollars, E.

    a. If you know how many hours Polly works, can you determine how much money she earned? Write the corresponding expression.

    b. Use your expression to determine how much Polly earned after working for $3\frac{1}{2}$ hours.

    c. If you know how much money Polly earned, can you determine how long she worked? Write the corresponding expression.

    d. Use your expression to determine how long Polly worked if she earned $52.50.

4. Mitchell delivers newspapers after school, for which he earns $0.09 per paper. Create a table of values that shows the relationship between the number of papers that Mitchell delivers, P, and the amount of money Mitchell earns in dollars, E.

a. If you know how many papers Mitchell delivers, can you determine how much money he earned? Write the corresponding expression.

b. Use your expression to determine how much Mitchell earned by delivering 300 newspapers.

c. If you know how much money Mitchell earned, can you determine how many papers he delivered? Write the corresponding expression.

d. Use your expression to determine how many papers Mitchell delivered if he earned $58.50 last week.

5. Randy is an art dealer who sells reproductions of famous paintings. Copies of the *Mona Lisa* sell for $475.

a. Last year Randy sold $9,975.00 worth of *Mona Lisa* reproductions. How many did he sell?

b. If Randy wants to increase his sales to at least $15,000 this year, how many copies will he need to sell (without changing the price per painting)?

Lesson 21: Writing and Evaluating Expressions—Multiplication and Addition

Classwork

Exercise 1

The Italian Villa Restaurant has square tables that the servers can push together to accommodate the customers. Only one chair fits along the side of the square table. Make a model of each situation to determine how many seats will fit around various rectangular tables.

Number of Square Tables	Number of Seats at the Table
1	
2	
3	
4	
5	
50	
200	
T	

Are there any other ways to think about solutions to this problem?

It is impractical to make a model of pushing 50 tables together to make a long rectangle. If we did have a rectangle that long, how many chairs would fit on the long sides of the table?

How many chairs fit on the ends of the long table?

How many chairs fit in all? Record it.

Work with your group to determine how many chairs would fit around a very long rectangular table if 200 square tables were pushed together.

If we let T represent the number of square tables that make one long rectangular table, what is the expression for the number of chairs that will fit around it?

Example 2

Look at Example 2 with your group. Determine the cost for various numbers of pizzas, and also determine the expression that describes the cost of having P pizzas delivered.

a. Pizza Queen has a special offer on lunch pizzas: $4.00 each. They charge $2.00 to deliver, regardless of how many pizzas are ordered. Determine the cost for various numbers of pizzas, and also determine the expression that describes the cost of having P pizzas delivered.

Number of Pizzas Delivered	Total Cost in Dollars
1	
2	
3	
4	
10	
50	
P	

What mathematical operations did you need to perform to find the total cost?

Suppose our principal wanted to buy a pizza for everyone in our class? Determine how much this would cost.

b. If the booster club had $400 to spend on pizza, what is the greatest number of pizzas they could order?

c. If the pizza price was raised to $5.00 and the delivery price was raised to $3.00, create a table that shows the total cost (pizza plus delivery) of 1, 2, 3, 4, and 5 pizzas. Include the expression that describes the new cost of ordering P pizzas.

Number of Pizzas Delivered	Total Cost in Dollars
1	
2	
3	
4	
5	
P	

Problem Set

1. Compact discs cost $12 each at the Music Emporium. The company charges $4.50 for shipping and handling, regardless of how many compact discs are purchased.

   a. Create a table of values that show the relationship between the number of compact discs that Mickey buys, D, and the amount of money Mickey spends, C, in dollars.

Number of CDs Mickey Buys (D)	Total Cost in Dollars (C)
1	
2	
3	

   b. If you know how many CDs Mickey orders, can you determine how much money he spends? Write the corresponding expression.

   c. Use your expression to determine how much Mickey spent buying 8 CDs.

2. Mr. Gee's class orders paperback books from a book club. The books cost $2.95 each. Shipping charges are set at $4.00, regardless of the number of books purchased.

   a. Create a table of values that show the relationship between the number of books that Mr. Gee's class buys, B, and the amount of money they spend, C, in dollars.

Number of Books Ordered (B)	Amount of Money Spent in Dollars (C)
1	
2	
3	

   b. If you know how many books Mr. Gee's class orders, can you determine how much money they spend? Write the corresponding expression.

   c. Use your expression to determine how much Mr. Gee's class spent buying 24 books.

3. Sarah is saving money to take a trip to Oregon. She received $450 in graduation gifts and saves $120 per week working.

   a. Write an expression that shows how much money Sarah has after working W weeks.

   b. Create a table that shows the relationship between the amount of money Sarah has (M) and the number of weeks she works (W).

Amount of Money Sarah Has (M)	Number of Weeks Worked (W)
	1
	2
	3
	4
	5
	6
	7
	8

   c. The trip will cost $1,200. How many weeks will Sarah have to work to earn enough for the trip?

4. Mr. Gee's English Language Arts class keeps track of how many words per minute are read aloud by each of the students. They collect this Oral Reading Fluency data each month. Below is the data they collected for one student in the first four months of school.

a. Assume this increase in Oral Reading Fluency continues throughout the rest of the school year. Complete the table to project the reading rate for this student for the rest of the year.

Month	Number of Words Read Aloud in One Minute
September	126
October	131
November	136
December	141
January	
February	
March	
April	
May	
June	

b. If this increase in Oral Reading Fluency continues throughout the rest of the school year, when would this student achieve the goal of reading 165 words per minute?

c. The expression for this student's Oral Reading Fluency is $121 + 5m$, where m represents the number of months during the school year. Use this expression to determine how many words per minute the student would read after 12 months of instructions.

5. When corn seeds germinate, they tend to grow 5 inches in the first week, then 3 inches per week for the remainder of the season. The relationship between height (H) and number of weeks since germination (W) is shown below.

a. Complete the missing values in the table.

Number of Weeks Since Germination (W)	Height of Corn Plant (H)
1	5
2	8
3	11
4	14
5	
6	

b. The expression for this height is $2 + 3W$. How tall will the corn plant be after 15 weeks of growth?

6. The Honeymoon Charter Fishing Boat Company only allows newlywed couples on their sunrise trips. There is a captain, a first mate, and a deck hand manning the boat on these trips.

a. Write an expression that shows the number of people on the boat when there are C couples booked for the trip.

b. If the boat can hold a maximum of 20 people, how many couples can go on the sunrise fishing trip?

Lesson 22: Writing and Evaluating Expressions: Exponents

Classwork

Example 1: Folding Paper

Exercises

1. Predict how many times you can fold a piece of paper in half.

   My Prediction: _____

2. Before any folding (zero folds), there is only one layer of paper. This is recorded in the first row of the table.
   Fold your paper in half. Record the number of layers of paper that result. Continue as long as possible.

Number of Folds	Number of Paper Layers That Result	Number of Paper Layers Written as a Power of 2
0	1	2^0
1		
2		
3		
4		
5		
6		
7		
8		

   a. Are you able to continue folding the paper indefinitely? Why or why not?

   b. How could you use a calculator to find the next number in the series?

   c. What is the relationship between the number of folds and the number of layers?

   d. How is this relationship represented in the exponential form of the numerical expression?

   e. If you fold a paper f times, write an expression to show the number of paper layers.

3. If the paper were to be cut instead of folded, the height of the stack would double at each successive stage, and it would be possible to continue.

   a. Write an expression that describes how many layers of paper result from 16 cuts.

   b. Evaluate this expression by writing it in standard form.

Example 2: Bacterial Infection

Bacteria are microscopic one-celled organisms that reproduce in a couple of different ways, one of which is called binary fission. In binary fission, a bacterium increases its size until it is large enough to split into two parts that are identical. These two grow until they are both large enough to split into two individual bacteria. This continues as long as growing conditions are favorable.

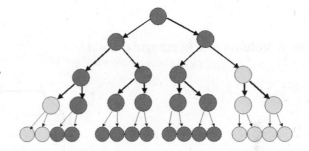

a. Record the number of bacteria that result from each generation.

Generation	Number of bacteria	Number of bacteria written as a power of 2
1	2	2^1
2	4	2^2
3	8	2^3
4		
5		
6		
7		
8		
9		
10		
11		
12		
13		
14		

b.   How many generations would it take until there were over one million bacteria present?

c.   Under the right growing conditions, many bacteria can reproduce every 15 minutes. Under these conditions, how long would it take for one bacterium to reproduce itself into more than one million bacteria?

d.   Write an expression for how many bacteria would be present after g generations.

Example 3: Volume of a Rectangular Solid

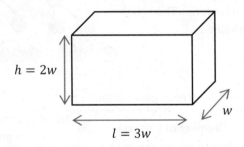

This box has a width, w. The height of the box, h, is twice the width. The length of the box, l, is three times the width. That is, the width, height, and length of a rectangular prism are in the ratio of $1:2:3$.

For rectangular solids like this, the volume is calculated by multiplying length times width times height.

$$V = l \cdot w \cdot h$$
$$V = 3w \cdot w \cdot 2w$$
$$V = 3 \cdot 2 \cdot w \cdot w \cdot w$$
$$V = 6\,w^3$$

Follow the above example to calculate the volume of these rectangular solids, given the width, w.

Width in centimeters (cm)	Volume in cubic centimeters (cm³)
1	
2	
3	
4	
w	

Problem Set

1. A checkerboard has 64 squares on it.

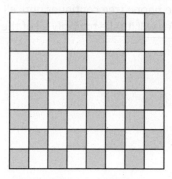

a. If a grain of rice is put on the first square, 2 grains of rice on the second square, 4 grains of rice on the third square, 8 grains of rice on the fourth square, etc. (doubling each time), how many grains of rice would be on the last square? Represent your answer first in exponential form. Use the table below to help solve the problem.

Checkerboard Square	Grains of Rice	Checkerboard Square	Grains of Rice	Checkerboard Square	Grains of Rice	Checkerboard Square	Grains of Rice
1		17		33		49	
2		18		34		50	
3		19		35		51	
4		20		36		52	
5		21		37		53	
6		22		38		54	
7		23		39		55	
8		24		40		56	
9		25		41		57	
10		26		42		58	
11		27		43		59	
12		28		44		60	
13		29		45		61	
14		30		46		62	
15		31		47		63	
16		32		48		64	

b. Would it have been easier to write your answer to part (a) in exponential form or standard form?

2. If an amount of money is invested at an annual interest rate of 6%, it doubles every 12 years. If Alejandra invests $500, how long will it take for her investment to exceed $2,000 (assuming she doesn't contribute any additional funds)?

3. The athletics director at Peter's school has created a phone tree that is used to notify team players in the event that all games have to be canceled or rescheduled. The phone tree is initiated when the director calls two captains. During the second stage of the phone tree, the captains each call two players. During the third stage of the phone tree, these players each call two other players. The phone tree continues until all players have been notified. If there are 50 players on the teams, how many stages will it take to notify all of the players?

Lesson 23: True and False Number Sentences

Opening Exercise

Determine what each symbol stands for and provide an example.

Symbol	What the Symbol Stands For	Example
=		
>		
<		
≤		
≥		

Example 1

For each inequality or equation your teacher displays, write the equation or inequality, then substitute 3 for every x. Determine if the equation or inequality results in a true number sentence or a false number sentence.

1.

2.

3.

4.

5.

6.

Exercises

Substitute the value into the variable and state (in a complete sentence) whether the resulting number sentence is true or false. If true, find a value that would result in a false number sentence. If false, find a value that would result in a true number sentence.

1. $4 + x = 12$. Substitute 8 for x.

2. $3g > 15$. Substitute $4\frac{1}{2}$ for g.

3. $\frac{f}{4} < 2$. Substitute 8 for f.

4. $14.2 \le h - 10.3$. Substitute 25.8 for h.

5. $4 = \frac{8}{d}$. Substitute 6 for d.

6. $3 > k + \frac{1}{4}$. Substitute $1\frac{1}{2}$ for k.

7. $4.5 - d > 2.5$. Substitute 2.5 for d.

8. $8 \ge 32p$. Substitute $\frac{1}{2}$ for p.

9. $\frac{w}{2} < 32$. Substitute 16 for w.

10. $18 \le 32 - b$. Substitute 14 for b.

	Lesson 23:	True and False Number Sentences
	Date:	12/16/13

Problem Set

Substitute the value into the variable and state (in a complete sentence) whether the resulting number sentence is true or false. If true, find a value that would result in a false number sentence. If false, find a value that would result in a true number sentence.

1. $3\frac{5}{6} = 1\frac{2}{3} + h$. Substitute $2\frac{1}{6}$ for h.

2. $39 > 156g$. Substitute $\frac{1}{4}$ for g.

3. $\frac{f}{4} \leq 3$. Substitute 12 for f.

4. $121 - 98 \geq r$. Substitute 23 for r.

5. $\frac{54}{q} = 6$. Substitute 10 for q.

Create a number sentence using the given variable and symbol. The number sentence you write must be true for the given value of the variable.

6. Variable: d Symbol: $\geq$ The sentence is true when 5 is substituted for d.

7. Variable: y Symbol: $\neq$ The sentence is true when 10 is substituted for y.

8. Variable: k Symbol: $<$ The sentence is true when 8 is substituted for k.

9. Variable: a Symbol: $\leq$ The sentence is true when 9 is substituted for a.

Lesson 24: True and False Number Sentences

Classwork

Opening Exercise

State whether each number sentence is true or false. If the number sentence is false, explain why.

1. $4 + 5 > 9$

2. $3 \cdot 6 = 18$

3. $32 > \frac{64}{4}$

4. $78 - 15 < 68$

5. $22 \geq 11 + 12$

Example 1

Write true or false if the number substituted for g results in a true or false number sentence.

Substitute g with	$4g = 32$	$g = 8$	$3g \geq 30$	$g \geq 10$	$\frac{g}{2} > 2$	$g > 4$	$30 \geq 38 - g$	$g \geq 8$
8								
4								
2								
0								
10								

Exercises

Complete the following problems in pairs. State when the following equations and inequalities will be true and when they will be false.

1. $15c > 45$

2. $25 = d - 10$

3. $56 \geq 2e$

4. $\dfrac{h}{5} \geq 12$

5. $45 > h + 29$

6. $4a \leq 16$

7. $3x = 24$

Identify all equality and inequality signs that can be placed into the blank to make a true number sentence.

8. $15 + 9$ _____ 24

9. $8 \cdot 7$ _____ 50

10. $\dfrac{15}{2}$ _____ 10

11. 34 _____ $17 \cdot 2$

12. 18 _____ $24.5 - 6$

Problem Set

State when the following equations and inequalities will be true and when they will be false.

1. $36 = 9k$

2. $67 > f - 15$

3. $\dfrac{v}{9} = 3$

4. $10 + b > 42$

5. $d - 8 \geq 35$

6. $32f < 64$

7. $10 - h \leq 7$

8. $42 + 8 \geq g$

9. $\dfrac{m}{3} = 14$

Lesson 25: Find Solutions to Make Equations True

Classwork

Opening Exercise

Identify a value for the variable that would make each equation or inequality into a true number sentence. Is this the only possible answer? State when the equation or inequality is true using equality and inequality symbols.

1. $3 + g = 15$

2. $30 > 2d$

3. $\dfrac{15}{f} > 5$

4. $42 \leq 50 - m$

Example 1

Each of the following numbers, if substituted for the variable, makes one of the equations below into a true number sentence. Match the number to that equation: 3, 6, 15, 16, 44.

a. $n + 26 = 32$

b. $n - 12 = 32$

c. $17n = 51$

d. $4^2 = n$

e. $\dfrac{n}{3} = 5$

Lesson Summary

Variable: A *variable* is a symbol (such as a letter) that represents a number (i.e., it is a placeholder for a number). A variable is a placeholder for "a" number that does not "vary."

Expression: An *expression* is a numerical expression, or a result of replacing some (or all) of the numbers in a numerical expression with variables.

Equation: An *equation* is a statement of equality between two expressions. If A and B are two expressions in the variable x, then $A = B$ is an equation in the variable x.

Problem Set

Find the solution to each equation.

1. $4^3 = y$

2. $8a = 24$

3. $32 = g - 4$

4. $56 = j + 29$

5. $\dfrac{48}{r} = 12$

6. $k = 15 - 9$

7. $x \cdot \dfrac{1}{5} = 60$

8. $m + 3.45 = 12.8$

9. $1 = a^5$

Lesson 26: One-Step Equations—Addition and Subtraction

Classwork

Exercise 1

Solve each equation. Use both tape diagrams and algebraic methods for each problem. Use substitution to check your answers.

    a. $b + 9 = 15$

    b. $12 = 8 + c$

Exercise 2

Given the equation $d - 5 = 7$:

   a.   Demonstrate how to solve the equation using tape diagrams.

   b.   Demonstrate how to solve the equation algebraically.

   c.   Check your answer.

Exercise 3

Solve each problem and show work. You may choose which method (tape diagrams or algebraically) you prefer. Check your answers after solving each problem.

a. $e + 12 = 20$

b. $f - 10 = 15$

c. $g - 8 = 9$

Problem Set

1. Find the solution to the equation below using tape diagrams. Check your answer.

$$m - 7 = 17$$

2. Find the solution of the equation below algebraically. Check your answer.

$$n + 14 = 25$$

3. Find the solution of the equation below using tape diagrams. Check your answer.

$$p + 8 = 18$$

4. Find the solution to the equation algebraically. Check your answer.

$$g - 62 = 14$$

5. Find the solution to the equation using the method of your choice. Check your answer.

$$m + 108 = 243$$

6. Identify the mistake in the problem below. Then, correct the mistake.

$$p - 21 = 34$$
$$p - 21 - 21 = 34 - 21$$
$$p = 13$$

7. Identify the mistake in the problem below. Then, correct the mistake.

$$q + 18 = 22$$
$$q + 18 - 18 = 22 + 18$$
$$q = 40$$

8. Match the equation with the correct solution on the right.

$r + 10 = 22$	$r = 10$
$r - 15 = 5$	$r = 20$
$r - 18 = 14$	$r = 12$
$r + 5 = 15$	$r = 32$

Lesson 27: One-Step Equations—Multiplication and Division

Example 1

Solve $3z = 9$ using tape diagrams and algebraically and then check your answer.

First draw two tape diagrams, one to represent each side of the equation.

If 9 had to be split into three groups, how big would each group be?

Demonstrate the value of z using tape diagrams.

How can we demonstrate this algebraically?

How does this get us the value of z?

How can we check our answer?

Example 2 (5 minutes)

Solve $\frac{y}{4} = 2$ using tape diagrams and algebraically. Then, check your answer.

First, draw two tape diagrams, one to represent each side of the equation.

If the first tape diagram shows the size of $y \div 4$, how can we draw a tape diagram to represent y?

Draw this tape diagram.

What value does each $y \div 4$ section represent? How do you know?

How can you use a tape diagram to show the value of y?

How can we demonstrate this algebraically?

How does this help us find the value of y?

How can we check our answer?

Exercises

1. Use tape diagrams to solve the following problem: $3m = 21$.

2. Solve the following problem algebraically: $15 = \frac{n}{5}$.

3. Calculate the solution of the equation using the method of your choice: $4p = 36$.

4. Examine the tape diagram below and write an equation it represents. Then, calculate the solution to the equation using the method of your choice.

70

q	q	q	q	q	q	q

5. Write a multiplication equation that has a solution of 12. Use tape diagrams to prove that your equation has a solution of 12.

6. Write a division equation that has a solution of 12. Prove that your equation has a solution of 12 using algebraic methods.

Problem Set

1. Use tape diagrams to calculate the solution of $30 = 5w$. Then, check your answer.

2. Solve $12 = \frac{x}{4}$ algebraically. Then, check your answer.

3. Use tape diagrams to calculate the solution of $\frac{y}{5} = 15$. Then, check your answer.

4. Solve $18z = 72$ algebraically. Then, check your answer.

5. Write a division equation that has a solution of 8. Prove that your solution is correct by using tape diagrams.

6. Write a multiplication equation that has a solution of 8. Solve the equation algebraically to prove that your solution is correct.

7. When solving equations algebraically, Meghan and Meredith each got a different solution. Who is correct? Why did the other person not get the correct answer?

Meghan	Meredith
$\frac{y}{2} = 4$	$\frac{y}{2} = 4$
$\frac{y}{2} \cdot 2 = 4 \cdot 2$	$\frac{y}{2} \div 2 = 4 \div 2$
$y = 8$	$y = 2$

Lesson 28: Two-Step Problems—All Operations

Classwork

Mathematical Modeling Exercise

Juan has gained 20 lb. since last year. He now weighs 120 lb. Rashod is 15 lb. heavier than Diego. If Rashod and Juan weighed the same amount last year, how much does Diego weigh? Allow j to be Juan's weight last year (in lb.) and d to be Diego's weight (in lb.).

Draw a tape diagram to represent Juan's weight.

Draw a tape diagram to represent Rashod's weight.

Draw a tape diagram to represent Diego's weight.

What would combining all three tape diagrams look like?

Write an equation to represent Juan's tape diagram.

Write an equation to represent Rashod's tape diagram.

How can we use the final tape diagram or the equations above to answer the question presented?

Calculate Diego's weight.

We can use identities to defend our thought that $d + 35 - 35 = d$.

Does your answer make sense?

Example 1

Marissa has twice as much money as Frank. Christina has $20 more than Marissa. If Christina has $100, how much money does Frank have? Let f represent the amount of money Frank has in dollars and m represent the amount of money Marissa has in dollars.

Draw a tape diagram to represent the amount of money Frank has.

Draw a tape diagram to represent the amount of money Marissa has.

Draw a tape diagram to represent the amount of money Christina has.

Which tape diagram provides enough information to determine the value of the variable now?

Write and solve the equation.

The identities we have discussed throughout the module solidify that $m + 20 - 20 = m$.

What does the 80 represent?

Now that we know Marissa has $80, how can we use this information to find out how much money Frank has?

Write an equation.

Solve the equation.

Once again, the identities we have used throughout the module can solidify that $2f \div 2 = f$.

What does the 40 represent?

Does 40 make sense in the problem?

Station One: Use tape diagrams to solve the problem.

Raeana is twice as old as Madeline and Laura is 10 years older than Raeana. If Laura is 50 years old, how old is Madeline? Let m represent Madeline's age in years and let r represent Raeana's age in years.

Station Two: Use tape diagrams to solve the problem.

Carli has 90 apps on her phone. Braylen has half the amount of apps as Theiss. If Carli has three times the amount of apps as Theiss, how many apps does Braylen have? Let b represent the number of Braylen's apps and t represent the number of Theiss' apps.

Station Three: Use tape diagrams to solve the problem.

Reggie ran for 180 yards during the last football game, which is 40 more yards than his previous personal best. Monte ran 50 more yards than Adrian during the same game. If Monte ran the same amount of yards Reggie ran for his previous personal best, how many yards did Adrian run? Let r represent the number yards Reggie ran during his previous personal best and a represent the number of yards Adrian ran.

Station Four: **Use tape diagrams to solve the problem.**

Lance rides his bike at a pace of 60 miles per hour down hills. When Lance is riding uphill, he rides 8 miles per hour slower than on flat roads. If Lance's downhill speed is 4 times faster than his flat road speed, how fast does he travel uphill? Let f represent Lance's pace on flat roads in miles per hour and u represent Lance's pace uphill in miles per hour.

Problem Set

Use tape diagrams to solve each problem.

1. Dwayne scored 55 points in the last basketball game, which is 10 points more than his personal best. Lebron scored 15 points more than Chris in the same game. Lebron scored the same number of points as Dwayne's personal best. Let d represent the number of points Dwayne scored during his personal best and c represent the number of Chris' points.

   a. How many points did Chris score during the game?

   b. If these are the only three players who scored, what was the team's total number of points at the end of the game?

2. The number of customers at Yummy Smoothies varies throughout the day. During the lunch rush on Saturday, there were 120 customers at Yummy Smoothies. The number of customers at Yummy Smoothies during dinnertime was 10 customers less than the number during breakfast. The number of customers at Yummy Smoothies during lunch was 3 times more than during breakfast. How many people were at Yummy Smoothies during breakfast? How many people were at Yummy Smoothies during dinner? Let d represent the number of customers at Yummy Smoothies during dinner and b represent the number of customers at Yummy Smoothies during breakfast.

3. Karter has 24 t-shirts. The number of pairs of shoes Karter has is 8 less than the number of pants he has. If the number of shirts Karter has is double the number of pants he has, how many pairs of shoes does Karter have? Let p represent the number of pants Karter has and s represent the number of pairs of shoes he has.

4. Darnell completed 35 push-ups in one minute, which is 8 more than his previous personal best. Mia completed 6 more push-ups than Katie. If Mia completed the same amount of push-ups as Darnell completed during his previous personal best, how many push-ups did Katie complete? Let d represent the number of push-ups Darnell completed during his previous personal best and k represent the number of push-ups Katie completed.

5. Justine swims freestyle at a pace of 150 laps per hour. Justine swims breaststroke 20 laps per hour slower than she swims butterfly. If Justine's freestyle speed is three times faster than her butterfly speed, how fast does she swim breaststroke? Let b represent Justine's butterfly speed and r represent Justine's breaststroke speed.

Lesson 29: Multi-Step Problems—All Operations

Classwork

Example 1

The school librarian, Mr. Marker, knows the library has 1,400 books, but wants to reorganize how the books are displayed on the shelves. Mr. Marker needs to know how many fiction, nonfiction, and resource books are in the library. He knows that the library has four times as many fiction books as resource books and half as many nonfiction books as fiction books. If these are the only types of books in the library, how many of each type of book are in the library?

Draw a tape diagram to represent the total number of books in the library.

Draw two more tape diagrams, one to represent the number of fictions books in the library and one to represent the number of resource books in the library.

- ▪ Resource Books:

- ▪ Fiction Books:

What variable should we use throughout the problem?

Write the relationship between resource books and fiction books algebraically.

Draw a tape diagram to represent the number of nonfiction books.

How did you decide how many sections this tape diagram would have?

Represent the number of nonfiction books in the library algebraically.

Use the tape diagrams we drew to solve the problem.

Write an equation that represents the tape diagram.

Determine the value of r.

How many fiction books are in the library?

How many nonfiction books are in the library?

Set up a table with four columns and label each column.

How many fiction books are in the library?

How many nonfiction books are in the library?

How many resource books are in the library?

Does the library have four times as many fiction books as resource books?

Does the library have half as many nonfiction books as fiction books?

Does the library have 1,400 books?

Exercises

Solve each problem below. Then check your answer with the word problem.

1. Indian Ridge Middle School wanted to add a new school sport, so they surveyed the students to determine which sport is most popular. Students were able to choose between soccer, football, lacrosse, or swimming. The same number of students chose lacrosse and swimming. The number of students who chose soccer was double the number of students who chose lacrosse. The number of students who chose football was triple the number of students who chose swimming. If 434 students completed the survey, how many students chose each sport?

2. At Prairie Elementary School, students are asked to pick their lunch ahead of time so the kitchen staff will know what to prepare. On Monday, 6 times as many students chose hamburgers as chose salads. The number of students who chose lasagna was one third the number of students who chose hamburgers. If 225 students ordered lunch, how many students chose each option if hamburger, salad, and lasagna were the only three options?

Lesson 29: Multi-Step Problems—All Operations
Date: 12/16/13

S.130

3. The art teacher, Mr. Gonzalez, is preparing for a project. In order for students to have the correct supplies, Mr. Gonzalez needs 10 times more markers than pieces of construction paper. He needs the same number of bottles of glue as pieces of construction paper. The number of scissors required for the project is half the number of piece of construction paper. If Mr. Gonzalez collected 400 items for the project, how many of each supply did he collect?

4. The math teacher, Ms. Zentz, is buying appropriate math tools to use throughout the year. She is planning on buying twice as many rulers as protractors. The number of calculators Ms. Zentz is planning on buying is one quarter of the number of protractors. If Ms. Zentz buys 65 items, how many protractors does Ms. Zentz buy?

Problem Set

Solve the problems and then check your answers with the word problem.

1. On average, a baby uses three times the number of large diapers as small diapers, and double the number of medium diapers as small diapers.
   a. If the average baby uses 2,940 diapers size large and smaller, how many of each size would be used?
   b. Support your answer with equations.

2. Tom has three times as many pencils as pens, but has a total of 100 writing utensils.
   a. How many pencils does Tom have?
   b. How many more pencils than pens does Tom have?

3. Serena's mom is planning her birthday party. She bought balloons, plates, and cups. Serena's mom bought twice as many plates as cups. The number of balloons Serena's mom bought was half the number of cups.
   a. If Serena's mom bought 84 items, how many of each item did she buy?
   b. Tammy brought 12 balloons to the party. How many total balloons were at Serena's birthday party?
   c. If half the plates and all but four cups were used during the party, how many plates and cups were used?

4. Elizabeth has a lot of jewelry. She has four times as many earrings as watches, but half the number of necklaces as earrings. Elizabeth has the same number of necklaces as bracelets.
   a. If Elizabeth has 117 pieces of jewelry, how many earrings does she have?
   b. Support your answers with an equation.

5. Claudia was cooking breakfast for her entire family. She made double the amount of chocolate chip pancakes as she did regular pancakes. She only made half as many blueberry pancakes as she did regular pancakes. Claudia also knows her family loves sausage, so she made triple the amount of sausage as blueberry pancakes.
   a. How many of each breakfast item did Claudia make if she cooked 90 items in total?
   b. After everyone ate breakfast, there were 4 chocolate chip pancakes, 5 regular pancakes, 1 blueberry pancake, and no sausage left. How many of each item did the family eat?

6. During a basketball game, Jeremy scored triple the number of points as Donovan. Kolby scored double the number of points as Donovan.
   a. If the three boys scored 36 points, how many points did each boy score?
   b. Support your answer with an equation.

Lesson 30: One-Step Problems in the Real World

Opening Exercise

Draw an example of each term and write a brief description.

Acute

Obtuse

Right

Straight

Reflex

Example 1

$\angle ABC$ measures 90°. The angle has been separated into two angles. If one angle measures 57°, what is the measure of the other angle?

How are these two angles related?

What equation could we use to solve for x.

Now let's solve.

Example 2

Michelle is designing a parking lot. She has determined that one of the angles should be 115°. What is the measure of angle x and angle y?

How is angle x related to the 115° angle?

What equation would we use to show this?

How would you solve this equation?

How is angle y related the angle that measures 115° ?

Example 3

A beam of light is reflected off of a mirror. Below is a diagram of the reflected beam. Determine the missing angle measure.

How are the angles in this question related?

What equation could we write to represent the situation?

How would you solve an equation like this?

Exercises

Write and solve an equation in each of the problems.

1. $< ABC$ measures $90°$. It has been split into two angles, $< ABD$ and $< DBC$. The measure of the two angles is in a ratio of $2 : 1$. What are the measures of each angle?

2. Solve for x.

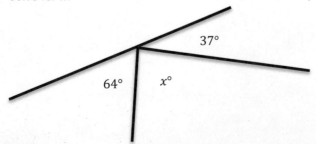

3. Candice is building a rectangular piece of fence according to the plans her boss gave her. One of the angles is not labeled. Write an equation and use it to determine the measure of the unknown angle.

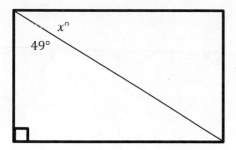

4. Rashid hit a hockey puck against the wall at a 38° angle. The puck hit the wall and traveled in a new direction. Determine the missing angle in the diagram.

5. Jaxon is creating a mosaic design on a rectangular table. He has added two pieces to one of the corners. The first piece has an angle measuring 38° that is placed in the corner. A second piece has an angle measuring 27° that is also placed in the corner. Draw a diagram to model the situation. Then, write an equation and use it to determine the measure of the unknown angle in a third piece that could be added to the corner of the table.

Problem Set

1. Solve for x.

2. $< BAE$ measures 90°. Solve for x.

3. Thomas is putting in a tile floor. He needs to determine the angles that should be cut in the tiles to fit in the corner. The angle in the corner measures 90°. One piece of the tile will have a measure of 24°. Write an equation and use it to determine the measure of the unknown angle.

4. Solve for x.

5.　Aram has been studying the mathematics behind pinball machines. He made the following diagram of one of his observations. Determine the measure of the missing angle.

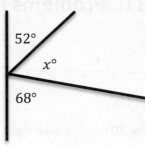

6.　The measures of two angles have a sum of 90°. The measures of the angles are in a ratio of 2: 1. Determine the measures of both angles.

7.　The measures of two angles have a sum of 180°. The measures of the angles are in a ratio of 5: 1. Determine the measures of both angles.

Lesson 31: Problems in Mathematical Terms

Classwork

Example 1

Marcus reads for 30 minutes each night. He wants to determine the total number of minutes he will read over the course of a month. He wrote the equation $t = 30d$ to represent the total amount of time that he has spent reading, where t represents the total number of minutes read and d represents the number of days that he read during the month. Determine which variable is independent and which is dependent. Then create a table to show how many minutes he has read in the first seven days.

Independent variable _____

Dependent variable _____

Example 2

Kira designs websites. She can create three different websites each week. Kira wants to create an equation that will give her the total number of websites she can design given the number of weeks she works. Determine the independent and dependent variables. Create a table to show the number of websites she can design over the first 5 weeks. Finally, write an equation to represent the number of websites she can design when given any number of weeks.

Independent variable _____

Dependent variable _____

Equation _____

Example 3

Priya streams movies through a company that charges her a $5 monthly fee plus $1.50 per movie. Determine the independent and dependent variables, write an equation to model the situation and create a table to show the total cost per month given that she might stream between 4 and 10 movies in a month.

Independent variable _____

Dependent variable _____

Equation _____

Exercises

1. Sarah is purchasing pencils to share. Each package has 12 pencils. The equation $n = 12p$, where n is the number of pencils and p is the number of packages can be used to determine the total number of pencils Sarah purchased. Determine which variable is dependent and which is independent. Then make a table showing the number of pencils purchased for 3–7 packages.

2. Charlotte reads 4 books each week. Let b be the number of books she reads each week and let w be the number of weeks that she reads. Determine which variable is dependent and which is independent. Then write an equation to model the situation, and make a graph that shows the number of books read in under 6 weeks.

3. A miniature golf course has a special group rate. You can pay $20 plus $3 per person when you have a group of 5 or more friends. Let f be the number of friends and c be the total cost. Determine which variable is independent and which is dependent, and write an equation that models the situation. Then make a table to show the cost for 5 to 12 friends.

4. Carlos is shopping for school supplies. He bought a pencil box for $3 and he also needs to buy notebooks. Each notebook is $2. Let $t =$ the total cost of the supplies and n be the number of notebooks. Determine which variable is independent and which is dependent, and write an equation that models the situation. Then make a table to show the cost for 1 to 5 notebooks.

Problem Set

1. Jaziyah sells 3 houses each month. To determine the number of houses she can sell in any given number of months she uses the equation $t = 3m$, where t is the total number of houses sold and m is the number of months. Name the independent and dependent variables. Then create a table to show how many houses she sells in less than 6 months.

2. Joshua spends 25 minutes of each day reading. Let d be the number of days that he reads and let m represent the total minutes of reading. Determine which variable is independent and which is dependent. Then write an equation that will model the situation. Make a table showing the number of minutes spent reading over 7 days.

3. Each package of hot dog buns contains 8 buns. Let p be the number of packages and b be the total number of buns. Determine which variable is independent and which is dependent. Then write an equation that will model the situation and make a table showing the number of hot dog buns in 3 to 8 packages.

4. Emma was given 5 sea shells. Each week she collected 3 more. Let w be the number of weeks and s be the number of sea shells she has total. Which variable is independent and which is dependent? Write an equation to model the relationship, and make a table to show how many shells she has from week 4 to week 10.

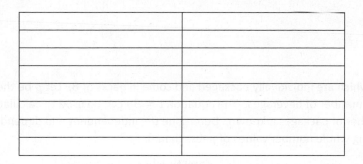

5. Emilia is shopping for fresh produce at a farmer's market. She bought a watermelon for $5 and she also wants to buy peppers. Each pepper is $0.75. Let $t =$ the total cost of the produce and n be the number of peppers bought. Determine which variable is independent and which is dependent, and write an equation that models the situation. Then make a table to show the cost for 1 to 5 peppers.

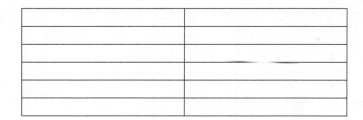

6. A taxi cab service charges a flat fee of $7 plus an additional $1.25 per mile. Show the relationship between the total cost and the number of miles. Which variable is independent and which is dependent? Write an equation to model the relationship, and make a table to show the cost of 4 to 10 miles.

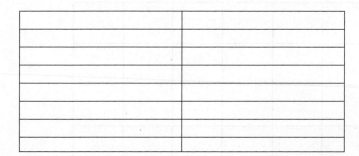

Lesson 32: Multi-Step Problems in the Real World

Classwork

Opening Exercise

Xin is buying beverages for a party, which are individually packaged and come in packs of 8. Let p be the number of packages Xin buys and t be the total number of beverages. The equation $t = 8p$ can be used to calculate the total number of beverages when the number of packages is known. Determine the independent and dependent variable in this scenario. Then make a table using whole number values of p less than 6.

Number of Packages (p)	Total Number of Beverages ($t = 8p$)
0	
1	
2	
3	
4	
5	

Example 1

Make a graph for the table in the Opening Exercise.

Example 2

Use the graph to determine which variable is the independent variable and which is the dependent variable. Then state the relationship between the quantities represented by the variables.

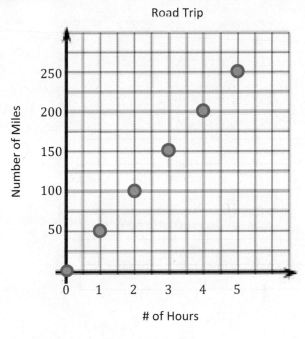

Road Trip

Exercises

1. Each week Quentin earns $30. If he saves this money, create a graph that shows the total amount of money Quentin has saved from week 1 through week 8. Write an equation that represents the relationship between the number of weeks that Quentin has saved his money (w) and the total amount of money he has saved (s). Then name the independent and dependent variable. Write a sentence that shows this relationship.

2. Zoe is collecting books to donate. She started with 3 and collects two more each week. She is using the equation $b = 2w + 3$, where b is the total number of books collected and w is the number of weeks she has been collecting. Name the independent and dependent variables. Then create a graph to represent how many books Zoe has collected when w is 5 or less.

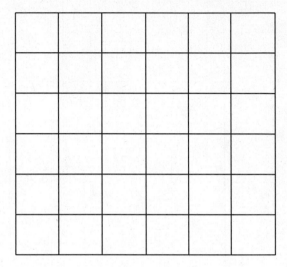

3. Eliana plans to visit the fair. She must pay $5 to enter the fair grounds and an additional $3 per ride. Write an equation to show the relationship between r, the number of rides, and t, the total cost. State which variable is dependent and which is independent. Then create a graph that models the equation.

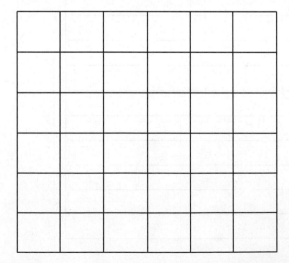

1. Caleb started saving money in a cookie jar. He started with $25. He adds $10 to the account each week. Write an equation where w is the number of weeks and t is the total amount in the account. Determine which variable is independent and which is dependent. Then graph the total amount in the account for w being less than 6 weeks.

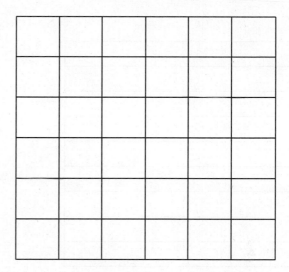

2. Kevin is taking a taxi from the airport to his home. There is a $6 flat fee for riding in the taxi. In addition, Kevin must also pay $1 per mile. Write an equation where m is the number of miles and t is the total cost of the taxi ride. Determine which variable is independent and which is dependent. Then graph the total cost for m being less than 6 miles.

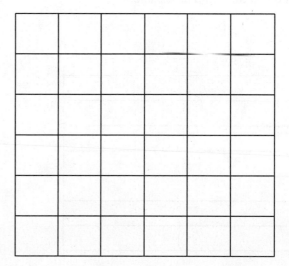

3. Anna started with $10. She saved an additional $5 each week. Write an equation that can be used to determine the total amount saved, t, after a given number of weeks, w. Determine which variable is independent and which is dependent. Then graph the total amount saved for first 8 weeks.

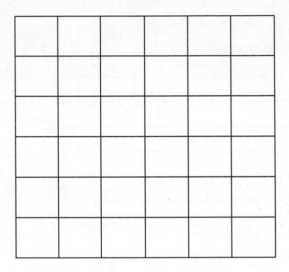

4. Aliyah is purchasing produce at the farmers' market. She plans to buy $10 worth of potatoes and some apples. The apples cost $1.50 per pound. Write an equation to show the total cost of the produce, where T is the total cost and a is the number of pounds of apples. Determine which variable is dependent and independent. Then graph the equation on the coordinate plane.

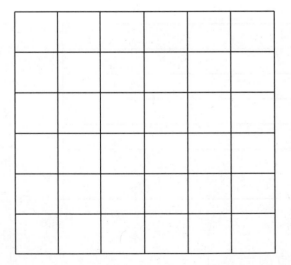

Lesson 33: From Equations to Inequalities

Classwork

Example 1

What value(s) does the variable have to represent for the number sentence to be a true statement? What value(s) does the variable have to represent for the number sentence to be a false statement?

a. $y + 6 = 16$

b. $y + 6 > 16$

c. $y + 6 \geq 16$

d. $3y = 15$

e. $3g < 15$

f. $3g \leq 15$

Example 2

Which of the following numbers make the equation true? $\{0, 3, 5, 8, 10, 14\}$

a. $m + 4 = 12$

b. $m + 4 < 12$

c. $f - 4 = 2$

d. $f - 4 > 2$

e. $\frac{1}{2}h = 8$

f. $\frac{1}{2}h \geq 8$

Exercises

Choose the numbers that make the equation or inequality true from the following set of numbers: $\{0, 1, 5, 8, 11, 17\}$.

1. $m + 5 = 6$

2. $m + 5 \leq 6$

3. $5h = 40$

4. $5h > 40$

5. $\frac{1}{2}y = 5$

6. $\frac{1}{2}y \leq 5$

7. $k - 3 = 20$

8. $k - 3 > 20$

Problem Set

Choose the numbers that make the equation or inequality true from the following set of numbers: $\{0, 3, 4, 5, 9, 13, 18, 24\}$.

1. $h - 8 = 5$

2. $h - 8 < 5$

3. $4g = 36$

4. $4g \geq 36$

5. $\frac{1}{4}y = 7$

6. $\frac{1}{4}y > 7$

7. $m - 3 = 10$

8. $m - 3 \leq 10$

Lesson 34: Writing and Graphing Inequalities in Real-World Problems

Classwork

Example 1

Statement	Inequality	Graph

a. Caleb has at least $5.   _____

b. Tarek has more than $5.   _____

c. Vanessa has at most $5.   _____

d. Li Chen has less than $5.   _____

Example 2

Kelly works for Quick Oil Change. If customers have to wait longer than 20 minutes for the oil change the company does not charge for the service. The fastest oil change that Kelly has ever done took 6 minutes. Show the possible customer wait times in which the company charges the customer.

Example 3

Gurnaz has been mowing lawns to save money for a concert. Gurnaz will need to work for at least six hours to save enough money but he must work less than 16 hours this week. Write an inequality to represent this situation, and then graph the solution.

Exercises

Write an inequality to represent each situation. Then graph the solution.

1. Blayton is at most 2 meters above sea level.

2. Edith must read for a minimum of 20 minutes.

3. Travis milks his cows each morning. He has never gotten less than 3 gallons of milk however he always gets less than 9 gallons of milk.

4. Rita can make 8 cakes for a bakery each day. So far she has orders for more than 32 cakes. Right now, Rita needs more than four days to make all 32 cakes.

5. Rita must have all the orders placed right now done in 7 days or less. How will this change your inequality and your graph?

Extension

6. Kasey has been mowing lawns to save up money for a concert. He earns $15 per hour and needs at least $90 to go to the concert. How many hours should he mow?

7. Rachel can make 8 cakes for a bakery each day. So far she has orders for more than 32 cakes. How many days will it take her to complete the orders?

8. Ranger saves $70 each week. He needs to save at least $2,800 to go on a trip to Europe. How many weeks will he need to save?

9. Clara has less than $75. She wants to buy 3 pairs of shoes. What price shoes can Clara afford if all the shoes are the same price?

10. A gym charges $25 per month plus $4 extra to swim in the pool for an hour. If a member only has $45 to spend each month, at most how many hours can the member swim?

Problem Set

Write and graph an inequality for each problem.

1. At least 13.

2. Less than 7.

3. Chad will need at least 24 minutes to complete the 5K race. However, he wants to finish in under 30 minutes.

4. Eva saves $60 each week. Since she needs to save at least $2,400 to go on a trip to Europe, she will need to save for at least 40 weeks.

5. Clara has $100. She wants to buy 4 pairs of the same pants. Due to tax, Clara can afford pants that are less than $25.

6. A gym charges $30 per month plus $4 extra to swim in the pool for an hour. Because a member has just $50 to spend at the gym each month, the member can swim 5 hours at most.

Copy Ready Materials

Name _____   Date _____

Lesson 1: The Relationship of Addition and Subtraction

Exit Ticket

1. Draw tape diagrams to represent each of the following number sentences.

   a. $3 + 5 - 5 = 3$

   b. $8 - 2 + 2 = 8$

2. Fill in each blank.

   a. $65 + \underline{\hspace{1cm}} - 15 = 65$

   b. $\underline{\hspace{1cm}} + g - g = k$

   c. $a + b - \underline{\hspace{1cm}} = a$

   d. $367 - 93 + 93 = \underline{\hspace{1cm}}$

$$w + x$$

$$w$$

$$x$$

$$w$$

$$x$$

$$w + x$$

$$w$$

$$x$$

$$w$$

$$x$$

Name _____   Date _____

Lesson 2: The Relationship of Multiplication and Division

Exit Ticket

1. Fill in the blank to make each number sentence true.

   a. $12 \div 3 \times \underline{\hspace{1cm}} = 12$

   b. $f \times h \div h = \underline{\hspace{1cm}}$

   c. $45 \times \underline{\hspace{1cm}} \div 15 = 45$

   d. $\underline{\hspace{1cm}} \div r \times r = p$

2. Draw a series of tape diagrams to represent the following number sentences.
   a. $12 \div 3 \times 3 = 12$

   b. $4 \times 5 \div 5 = 4$

Division of Fractions – Round 1

Number Correct: _____

Directions: Determine the quotient of the fractions.

1.	$\dfrac{1}{2} \div \dfrac{3}{5}$		16.	$6\dfrac{7}{8} \div 11\dfrac{2}{3}$	
2.	$\dfrac{5}{6} \div \dfrac{1}{5}$		17.	$5\dfrac{5}{6} \div 3\dfrac{1}{2}$	
3.	$\dfrac{3}{7} \div \dfrac{6}{11}$		18.	$10\dfrac{5}{8} \div 12\dfrac{3}{7}$	
4.	$\dfrac{2}{5} \div \dfrac{8}{9}$		19.	$9\dfrac{1}{3} \div 8\dfrac{2}{5}$	
5.	$\dfrac{1}{6} \div \dfrac{9}{10}$		20.	$\dfrac{3}{4} \div 6\dfrac{7}{10}$	
6.	$\dfrac{11}{12} \div \dfrac{8}{9}$		21.	$2\dfrac{1}{3} \div 3\dfrac{5}{6}$	
7.	$\dfrac{5}{6} \div \dfrac{10}{13}$		22.	$2\dfrac{4}{5} \div 7\dfrac{9}{10}$	
8.	$\dfrac{7}{8} \div \dfrac{13}{15}$		23.	$5\dfrac{8}{9} \div 3\dfrac{3}{5}$	
9.	$\dfrac{3}{5} \div \dfrac{7}{9}$		24.	$12\dfrac{5}{9} \div 5$	
10.	$\dfrac{14}{17} \div \dfrac{13}{20}$		25.	$1\dfrac{5}{6} \div 2\dfrac{6}{7}$	
11.	$3\dfrac{1}{2} \div 4\dfrac{4}{5}$		26.	$10 \div 5\dfrac{8}{9}$	
12.	$6\dfrac{1}{5} \div 6\dfrac{3}{4}$		27.	$14\dfrac{3}{5} \div 10$	
13.	$2\dfrac{1}{4} \div 3\dfrac{1}{8}$		28.	$7\dfrac{9}{11} \div 1\dfrac{9}{10}$	
14.	$1\dfrac{3}{5} \div \dfrac{7}{8}$		29.	$15\dfrac{2}{3} \div 24$	
15.	$\dfrac{1}{5} \div 4\dfrac{1}{2}$		30.	$32 \div 12\dfrac{6}{7}$	

Division of Fractions – Round 2

Number Correct: _____

Improvement: _____

Directions: Determine the quotient of the fractions.

1.	$\dfrac{1}{2} \div \dfrac{3}{4}$	
2.	$\dfrac{3}{5} \div \dfrac{1}{7}$	
3.	$\dfrac{5}{6} \div \dfrac{1}{8}$	
4.	$\dfrac{3}{8} \div \dfrac{5}{9}$	
5.	$\dfrac{1}{4} \div \dfrac{2}{5}$	
6.	$\dfrac{7}{8} \div \dfrac{9}{10}$	
7.	$\dfrac{8}{11} \div \dfrac{4}{5}$	
8.	$\dfrac{5}{6} \div \dfrac{7}{12}$	
9.	$\dfrac{3}{4} \div \dfrac{8}{9}$	
10.	$\dfrac{7}{11} \div \dfrac{4}{7}$	
11.	$1\dfrac{3}{4} \div \dfrac{1}{2}$	
12.	$\dfrac{1}{10} \div 2\dfrac{3}{4}$	
13.	$5\dfrac{2}{3} \div \dfrac{7}{9}$	
14.	$\dfrac{5}{6} \div 6\dfrac{1}{2}$	
15.	$\dfrac{6}{7} \div 2\dfrac{1}{3}$	

16.	$\dfrac{7}{8} \div 2\dfrac{1}{4}$	
17.	$\dfrac{3}{4} \div 2\dfrac{3}{5}$	
18.	$4\dfrac{1}{5} \div 2\dfrac{1}{3}$	
19.	$4\dfrac{3}{8} \div \dfrac{2}{7}$	
20.	$\dfrac{4}{5} \div 2\dfrac{1}{8}$	
21.	$1\dfrac{1}{2} \div 3\dfrac{5}{6}$	
22.	$3\dfrac{2}{3} \div 2\dfrac{1}{4}$	
23.	$4\dfrac{3}{5} \div 1\dfrac{3}{4}$	
24.	$7\dfrac{1}{2} \div 6\dfrac{1}{3}$	
25.	$3\dfrac{4}{5} \div 2\dfrac{9}{10}$	
26.	$3\dfrac{5}{6} \div 2\dfrac{1}{2}$	
27.	$3\dfrac{3}{4} \div 4\dfrac{1}{8}$	
28.	$5 \div 4\dfrac{5}{6}$	
29.	$3\dfrac{1}{4} \div 2$	
30.	$8 \div 5\dfrac{1}{3}$	

Name _____   Date _____

Lesson 3: The Relationship of Multiplication and Addition

Exit Ticket

Write an equivalent expression to show the relationship of multiplication and addition.

1. $8 + 8 + 8 + 8 + 8 + 8 + 8 + 8 + 8$

2. 4×9

3. $6 + 6 + 6$

4. $7h$

5. $j + j + j + j + j$

6. $u + u + u + u + u + u + u + u + u + u$

Name _____   Date _____

Lesson 4: The Relationship of Division and Subtraction

Exit Ticket

1.   Represent $56 \div 8 = 7$ using subtraction. Explain your reasoning.

2.   Explain why $30 \div x = 6$ is the same as $30 - x - x - x - x - x - x = 0$. What is the value of x in this example?

Graphic Organizer Reproducible

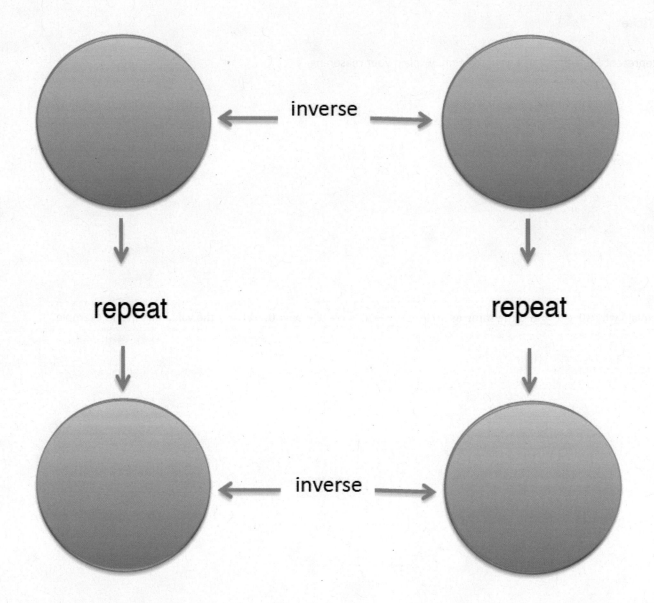

Name _____   Date_____

Lesson 5: Exponents

Exit Ticket

1. What is the difference between $6z$ and z^6?

2. Write 10^3 as a multiplication expression having repeated factors.

3. Write $8 \times 8 \times 8 \times 8$ using exponents.

Name _____   Date _____

Lesson 6: Order of Operations

Exit Ticket

1. Evaluate this expression: $39 \div (2 + 1) - 2 \times (4 + 1)$

2. Evaluate this expression: $12 \times (3 + 2^2) \div 2 - 10$

3. Evaluate this expression: $12 \times (3 + 2)^2 \div 2 - 10$

Name _____ Date _____

Lesson 7: Replacing Letters with Numbers

Exit Ticket

1. In the drawing below, what do the letters *l* and *w* represent?

2. What does the expression $l + w + l + w$ represent?

3. What does the expression $l \cdot w$ represent?

4. The rectangle below is congruent to the rectangle shown in Problem 1. Use this information to evaluate the expressions from Problems 2 and 3.

Name _____   Date _____

Lesson 8: Replacing Numbers with Letters

Exit Ticket

1. State the commutative property of addition, and provide an example using two different numbers.

2. State the commutative property of multiplication, and provide an example using two different numbers.

3. State the additive property of zero, and provide an example using any other number.

4. State the multiplicative identity property of one, and provide an example using any other number.

Division of Fractions – Round 1

Number Correct: _____

Directions: Determine the quotient of the fractions.

1.	$\dfrac{4}{10} \div \dfrac{2}{10}$	
2.	$\dfrac{9}{12} \div \dfrac{3}{12}$	
3.	$\dfrac{6}{10} \div \dfrac{4}{10}$	
4.	$\dfrac{2}{8} \div \dfrac{3}{8}$	
5.	$\dfrac{2}{7} \div \dfrac{6}{7}$	
6.	$\dfrac{11}{9} \div \dfrac{8}{9}$	
7.	$\dfrac{5}{13} \div \dfrac{10}{13}$	
8.	$\dfrac{7}{8} \div \dfrac{13}{16}$	
9.	$\dfrac{3}{5} \div \dfrac{7}{10}$	
10.	$\dfrac{9}{30} \div \dfrac{3}{5}$	
11.	$\dfrac{1}{3} \div \dfrac{4}{5}$	
12.	$\dfrac{2}{5} \div \dfrac{3}{4}$	
13.	$\dfrac{3}{4} \div \dfrac{5}{9}$	
14.	$\dfrac{4}{5} \div \dfrac{7}{12}$	
15.	$\dfrac{3}{8} \div \dfrac{5}{2}$	

16.	$3\dfrac{1}{8} \div \dfrac{2}{3}$	
17.	$1\dfrac{5}{6} \div \dfrac{1}{2}$	
18.	$\dfrac{5}{8} \div 2\dfrac{3}{4}$	
19.	$\dfrac{1}{3} \div 1\dfrac{4}{5}$	
20.	$\dfrac{3}{4} \div 2\dfrac{3}{10}$	
21.	$2\dfrac{1}{5} \div 1\dfrac{1}{6}$	
22.	$2\dfrac{4}{9} \div 1\dfrac{3}{5}$	
23.	$1\dfrac{2}{9} \div 3\dfrac{2}{5}$	
24.	$2\dfrac{2}{3} \div 3$	
25.	$1\dfrac{3}{4} \div 2\dfrac{2}{5}$	
26.	$4 \div 1\dfrac{2}{9}$	
27.	$3\dfrac{1}{5} \div 6$	
28.	$2\dfrac{5}{6} \div 1\dfrac{1}{3}$	
29.	$10\dfrac{2}{3} \div 8$	
30.	$15 \div 2\dfrac{3}{5}$	

Division of Fractions – Round 2

Number Correct: _____

Improvement: _____

Directions: Determine the quotient of the fractions.

1.	$\dfrac{10}{2} \div \dfrac{5}{2}$	
2.	$\dfrac{6}{5} \div \dfrac{3}{5}$	
3.	$\dfrac{10}{7} \div \dfrac{2}{7}$	
4.	$\dfrac{3}{8} \div \dfrac{5}{8}$	
5.	$\dfrac{1}{4} \div \dfrac{3}{12}$	
6.	$\dfrac{7}{5} \div \dfrac{3}{10}$	
7.	$\dfrac{8}{15} \div \dfrac{4}{5}$	
8.	$\dfrac{5}{6} \div \dfrac{5}{12}$	
9.	$\dfrac{3}{5} \div \dfrac{7}{9}$	
10.	$\dfrac{3}{10} \div \dfrac{3}{9}$	
11.	$\dfrac{3}{4} \div \dfrac{7}{9}$	
12.	$\dfrac{7}{10} \div \dfrac{3}{8}$	
13.	$4 \div \dfrac{4}{9}$	
14.	$\dfrac{5}{8} \div 7$	
15.	$9 \div \dfrac{2}{3}$	

16.	$\dfrac{5}{8} \div 1\dfrac{3}{4}$	
17.	$\dfrac{1}{4} \div 2\dfrac{2}{5}$	
18.	$2\dfrac{3}{5} \div \dfrac{3}{8}$	
19.	$1\dfrac{3}{5} \div \dfrac{2}{9}$	
20.	$4 \div 2\dfrac{3}{8}$	
21.	$1\dfrac{1}{2} \div 5$	
22.	$3\dfrac{1}{3} \div 1\dfrac{3}{4}$	
23.	$2\dfrac{2}{5} \div 1\dfrac{1}{4}$	
24.	$3\dfrac{1}{2} \div 2\dfrac{2}{3}$	
25.	$1\dfrac{4}{5} \div 2\dfrac{3}{4}$	
26.	$3\dfrac{1}{6} \div 1\dfrac{3}{5}$	
27.	$3\dfrac{3}{5} \div 2\dfrac{1}{8}$	
28.	$5 \div 1\dfrac{1}{6}$	
29.	$3\dfrac{3}{4} \div 5\dfrac{1}{2}$	
30.	$4\dfrac{2}{3} \div 5\dfrac{1}{4}$	

Name _____   Date _____

Lesson 9: Writing Addition and Subtraction Expressions

Exit Ticket

1.   Write an expression showing the sum of 8 and a number f.

2.   Write an expression showing 5 less than the number k.

3.   Write an expression showing the sum of a number h and a number w minus 11.

Name _____   Date _____

Lesson 10: Writing and Expanding Multiplication Expressions

Exit Ticket

1. Rewrite the expression using the fewest number of symbols and characters possible.

    a. $5g \cdot 7h$

    b. $3 \cdot 4 \cdot 5 \cdot m \cdot n$

2. Name the parts of the expression. Then expand.

    a. $14b$

    b. $30jk$

$2 \bullet 5 \bullet m$				$35mpt$
$45mp$	$40p$		$24m$	$2 \bullet 3 \bullet 3 \bullet p \bullet t$
	$2 \bullet 7 \bullet m \bullet p$	★		$11mp$
$28pt$			$22mp$	$2 \bullet 2 \bullet 3 \bullet 3 \bullet m$
$27mp$		$5mpt$		$45mpt$

$22mp$		$40p$		
	$28pt$		$2 \bullet 5 \bullet m$	$2 \bullet 2 \bullet 3 \bullet 3 \bullet m$
	$45mp$	★		$35mpt$
$24m$			$45mpt$	$27mp$
$2 \bullet 7 \bullet m \bullet p$	$5mpt$		$11mp$	$2 \bullet 3 \bullet 3 \bullet p \bullet t$

COMMON CORE™

Lesson 10:   Writing and Expanding Multiplication Expressions
Date: 12/11/13

$45mp$	$40p$			$24m$
$2 \bullet 3 \bullet 3 \bullet p \bullet t$	$5mpt$	$22m$		
$11mp$		★	$45mpt$	$2 \bullet 2 \bullet 3 \bullet 3 \bullet m$
	$27mp$	$2 \bullet 7 \bullet m \bullet p$		$28pt$
	$2 \bullet 5 \bullet m$		$35mpt$	

Name _____   Date _____

Lesson 11: Factoring Expressions

Exit Ticket

Use greatest common factor and the distributive property to write equivalent expressions.

1. $2x + 8y$

2. $13ab + 15ab$

3. $20g + 24h$

Greatest Common Factor – Round 1

Number Correct: _____

Directions: Determine the greatest common factor of each pair of numbers.

1.	GCF of 10 and 50	
2.	GCF of 5 and 35	
3.	GCF of 3 and 12	
4.	GCF of 8 and 20	
5.	GCF of 15 and 35	
6.	GCF of 10 and 75	
7.	GCF of 9 and 30	
8.	GCF of 15 and 33	
9.	GCF of 12 and 28	
10.	GCF of 16 and 40	
11.	GCF of 24 and 32	
12.	GCF of 35 and 49	
13.	GCF of 45 and 60	
14.	GCF of 48 and 72	
15.	GCF of 50 and 42	

16.	GCF of 45 and 72	
17.	GCF of 28 and 48	
18.	GCF of 44 and 77	
19.	GCF of 39 and 66	
20.	GCF of 64 and 88	
21.	GCF of 42 and 56	
22.	GCF of 28 and 42	
23.	GCF of 13 and 91	
24.	GCF of 16 and 84	
25.	GCF of 36 and 99	
26.	GCF of 39 and 65	
27.	GCF of 27 and 87	
28.	GCF of 28 and 70	
29.	GCF of 26 and 91	
30.	GCF of 34 and 51	

Greatest Common Factor – Round 2

Number Correct: _____

Improvement: _____

Directions: Determine the greatest common factor of each pair of numbers.

1.	GCF of 20 and 80	
2.	GCF of 10 and 70	
3.	GCF of 9 and 36	
4.	GCF of 12 and 24	
5.	GCF of 15 and 45	
6.	GCF of 10 and 95	
7.	GCF of 9 and 45	
8.	GCF of 18 and 33	
9.	GCF of 12 and 32	
10.	GCF of 16 and 56	
11.	GCF of 40 and 72	
12.	GCF of 35 and 63	
13.	GCF of 30 and 75	
14.	GCF of 42 and 72	
15.	GCF of 30 and 28	

16.	GCF of 33 and 99	
17.	GCF of 38 and 76	
18.	GCF of 26 and 65	
19.	GCF of 39 and 48	
20.	GCF of 72 and 88	
21.	GCF of 21 and 56	
22.	GCF of 28 and 52	
23.	GCF of 51 and 68	
24.	GCF of 48 and 84	
25.	GCF of 21 and 63	
26.	GCF of 64 and 80	
27.	GCF of 36 and 90	
28.	GCF of 28 and 98	
29.	GCF of 39 and 91	
30.	GCF of 38 and 95	

Name _____   Date _____

Lesson 12: Distributing Expressions

Exit Ticket

Use the distributive property to expand the following expressions.

1. $2(b + c)$

2. $5(7h + 3m)$

3. $e(f + g)$

Name _____   Date _____

Lesson 13: Writing Division Expressions

Exit Ticket

Rewrite the expressions using the division symbol and as a fraction.

1. The quotient of m and 7.

2. Five divided by the sum of a and b.

3. The quotient of k decreased by 4 and 9.

Name _____ Date _____

Lesson 14: Writing Division Expressions

Exit Ticket

1. Write the division expression in words and as a fraction.

$$(g + 12) \div h$$

2. Write the following division expression using the division symbol and as a fraction: f divided by the quantity h minus 3.

Exercise Handout

Set A

1. $5 \div p$
2. The quotient of g and h
3. $w\overline{)23}$
4. $\dfrac{y}{x+8}$
5. 7 divided by the quantity a minus 6
6. $3\overline{)m+11}$
7. $(f + 2) \div g$
8. $\dfrac{c-9}{d+3}$

Set B

1. $h \div 11$
2. The quotient of m and n
3. $5\overline{)j}$
4. $\dfrac{h}{m-4}$
5. f divided by the quantity g minus 11
6. $18\overline{)a+5}$
7. $(y - 3) \div x$
8. $\dfrac{(g+5)}{(h-11)}$

Set C

1. $6 \div k$
2. The quotient of j and k
3. $10\overline{)a}$
4. $\dfrac{15}{f-2}$
5. 13 divided by the sum of h and 1
6. $3\overline{)c+18}$
7. $(h - 2) \div m$
8. $\dfrac{4-m}{n+11}$

Name _____   Date _____

Lesson 15: Read Expressions in Which Letters Stand for Numbers

Exit Ticket

1. Write two word expressions for each problem using different math vocabulary for each expression.

    a. $5d - 10$

    b. $\dfrac{a}{b+2}$

2. List five different math vocabulary words that could be used to describe each given expression.

    a. $3(d - 2) + 10$

    b. $\dfrac{ab}{c}$

Name _____   Date _____

Lesson 16: Write Expressions in which Letters Stand for Numbers

Exit Ticket

Mark the text by underlining key words, and then write an expression using variables and numbers for each of the statements below.

1. Omaya picked x amount of apples, took a break, and then picked v more. Write the expression that models the total number of apples Omaya picked.

2. A number h is tripled and then decreased by 8.

3. Sidney brings s carrots to school and combines them with Jenan's j carrots. She then splits them equally between 8 friends.

4. 15 less than the quotient of e and d.

5. Marissa's hair was 10 inches long, and then she cut h inches.

Name _____   Date _____

Lesson 17: Write Expressions in which Letters Stand for Numbers

Exit Ticket

Write an expression using letters and numbers for each problem below.

1. d squared.

2. A number x increased by 6 and then the sum is doubled.

3. The total of h and b is split into 5 equal groups.

4. Jazmin has increased her $45 by m dollars and then spends a third of the entire amount.

5. Bill has d more than 3 times the number of baseball cards as Frank. Frank has f baseball cards.

Addition of Decimals – Round 1

Number Correct: _____

Directions: Determine the sum of the decimals.

1.	$1.3 + 2.1$			18.	$14.08 + 34.27$	
2.	$3.6 + 2.2$			19.	$24.98 + 32.05$	
3.	$8.3 + 4.6$			20.	$76.67 + 40.33$	
4.	$14.3 + 12.6$			21.	$46.14 + 32.86$	
5.	$21.2 + 34.5$			22.	$475.34 + 125.88$	
6.	$14.81 + 13.05$			23.	$561.09 + 356.24$	
7.	$32.34 + 16.52$			24.	$872.78 + 135.86$	
8.	$56.56 + 12.12$			25.	$788.04 + 324.69$	
9.	$78.03 + 21.95$			26.	$467 + 32.78$	
10.	$32.14 + 45.32$			27.	$583.84 + 356$	
11.	$14.7 + 32.8$			28.	$549.2 + 678.09$	
12.	$24.5 + 42.9$			29.	$497.74 + 32.1$	
13.	$45.8 + 32.4$			30.	$741.9 + 826.14$	
14.	$71.7 + 32.6$			31.	$524.67 + 764$	
15.	$102.5 + 213.7$			32.	$821.3 + 106.87$	
16.	$365.8 + 127.4$			33.	$548 + 327.43$	
17.	$493.4 + 194.8$			34.	$108.97 + 268.03$	

Addition of Decimals – Round 2

Number Correct: _____

Improvement: _____

Directions: Determine the sum of the decimals.

1.	3.4 + 1.2	
2.	5.6 + 3.1	
3.	12.4 + 17.5	
4.	10.6 + 11.3	
5.	4.8 + 3.9	
6.	4.56 + 1.23	
7.	32.3 + 14.92	
8.	23.87 + 16.34	
9.	102.08 + 34.52	
10.	35.91 + 23.8	
11.	62.7 + 34.89	
12.	14.76 + 98.1	
13.	29.32 + 31.06	
14.	103.3 + 32.67	
15.	217.4 + 87.79	
16.	22.02 + 45.8	
17.	168.3 + 89.12	

18.	67.82 + 37.9	
19.	423.85 + 47.5	
20.	148.9 + 329.18	
21.	4 + 3.25	
22.	103.45 + 6	
23.	32.32 + 101.8	
24.	62.1 + 0.89	
25.	105 + 1.45	
26.	235.91 + 12	
27.	567.01 + 432.99	
28.	101 + 52.3	
29.	324.69 + 567.31	
30.	245 + 0.987	
31.	191.67 + 3.4	
32.	347.1 + 12.89	
33.	627 + 4.56	
34.	0.157 + 4.56	

Name _____   Date _____

1. Yolanda is planning out her vegetable garden. She decides that her garden will be square. Below are possible sizes of the garden she will create.

    a. Complete the table by continuing the pattern.

Side length	1 foot	2 feet	3 feet	4 feet	5 feet	x feet
Notation	$1^2 = 1 \cdot 1 = 1$					
Formula	$A = l \cdot w$ $A = 1 \cdot 1$ $A = 1^2$ ft^2 $A = 1$ ft^2					
Representation	▢	⊞				

    b. Yolanda decides the length of her square vegetable garden will be 17 ft. She calculates that the area of the garden is 34 ft^2. Determine if Yolanda's calculation is correct. Explain.

2. Yolanda creates garden cubes to plant flowers. She will fill the cubes with soil and needs to know the amount of soil that will fill each garden cube. Volume is determined by the following formula: $V = s^3$, where s represents the side length.

       32 inches

    a.   Represent the volume of the garden cube above using a numerical expression.

    b.   Evaluate the expression to determine the volume of the garden cube, and the amount of soil she will need for each cube.

3. Explain why $\left(\dfrac{1}{2}\right)^4 = \dfrac{1}{16}$.

4. Yolanda is building a patio in her back yard. She is interested in using both brick and wood for the flooring of the patio. Below is the plan she has created for the patio. All measurements are in feet.

    a. Create an expression to represent the area of the patio.

    b. Yolanda's husband develops another plan for the patio because he prefers the patio to be much wider than Yolanda's plan. Determine the length of the brick section and the length of the wood section. Then use the dimensions to write an expression that represent the area of the entire patio.

    24   48x 96

5. The landscaper hired for Yolanda's lawn suggests a patio that has the same measure of wood as it has brick.

    a. Express the perimeter of the patio in terms of x first using addition, and then using multiplication.

    b. Use substitution to determine if your expressions are equivalent. Explain.

---

6. Elena and Jorge have similar problems and find the same answer. Each determines that the solution to their problem is 24.

    Elena: $(14 + 42) \div 7 + 4^2$ Jorge: $14 + (42 \div 7) + 4^2$

    a. Evaluate each expression to determine if both Elena and Jorge are correct.

    b. Why would each find the solution of 24? What mistakes were made, if any?

7. Jackson gave Lena this expression to evaluate: $14(8 + 12)$. Lena said that to evaluate the expression was simple; just multiply the factors 14 and 20. Jackson told Lena she was wrong. He solved it by finding the product of 14 and 8, then adding that to the product of 14 and 12.

    a. Evaluate the expression using each student's method.

Lena's Method	Jackson's Method

    b. Who was right in this discussion? Why?

Name _____   Date _____

Lesson 18: Writing and Evaluating Expressions—Addition and Subtraction

Exit Ticket

1. Kathleen lost a tooth today. Now she has lost 4 more than her sister Cara lost.
    Write an expression to represent the number of teeth Cara has lost. Let K = the number of teeth Kathleen lost.

    Expression:

2. Write an expression to represent the number of teeth Kathleen has lost. Let C = the number of teeth Cara lost.

    Expression:

3. If Cara lost 3 teeth, how many teeth has Kathleen lost?

Name _____　　　Date _____

Lesson 19: Substituting to Evaluate Addition and Subtraction Expressions

Exit Ticket

1. Jenna and Allie work together at a piano factory. They both were hired on January 3, but Jenna was hired in 2005, and Allie was hired in 2009.

   a. Fill in the table below to summarize the two workers' experience totals.

Year	Allie's Years of Experience	Jenna's Years of Experience
2010		
2011		
2012		
2013		
2014		

   b. If both workers continue working at the piano factory, when Allie has A years of experience on the job, how many years of experience will Jenna have on the job?

   c. If both workers continue working at the piano factory, when Allie has 20 years of experience on the job, how many years of experience will Jenna have on the job?

Subtraction of Decimals – Round 1

Number Correct: _____

Directions: Subtract the decimals to determine the difference.

1.	9.4 – 4.1	
2.	7.4 – 3.2	
3.	49.5 – 32.1	
4.	20.9 – 17.2	
5.	9.2 – 6.8	
6.	7.48 – 2.26	
7.	58.8 – 43.72	
8.	38.99 – 24.74	
9.	116.32 – 42.07	
10.	46.83 – 35.6	
11.	54.8 – 43.66	
12.	128.43 – 87.3	
13.	144.54 – 42.09	
14.	105.4 – 68.22	
15.	239.5 – 102.37	

16.	41.72 – 33.9	
17.	354.65 – 67.5	
18.	448.9 – 329.18	
19.	8 – 5.38	
20.	94.21 – 8	
21.	134.25 – 103.17	
22.	25.8 – 0.42	
23.	115 – 1.65	
24.	187.49 – 21	
25.	345.77 – 248.69	
26.	108 – 54.7	
27.	336.91 – 243.38	
28.	264 – 0.742	
29.	174.38 – 5.9	
30.	323.2 – 38.74	

Subtraction of Decimals – Round 2

Number Correct: _____

Improvement: _____

Directions: Subtract the decimals to determine the difference.

1.	8.4 − 5.4		16.	14 − 10.32	
2.	5.6 − 3.1		17.	43.37 − 28	
3.	9.7 − 7.2		18.	24.56 − 18.88	
4.	14.3 − 12.1		19.	33.55 − 11.66	
5.	34.5 − 13.2		20.	329.56 − 284.49	
6.	14.86 − 13.85		21	574.3 − 342.18	
7.	43.27 − 32.14		22.	154 − 128.63	
8.	48.48 − 27.27		23.	247.1 − 138.57	
9.	64.74 − 31.03		24.	12 − 3.547	
10.	98.36 − 24.09		25.	1.415 − 0.877	
11.	33.54 − 24.4		26.	185.774 − 154.86	
12.	114.7 − 73.42		27.	65.251 − 36.9	
13.	45.2 − 32.7		28.	144.2 − 95.471	
14.	74.8 − 53.9		29.	2.11 − 1.949	
15.	238.4 − 114.36		30.	100 − 34.746	

Name _____   Date _____

Lesson 20: Writing and Evaluating Expressions—Multiplication and Division

Exit Ticket

1. Anna charges $8.50 per hour to babysit. Complete the table and answer the questions below.

Number of Hours	Amount Anna Charges in Dollars
1	
2	
5	
8	
H	

a. Write an expression describing her earnings for working H hours.

b. How much will she earn if she works for $3\frac{1}{2}$ hours?

c. How long will it take Anna to earn $51.00?

Name _____   Date _____

Lesson 21: Writing and Evaluating Expressions—Multiplication and Addition

Exit Ticket

1. Krystal Klear Cell Phone Company charges $5.00 per month for service. The company also charges $0.10 for each text message sent.

    a. Complete the table below to calculate the monthly charges for various numbers of text messages sent.

Number of Text Messages Sent (T)	Total Monthly Bill in Dollars
0	
10	
20	
30	
T	

    b. If Suzannah's budget limit is $10 per month, how many text messages can she send in one month?

Name _____   Date _____

Lesson 22: Writing and Evaluating Expressions—Exponents

Exit Ticket

1. Naomi's allowance is $2.00 per week. If she convinces her parents to double her allowance each week for two
    months, what will her weekly allowance be at the end of the second month (week 8)?

Week Number	Allowance
1	$2.00
2	
3	
4	
5	
6	
7	
8	
w	

2. Write the expression that describes Naomi's allowance during week w, in dollars.

Name _____   Date _____

Lesson 23: True and False Number Sentences

Exit Ticket

Substitute the value for the variable and state (in a complete sentence) whether the resulting number sentence is true or false. If true, find a value that would result in a false number sentence. If false, find a value that would result in a true number sentence.

1. $15a \geq 75$. Substitute 5 for a.

2. $23 + b = 30$. Substitute 10 for b.

3. $20 > 86 - h$. Substitute 45 for h.

4. $32 \geq 8m$. Substitute 5 for m.

Name _____   Date _____

Lesson 24: True and False Number Sentences

Exit Ticket

State when the following equations and inequalities will be true and when they will be false.

1. $5g > 45$

2. $14 = 5 + k$

3. $26 - w < 12$

4. $32 \leq a + 8$

5. $2 \cdot h \leq 16$

Name _____   Date _____

Lesson 25: Finding Solutions to Make Equations True

Exit Ticket

Find the solution to each equation.

1. $7f = 49$

2. $1 = \dfrac{r}{12}$

3. $1.5 = d + 0.8$

4. $9^2 = h$

5. $q = 45 - 19$

6. $40 = \dfrac{1}{2}p$

$a + 14 = 36$	22	$3^3 = b$
27	$\dfrac{c}{5} = 3$	15
$d - 10 = 32$	42	$24 = e + 11$
13	$32 = 4 \cdot f$	8
$9 = \dfrac{45}{g}$	5	$43 = h - 17$

　Lesson 25:　Finding Solutions to Make Equations True
Date:　12/16/13

60	$1.5 + 0.5 = j$	2
$9 \cdot \dfrac{1}{3} = k$	3	$m = \dfrac{56}{8}$
7	$n = 35.5 - 9.5$	26
$p + 13\dfrac{3}{4} = 32\dfrac{3}{4}$	19	$4 = \dfrac{1}{4}q$
16	$\dfrac{63}{r} = 7$	9

$$99 - u = 45 \qquad \bigg| \qquad 54$$

Division of Fractions – Round 1

Number Correct: _____

Directions: Determine the quotients of the fractions.

1.	$\dfrac{1}{2} \div \dfrac{3}{5}$	
2.	$\dfrac{5}{6} \div \dfrac{1}{5}$	
3.	$\dfrac{3}{7} \div \dfrac{6}{11}$	
4.	$\dfrac{2}{5} \div \dfrac{8}{9}$	
5.	$\dfrac{1}{6} \div \dfrac{9}{10}$	
6.	$\dfrac{11}{12} \div \dfrac{8}{9}$	
7.	$\dfrac{5}{6} \div \dfrac{10}{13}$	
8.	$\dfrac{7}{8} \div \dfrac{13}{15}$	
9.	$\dfrac{3}{5} \div \dfrac{7}{9}$	
10.	$\dfrac{14}{17} \div \dfrac{13}{20}$	
11.	$3\dfrac{1}{2} \div 4\dfrac{4}{5}$	
12.	$6\dfrac{1}{5} \div 6\dfrac{3}{4}$	
13.	$2\dfrac{1}{4} \div 3\dfrac{1}{8}$	
14.	$1\dfrac{3}{5} \div \dfrac{7}{8}$	
15.	$\dfrac{1}{5} \div 4\dfrac{1}{2}$	

16.	$6\dfrac{7}{8} \div 11\dfrac{2}{3}$	
17.	$5\dfrac{5}{6} \div 3\dfrac{1}{2}$	
18.	$10\dfrac{5}{8} \div 12\dfrac{3}{7}$	
19.	$9\dfrac{1}{3} \div 8\dfrac{2}{5}$	
20.	$\dfrac{3}{4} \div 6\dfrac{7}{10}$	
21.	$2\dfrac{1}{3} \div 3\dfrac{5}{6}$	
22.	$2\dfrac{4}{5} \div 7\dfrac{9}{10}$	
23.	$5\dfrac{8}{9} \div 3\dfrac{3}{5}$	
24.	$12\dfrac{5}{9} \div 5$	
25.	$1\dfrac{5}{6} \div 2\dfrac{6}{7}$	
26.	$10 \div 5\dfrac{8}{9}$	
27.	$14\dfrac{3}{5} \div 10$	
28.	$7\dfrac{9}{11} \div 1\dfrac{9}{10}$	
29.	$15\dfrac{2}{3} \div 24$	
30.	$32 \div 12\dfrac{6}{7}$	

Division of Fractions – Round 2

Number Correct: _____

Improvement: _____

Directions: Determine the quotients of the fractions.

1.	$\dfrac{1}{2} \div \dfrac{3}{4}$	
2.	$\dfrac{3}{5} \div \dfrac{1}{7}$	
3.	$\dfrac{5}{6} \div \dfrac{1}{8}$	
4.	$\dfrac{3}{8} \div \dfrac{5}{9}$	
5.	$\dfrac{1}{4} \div \dfrac{2}{5}$	
6.	$\dfrac{7}{8} \div \dfrac{9}{10}$	
7.	$\dfrac{8}{11} \div \dfrac{4}{5}$	
8.	$\dfrac{5}{6} \div \dfrac{7}{12}$	
9.	$\dfrac{3}{4} \div \dfrac{8}{9}$	
10.	$\dfrac{7}{11} \div \dfrac{4}{7}$	
11.	$1\dfrac{3}{4} \div \dfrac{1}{2}$	
12.	$\dfrac{1}{10} \div 2\dfrac{3}{4}$	
13.	$5\dfrac{2}{3} \div \dfrac{7}{9}$	
14.	$\dfrac{5}{6} \div 6\dfrac{1}{2}$	
15.	$\dfrac{6}{7} \div 2\dfrac{1}{3}$	

16.	$\dfrac{7}{8} \div 2\dfrac{1}{4}$	
17.	$\dfrac{3}{4} \div 2\dfrac{3}{5}$	
18.	$4\dfrac{1}{5} \div 2\dfrac{1}{3}$	
19.	$4\dfrac{3}{8} \div \dfrac{2}{7}$	
20.	$\dfrac{4}{5} \div 2\dfrac{1}{8}$	
21.	$1\dfrac{1}{2} \div 3\dfrac{5}{6}$	
22.	$3\dfrac{2}{3} \div 2\dfrac{1}{4}$	
23.	$4\dfrac{3}{5} \div 1\dfrac{3}{4}$	
24.	$7\dfrac{1}{2} \div 6\dfrac{1}{3}$	
25.	$3\dfrac{4}{5} \div 2\dfrac{9}{10}$	
26.	$3\dfrac{5}{6} \div 2\dfrac{1}{2}$	
27.	$3\dfrac{3}{4} \div 4\dfrac{1}{8}$	
28.	$5 \div 4\dfrac{5}{6}$	
29.	$3\dfrac{1}{4} \div 2$	
30.	$8 \div 5\dfrac{1}{3}$	

Lesson 25:
Date:

Finding Solutions to Make Equations True
12/16/13

Name _____ Date _____

Lesson 26: One-Step Equations—Addition and Subtraction

Exit Ticket

1. If you know the answer, state it. Then use a tape diagram to demonstrate why this is the correct answer. If you do not know the answer, find the solution using a tape diagram.

$$j + 12 = 25$$

2. Find the solution to the equation algebraically. Check your answer.

$$k - 16 = 4$$

Name _____   Date _____

Lesson 27: One-Step Equations—Multiplication and Division

Exit Ticket

Calculate the solution to each equation below using the indicated method. Remember to check your answers.

1. Use tape diagrams to find the solution of $\dfrac{r}{10} = 4$.

2. Find the solution of $64 = 16u$ algebraically.

3. Use the method of your choice to find the solution of $12 = 3v$.

Name _____   Date _____

Lesson 28: Two-Step Problems—All Operations

Exit Ticket

Use tape diagrams and equations to solve the problem with visual models and algebraic methods.

Alyssa is twice as old as Brittany, and Jazmyn is 15 years older than Alyssa. If Jazmyn is 35 years old, how old is Brittany? Let a represent Alyssa's age in years and b reprerent Brittany's age in years.

Addition of Decimals – Round 1   Number Correct: _____

Directions: Determine the sum of the decimals.

1.	1.3 + 2.1		18.	14.08 + 34.27	
2.	3.6 + 2.2		19.	24.98 + 32.05	
3.	8.3 + 4.6		20.	76.67 + 40.33	
4.	14.3 + 12.6		21.	46.14 + 32.86	
5.	21.2 + 34.5		22.	475.34 + 125.88	
6.	14.81 + 13.05		23.	561.09 + 356.24	
7.	32.34 + 16.52		24.	872.78 + 135.86	
8.	56.56 + 12.12		25.	788.04 + 324.69	
9.	78.03 + 21.95		26.	467 + 32.78	
10.	32.14 + 45.32		27.	583.84 + 356	
11.	14.7 + 32.8		28.	549.2 + 678.09	
12.	24.5 + 42.9		29.	497.74 + 32.1	
13.	45.8 + 32.4		30.	741.9 + 826.14	
14.	71.7 + 32.6		31.	524.67 + 764	
15.	102.5 + 213.7		32.	821.3 + 106.87	
16.	365.8 + 127.4		33.	548 + 327.43	
17.	493.4 + 194.8		34.	108.97 + 268.03	

Addition of Decimals – Round 2

Number Correct: _____

Improvement: _____

Directions: Determine the sum of the decimals.

1.	3.4 + 1.2		18.	67.82 + 37.9	
2.	5.6 + 3.1		19.	423.85 + 47.5	
3.	12.4 + 17.5		20.	148.9 + 329.18	
4.	10.6 + 11.3		21.	4 + 3.25	
5.	4.8 + 3.9		22.	103.45 + 6	
6.	4.56 + 1.23		23.	32.32 + 101.8	
7.	32.3 + 14.92		24.	62.1 + 0.89	
8.	23.87 + 16.34		25.	105 + 1.45	
9.	102.08 + 34.52		26.	235.91 + 12	
10.	35.91 + 23.8		27.	567.01 + 432.99	
11.	62.7 + 34.89		28.	101 + 52.3	
12.	14.76 + 98.1		29.	324.69 + 567.31	
13.	29.32 + 31.06		30.	245 + 0.987	
14.	103.3 + 32.67		31.	191.67 + 3.4	
15.	217.4 + 87.79		32.	347.1 + 12.89	
16.	22.02 + 45.8		33.	627 + 4.56	
17.	168.3 + 89.12		34.	0.157 + 4.56	

Name _____   Date _____

Lesson 29: Multi-Step Problems—All Operations

Exit Ticket

Solve the problem using tables and equations and then check your answer with the word problem. Try to find the answer only using two rows of numbers on your table.

A pet store owner, Byron, needs to determine how much food he needs to feed the animals. Byron knows that he needs to order the same amount of bird food as hamster food. He needs four times as much dog food as bird food, and needs half the amount of cat food as dog food. If Byron orders 600 packages of animal food, how much dog food does he buy? Let b represent the amount of bird food.

Name _____   Date _____

Lesson 30: One-Step Problems in the Real World

Exit Ticket

Write an equation and solve for the missing angle in each question.

1. Alejandro is repairing a stained glass window. He needs to take it apart to repair it. Before taking it apart he makes a sketch with angle measures to put it back together.

   Write an equation and use it to determine the measure of the unknown angle.

2. Hannah is putting in a tile floor. She needs to determine the angles that should be cut in the tiles to fit in the corner. The angle in the corner measures 90°. One piece of the tile will have a measure of 38°. Write an equation and use it to determine the measure of the unknown angle.

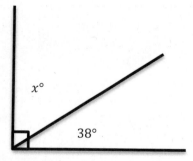

Subtraction of Decimals – Round 1

Number Correct: _____

Directions: Subtract the decimals to determine the difference.

1.	9.4 – 4.1		16.	41.72 – 33.9	
2.	7.4 – 3.2		17.	354.65 – 67.5	
3.	49.5 – 32.1		18.	448.9 – 329.18	
4.	20.9 – 17.2		19.	8 – 5.38	
5.	9.2 – 6.8		20.	94.21 – 8	
6.	7.48 – 2.26		21.	134.25 – 103.17	
7.	58.8 – 43.72		22.	25.8 – 0.42	
8.	38.99 – 24.74		23.	115 – 1.65	
9.	116.32 – 42.07		24.	187.49 – 21	
10.	46.83 – 35.6		25.	345.77 – 248.69	
11.	54.8 – 43.66		26.	108 – 54.7	
12.	128.43 – 87.3		27.	336.91 – 243.38	
13.	144.54 – 42.09		28.	264 – 0.742	
14.	105.4 – 68.22		29.	174.38 – 5.9	
15.	239.5 – 102.37		30.	323.2 – 38.74	

Subtraction of Decimals – Round 2

Number Correct: _____

Improvement: _____

Directions: Subtract the decimals to determine the difference.

1.	8.4 – 5.4	
2.	5.6 – 3.1	
3.	9.7 – 7.2	
4.	14.3 – 12.1	
5.	34.5 – 13.2	
6.	14.86 – 13.85	
7.	43.27 – 32.14	
8.	48.48 – 27.27	
9.	64.74 – 31.03	
10.	98.36 – 24.09	
11.	33.54 – 24.4	
12.	114.7 – 73.42	
13.	45.2 – 32.7	
14.	74.8 – 53.9	
15.	238.4 – 114.36	

16.	14 – 10.32	
17.	43.37 – 28	
18.	24.56 – 18.88	
19.	33.55 – 11.66	
20.	329.56 – 284.49	
21.	574.3 – 342.18	
22.	154 – 128.63	
23.	247.1 – 138.57	
24.	12 – 3.547	
25.	1.415 – 0.877	
26.	185.774 – 154.86	
27.	65.251 – 36.9	
28.	144.2 – 95.471	
29.	2.11 – 1.949	
30.	100 – 34.746	

Name _____   Date _____

Lesson 31: Problems in Mathematical Terms

Exit Ticket

For each problem, determine the independent and dependent variables, write an equation to represent the situation, and then make a table with at least 5 values that models the situation.

1. Kyla spends 60 minutes of each day exercising. Let d be the number of days, and let m represent the total minutes of exercise in a given time frame. Show the relationship between the number of days and the total minutes of exercise.

Independent Variable _____

Dependent Variable _____

Equation _____

2. A taxi cab service charges a flat fee of $8 plus an additional $1.50 per mile. Show the relationship between the total cost and the number of miles driven.

Independent Variable _____

Dependent Variable _____

Equation _____

Name _____   Date _____

Lesson 32: Multistep Problems in the Real World

Exit Ticket

Determine which variable is the independent variable and the dependent variable. Write an equation, make a table and plot the points from the table on the graph.

Enoch can type 40 words per minute. Let w be the number of words and m be the number of minutes.

Independent variable _____

Dependent variable _____

Equation _____

Name _____   Date _____

Lesson 33: From Equations to Inequalities

Exit Ticket

Choose the numbers that make the equation or inequality true from the following set of numbers: $\{3, 4, 7, 9, 12, 18, 32\}$.

1. $\frac{1}{3}f = 4$

2. $\frac{1}{3}f < 4$

3. $m + 7 = 20$

4. $m + 7 \geq 20$

Name _____   Date _____

Lesson 34: Writing and Graphing Inequalities in Real-World Problems

Exit Ticket

For each question, write an inequality. Then graph your solution.

1.   Keisha needs to make at least 28 costumes for the school play. Since she can make four costumes each week, Keisha plans on working on the costumes for at least 7 weeks.

2.   If Keisha has to have the costumes complete in 10 weeks or less, how will our solution change?

Name _____   Date _____

1. Gertrude is deciding which cell phone plan is the best deal for her to buy. Super Cell charges a monthly fee of $10 and also charges $0.15 per call. She makes a note that the equation is $M = 0.15\,C + 10$, where M is the monthly charge and C is the number of calls placed. Global Cellular has a plan with no monthly fee, but charges $0.25 per call. She makes a note that the equation is $M = 0.25\,C$, where M is the monthly charge and C is the number of calls placed. Both companies offer unlimited text messages.

   a. Make a table for both companies showing the cost of service, M, for making from 0 to 200 calls per month. Use multiples of 20.

Number of Calls, C	Super Cell $M = 0.15C + 10$	Global Cellular $M = 0.25C$

   b. Construct a graph for the two equations on the same graph. Use the number of calls, C, as the independent variable, and the monthly charge, M, as the dependent variable.

c.   Which cell phone plan is the best deal for Gertrude? Defend your answer with specific examples.

2. Sadie is saving her money to buy a new pony, which costs $600. She has already saved $75. She earns $50 per week working at the stables and wonders how many weeks it will take to earn enough for a pony of her own.

a.   Make a table showing the week number, W, and total savings, S, in Sadie's savings account.

Number of Weeks											
Total Savings											

b.   Show the relationship between the number of weeks and Sadie's savings using an expression.

c.   How many weeks will Sadie have to work to earn enough to buy the pony?

3. The elevator at the local mall has a weight limit of 1,800 pounds and requires that the maximum person allowance be no more than nine people.

   a. Let x represent the number of people. Write an inequality to describe the maximum allowance of people allowed in the elevator at one time.

   b. Draw a number line diagram to represent all possible solutions to part (a).

   c. Let w represent the amount of weight. Write an inequality to describe the maximum weight allowance in the elevator at one time.

   d. Draw a number line diagram to represent all possible solutions to part (c).

4. Devin's football team carpools for practice every week. This week is his parents' turn to pick up team members and take them to the football field. While still staying on the roads, Devin's parents always take the shortest route in order to save gasoline. Below is a map of their travels. Each gridline represents a street and the same distance.

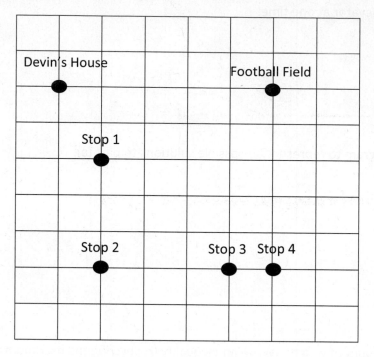

Devin's father checks his mileage and notices that he drove 18 miles between his house and Stop 3.

a. Create an equation and determine the amount of miles each gridline represents.

b. Using this information, determine how many total miles Devin's father will travel from home to the football field, assuming he made every stop. Explain how you determined the answer.

c. At the end of practice, Devin's father dropped off team members at each stop and went back home. How many miles did Devin's father travel altogether?

5. For a science experiment, Kenneth reflects a beam off a mirror. He is measuring the missing angle created when the light reflects off the mirror. (Note: figure is not drawn to scale.)

Use an equation to determine the missing angle, labeled x in the diagram.